Crises in the British State
1880–1930

Crises in the British State 1880–1930

Edited by Mary Langan and Bill Schwarz

Hutchinson
London   Melbourne   Sydney   Auckland   Johannesburg

in association with
the Centre for Contemporary Cultural Studies
University of Birmingham

Hutchinson and Co. (Publishers) Ltd

An imprint of the Hutchinson Publishing Group

17–21 Conway Street, London W1P 6JD
and 51 Washington Street, Dover, New Hampshire 03820, USA

Hutchinson Publishing Group (Australia) Pty Ltd
16–22 Church Street, Hawthorn, Melbourne, Victoria 3122

Hutchinson Group (N Z) Ltd
32–34 View Road, P O Box 40–086, Glenfield, Auckland 10

Hutchinson Group (S A) (Pty) Ltd
PO Box 337, Bergvlei 2012, South Africa

First published 1985

Set by Colset Private Limited in Singapore

Printed and bound in Great Britain by
Anchor Brendon Ltd,
Tiptree, Essex

British Library Cataloguing in Publication Data

Crises in the British state 1880–1930.
    1. State, The   2. Great Britain——Politics and government——1837–1901
    3. Great Britain——Politics and government——1901–1936
    I. Langan, Mary   II. Schwarz, Bill
    III. University of Birmingham, *Centre for Contemporary Cultural Studies*
    320.1′0941   JN216

Library of Congress Cataloging in Publication Data
Main entry under title:

Crises in the British state, 1880–1930.

    Includes bibliographies and index.
    1. Great Britain—Politics and government—19th century—Addresses, essays, lectures.
2. Great Britain—Politics and government—1901–1936—Addresses, essays, lectures.
3. Great Britain—Economic policy—Addresses, essays, lectures. 4. Great Britain—Social
policy—Addresses, essays, lectures. I. Langan, Mary II. Schwarz, Bill.
JN216.C75   1985   941.08   85–14311

ISBN 0 09 154681 8

Contents

Acknowledgements

Many thanks to Richard Johnson from whom we have all learned much, and who has taken much time and trouble to read successive drafts of many of the individual chapters as well as the completed manuscript; to Penny Gardiner for her superb typing and sustained support in ensuring the completion of the book; and as ever to Claire L'Enfant for her encouragement, patience and goodwill.

1 State and society, 1880–1930

Stuart Hall and Bill Schwarz

The main theme of this volume is the recomposition of British society, politics and the state from the 1880s to the 1920s. Central is the emphasis we give to the state. Most of the recent literature on the state has been concerned with theoretical elaboration, often at a very high level of abstraction. Much of this work has been impressive in its conceptual sophistication. But there is little evidence of this theoretical work being integrated with empirical and historical investigation. This seems to be especially true of inquiry into the history of contemporary British politics, a field largely dominated by intellectual traditions which do not appear to be particularly concerned with questions of state power. The purpose of this volume is to work *from* the theories, to bend the stick the other way and to study the state in its historical and concrete instances.

The recourse to Gramsci, in this introduction and in our interpretation as a whole, will be clear. One of the features of Gramsci's investigations which we have found useful is the level of abstraction at which he worked, specifically his attempts to think through developments in the field of state and politics. What might be called his 'historicized' concepts and abstractions have shaped our own analysis at almost every stage.

The individual chapters which follow necessarily draw heavily on existing historical material and do not claim to present the fruits of original research. The chapters are, however, linked by certain common themes and are underpinned by a common argument. The aim of this introductory chapter is to elaborate on this common ground and review some of the main features of the arguments which support our interpretation of the state in this period. The general approach is then more fully sustained in the individual chapters.

The broad lines of this interpretation can be summarized by the following points. First, from the 1880s there occurred a profound crisis of the British state which became acute from 1910 to 1926. The general crisis of the state marked a sharp historical *discontinuity* from the period which preceded it. One important way in which we characterize this crisis is as a 'crisis of liberalism'.

Second, out of this crisis, or succession of crises, there developed a transition to new 'collectivist' forms of state organization and social regulation which were qualitatively distinct from the *laissez-faire* individualism of the mid Victorian period. This new form of the state can be described as the interventionist state.

Third, although we insist that a transition from individualism to collectivism (or *laissez-faire* to monopoly capitalism) was accomplished in Britain by the end of the 1920s, we reject the idea of any adequate general theory of the state from which British particulars can be deduced. Rather we wish to stress the necessarily contingent dimensions of the political forces which constituted both the 'crisis' and the 'transition'. This means emphasizing the peculiarities of the British route and – in contrast to Germany and Italy – the differences which led, in the British case, not to a fascist but to a democratic-interventionist 'solution'.

Fourth, the form of the state and the main agencies for mass political representation which are now seen as characteristically 'modern' first appeared between the 1880s and the 1920s. In this sense the major political forces of our own period first arose in these years. In the analyses of the crisis of the state which now confronts us in the 1980s, the 1880s to the 1920s remain the 'crucible years'.

Fifth, and last, we argue that the political solutions and compromises of the 1920s and the decades which followed carried with them new antagonisms and contradictions; these have become especially apparent from the perspective of the crisis of the state of the 1970s and 1980s. Each of these points needs to be discussed in turn.

Crises

The apparently precise period we have adopted – 1880 to 1930 – is only an approximate indication of the historical boundaries of our subject. Within these decades the first, formative moment in the consolidation of monopoly capitalism was completed. This was a transition which stamps the historical development of Britain as surely, but perhaps not as visibly, as the 1640s–60s (the establishment of the revolutionary constitutional regime) or the period from the 1770s to the 1840s (the formation of industrial capitalism). Each of these periods was an epochal moment, a time of organic crisis when the society as a whole was structurally re-formed. The significance of the 1880s–1920s, however, is that although its epochal character is not so well established or studied, it is, nevertheless, the period most immediately formative *for us*.

Epochal transitions, in the sense used above, are notoriously difficult to theorize and specify. The key lies in the concept of crisis. Crisis is a term which has been weakened through over-use, forming the very staple of journalistic punditry. But none the less it has pertinence, and is peculiarly applicable to the analysis of the British state since the 1880s. It is however necessary to distinguish a short-term crisis of the state – one which is relatively localized and confined to the formal institutional apparatuses of the state – from a crisis which breaks across the social formation as a whole and threatens the hegemony of the dominant order. From the 1880s there occurred a *succession* of crises of the state, each only incompletely and partially resolved before new antagonisms arose, which in their combination amounted to a crisis of the social order itself. Crises occur when the social formation can no longer be reproduced on the basis of the pre-existing system of social relations. To be more specific, in the closing decades of the nineteenth century the liberal state and its attendant modes for regulating civil society could no longer be reproduced by means of liberal policies, practices and objectives. That is why the crisis was general – and also why it was a crisis of liberalism.

The onset of this crisis in the 1880s marked a deep rupture and discontinuity in British social and political development. This needs to be emphasized, given the continuing predominance of evolutionist explanations both within contemporary political ideologies and within historiography. Theories which are predicated on a fundamental continuity between the mid Victorian period and the early decades of the twentieth century – such as seeing the Labour Party as the natural successor to the Liberals, or the 'growth' of the welfare state – fail to grasp the immediate determinations which *impelled* a change of course and the desperate attempts to organize new solutions. After the cataclysmic impact of the war the state formation which emerged in the 1920s was quite new, both in its internal organization and in the set of social relations in which it existed. No return to older forms was possible.

One reason why some commentators are so keen to assert an essential continuity in these years may be to distance themselves from the excesses of the thesis developed by George Dangerfield in his book *The Strange Death of Liberal England*, published some fifty years ago but which (with Halévy's monumental account, to which Dangerfield owed a great deal) still largely defines the terms of current debate.[1]* This is a racy book, written with stylistic verve, stronger on anecdotes than it is on historiographical research. His argument, which he pursues in uncompromising terms, is that in the years from 1910 to 1914 the multiple threat to the social order – manifest in the struggles of the syndicalists, the suffragettes and the opponents of Irish Home Rule – had, even before the outbreak of war, brought about the death of liberal England. In their different ways, he contends, these struggles expressed the fundamental 'spirit of the age' in tearing to the ground the institutions and assumptions of high Victorianism. Historians have attacked his method as hopelessly idealist and his conclusions as extreme. They demonstrate, for example, that the Liberal Party still remained a major electoral contender until the end of the 1920s, and liberal social theory and

---

* Superior figures refer to Notes and references section at the end of each chapter.

philosophy, far from dying out before 1914, was an active force long after the First World War. These qualifications and counter-examples, however, may not be as damaging to the quality of his historical insight as his critics imagine. The Dangerfield thesis, in its pure form, cannot stand. Yet there is none the less a profound historical imagination at work in Dangerfield's account, for all its over-dramatization. He grasps the fact and the depth of the crisis and he sees its connection to liberalism. If only as a marker in a complicated debate, his analysis provides the account offered in this volume with its initial bearing.

It is, however, necessary to have some indication of the various meanings attached to the term liberalism. First and most obviously it refers to the rule of the Liberal Party. As a party of government and as a major political force in the country the Liberals did not survive the coalitions of Asquith (1915–16) and Lloyd George (1916–22), even when the shell of the party survived. The party suffered two great splits in this period, in 1886 over Home Rule and in 1916 over the conduct of the war. The decline of the Liberal Party was long and complex, and it was by no means out of the running until the early 1930s. Yet a decline it indisputably was, and as such must mark an important element in the crisis of liberalism.

But liberalism always carried much deeper connotations than the designation of a single party. It defined the relationship between state and civil society. In this area the key concept of classical liberalism was 'individualism' (to which the new term 'collectivism' was explicitly a counter). The sovereign individual in civil society, with his right to property and to his liberties of action and movement, was the central ideological figure. Individual liberty was determined by the workings of the free market, sanctioned and protected by the rule of law. The role of the state was to oversee the free play of the market and thereby serve as the defender of individual liberties: it should assume the role of 'nightwatchman', intervening in the market economy as little as possible. This, briefly described, formed the ideals of *laissez-faire* government, even when modified in actual practice. The identifications forged in this system between the free individual in civil society, the free market, private property and the patriarchal domestic household formed one of the most powerful and durable popular conceptions of state and society. But as many of the conventional histories demonstrate, as do the chapters in this book, the tempo of state intervention increased sharply in the 1880s and 1890s; the boundaries between state and civil society began to be redefined; and the nightwatchman role of the state began to be steadily eroded. In this sense, too, liberalism was in crisis in the last two decades of the nineteenth century.

A third, broader meaning attached to the idea of liberalism is the notion of a liberal social *system* referring not only to the relationship between state and civil society (concisely if too simply described by the term *laissez-faire*) but also to the constitutive features of civil society itself. This includes the formal, philosophical elaborations of liberalism, as well as the lived, civic ideologies and practices which drew on liberal philosophy and which, by the 1860s, constituted the common sense of the mid Victorian age. Crucial in this context are the conceptions which were dominant in the period – of the individual, family, constitution, law and nation – which defined the very core of liberal thought. These formed not a codified 'philosophy' or body of political thought, but the common-sense ideas, the taken-for-granted points of moral reference, the practical ideologies of the leading classes in English society. The crisis of liberalism in the closing decades of the century was, therefore, also a crisis of confidence and of continuity in these practical-ideological conceptions. Each of the leading ideas noted earlier is challenged and redefined in our period – and not only by new conceptions but in practice and in social organization.

The fissures and breaks in the practical organization of common sense represented – as Gramsci has argued – no mere shift in the 'spirit of the age'. They have a direct bearing on the mechanisms of power in both civic life and in political institutions. They lead us directly to the questions concerning the maintenance of social authority or hegemony. The question of liberalism in mid Victorian society was, in the end, always a question of how the delicate power balance was maintained and reinforced in a rapidly changing society. The crisis of liberalism was, therefore, ultimately connected with a crisis of hegemony in the whole social formation.

Thus the crisis of liberalism was not just a crisis of the state, narrowly conceived (concerning the fortunes of the Liberal Party), nor simply of the technical relationship between state and civil society (the demise of *laissez-faire* as a practical objective) but rather of the very *ideas* of state and civil society, of public and private. It is legitimate, then, to refer also to a crisis in liberal philosophy, and to note that this had direct effects on the intellectual and moral leadership of the dominant classes.[2] From this point of view it is possible to return to the original Dangerfield thesis and to rework and reappropriate it as an insight into the crisis of *liberal hegemony*.

From this historical moment the very means and modes by which hegemony is exerted in the metropolitan nations undergo a significant alteration. There is a shift not just in the disposition of forces but in the terrain of struggle itself. The nature of 'the political' underwent a profound transformation. Indeed, there is a strong sense in which Gramsci's own notion of hegemony was specified historically. In distinguishing between the working-class movement of 1848, which relied only on direct confrontation with the power centres of the state, and the strategic questions facing the socialist movement of his own time in the 1920s and 1930s, Gramsci noted:

In the period after 1870, with the colonial expansion of Europe . . . the internal and international organisational relations of the State became more complex and massive, and the Forty-Eightist formula of the 'Permanent Revolution' is expanded and transcended in political science by the formula of 'civil hegemony'. . . . The massive structures of the modern democracies, both as State organisations and as complexes of associations in civil society, constitute for the art of politics as it were the 'trenches' and the permanent fortifications of the front in the war of position: they render merely 'partial' the element of movement which before used to be 'the whole' war. . . .[3]

It is this deepening complexity of state power which led Gramsci to adopt the idea of a war of position, in which the overthrow of the state is conceptualized as a protracted struggle waged on all fronts, cultural as well as political, economic and military, engaging with the '*focos*' of power distributed through political *and* civil society. The significance of this, for our purpose, is the idea that Gramsci conveys of the reconstitution of the relations between state and civil society, the expansion of the very idea of 'politics' and the incorporation of the masses in the nation states of the late nineteenth century.

Political representation

Fundamental to this process was the means by which formal representation of the popular masses was secured. The second Reform Act of 1867 clearly demonstrated that the liberal state was organized to counter mass democracy and universal suffrage. The masses were to be incorporated in the nation, but indirectly, on the basis of a limited suffrage. It was along this fault-line that the disintegration of liberal hegemony first occurred.[4] This signalled the end of the period of relative stability in the mid Victorian political order.

From the 1880s established constitutionalism could no longer ensure the representation of the nation. Indeed, what social and political elements composed 'the nation' became a pressing political question. The pressures for the democratization and universalization of the political nation (such that every adult member had formal and equal rights of citizenship) undermined the established unity, organized by and through the state, of the liberal alliance. In the early moments of this collapse, party organization loosened and political affiliation became increasingly volatile. Gramsci's account of what he called an 'organic' crisis is instructive:

At a certain point in their historical lives, social classes become detached from their traditional parties. In other words, the traditional parties in that particular organisational form, with the particular men who constitute, represent and lead them, are no longer recognised by their class (or fraction of a class) as its expression. When such crises occur, the immediate situation becomes delicate and dangerous, because the field is open for violent solutions, for the activities of unknown forces, represented by charismatic 'men of destiny'.[5]

The reference here to the 'men of destiny' is one to which we must return. But the emergent political forces which, from the 1880s, weakened the traditional organizations which had hitherto represented and constituted social classes need first to be located.

Perhaps the most significant factor in the political realignments of the late nineteenth century is the least researched: the recomposition of the capitalist class. The expansion of capital accumulation and the increasing opportunities for the diversification of investment tended to undercut traditional divisions between those who secured their wealth from capitalist agriculture and those whose primary concerns lay in manufacturing. These social distinctions had been reproduced in the political alliances of the Conservative Party and the Liberal Party respectively, giving each its distinctive social character. But in the period up to the First World War these divisions rapidly diminished in significance. As the process of capital accumulation became more complex, so the various functions within the ownership and management of capital increased. One feature of this was the emergence of a new plutocracy – bankers, stockbrokers, investors and so on – who through their spectacular wealth commanded immense prestige in Edwardian society, and who gravitated to the Conservative Party, especially from the 1890s. Despite the continued presence of the political grandees, an effective social revolution took place within the Conservative Party, allowing into its inner councils those whose wealth and position was directly dependent on the day-to-day fluctuations of business.

Yet the immediate trigger for this transformation of alignment stemmed from the disarray of the Liberal Party, provoked by the antagonism between Joseph Chamberlain's Radicalism and Gladstone's more cautious conception of liberalism. This came to a head in 1886 when Chamberlain formed an organized Liberal Unionist grouping in order to oppose Gladstone's Home Rule Bill. This represented not only a disaster for the Liberal Party, but a grave split inside the ruling bloc as a whole. It was a break which permanently shifted the political terrain. In the following thirty years the Unionist (Conservative) alliance was to emerge as the all but exclusive representative of the varied interests which made up capital 'in general'.

The issue which drove Chamberlain towards Conservatism was *imperial* – the rejection of Home Rule for Ireland. Throughout the period covered by this volume Ireland was perceived first and foremost as an imperial issue, with an immediate, continuous and overbearing impact on domestic politics. The issue of Ireland condensed the anxieties about Britain's imperial position as no other could, for if the empire were to be dislocated at its very centre its prospects looked bleak. In the last quarter of the century the concept of empire assumed radically new connotations. Behind this shift lay the recognition that the rise of industrialized competitors for the first time decisively threatened both Britain's trade and its informal spheres of colonial interest. From this point on Britain could no longer run on the steam of its own economic power, founded on the principles of free trade. British manufacturers were perplexed by the sustained period of stagnation and paralysis in capital accumulation which characterized much of the last quarter of the last century and which later came to be known as the Great Depression. This decline in the rate of growth was striking compared both with the pace of Britain's earlier economic expansion and with the astonishing acceleration of industrial output of Germany, Russia, Japan and the USA. Britain passed in this period from being the strongest to becoming one of the weaker links in the chain of industrial nations. This did not, in most cases, compel businessmen to adopt radically new solutions; but it did exert a new set of political pressures on those who most directly represented capital in the state. Chamberlain's conversion to Empire and tariff reform was the most celebrated instance.

Just as from the 1880s the dominant class underwent an important phase in recomposition, so too the working class was 'remade'. The drive of capital to break down the skills of those workers strategically placed in the production process had crucial implications in the restructuring of the division of labour and in fracturing and disorganizing the cultural and political ties which had held skilled labourers to Liberalism. But equally important the socialist revival (conventionally dated from the great Dock Strike of 1889), combining with forces pressing from below for a system of *mass* democracy, coincided with the political splits in the dominant bloc and gave a strategic leverage to those political movements emerging outside the state.

The Dock Strike was the first major sign of the organized workers' movement disengaging from the Liberal Party and seeking to win independent political representation. In the socialist movement of the late nineteenth century up to the First World War political opposition to the state cohered as it had not done since Chartism. In these years, as in no other period before or since, the different strands of the 'socialisms' appeared as organic expressions of proletarian experience, though this process was always manifestly uneven and heterogeneous. One common impetus which lay behind these experiences, however, derived from the incipient internal collapse of the administrative solutions which had been institutionalized as state policy in the 1830s. The most obvious example of this is the New Poor Law, which demonstrated with singular force the inability of such administrative reforms to resolve or even mitigate structural economic problems. In such a climate, socialist and collectivist alternatives took on a more acceptable and positive profile.

The pressures for the expansion of democratic participation were not confined to the male working-class movement. For the first time there arose a mass feminist movement, organized initially as a campaign to repeal the Contagious Diseases Acts. By the early 1880s the repeal movement had moved to the centre of the public stage and feminism had become established as a major political force. The dynamic of popular and public concern over sexual matters reached a peak in 1885, the year which Jeffrey Weeks has called 'an *annus mirabilis* of sexual politics'.[6] A fundamental objective of this and later campaigns was concentrated on the suffrage. The aim was to win a political voice and thus articulate such matters on the parliamentary stage. The rationale for this objective was drawn in part from liberal philosophy, but at the same time challenged a principled liberalism on its own terms. The long-term effect of these struggles was to impose a further degree of fragmentation on the political and social alliances organized around the Liberal Party. In the later years, at the height of suffragette activity, this was symbolized in the most dramatic terms, when male political leaders looked out from the Palace of Westminster to see their female relatives and social acquaintances breaking through the police cordons in order to reach the Parliament building and demonstrate their passionate and public condemnation of that exclusively masculine bastion of political power.

However, liberal hegemony was broken not only by an array of alternative political forces, but also by an alternative and expanded conception of politics. Liberty to sell one's labour in the market, and even to choose a parliamentary representative, was challenged in the name of *social* rights. This was made explicit in the socialist groupings of the time – which were insistent in their claims that they could supersede liberalism – and even more so in the feminist movement. This is not to suggest that there occurred a spontaneous alliance between the socialist and feminist movements. Quite the reverse. The effect of the feminist campaign was to activate new sources of contention and antagonism, as well as new potentialities for alliances, *across* the popular movements of the day. Feminism challenged the apparent unity of the male labour movement, just as the impact of socialism disrupted the women's organizations. The intellectual resources of feminism may have drawn from the socialist tradition as well as from liberalism, but they were primarily constituted by women's distinctive histories and concerns. The struggle for the vote was only one very particular aspect of a much wider conception of women's emancipation.

The political forces which broke up the liberal system at the end of the century were thus not premised on shared objectives; neither was there a common idea of what would be the most satisfactory political solutions to the varying conceptions of 'the crisis'. Nevertheless, the new political forces which arose in the 1880s were all positioned in different ways *against* the state and existing institutions of power. In varying degrees they all addressed popular constituencies in a bid to recruit them in reconstructing the forms and boundaries of the state. This included not only the socialist and feminist movements but also elements which, under the aegis of jingoism or Orangeism, became seriously involved in building mass movements of the right. There is a sense in which Dangerfield is correct in seeing these different movements, from diverse sources, all coming to a head on the eve of the war. Although the fissures and breaks in the liberal system originated from distinct antagonisms, in terms of their effects they began to converge. The combined effect was to precipitate and then deepen the crisis of liberalism. Liberal constitutionalism and mass democracy, far from being evolutionary successors to one another, could not coexist in one state without there first being a major upheaval. Victorian constitutionalism consequently broke apart. Inside Parliament new mechanisms for compromise evolved for managing the pressing issues of the day; outside the constitutional arena, political forces generated by new mass movements assumed a radically new profile. The liberal state could no longer serve as a means to represent the new social forces, nor reproduce itself as a point of political and social stability. The issue at stake was how a new type of state could be constructed, capable of sustaining these new forces.

For each specific crisis innumerable new solutions, at once political and ethical, were proposed. A hundred different positions, philosophies and formations vied with one another to win ascendancy in defining the new rules of the game. Some politicians still hoped to save liberal society, even if this required illiberal means. Others subscribed to versions of a new social order. However, the social system was not so finely and functionally balanced that all the elements which composed the crisis were at some point resolved. The relations between state and society were dramatically reconstituted. But in some senses certain features of the British crisis were permanent, and in any fundamental sense, remained – and remain – unresolved.

Collectivism

The picture gets more complex when we see that each moment of crisis *is also* a moment of reconstruction: crises are the means by which social relations are reconstituted. The destructive and the reconstructive moments are parts of a single process of social transformation. Thus the emphasis on crisis is at the same time an emphasis on the remaking of the social formation. This process of reconstruction – 'reconstruction in the very moment of destruction' as Gramsci once put it – at the end of the last century was one in which many new possible solutions appeared on the horizon, each carrying potentially new dangers and contradictions. A central feature of many of the emergent solutions was the idea of collectivism.

There is a substantial but varied body of journalistic, theoretical and historical work, spanning contemporary liberal theorists such as A. V. Dicey and marxists such as Lenin, which locates the crucial transformation in the metropolitan nations of the period in the transition from *laissez-faire* to collectivism. Collectivism is as ambiguous a term as individualism. It refers to the process by which state policy became organized around class or corporate rather than individual interests. Thus, within the collectivist perspective, the state was seen as representing particular collective interests, and thereby required to intervene positively in civil society on behalf of these, rather than holding the ring within which individual interests compete. Underlying these theories was the idea that the state was linked to the organic interests of class, community or nation. It followed that the state should forsake its night-watchman role and become more actively interventionist, regulating more directly the civic and private spheres of individual decision. This tendency, explicitly counterposed as it was to the liberal conception of the state, gathered pace in our period, supported by a diverse and heterogeneous set of social forces. Some welcomed the drift to collectivism. To others, who feared the erosion of individual liberties, it was the cause for deep despair.

That was at the level of political theory, public philosophy, social attitudes and legislation. At a higher theoretical level, and within the specifically marxist framework deployed by Lenin, the new collectivist system represented not simply a new form of state but a new phase of capitalism – monopoly capitalism – in which the contradictions inherent in the capitalist mode of production reached a new level. This Lenin conceptualized as the highest and last stage of capitalism, in which the state assumed a central role as the direct organizer of capital.

Those committed to liberal individualism frequently indulged in unwarranted hyperbole in making their case, unearthing the makings of a revolution in political and civil society, pioneered not by wild extremists from the barricades but from within the very citadel of Parliament itself. However the publicists indulging in these polemics were never simply scare-mongering. The pressures for collectivism *were* strengthening, as was the tendency for more direct regulation of civil society. The chapters which follow attempt to identify and explain this process in particular areas of social life. The *fact* of a 'transition to collectivism' in this period in Britain needs to be established. What must to be added are the extremely diverse points in the political compass from which the collectivist impulse arose, and their highly contradictory outcomes.

The prior question remains, however, as to the qualitative shift in the actual position and role of the state to which the polemicists and theorists drew attention. How did the forms of state regulation emerging in the early part of the twentieth century differ from state regulation in the period of *laissez-faire*? This touches on a major historical debate which we can only deal with in a very summary way in this introductory chapter. We have so far accepted a rather simple equation between classical nineteenth-century liberalism and *laissez-faire*. Yet the ideal of such limited state intervention never came anywhere near realization in practice. In social terms, 'the population' had been the constant object of state regulation and surveillance since the early decades of industrialization, especially in matters of health, sanitation and hygiene which could be incorporated within the very broad rubric of medical discourses. Even in terms of the market, those most often committed to the principles of *laissez-faire* were frequently, as state officials and administrators, the most inveterate 'interveners'. Those involved with the legislation on poor relief provide a striking example. By the mid century the impetus of reform, involving a steady 'growth in government intervention' was in full spate.

Two general points which help to distinguish liberal from collectivist regulation can be made. First, the liberal reformers of the 1830s and 1840s were concerned above all to dislodge and break up the social institutions and practices inherited from an older social system which they perceived as inhibiting the free currency of market relations. Their objectives were in a sense, then, negative: to intervene in order to secure the conditions for regulation by economic or market compulsion. Second, the market and the conditions of wage-labour are *always* politically constituted, even if the role of the state is only remedial and deterrent. In this sense the state always has a positive role to play, even if that role is 'only' to ensure that the law of the free market prevails. We can therefore modify our definition of the key contrasting term to collectivism. *Laissez-faire* describes not an absence of controls, but a specific means by which market forces are politically regulated.

In the process of capital accumulation itself there exists a tendency for the progressive socialization of the means of production (larger and more closely integrated units of production) and also for greater collectivization of owners on the one hand and workers on the other. In the later stages of capitalist development there arises the tendency towards the organization of cartels of capitalists, overriding the laws of the market through price-fixing and trade agreements, ultimately leading to monopoly enterprises. Similarly, there develops a greater concentration of workers at the workplace (and in the great industrial cities) who attempt to protect their collective interests by regulating the price of labour, principally through trade unions. These pressures, inseparable from the process of capital accumulation itself, have the effect of destroying the classical rule of the 'free' market in its pure form, and with it the basis of a systematic and thoroughgoing *laissez-faire*. Yet the decomposition of market relations can be counteracted by the reconstitution of the market, in new forms, by the state. Indeed it must be reconstituted since it is an essential condition for the realization of value and the reproduction of capital. Thus direct state regulation of the market in one sector tends to occur *in order to preserve* the system of 'unfettered' relations in another. Far from the reproduction of market relations depending on the state absenting itself from the free play of the economy, it now comes to depend on a certain level of positive intervention by the state in the economy. This is one of the great contradictions on which intervention by the capitalist state is founded. The state tends to become an *active* and more direct agent in the process of 'decomposition and recomposition' of the social relations of production.

For example, at the turn of the century William Beveridge devised a scheme for state-sponsored national insurance (to aid those temporarily outside paid employment) and for labour exchanges. To be effective these plans required direct state intervention in the labour market. Indeed, they were premised on the belief that free-market relations were *no longer able* to direct a particular worker to the job to which he (the worker was generally thought of as male) was best suited or trained. In part, the objective was to use state intervention to overcome blockages in the labour market, particularly those resulting from the system of casual labour. But this was accompanied by a more positive conception in which the state was to secure both the maximization of the mobility of labour power and the cultivation of labour power of a particular quality. These policies necessarily involved not only the direct constitution of the market by the state but also the direct intervention of the state in the qualitative reproduction of social labour. The spectre of the casual poor as a stagnant pool of labour in the East End of London was the image which reverberated through these debates. Such blockages in the market could only be overcome by state agencies substituting direct regulation for the rule of the market in order to reconstitute the market *as a whole*. The immediate imperatives behind these schemes were not, as in the 1840s, to clear away specific, perceived inhibitions, but rather to ensure the survival of the market as such.

The transformation in state regulation was not merely quantitative but effectively produced a new idea of the 'social' (as in the term 'social reform'), a new discourse of social regulation, in which there arose new objects and targets for intervention. Thus, to continue with our earlier example, Beveridge saw his job as one of classification, determining the various causes of poverty and how these affected any particular group at any particular moment. The motive-force of his investigations was to disaggregate what had previously been seen as the undifferentiated mass of the labouring poor. Within the enlarged sphere of action of the state, new categories and new social identities were produced in opposition to the generalized notions of poverty and pauperism: the unemployed man, the old age pensioner, the incorrigible loafer, the destitute alien, and so on. Each 'problem' needed a *specific* form of intervention and regulation.

This process of breaking down the 'social problem' into component parts, each corresponding to a specific practice of regulation by some apparatus of the state developed for the purpose, can be taken as an example of Foucault's 'proliferation of discourses' in which new social subjects appear as potential objects for state concern. Other examples in other domains of social reproduction can be cited – the common prostitute (in the moment of the contagious diseases legislation of the 1860s and 1870s) and slightly later the 'amateur prostitute'; the unfit mother; the male juvenile delinquent and the hooligan. Each social category required a whole battery of state and/or voluntary agencies in order to ameliorate the effects of each particular 'disorder'. As the state was progressively enmeshed in resolving, or attempting to resolve, these dysfunctions in the social system so specific bureaucracies and departments of state were adopted for their regulation. These apparatuses, together with the experts and administrators – the 'organic state intellectuals' of the period – assumed the positive role of producing and accumulating new knowledge about the specific subjects and categories which came under their disciplinary regimes. The formation, expansion and diversification of particular state departments and ministries, the arrival of the powerful state administrator-intellectuals like Hubert Llewellyn Smith or Robert Morant, and the use of a new philosophy of scientific administration were all institutional expressions of this process. In this way the machinery of state began to be transformed and reorganized.

Although the necessary emphasis here is on the particularity of each response, and of the theories and agencies constituted in each instance, there were certain common features. The emerging welfare and collectivist ideologies which came to be channelled most directly through the state were primarily organized around particular forms of knowledge: explicitly psychology and eugenics – the sciences of social engineering often summarized in the phrase 'social Darwinism'. The means by which the various categories of the 'unfit' could be identified was through the mechanistic utilitarianism of 'mental measurement'. Psychological and statistical criteria could pin-point those deemed to be a social burden. Eugenics was the means by which the socially unfit would be bred out of the nation. The discursive polarities separating the deficient from the efficient, the deprived from the depraved, the healthy from the unfit, became an organizing principle for many of the new collectivist projects. For the deficient, especially those categorized as the residuum, the sternest disciplinary measures were evolved within the expanding administrative arenas of state action.

Yet it would be misleading to attribute the impulse to collectivism within the state exclusively to this expansion of state practices and apparatuses. Collectivism had deep roots, too, in pressures from below. The labour movement, clearly, was an emergent organic social interest with which the state would have to deal. The broadening of the theories of social, as against individual rights, led not only the organized labour movement but other sections of the population – the poor, the homeless, the residuum, and, after the great feminist revival, women – to lay claims to a more equal share in the social goods to which citizenship entitled them. There was, by and large, only one force capable of intervening against the logic of the market and of individual interest in the cause of social reform, redistributive justice and the guarantee of social rights. That power was the state. This conception of rights was therefore of the utmost importance in the early struggles in this period for reform. These struggles from below constituted a powerful complementary force to that of disciplinary regulation in the growth of those forms of collectivist expansion which were implemented first in our period and which culminated in the welfare state. In combination these two streams – those which looked to the state for an organic solution to the crisis of reproduction, from 'above', and those which looked to the state to intervene in the name of the collective good against the imperatives of the free market – not only powered the transition to collectivism, but helped to form the contradictory parameters which, ever since, have enclosed modern welfare programmes.[7]

But collectivism, too, was linked to the struggles for mass democracy. If we put together the struggles for the extension of the male franchise, the great engagement around women's suffrage and the new forms of industrial and political representation, we can see that perhaps the most significant underlying social force threatening the delicate balancing-act of mid century liberalism was the pressure for mass democracy. The emergence of mass democracy could not be contained within the limiting forms of representation of the liberal state. What the democratic challenge carried was nothing more nor less than a new set of claims on the state by the unenfranchised masses, a new conception of citizenship and, indeed, an expansion of the rights of citizenship from the sphere of legal and political to economic and social rights.

The political forces of collectivism

For the purposes of this introduction three of the dominant collectivist currents can be identified here: imperialist, new liberal and Fabian – emphasizing the *political* and contingent constitution of these collectivist forces.

First, the social–imperialist position. There already existed a long Tory tradition of commitment to a strong state; in this period diehards inside the Conservative Party attempted to resist the 'capitulation' of their party to liberalism, arguing the essential continuity between Tory paternalism and the organic interventionist state. The alliance between Joseph Chamberlain's Unionists, and the eventual dominance in the party of a Unionist bloc which aimed to construct a vigorous imperial regime, resulted in the formation of an authentically Conservative and imperialist collectivism. The politics of imperialist collectivism were most characteristically of the radical right, envisaging drastic solutions, imposed from above, to resolve Britain's ills, and scarcely restrained by the constraints of parliamentary constitutionalism. The language was formed in the syntax of 'national efficiency' and 'social imperialism' – the former pin-pointing liberalism's inadequacy in facing the task of national renovation, the latter designating a set of policies which, by combining imperialist development abroad with welfare and economic reforms at home, would build up the strength, efficiency and fitness of the British race as an imperial power. In this the martial spirit of Prussia and Japan were held as ideals. Although deeply authoritarian in their drive for leadership and efficiency, and threatening to uproot many of the established constitutional practices of a parliamentary democracy, these collectivists of the right worked energetically to enlist a populist movement in the country. Social imperialism did not so much deny citizenship as recast it in a populist and activist idiom: the new citizen was to be a *participant* absorbed into the larger organic unities of race, empire and nation.

To the new liberals – our second current – this *dirigisme* was abhorrent.

The new liberals, a group of highly gifted professional intellectuals, evolved a conception of collectivism which was constitutional and communitarian, ethical rather than utilitarian, and which aimed to preserve individual liberties *through greater state intervention*. New liberalism was a body of thought based on the determination to devise forms of collectivist control which could complement and extend, rather than negate, the inherited ethos of liberalism. Its trajectory was evolutionary, its driving-force idealist and ethical. In this respect and others, it played an inestimable role in the formation of British social democracy.

Its concept of citizenship was uncompromisingly constitutional, but principled in its desire to elevate the citizen as a full member of the political nation and the community, as a moral being, with duties as well as rights. The new liberal perspective shared the imperialist belief that citizenship not only conferred legal rights but signified a *potential* which could be realized in each individual through an educative political participation. To ensure that the majority could be educated in this way was therefore taken to be one of the *moral* functions of the state – hence the justification for state-sponsored public education. Yet, for all their formal adherence to constitutionalism their attitude to democracy was ultimately rather more guarded. Democracy was a term which came frequently to their lips and they were often insistent on the need to democratize from top to bottom state and civil society. But this was often counterbalanced, even among the most generous of these theorists (like J. A. Hobson or John or Barbara Hammond) by a residual utilitarianism and by the fear of outright socialism. Socialism they conceived as representing a particular class interest as against the general interest of the 'common good'. This counterposition – liberalism not socialism – was a structural feature of their conception of citizenship.

The new liberal idea of democracy was subject to the persistent undertow of a fluctuating but recurrent spirit of inegalitarianism. The significance of the new position within the liberal tradition articulated by the new liberals lies most of all in their advocacy of the provision of *universal* social rights. But this was tempered and qualified by their identification of those whom they deemed were unfit for the purposes of citizenship – an exception to universalism within the discourses of new liberalism which was not perceived as contentious. However, the commitment to universalism was given a negative inflexion – the right, in other words, *not* to be impoverished, or ill-educated and so on. It was a negative conception of rights which left intact, as a system, the positive relations of private competition. In fact the new liberalism was premised on this assumption for, quite consistently, it aimed to compensate those who visibly suffered gross privation on account of their being unable, for whatever reason, to participate fully in market relations. The structural inequalities of class relations, however, did not come within the compass of new liberal investigations – not because they were forgotten, but because they were positively excluded. Their whole theorization was antipathetical to any analysis which privileged class relations for they reasoned that this was to succumb to the dictates of a singular social interest rather than elaborating a view of society which could accommodate the full spectrum of different interests. This can be put more strongly, if polemically. The new liberals endeavoured to recast and rearticulate classical liberalism within the imperatives of a collectivist and democratic age. In so doing they preserved much of the liberal tradition and inheritance by partially transforming it. But it also represented precisely the response by humane and liberal social theorists to the combined threat of socialism and mass democracy. They attempted to deal with that threat by appropriating and incorporating the language of universalism into their own discourse and making it their own.

The third and perhaps most intriguing collectivist grouping were the Fabians. The Fabians represented the contradictory thrust of collectivism at the very heart of socialism itself. Unlike those who adhered to a Tory imperialism or the new liberalism, the most prominent of the Fabians (like Bernard Shaw and Beatrice and Sidney Webb) were socialists: they wished to destroy the anarchy of the capitalist market and achieve a classless society. But there were many 'socialisms' contending for ascendancy within the working-class movement at this time and for decades there was no guarantee which current would prevail in English socialism. Fabian socialism was the reformist, bureaucratic, anti-democratic and illiberal variety. Their dream was of a fully regulated, fully administered collectivist society in which state surveillance would be an essential condition of civic conduct. Regulated collectivism should replace the regime of unregulated individualism. This variant of socialism was deeply at odds with other socialist currents and with the spirit of self-activism which animated the proletarian socialist organizations of the period. The drift of Fabianism even to the Labour Party was protracted and reluctant, and only finally accomplished on tactical grounds. Like the new liberals, with whom they had much in common in terms of their class position, the Fabians were not only members of a newly professionalized intelligentsia; they elevated the bureaucrat, the expert and the administrator to the position of the leading *cadre* of their struggle for a new society. Whereas the defining impulse of the new liberals was mainly ethical, the Fabians were utilitarian. If the new liberals played a key role in defining the character of the welfare state, it was Fabianism which fashioned the ideology of rational efficiency and administrative neutrality which characterized welfarism in practice.

It is important at this point to emphasize the authoritarianism of the collectivist project. There was the clear anti-constitutionalism of the imperialist and Conservative tradition. But more importantly, perhaps, was the *statist* nature of their vision – a common denominator of all the collectivist tendencies, including the new liberals. The new regime, it was supposed, would be imposed from above. The main agent of transformation would not be the masses but the agencies of the state itself. How would these agencies in turn be transformed? For Conservatives the main figures were the adventurist political leaders and charismatic imperial impresarios who hovered in the wings and on stage. For the new liberals and Fabians it was the state administrators and experts, the organic intellectuals who aligned themselves with the collectivist impulse, who would devise one blueprint after another according to rational and scientific procedures alone. The dominance of state over civil society inscribed in all these programmes gave a legitimate case to the uncompromising liberal critics of collectivism who argued convincingly that they could not imagine a collectivism which did not also result in an illiberal state.

The designation of the currents of collectivism sketched here can only be preliminary, indicating the major intellectual tendencies. More important was how these ideological formations became organized politically. *All* the collectivist groupings opposed the established party labels to varying degrees; all hoped to construct alliances with other collectivist groupings or cells. This rejection of Victorian liberalism was often sufficient, in its own right, to promote alliances between groupings which, according to the more familiar, standard political classifications of today, appear to have little in common. The main institutional form for social imperialism was the Tariff Reform League; but a number of Fabians (not to mention a small but important coterie of Liberals) were also deeply committed to the imperial idea, a fact which created an enormous split in their ranks. Fabians and collectivist liberals, like many social imperialists, were doctrinaire supporters of national efficiency. On many political issues Fabians and new liberals were virtually indistinguishable: both had immense influence in defining socialism, in fixing the character of labourism, and in setting the targets of what could be achieved politically by the nascent Labour Party. Collectivism thus took no clear party or doctrinal form. On the contrary, it was instrumental in dismantling established party allegiances and formations. For a considerable number of politicians in this period, party labels came to appear an insubstantial and unnecessary irrelevance. As Beatrice Webb, writing in 1893, remarked: 'Collectivism will spread, but it will spread from no one centre.'[8]

Peculiarities of the British case

'The crisis' and 'the transition' were *constituted* by political forces, and their outcomes were determined in the first instance by political struggle. Explanation needs to concentrate on the peculiarities of each particular social formation, and on the national features of a political culture. A number of such concepts from recent theories of the state have shaped and informed our empirical investigations in this respect. One such concept is the notion, again drawn from Gramsci, of 'passive revolution'.

In his fragmentary notes on 'Americanism and Fordism' Gramsci considered the problem of identifying 'the links in the chain marking the passage from the old economic individualism to the planned economy'. Two aspects of this question particularly concerned him. The first was whether the model of the United States as the most advanced capitalist society could be followed by the nations of western Europe, and what cultural and political conditions would be necessary for this to occur. Second, if this were possible, what kind of social transformation would it involve. Gramsci proposed two alternatives to this question. On the one hand he saw the possibilities for 'a gradual evolution of the same type as the "passive revolution" '; on the other, he foresaw a more cataclysmic transformation which he described as 'the molecular accumulation of elements destined to produce an "explosion", that is, an upheaval on the French pattern' – this last reference alluding to the revolutionary traditions of French political culture.[9] These notes comprise little more than perceptive musings. Their relevance to this volume lies in the fact that Gramsci's object of analysis is very close to our own – which accounts, in part, for our persistent return to his inquiries. His ideas on the relationship between a passive revolution and the formation of monopoly capitalism are especially fruitful in understanding developments in British society during this period.

By passive revolution Gramsci referred to historical occasions in which a 'revolution' was installed from above, in order to forestall a threat from below but in which the popular masses did not take or win the political initiative. He thought of such transformations as marking both an important re-ordering of state and civil society and as a restoration of the fundamental social relations of production on a more stable basis for the future.

The defining feature of a passive transformation of this type is the success of the dominant groups in maximizing the *exclusion* of the masses from determining political affairs and the reconstruction of the state. Such a strategy constrains the scope and extent of the recomposition of the state, favouring overall those elements which contribute to restoration and continuity. This suggests methodologically the need to examine not only the measure of popular activity, but also the strategic *position* of mass movements in their relation to the state in this period.

In Britain the political strategies which predominated after the First World War formed a distinctive passive transformation. There were, however, organizations and parties which attempted to transcend these limits, drawing upon a radical popular movement in order to break the hold of the existing state. These political movements were of both the left and the right. The majority of socialist organizations, determined to overturn the state by pressure from below and create a more just and democratic alternative, imagined not a passive but an active remaking of society. But the populist organizations of the radical right – most notably the various currents inside the Tariff Reform League – also had as their objectives the construction of an alternative regime, albeit an authoritarian and imperial one. The ideal of the radical right was a state which would maximize, not the exclusion, but the *incorporation* of populist organizations into the composition of the state apparatuses. A clearer example of this harnessing of the masses in the reconstruction of the state during the formative moments of monopoly capitalism, in an explosive manner, were the mass fascist movements in Italy and Germany, in which the relation between popular organizations and the state was intensified and maximized to an unprecedented degree.

In Britain these radical movements were either defeated or marginalized. The mass movements of the time exerted pressure on the state, from a position outside the state. Characteristically, this resulted in the *internal* reconstitution of state institutions. To those on the radical right this often appeared no more than an appalling compromise, failing to face the drastic consequences of the new global balance of forces and of the need for a complete overhaul of the machinery of the British state. Yet the compromises compounded the passive character of the transformation. From the predominance of these compromises derives the significance in the British state of the reforming state bureaucrats, the new breed of state intellectuals informed by the Fabian or new liberal ideals. Internal administrative reform became a key mechanism for transforming the state with the minimum upheaval and catastrophe. Challenges for reform from below were first defined in public discourse by new liberal or Fabian social theorists, taken up by progressive state administrators, reconstituted in a bureaucratic mould, installed as state policy and at that point presented back to the people. This was a process which lay at the very core of an administrative type of passive reform and led to the consolidation of statism. As a personification of this process the conservative administrative radical, Beveridge, stands out.

This suggests that the ideologies of new liberalism and Fabianism were in fact theorizations of *passive* transformation. The new liberal idea of citizenship, although never simply legalistic, was limited to the extent that it positioned political subjects either as public servants or as rational and discriminating participants in the electoral process. Any greater sense of collective political action, based on a more popular sense of social needs, or of a politics capable of transcending the limits of the lecture-room and the *Manchester Guardian*, appeared not only remote and a touch irrational, but also threatening. An even greater testimony to the depth and penetration of this passive transformation was the fact that this commitment to constitutionalism also came ultimately to define the objective and political practice of the Labour Party. It was on this ground, in the 1920s, that the renowned 'historic compromise' was elaborated between the major social classes. Within the limits of the deals concluded, the typical contours of British social democracy emerged. Of the many 'socialisms' which made themselves available in this period, it was this variant, with its commitments to statism and social engineering, which prevailed – not least because of the critical role played by the state itself in containing the more 'extreme' elements in the Labour formation, while educating the more accommodative elements into a safe place within the pale of the constitution.

The significance of new liberalism in these developments, as a political–intellectual formation, must lead us to qualify substantially the Dangerfield thesis. Classic mid century liberalism was deconstructed. But liberalism did not 'die' in the years between 1910 and 1914. On the contrary, under the impact of the struggles which Dangerfield described there occurred the *redeployment* of liberal philosophy. An extensive labour of philosophical renovation was achieved to adapt it to a new democratic age. Yet many elements of the new ideology were recognizably those of classical liberalism, with constitutionalism and individual rights a prominent feature, transformed into the syntax of social democracy. It was the language of new liberalism which then effectively defined the collectivist, social-democratic project in Britain for the next four or five decades. The 'peculiarity' of the British case rests on these facts: on the passive transformation of liberalism and on the consequent elements of continuity and displacement. The fact that the dominant conception of collectivism remained within the discursive traditions of liberalism and constitutionalism should not conceal the profound crisis of Victorian liberalism and, in practice, the interruptions and breaks in social and political developments which followed in its wake. The transition to a collectivist regime was partial and uneven. But it remained (for the most part) within the constitutional boundaries. It is this underlying persistence which provides the staple argument for those dedicated to proclaiming the historic continuity of British political life. But this perception fails to see that what survived did so only at the cost of a sometimes frenzied reconstruction of constitutional liberalism and only through its displacement into a new and specific formation in the 1920s. Liberalism, as a system, was dismantled.

The making of contemporary politics

The first steps in the creation of a mass democratic culture were made in the 1880s (the 1884 Reform Act, the 1885 Redistribution Act, the 1888 Local Government Act). They were followed in the next decades by the development of commensurate civic institutions (the provincial universities for example). This movement was cautious and protracted. Resistance to democratic progress – above all to the enfranchisement of women – remained bitterly fierce. Nevertheless these early political concessions, organized in the first moments of the crisis of liberalism, formed the preconditions for the emergence of mass democracy *before* the onset of the succession of crises which marked political developments until the mid 1920s. Undoubtedly the successive stages of incorporation within the democratic framework, however long resisted, afforded the political system an increased flexibility and manoeuvrability. It undermined the traditions of patronage and thereby broadened, if only within very definite limits, the power centres of the state. The break-up of the old alliances and the construction of a new political system facilitated the movement towards a new type of democratic political order. The long, defensive period of coalition governments from 1915–22 (including the exceptional circumstances of the war, during which many of the new modes of state-collectivist regulation were first pioneered) played a key role. It was in that period that the old party formations finally dissolved and regrouped; the syndicalist challenge was confronted and repelled; labour, its internationalism broken by the war, was constitutionalized into the alternative party of government; state intervention in ·the economy hastened the transition to monopoly forms in some sectors; and the system of industrial conciliation, with the state as 'neutral' mediator between capital and labour, was fully institutionalized. In the end the Conservatives could not live with the vagaries of the architect of this transformation – Lloyd George. But by the time they sent him and the coalition packing their historic mission had been achieved.

The major breakthrough in winning a system of universal suffrage also came about in this moment, as a direct result of the war. The Representation of the People Act of 1918 enfranchised all male adults of 21 and over and all women aged 30 and over. Issues which had caused the deepest passion before 1914 were quietly if reluctantly conceded by diehards in the course of the war. The Representation of the People Act instituted the universalist state, formally representative of the totality of interests which composed the nation. It was within this framework that its complement, 'universal' social provision, began slowly to develop, if only as a formal commitment of state policy. With universalism too came the triumph of the electoralist version of democracy: the individual voting subject became the lynchpin within all official state discourses. In turn the act shaped the conditions which made possible the strategic reassertion of the absolute centrality of Parliament and constitutional politics. It provided the resources for the emergence of a new political language based not on interest but on the more expansive category of 'citizenship'. The precise forms of this language remained indeterminate and open until the period of the most intense industrial and class confrontations in 1925–6. In those years the democratic advances embodied in the act were finally absorbed into Baldwinite Conservatism and any hopes for a more assertive, radical and popular conception of democracy – either representative or direct – disappeared. Democracy was contained within the confines of electoralism and a very specific variant of national constitutionalism. The containment of labour and of other democratic forces also had international conditions of existence – the post-war proletarian upsurge and its large-scale defeats in Europe. In this context Britain continued in its role as European and global *gendarme*, a policy pursued with vigour and almost without interruption by Conservative and coalition leaders, from military intervention against the nascent Soviet Union to the appalling débâcle of Munich. In the turbulent years of insurgent socialist and anarchist movements in Europe from 1917 to 1923 the British formation could still be counted as the strongest link in the European chain, the one least vulnerable to the socialist offensive.

This constitutionalist framework remained intact for the next four or five decades, 'a continuum almost without precedence in post-Reformation history'.[10] The dominant features of the new organization of the state can be briefly summarized, indicating at the same time the discontinuity between the settlement of the 1920s and classic Victorian liberalism. First there was the universalist ordering of the institutions of political life, in terms both of legal and social rights, the latter giving rise to early welfare policies. It is this 'universalism' which underpinned Gramsci's understanding of the transformed conditions for the winning of hegemony 'in the period after 1870' and the new position of the masses in relation to the state.

Second, the Labour Party achieved the position of the political representative of the working class and, as 1924 showed, legitimately earned its constitutional credentials as the very junior partner in the new historic settlement. Alongside this there developed the constellation of corporatist institutions in which representatives of the collective interests of capital and labour were directly placed within the sphere of the state. To quote the major theorist of this process, 'what had been merely interest groups crossed the political threshold and became part of the extended state'.[11]

Third, the hesitant process of reforming the *imperial* state was initiated. The partition of Ireland in 1921 destroyed the unity of the old imperial regime. As a response to the sometimes insurgent movements for colonial liberation the majority of British politicians gradually came to the conclusion that, in order to save the empire as best they could, they had no option but to begin to constitutionalize the directive role of the imperial government. The first formal declaration of this recognition can be dated from the Montagu-Chelmsford reforms of 1919, anticipating a future of 'responsible government' for India, although it was not until the 1930s that the role of the imperial government itself was the object of legislation and not until the post-war period that decolonization as such was set in motion.

This political settlement represented an unequivocal victory for the forces of constitutionalism but a much more ambivalent outcome for democracy. Nevertheless, the significance of the defeat of the radical right as an organized movement must be stressed. The radical right cannot be consigned to the occasional footnote as simply an immoderate outburst of diehard spleen with no lasting significance. Its presence was a dominant component of the period and its logic, if unchecked, led directly to the possibility of an authentic proto-fascism. The marching and the counter-marching of the pro-consuls and other would-be 'Napoleons' waiting to be summoned to their destinies, the cynical manoeuvrings for power in the corridors of government, the sudden reappearances in Ulster of these figures at the head of an Orange troop, the repeated calls for a solution to be imposed from above, the very language of authoritarianism, were ingrained elements in the disintegrating political culture of those years. Despite widespread illusions to the contrary, the progression of English constitutionalism was not under-written by some providential historical law. If the radical right had gained ascendancy there would have occurred not the redeployment but the destruc-tion of liberalism. Even so, its characteristic ideologies have never dis-appeared as active dimensions of the political culture of Conservatism and have continued to shape its very project to this day.

The failure of the radical right and the fall of Lloyd George nevertheless ensured that by the 1920s the dominant political forces crystallized within a constitutionalized Conservatism, accommodated to the imperatives of mass democracy and universal suffrage. The only *legitimate* alternatives were the more actively assertive collectivisms of new liberalism and Fabianism, which transmuted into the 'middle opinion' of the 1930s and later into social demo-cracy in the political debates of the 1940s; and an evolutionary socialist statism, whose organizational basis was the TUC and the Labour Party. This is how the configurations of a specifically contemporary set of political and ideological dispositions finally emerged from the crisis.

These were the currents in which a peculiarly British collectivism was articulated. Liberal opposition to collectivism, however, did not collapse. *Neo*-liberalism, the term which designates the continuing persistence within these other formations of the individualist critique of collectivism, had a submerged but critical presence in the political field. Neo-liberalism (not to be confused with new liberalism) was co-extensive with the formation of collectivist ideologies, and its history also begins in the 1880s. Even in the moment of its formation it was not simply an ideology whose adherents advocated a return to classical liberalism; with the eventual dominance of collectivist forces it became progressively less so. On the contrary the project of neo-liberalism was systematically to contest and where possible to *uproot* the political conditions in which collectivism flourished. This called for a strong state (little resembling the Gladstonian model) and a particular kind of interventionism which could *enforce* free-market relations. State regula-tion of the market was defined as no more and no less than socialism and thus inimical in itself. The neo-liberal analysis was sound only in so far as com-mitment to state-organized welfare did impose great fiscal burdens on the state, leading to that 'overload' which neo-liberals of our own day are so keen to reverse. It was partial, however, to the extent that advanced capi-alism could scarcely have continued without the existence of such state velfare programmes to compensate for the damaging social effects of the narket. Neo-liberalism was nevertheless forced to adopt an increasingly adical posture at each moment of the consolidation of collectivism, as the imited forms of intervention and welfarism became established within all the major parties contending for government. As its objectives became increasingly defined not by particular pieces of legislation but by the very foundations of a regime which it hoped at some point to destroy, so its rhetoric became more strident. This too registers a strand in the dispersal of liberalism.

Resolutions and contradictions

In rudimentary form two-party constitutionalism based on universalism, an institutional framework for corporatist bargaining and a system of state welfare were all in place by the mid 1920s. Each had a fragile existence, at times seeming to disappear altogether; for the most part, each was justified pragmatically rather than on grounds of principle. Only under the impact of the radical populism generated by the Second World War did these elements fuse into a developed political system capable of winning a broad degree of popular consent for a programme which temporarily deepened in democratic content. This was symbolized by the invocation of the date 1945.

The major elements which came together in 1945 were – we would argue – first formed in the conjuncture of events of the 1880s–1920s. This longer history is necessary in order to dispel the myths surrounding current interpretations and to contextualize and explain the profound ambiguities in the social-democratic experiment of the 1940s and 1950s. The ideologies of collectivism and citizenship which were predominant in the 1940s still carried in them all the contradictory features which had characterized the collectivist aspirations of the 1880s. Most of all, the persistently statist inflexion of these ideologies and practices on the one hand indelibly stamped the forms of social democracy, and on the other, sustained neo-liberal antagonism. After a period in which neo-liberals appeared to be all but politically extinct, they began to coalesce once more into an organic political tendency. They ultimately forced a breach in the collectivist defences, and won back the political ground they had lost for so long. Thus the solutions to the crisis of liberalism at the end of the nineteenth century restored a degree of political stability to the British social formation for a number of decades. But they also created the conditions for their own ultimate destruction.

In other respects too it seems as if the crisis of the late nineteenth century has been more protracted and continuous. In the 1880s British capitalism entered a period of secular decline from which in any fundamental sense it has never recovered. After the First World War Britain became for the first time a debtor nation, subordinate in global terms to the USA. Owing to its concentration in the financial markets of the world, its continued commitment to its traditional imperial role, and the adaptation of the dominant institutions of capital to the defence of sterling as an international currency, the British economy became peculiarly vulnerable to the exigencies of the world market. Even during the height of the consumer boom and 'consensus' politics of the 1950s this long-term economic decline was not structurally reversed.

Over the past century a constitutive dimension of British politics has been the return to the centre of the political stage of this antagonism between collectivists and their opponents. In a broad sense the dominance of the collectivist forces by the 1920s created the conditions for the consolidation of monopoly capitalism, the settlement of the new social order and the emergence of the 'consensus' politics of social democracy. The forms in which the crisis was resolved or contained are the forces which constituted the structures of modern British politics today. The neo-liberal resurgence today is testimony to the unfinished trajectory of the crisis of that earlier period. Social democracy was formed out of the crisis of liberalism between the 1880s and the 1920s. We are now living through its successor – the crisis of social democracy.

Notes and references

1   George Dangerfield, *The Strange Death of Liberal England* (Paladin 1984); and see E. Halévy, *Imperialism and the Rise of Labour* and *The Rule of Democracy* (Ernest Benn 1961).

2   It is worth recalling that in his characterization of the 'culture and society' tradition Raymond Williams marked the period between Morris and Lawrence as an 'interregnum': *Culture and Society, 1780–1950* (Penguin 1971); and see too on this, Terry Eagleton, *Exiles and Emigrés* (Chatto and Windus 1970).

3   A. Gramsci, *The Prison Notebooks* (Lawrence and Wishart 1971), p. 243.

4   See especially C. B. Macpherson, *The Life and Times of Liberal Democracy* (Oxford University Press 1977).

5   Gramsci, p. 210.

6. Jeffrey Weeks, *Sex, Politics and Society. The regulation of sexuality since 1800* (Longman 1981), p. 87.

7   For some interesting reflections, Claus Offe, *Contradictions of the Welfare State* (Hutchinson 1984).

8   Quoted in W. H. Greenleaf, *The British Political Tradition* (Methuen 1983), **1**, p. 43.

9   Gramsci, pp. 279–80. In a different language, this 'molecular accumulation of elements destined to produce an "explosion" ' would be a crisis which was 'overdetermined'. The argument here is that the British crisis at the turn of the century was not one which was overdetermined in this way.

10 Keith Middlemas, *Politics in Industrial Society* (Deutsch 1979), p. 15.

11 ibid., p. 373.

2 Conservatism and 'caesarism', 1903-22

Bill Schwarz

The whole idea is wrong because it means the only alternatives to the Centre are the extremes   (*Shirley Williams, November 1980, on the concept of a centre party*).

There seems to be nothing so natural about British politics as the regular rotation of political parties. Whatever the fate of 'other parties' the Conservative Party always appears the fixed point on which all else is balanced, its presence as permanent as the Palace of Westminster itself. The Whigs have passed, Liberalism has died and Labour may currently be marching backwards, but Conservatism seems to carry on for ever.

This is not to say that the Conservatives always wish to see their party as the party of government. That wily old Conservative, Rab Butler, reflecting on his party's defeat of 1945 explained that

thirty years of almost uninterrupted power, such as we had exercised either alone or in coalition, must be regarded as unnatural in a properly functioning democracy. Such democracy does not necessarily require, like a tennis match, the regular alternation of service and defence; on the contrary, it is frequently strengthened by a lengthy continuity of experience in administration. But just as its post-war periods of office have mellowed and matured the Labour party, educating it out of many callower socialistic assumptions, so the Conservatives, when thrown into opposition, were provided with a healthy opportunity and a compelling motive for bringing their policies and their characteristic modes of expression up-to-date. The adaptations and adjustments of both sides were, on a long-term view, of benefit to the country.[1]

The confidence which lies behind this pragmatic assessment is revealing. Tories assume that the Conservative Party will always be there and that two-party constitutionalism is the condition for a 'properly functioning democracy'. In the words of Sir Ian Gilmour it is 'the highest form of political development'.[2] Butler's own politics were of the 'moderate centre'. Yet, as Brian Harrison has argued, it is a paradox that most centrists favour a regular rotation between a party of 'business' and a party of 'labour' rather than placing their bets on a single party of the centre.[3] Until very recently this commitment to two-party constitutionalism remained virtually unquestioned within the British political establishment. This above all had become the 'common sense' of the dominant classes.

Yet the principle of two-party constitutionalism based on universal suffrage is a relatively recent development. In part, as the liberal historiography persistently reminds us, the emergence of this as a principle was associated with the progressive widening of the electoral franchise from the mid nineteenth century. As more and more workers gained the vote, liberals increasingly recognized the need for the representatives of 'labour' to take their turn in governing. Yet it is also critical to see how two-party constitutionalism developed as a political strategy, in contention with a number of alternative strategies. Indeed this was an historical project which the political representatives of the dominant classes had to learn. They had to overcome a reflex which frequently favoured only an outright anti-socialism. Only in the course of struggles within and between the fundamental social classes could the two-party system become established as a new common sense. Even then, as one political crisis followed the next, the principles behind such a strategy were frequently compromised.

These issues were fiercely contested inside the Conservative Party. Most historians have taken for granted that the Conservatives emerged as the stable element in the political culture of the 1920s. But this could never have been assumed at the time. Rebellions against the leadership, factionalism, constant realignments imposed by the shifting bids for coalitions, and temptations to ditch the party for the lure of a national anti-socialist bloc – all continually mesmerized some of the most able Tory figures. Given the extent of these difficulties what needs to be explained is how the party managed to survive at all. Moreover, every single radical venture to regenerate the party failed in its immediate objectives. The efforts of Randolph Churchill in the 1880s, the tariff reform campaign from 1903 to 1910, the radical right and the diehard groundswell between 1910 and 1914, and the machinations of Austen Chamberlain and Lord Birkenhead from 1920 to 1922, all became unhinged. This too needs an explanation.

Contrary to the mythology of Conservatism, the death of liberal England eliminated not just the Liberal Party, but came close to killing off the Conservative Party too. The crisis was a crisis of the state, not just of one party. After 1910 both the major parties fragmented as the constitutional arrangements of mid Victorian Britain collapsed. The process by which the system was rebuilt, on the new foundations of universal suffrage, was exceedingly precarious for the dominant classes. Ultimate success was achieved only by blocking the rotation of parties, exerting a temporary freeze on the core representative institutions of the state (Parliament and party) and erecting in their place the defensive fortifications of coalition. In this process the Conservative Party was very nearly swallowed up.

Four particular episodes will be discussed in this chapter: the bid to win active working-class support by means of the Tariff Reform League; the dominance of the diehard or radical right; the alliance with Lloyd George; and the revolt instigated by the junior ministers, led by Stanley Baldwin, against continuation of the alliance with Lloyd George which temporarily reversed coalition government. The chronology of these developments is already well staked out in the official historiography with the usual precision to which historians of high politics are given: 15 May 1903 to 19 October 1922.

The Tariff Reform League 1903: the prospects

On 15 May 1903, Joseph Chamberlain, triumphant from the conquest of South Africa, declared to a tumultuous meeting in Birmingham his intention of launching a campaign for tariff reform. With evangelical fervour Chamberlain proclaimed his mission to replace free trade with a system based on the preferential treatment for British colonies. Chamberlain's radicalism had been heavily compromised but not entirely extinguished in his defection from Liberalism. He found no ready outlet for his energies in Lord Salisbury's administration, nor in that which followed it in 1902 under the leadership of Salisbury's nephew, Arthur Balfour. The cumulative effects of Unionist imperial and domestic policies had progressively narrowed popular support for the government party. Chamberlain found the vacillation he had encountered with Gladstone reproduced in the Conservative leadership, and he became increasingly reluctant to press home his positions inside the Cabinet. It was this immobilization inside the power centre of the imperial state and his irrepressible belief in the destiny of the 'white races' of the British Empire which drove him to move his sights beyond the established political institutions. Chamberlain set about creating through the Tariff Reform League his own mass movement of the right.

The tariff reform movement dominated Conservatism for the first thirty years of this century.[4] Support for protection could boast a long tradition within Conservatism, with pressure groups stretching back to the agricultural protectionists and Industrial Fair Traders of the 1880s. This Tory tradition held that behind a protective wall of tariffs the mechanisms of the domestic market could continue to function free from direct state interference and unfair foreign competition. Many of its supporters emphasized tariffs as a strategy to raise revenue, providing an alternative to the Liberal policy of directly squeezing capital through a combination of progressive taxation and land duties. Chamberlain's insistence on preferential tariffs did not always sit easily with the Tory tradition of protection. In his scheme Britain would offer preferential treatment to the other nations in the empire which in turn would be reciprocated. The aim was to produce an intermeshed economic bloc of global proportions, sufficiently powerful to challenge Britain's emerging industrial and imperial competitors.

The tariff issue held historic significance in defining the very nature of Conservatism. In 1846 the party had been devastated over the issue, and had only slowly and pragmatically come round to endorse free trade. From the

1880s, as the party took on the profile of the major representative of capital, the advocates of protection often appeared to be speaking from another age. Much of the party's growing support in the late nineteenth century depended on the Tories' new commitment to economic liberalism, as indeed did the evolving definition of Conservatism itself. There were many Conservatives, particularly those of Whig patrimony, who despised Chamberlain and his challenge. These Tories feared that they were about to witness a new outbreak of Chamberlain's old radicalism. They distrusted his reputation for coquetting with the proletariat, and particularly resented the fact that this threat now emanated from inside the party of tradition and order.

The effect of Chamberlain's tariff reform speech of 15 May was explosive, despite his calculated defence that he was merely 'opening up' the issue. On the same day, Balfour, the leader of the party and Prime Minister, publicly relegated imperial preference to the distant future. Unionist factionalism had been triggered.

Balfour had agreed beforehand that Chamberlain could once more broach the matter of tariffs. To this extent Balfour was showing his hand and cautiously sanctioning the initial sounding of public response to a more interventionist Unionism. None the less, Chamberlain adopted a much stronger stand than he had indicated to Balfour, and the whole episode was reported in the press as if it indicated a split between the two leaders. Having opened the debate Chamberlain proceeded to force the pace. Within the week, in debate with Lloyd George, he linked imperial aspirations to social reform. He made clear his view that tariffs could finance domestic reform and hence provide the Tories with a basis from which to challenge the Liberals' claim to be the party of progress. Within a fortnight Chamberlain had clarified his own position on tariffs sufficiently to incur the restraining hand of Balfour. Over the next six months he moved much closer to a policy in which imperial preference was to be coupled with systematic industrial protection.

Deep dissension resulted. Balfour was prepared to accept retaliatory protection for specific industries, but he feared the electoral damage which could result from food taxes. However, what rattled Balfour was not Chamberlain's espousal of preference and protection but rather the fact that his government was in the process of being torn to pieces. Balfour's problems in holding the party together absorbed all his energies until he was pushed out of the leadership in November 1911. On the one side he had Chamberlain and the tariff reformers fired as never before and attracting the most bellicose elements. On the other were the committed 'free-fooders'. These included the majority of the Unionists' most brilliant personalities: the old Whigs who had broken with Gladstone over Home Rule (Devonshire, Goschen, and St Loe Strachey), old guard Tories convinced of the iniquities of tariffs (Hicks Beach), and some representative Young Turks of Unionism (Lord Hugh Cecil and Winston Churchill). There were no possible grounds for permanent reconciliation. The creation of rival organizations at a national level indicated the gravity of the split. On 13 July the free-fooders, thrown off balance by the vigour of the tariff campaign and by Balfour's apparent sympathy, formed the Free Food League. A week later the Tariff Reform League was founded.

The situation came to a head in September. Balfour accepted the resignations of the leaders of both factions: from Ritchie and Devonshire, and from Chamberlain himself. But the remaking of the Cabinet was more favourable to the tariff reformers. In place of Ritchie at the Exchequer – a vital post in the fiscal controversy – Chamberlain's eldest son, Austen, was appointed. An informal alliance was sustained between Balfour and Chamberlain until the latter's stroke removed him from the political scene in July 1906.

Chamberlain had already had some experience, in 1886, of splitting a political party. There is no evidence that in 1903 he wished to repeat the trick with the Unionist Party. Yet through the summer and autumn he could hardly have been unaware of the consequences of his actions in creating havoc inside the Unionist ranks. In the older historiography it was argued that Chamberlain wrecked the party, or at least that he declared war on his Unionist colleagues.[5] Despite the immediate and very serious fragmentation which resulted, such assessments are exaggerated. The campaign has to be seen in the context of the desperate paralysis of the Toryism of Balfour and Salisbury.

The British Empire was threatened by powerful rivals; the military destruction of the defenceless Transvaal Republic turned out to be a long and disheartening slog, dogged by constant ineptitude which brought home to the British public the gross inefficiency of the imperial state; the party's will to formulate a programme of social reform never held steady. And over all there hung the spectre of labour. Salisbury's political formation had been as a Tory diehard. At first he saw the function of Conservatism simply to hold back democracy. After 1867 he arrived at the more astute perception that representative democracy did not entail 'the people' speaking for themselves. Nevertheless he was still troubled by his recurring nightmare of the mob storming through the French windows at Hatfield House. Balfour, when up against Fenian resistance in Ireland, earned himself the sobriquet 'Bloody Balfour'. Although he never thought to apply these methods widely at home, he was all but incapable of commanding a positive strategy for the accommodation of labour. Both Salisbury and Balfour believed that the task of the Unionist Party remained that of governing, for 'the people', but with the minimum of popular concessions. Thus, in an age which saw the birth of the socialist movements, Conservative fortunes rested heavily on Chamberlain who sought actively to integrate the masses into the Unionist Party and to harness a popular radicalism for the party. So far as the Conservatives were concerned Salisbury's alliance with Chamberlain had been an attempt to incorporate into the Unionist bloc a conservative popular politics for which Birmingham, Belfast and Liverpool were the models. However, on the national electoral scene there was little sign of the emergence of a stable inter-class alliance under Conservative hegemony. Indeed, the Whiggish elements inside the party were resolutely opposed to the conclusion of any such alliance.

Chamberlain was ultimately defeated by the Unionist leadership neither over his broad philosophy of Unionism nor in his quest for imperial reorganization, but on the consequences which he believed must follow. The Unionist leadership opposed the reconstruction and expansion of the domestic state and the construction of a political regime which was both active in its interventionism and universal in its provision of social rights.

Before the First World War there was a wide range of collectivist groupings of the right. The members of these groups included politicians, imperialist adventurers, civil servants, journalists, generals and admirals, all espousing their own brand of social imperialism. At times they had a considerable impact on party politics. But none of these groups emerged as more than a marginal intellectual coterie. Chamberlain, having a much deeper grasp of the development of working-class socialism, saw that the regeneration of Conservatism demanded a mass base. Furthermore, Chamberlain understood that if he could command a popular following he would have the strategic means by which to overcome the paralysis of the power bloc, and to outmanoeuvre the Unionist Cabinet in particular.

Tariff reform: the campaign

Unionism already claimed an impressive array of extra-parliamentary institutions before the formation of the Tariff Reform League. These included the Primrose League, the volunteer and militaristic youth movements and the press. After the tariff controversy broke out, control of the Unionist press became decisive for all factions in organizing support, both inside and outside the party. For the tariff reformers it presented the opportunity of uniting the various voluntary and informal imperialist organizations under the single banner of the League. Issues were manufactured and alliances made in the editorial offices. Newspaper magnates like Arthur Pearson, Lord Northcliffe and, slightly later, Max Aitken, came to occupy positions of unprecedented influence. The foremost Unionist editor, J. L. Garvin, became a self-appointed and indefatigable political fixer. The power accruing to the press at this time derived in part from the disruptive effect of the tariff issue on the established party organizations. Chamberlain was convinced of the need to organize working-class support and understood the importance of the press in securing it. By the autumn of 1903 the *Daily Mail* had been won to the tariff cause; within a couple of years Chamberlain had swung virtually all the newspapers against the Tory free-traders.

In addition to lobbying the press the League ran its own formidable propaganda machine producing millions of leaflets. Tariff Reform activities were funded in part by the personal finance of the major participants. They were also supported by some powerful capitalists, especially those who derived their wealth from the iron, steel and engineering trades of the West Midlands and Sheffield who found their traditional export markets shrinking. For these ironmasters and manufacturers a system of preferential tariffs made sound economic sense. The programme of the League avowed its commitment to the 'defence and development of the industrial interests of the British Empire'. However, support from capital was limited because many more capitalists feared that wages would rise with no tangible prospects of profits increasing in the same proportion. Others remained suspicious of the League's demagogic appeals to populist sentiments.

The League's propaganda, however, did more than attempt to persuade people that protection and preference would boost prosperity for all. It asserted that the issue of tariffs transcended traditional party alignments and that it went beyond 'ordinary' politics, as a truly national issue. The League's intellectuals prescribed not only an economic programme but also aimed to provide a moral structure for an imperial nation which had already glimpsed the beginnings of its own disintegration. The ambiguity in this discourse resulted from the contradictory relationship of the League to Unionism. The League itself was designed as an instrument to revitalize a populist Unionism. Yet its insistence on the exceptional nature of the imperial crisis and the doubts it registered about Britain's future as a great power increasingly suggested that a radically new political formation was required. This would be populist and right-wing, but 'above' party. In Chamberlain's view, this could be accommodated in a revamped Unionist Party. For others of a more radical temperament, there was but a short step from the Tariff Reform League to the conclusion that 'Unionism's' salvation could only be guaranteed by the destruction of the existing Unionist Party.

The Tariff Reform League had a major impact on the Unionist Party and on the traditions of Conservatism. In the short term severe internal bloodletting took place. The economic issue of protectionism remained unresolved until 1932. Until then it caused periodic rancour, upsetting the unstable compromises patched up by successive party managers. Despite these failures, the programme of the League was of fundamental significance in fashioning a distinctly Conservative collectivism. Chamberlain's erstwhile radicalism was sucked dry and reincarnated in a new Conservative form which took shape in combat against the forces of progressivism and socialism. Conservative collectivism proved ultimately of greater importance than the technical issue of tariffs. From 1911 until 1940 the Conservative Party was led by those who had been influenced and politically formed by the Chamberlain vision.

The refashioning of Conservatism did not however have an immediate popular appeal. The attempt to win the working class to Unionism and to stem the party's electoral losses was a failure. In 1903 the TUC promptly came out in opposition to the League. Occasional converts to the imperial programme turned out to be the exception rather than the rule, as Robert Blatchford was to show in 1909. It was with a note of desperation that Chamberlain declared in 1905: 'Unless I have the support of working people my movement is already condemned.'[6]

Very little study has been made of popular responses to tariff reform. Opposition to dear food is the most frequent explanation for its failure. But although this is of prime importance it tends to neglect the record of the Unionist governments and the accumulation of resentment which unified the labour movement, the Radicals and the progressives. The electoral fortunes of Unionism were receding before the Tariff Reform League was launched and the fate of the League was ultimately entwined with the fate of the party. Two factors are evident. First, the tariff programme was closely tied to the aspirations for political representation of capitalists whose long-term prosperity depended on indirect taxation, which placed the greatest burden on the working class. Second, the implementation of the League's policies would have led directly to social-imperialist and authoritarian prescriptions. Free trade, social reform and peace were not to be easily dislodged as the goals of the labour movement by a militant imperialism when economic benefits seemed so few and potential incursions into traditional constitutionalism so many.

The radical right

The populist aspirations of the Unionist radicals did not disappear in the face of the initial failures of the Tariff Reform League. No other viable political identity existed for Unionists. It was possible to leave the party altogether – as Churchill did in May 1904. He had long been a malcontent, nursing radical dreams and, like Chamberlain, despairing of the leadership. Yet he rejected any form of protection. Others hinted at the possibility of splitting the imperialists from the Liberal Party and setting up a party of the centre. This option became increasingly attractive as the political situation became more volatile. Alternatively, it was possible to stick with Balfour or the free-fooders, but occupy a subordinate position inside the Unionist Party.

Failure to build a popular movement did not prevent the Tariff Reform League from dominating the Unionist organizations. The more the tariff reformers gained ground, the more Balfour's position weakened and internecine factionalism sharpened. This success allowed radical members of the League, above all Leo Maxse and Garvin, to put pressure on Chamberlain which imposed further strains on his relations with Balfour.

In December 1905 Balfour resigned and the Liberals assumed office. In the ensuing election the Unionist defeat was devastating: the Unionist Party lost more than 200 seats, including Balfour's. After ruling for ten years Unionism fell apart. In the aftermath the tariff reformers, free from the blame attached to the leadership, again took the offensive inside the party. The position of the radicals gained momentum.

In February 1906, Chamberlain agreed that he would not challenge Balfour for the leadership providing the latter pledged himself and the party to tariff reform. Balfour's reply stated unequivocally that fiscal reform would remain 'the first constructive work' of the Unionists. This deal weakened the Balfour centre position. To Unionist members who feared that the Liberals were about to dismantle the empire at one blow the tariff reformers provided a ready defence for an enfeebled party. The most careful estimates suggest that by the end of 1906 the free-fooders could count on the support of thirty-one MPs. Balfour held on to forty-nine and the tariff reformers seventy-nine.[7]

Throughout 1906 the initiative passed increasingly to the tariff reform zealots. The concordat between Balfour and Chamberlain, the consequent isolation of the free-fooders and then, in July, Chamberlain's stroke, all strengthened the position of the more militant protectionists. The lack of positive working-class support had in the previous three years thrown Chamberlain back into the arms of Balfour and established Unionism. Where Chamberlain equivocated, Maxse and Milner pushed ahead. They were ready to try to link the imperialism and collectivism of the Tariff Reform League with the socialism of the labour movement in an anticipation of a national socialism. In this project the Unionist Party was ultimately expendable. This was the 'catastrophical' theory of politics which many Conservatives found distasteful and dangerous. The stakes were raised on both sides. The virulently sectarian *Morning Post* published a list of free-food MPs and called for their expulsion, a cry taken up by the *Express* and the *Globe*. On a similar impulse Henry Page Croft formed the Confederacy as a secret grouping of extremist tariff reformers. Guided by Leo Maxse and the future Unionist leader and Prime Minister, Andrew Bonar Law, it acted as the vigilante overseer of the tariff movement. Its aim was to seek out and expel any members who vacillated on the principle of tariffs. As Croft recollected:

It was started by three or four of us who held the view that nothing was worth fighting for except Chamberlain's battle. . . . Our idea was to endeavour to get large numbers of young men drawn from the aristocracy and county gentlemen who should devote themselves to the cause.[8]

The fortunes of these radical Unionists altered drastically in the course of 1909. Lloyd George's budget, first presented to the House of Commons in April, was probably not calculated to provoke the peerage into a fit of retribution. But the budget did permanently alter the political landscape. As a radical within his own party Lloyd George confronted an impasse not dissimilar to that encountered by Chamberlain. Lloyd George's attempt to construct an active and popular basis for Liberalism appeared a feasible strategy to regenerate the Liberal Party, create the conditions for a more interventionist state and halt the socialist threat. The radical clauses in the budget prepared the ground, unleashing a chain of events in which inter-party conflict rose to unseen heights.

In opposing the budget the fractious political and ideological forces of Unionism were temporarily regrouped under the standard of the Tariff Reform League. The budget was rejected by the Unionist-dominated House of Lords. As a result an election was called in January 1910 in which the Liberals lost their overall majority and power in the House of Commons shifted to the Irish Party. In April the budget finally became law. In December a second election was called to deal with the unresolved matter of the constitutional position of the peers. This returned an exact balance of Unionist and Liberal members. Impasse continued until the following summer when Balfour persuaded sufficient numbers of his party to concede on the issue of the Lords.

The significance of these events lies in the breakdown of constitutional precedent and practice, the need for extraordinary measures (such as the bi-partisan constitutional conference in the summer of 1910) and the struggles for the redistribution of power between the two chambers. It became evident in the course of 1910 that party conflict could no longer be satisfactorily contained in the parliamentary arena. Extra-parliamentary organizations were quickly set up in 1909 – the Budget League and the Budget Protest League – in an attempt to carry the fight on to the terrain of popular politics. There were many such Unionist organizations. The situation was made even more dangerous for the politicians by the fact that at the same time direct action by trade unionists and insurgent feminists dramatically indicated that the hold of Westminster on popular politics was in jeopardy. In addition the power of the Irish Party in the Commons forced the issue of Home Rule to the centre of the political stage.

To endorse a right-wing activism in the style of Chamberlain in this situation was to play the joker in the pack. The question for the established politicians was how they could retain control of what promised to be a volatile movement. The result of these pressures led to the break-up of the Tariff Reform League in 1910. Some drew back from populism and began to make overtures to their political-party opponents in the hope of building a parliamentary coalition to weather the storm. Others, however, still holding true to the original intentions of the Tariff Reform League, insisted the situation was so exceptional and the Unionist Party so unreliable that there was no alternative but to pursue the populist gamble despite the manifold dangers. For these reasons 1910 marks a profound break.

It was Garvin in the *Observer* who first formulated the stark choice facing Unionism – 'Tariff Reform or Socialism'. Garvin rightly sensed that his boss, Northcliffe, was beginning to waver from the Unionist position.

During 1909 Northcliffe had even contemplated a new radical alignment under the aegis of Lloyd George. Garvin was aghast. He swung Northcliffe back into the fold of imperial orthodoxy. He then did his utmost to persuade Balfour, Austen Chamberlain and F. E. Smith – the leading Unionist strategists – that it was the duty of the party to force the issue with the Liberals and raise the tempo of party conflict. But Northcliffe's alarming drift towards Lloyd George anticipated a strategic solution, through the convergence of political 'opposites', which became increasingly appealing.

It was paradoxically during this time of their greatest success inside the party that the programme of the tariff reformers began to crumble. Their success had only been accomplished by the League modifying its approach to one of plain anti-socialism. The tariff reform controversy embraced a number of separate conflicts which the reformers were no longer capable of containing.

The Tariff Reform League effectively came to an end in November 1910 when Balfour announced, under pressure from Garvin and Bonar Law, that the Unionist Party would not implement preferential tariffs without first winning a clear mandate from the people. That even tariff militants like Garvin and Law were prepared to back–peddle at this moment is significant. According to one commentator this move indicated that 'The working classes, to whom tariff reform was alleged to appeal, were in practice given up as lost.'⁹ The disintegration of the Tariff Reform League gave rise to the chaotic forces of the radical right.

The League had offered to the Unionists their greatest hope for winning the working class. This was now dashed. In response, the party as a whole shifted rapidly to the right, pulled by the attraction of a belligerent anti-socialism. Blatant disregard for the constitution became commonplace after the parliamentary impasse of 1910. The recent semi-official history of the party notes that 'the patriotic party became begetters of rebellion, the party of order suborned crime and mutiny, and the leader of the opposition in parliament approved and supported the destruction of both the practice and authority of parliament' – although the good sense of the author prevails when he reminds us, 'It should not be thought that the Unionists enjoyed such a situation, for they certainly did not.'¹⁰ Few sections of the party, still less the leadership, escaped this lurch to the right. As the syndicalist and suffragette movements gathered strength so the most reactionary tendencies within Unionism came into the open.

Militant Unionism found expression in resistance both to the Parliament Bill (which threatened to curtail the authority of the House of Lords and thus overturn the power structure on which Unionism rested) and to the Third Home Rule Bill. The first wave of resistance, which lasted until the defeat of the diehards in the Lords in August 1911, was mounted as a rebellion against the leadership of Balfour. The second, attempting to hold back Home Rule, carried with it the new leader, Bonar Law.

No single cause could reunite the party. Bonar Law opposed diehard resistance to the Parliament Bill, but was vocal in his support for a mutinous Ulster Unionism. Garvin and Austen Chamberlain (who fundamentally disagreed over tariffs) were both 'ditchers' on the issue of the Lords but much more muted in their support of the Ulster Volunteers. Some from the militant wing of Unionism – the Milnerite group of Garvin, Waldorf Astor and F. S. Oliver in particular – broadly agreed with Lloyd George and Churchill on Ireland with whom they reached a preliminary consensus (to the fury of the Ulster Unionist leader Sir Edward Carson). On the other hand Henry Page Croft and Willoughby de Broke (the latter dreaming of drilling his yeomen commandos up and down the Warwickshire countryside) formed the Reveille group in September 1910, hoping to raise the political temperature and open up the antagonisms separating Unionists from Liberals. While a minority considered breaking with the party altogether, others (such as Amery) were content to hang on and 'keep in touch'.[11] The vast majority, however, diehards included, were resolved to stay with Unionism.

All these personalities and factions were of the radical right in the sense that all were prepared to place the dictates of Unionism or empire above the demands of parliamentary and constitutional politics. Garvin made his stand on the Lords, Austen Chamberlain on tariffs, Carson on Ulster: where some were prepared to compromise, others believed the very integrity of Unionism to be at stake.[12]

The chaotic character of these developments is important, for the whole political ground moved in this period, leaving no secure guidelines. The radical right emerged not primarily to confront Liberalism, but to break and constrain popular democratic movements and above all to turn back the rise of socialism and Labour. The central problem was whether it was possible to hold back the independent representation of labour and remain within the constitution.

The increase in popular, extra-parliamentary opposition did not convince all radical Unionists that Chamberlain's strategy was reckless. Captains of the old movement like Amery and Maxse were sure that it was necessary to fight on. Croft and de Broke – constructing an amalgam of aristocratic Tory paternalism and a populism in the Chamberlain style – planned a new National Party, aiming to build a popular movement uncompromised by what they saw as the archaic structures of Unionism.

The old tariff radicals searched for new causes after 1910. It looked for a moment as if rejection of the Parliament Bill would provide the grounds for a remaking of old alliances. Opposition to the bill cohered in May 1911 with the organization of the 'last ditchers'. Lord Curzon was the first recognized leader of the ditchers, although other prominent Unionists were quick to rally – Lord Halsbury, de Broke, F. E. Smith, Garvin, Carson, Milner, Austen Chamberlain and Amery. The nucleus of the old tariff reformers worked alongside more cautious leaders like Curzon who stopped short of encouraging any concession to popular politics. Diehard resistance in the Lords fused with the radical right, developing a new perspective in which Balfourism, Liberalism and Labour would have no place.

The rebellion in the Lords did very little to bring any closer popular support for Unionism – but it spelt the end of Balfour's leadership. In November 1911 Bonar Law emerged as the successful compromise candidate for the leadership. Bonar Law's family roots lay in the Protestant fringe of the empire (Canada, Scotland, Ulster). His wealth came from his ironworks and directorship of the Clydeside Bank, his politics from Glasgow Unionism. His political elevation reversed the Conservative tradition of recruiting the leader from the patrician governing class. In November 1910 he had been largely responsible for modifying the party's formal position on tariffs. Bonar Law succeeded to the leadership because of his reputation as a tariff reform radical, not as a result of a continuing commitment to the letter of Chamberlain's programme.

Shortly after Bonar Law became leader, the radical right became convulsed in the second great Unionist cause of the day, Ulster. It would seem that the Ulster revolt and the mass recruitment both in Ulster and in Britain might have provided Unionism with its means for a decisive populist renewal. The Ulster issue appeared to condense and accentuate all the fears of social and moral collapse which had first given rise to Unionism. Some inside the Unionist ranks – Carson, F. E. Smith and Bonar Law – attempted to force the issue and use it to rebuild the party. But the divisions inside Unionism in the end proved decisive. Some of the most prominent British Unionists moved to jettison their Ulster allies and leave them to their fate. While some of the radical right were giving full support to Carson and the Ulster rebellion, the Milnerites were deep in consultation with the very perpetrators of Home Rule – Lloyd George and Churchill.

The emergence of coalition politics

From 1903 to 1910 Unionism had been dominated by the unsuccessful attempt to launch an active, popular imperial movement as a means to reconstruct the party and the state. From the outset many Unionists were fearful of such a strategy. But with Balfourism discredited, those who remained unpersuaded by these populist adventures began to call for a different solution, a coalition or centre government. After 1910, given Unionist inability to prevent the budget and the reform of the Lords, combined with the radicalization of popular movements outside Parliament, the idea of coalition government became more attractive. From the time of the formation of the Liberal Unionists in 1886 the idea of a centre party had been floated from time to time without attracting much support. But after the crisis of 1910 positions within the Unionist camp veered wildly from one crisis to the next, oscillating unpredictably between populist and coalitionist positions. From this moment a new configuration of political forces opened which, following Gramsci, can usefully be called 'caesarist'.

By caesarism I refer to a political situation characterized by the following features: first, a protracted crisis of representation; second, the strength of opposition forces ranged against the state; third, the exhaustion of the resources for the power bloc to construct and command its own popular interventions; and fourth, the concentration of power at one point in the state. These features led Gramsci to observe that 'every coalition government is the first stage of Caesarism'.[13] In such a situation the state representatives are captured by their own logic of constraining popular struggles and recomposing the apparatuses of the state internally and administratively. From this perspective comes the understanding of 'various gradations of caesarism' and of parliamentary caesarism without the classic hero, without the 'Caesar' or 'Bonaparte'.

Growing pressure from influential political figures for a centre or national party and for a solution to the crisis of representation to be imposed 'from above', followed by the actual coalition governments from 1915 to 1922, suggest that 'gradations' of caesarism are discernible in this period. However, caution is called for. From the late 1880s records of club chit-chat, scribbled letters and diary entries overflow with references to schemes for various centre parties or governments. These were generally phantoms, bred in political gossip or strategic frustration and only given life by excessive personal vanity. But they were also an index of the crisis of the state and of the sort of solutions devised to counter it, suggesting the declining appeal of the classic two-party model.

This process of incipient caesarism can be seen as the last moment in a long radical tradition which had its roots in Jacobinism and which even in the previous century had already become jaded and spiritless. This tradition was laid to rest by the *arriviste* provincial radicalism of Chamberlain and Lloyd George. And paradoxically Winston Churchill, born into one of the greatest of the aristocratic families, adopted for a time this radicalism as his own, his aristocratic romanticism momentarily taking on a distinctly radical and populist hue. But it was these figures who also became most closely identified with caesarist solutions. The final closure of this radical tradition meant an abrupt retreat from earlier positions, the spurning of 'the people' in favour of a national solution imposed by political leaders and the slow organization of new alliances: in short, a new strategy for reaction. The passage from a radical populism to a bonapartist regime is not, after all, unprecedented.

In January 1910 the *Morning Post* commented on the profound gulf separating the parties. Yet by June the Conservative and Liberal leaders were engaged in a joint constitutional conference. This took place outside the formal parliamentary arena in a search for compromises on the vital issues of the day. It was in the *Observer* of 8 May that the idea for a conference was first publicly proposed, and this clearly conformed to the switch in Garvin's own position. At the beginning of the year he had commented: 'My whole instinct for the moment is just as much for going steady as last autumn it was for going strong.'[14] The stature of the representatives at the conference showed the seriousness of the initiative: Balfour, Austen Chamberlain, Asquith and Lloyd George. They discussed Home Rule, the House of Lords, tariff reform and conscription. In the course of the meeting there occurred the first serious attempt to create a coalition. It is not clear how far the two party leaders followed this move, although both were kept informed and both endorsed the idea of exploratory discussions. Churchill, Lloyd George, Austen Chamberlain and F. E. Smith were those most directly involved. The crucial figure in these negotiations was Lloyd George. Smith believed that 'Lloyd George is done for unless he gradually inclines to our side in all things that permanently count'.[15] By the summer this shift had already started. From this time his hostility to labour increased and in July during the debate on the Conciliation Bill (on women's suffrage) both he and Churchill adopted a position of unexpectedly vehement and intransigent opposition. Garvin and Lloyd George were moving in tandem. In a reversal of the position of the previous year Garvin now had to persuade Northcliffe to accept this potential Unionist/Lloyd George regroupment. In the event the whole thing foundered on Home Rule. But according to Semmel if such a government had been formed it would have been 'a virtually complete amalgam of both Liberal and Tariff Reform social imperialisms'.[16]

Coalition governments, 1915–22

The forces opposed to the establishment of a coalition, however, remained formidable. The bulk of the Unionist and Liberal members saw greater reason to resist such moves than to support them. The usual invective of party politics ran as deep as ever in the years immediately preceding the outbreak of war. The foremost figures entertaining the idea of coalition were perceived by many back-benchers as little more than contemptible. Asquith had little regard for Bonar Law and no one trusted Lloyd George. Churchill was reviled by the Unionists and unnerved many Liberals. F. E. Smith had a reputation for being too clever by half. At the time war was declared the Milnerites remained influential, but they had no secure platform inside the Unionist Party itself. Garvin's star never rose again to the heights of 1910. And Max Aitken, the future Lord Beaverbrook, was intoxicated by the drama of behind-the-scenes power politics. When the prospect of coalition became a reality the apprehensions of the Unionist Walter Long were characteristic of the atmosphere of mutual distrust. In a letter to Carson he confided, 'I loathe the very idea of our good fellows sitting with those double-dyed traitors.'[17]

To understand how the countervailing pressures against coalition were finally overcome it is necessary to consider the wider historical issues. The

Lloyd George coalitions of 1916–22 responded to the imperatives of a nation fully mobilized for war by actively intervening in both civilian and military matters. They attracted the collectivist wings of both the parties, realizing the aspirations of the pre-war collectivist radicals.[18] The war itself was the critical final factor in creating the conditions which, in May 1915, made Asquith's coalition possible. But from that moment the pre-war process which had weakened the party structures accelerated. The political leaders were freed from party allegiances and the War Cabinets determined by a handful of individuals. As A. J. P. Taylor noted of Asquith's coalition, it resulted not from a consensus between the two major parties but from 'a pact between the two front benches'.[19]

Coalition was forced on Asquith partly because of pressures exerted by Lloyd George (who threatened resignation) and by the Unionist leader, Bonar Law. Bonar Law made it a condition of Unionist participation that Churchill should be sacked from the Admiralty, thus taking the opportunity to settle scores. But Asquith, although ready to ditch Churchill, had no desire to relinquish any further either his own power or that of his party. All the key posts remained with the Liberals and the significant task of Minister of Munitions fell to Lloyd George. On the whole the business of government proceeded much as it had done before.

To the Unionists who had been schooled in the traditions of the Tariff Reform League the Asquith coalition appeared a cowardly sham. First on the offensive were the Milnerites – Milner himself, Amery and one of Milner's most trusted cronies from South African days, Geoffrey Dawson, then editor of *The Times*. Two days after the coalition was established *The Times* carried a 'Call for Leadership', declaring the need for what it regarded as an authentic, active national leader. The Milnerites continued the campaign through the channels of the National Service League, an organization dear to the radical right from before the war. With its commitment to conscription it was a useful stick with which to beat the Liberals. Through its proprietor, Northcliffe, *The Times* was brought into the anti-Asquith fray. In the course of the summer and autumn of 1915 this unofficial Unionist opposition began to look like a potential regrouping of the radical right. Its status was enhanced by the resignation of Sir Edward Carson from the government to join the unofficial opposition. Although Lloyd George's unease was widely known, he refused to budge or openly to side with the disaffected Unionists.

By the end of the year the opposition was in a position of strength. Dawson and Astor controlled *The Times* and the *Observer*; Milner himself was a weighty presence in the House of Lords; and Carson was relentless from the back-benches. Nor was this opposition exclusively drawn from the Unionists. Christopher Addison, a Liberal and a radical, approved Lloyd George's comprehensive plans for social reform. He was not only frustrated by Asquith's vacillation, but identified a deeper problem in the organization of the state. In December he wrote in his diary: 'Good democrat as I am, I am beginning to change my mind and to think that it would be better for the nation at present if Parliament were not sitting.'[20]

Whatever their formal party affiliation, all the dissidents rallied around the potential alternatives to Asquith: Lloyd George, Bonar Law and Carson. The Milnerites did their best to keep contact with Lloyd George. But from the time of his resignation Carson set out on an uninhibited grab for power, believing that Bonar Law's status as a national and Unionist leader had been compromised by his association with Asquith. A ferocious trial of strength developed. The Milnerites wisely also kept in touch with Carson. Sir Max Aitken took it upon himself to act once more as Bonar Law's second. He realized that for Bonar Law to retain his authority it was necessary to split Carson from Milner and to cement the Lloyd George/Bonar Law relationship. Aitken's objective was to use Lloyd George to save Bonar Law and Unionism from the untempered diehardism of the Milnerites.

Asquith's unpopularity grew through 1916 and in November he barely survived a vote of confidence in the House. Within the fortnight, for the first time, Lloyd George, Bonar Law and Carson met secretly. Lloyd George was keen to press his idea for a war committee, independent of the Cabinet and without the Prime Minister at its head. Despite his continued suspicion of Lloyd George, Bonar Law was attracted by this plan and by the idea that his old rival Carson should be included as one of its three members, together with Bonar Law himself and Lloyd George as chairman. Over the next few days other meetings of this triumvirate took place and it was at this stage that Bonar Law's personal loyalty to Asquith finally gave way. Asquith refused to countenance the plan for the war committee. In response Aitken unleashed an effective press campaign against Asquith and, as in May the previous year, Lloyd George again threatened resignation. Bonar Law met with his Conservative ministers who insisted that Asquith be sent a resolution recommending the government's resignation. To preserve his premiership Asquith had no option but to capitulate. He accepted the war committee scheme and the reconstruction of his government. At this point, on 4 December, it seemed as if he were safe. However the next day *The Times* renewed the attack, drawing on confidential information of the recent negotiations. Not surprisingly Asquith suspected Lloyd George of double-dealing. Asquith withdrew his previous agreements and again joined battle with Lloyd George. But the power of the Unionists proved decisive. Balfour and Bonar Law had little option but to support Lloyd George and force Asquith's resignation. Bonar Law was asked to form an administration but Asquith refused to serve under him. Consequently on 6 December the King's invitation went to Lloyd George and he accepted. A major Conservative victory had been accomplished.

For the next six years the destiny of the Conservative Party depended on Lloyd George; equally Lloyd George depended on the Conservatives. He had no party organization to support him, for Asquith remained leader of the Liberal Party. No Liberal member of the 1915–16 cabinet was retained and once more the party whips had exercised virtually no influence on the formation of the coalition. Without the Unionists Lloyd George was badly isolated. What had effectively been secured by the events of December was a Conservative government, strengthened by a number of right-wing Liberals, most of whom were shortly to leave the Liberal Party. In 1916 a predominantly Liberal government was exchanged for one predominantly Conservative, not as the result of any electoral 'swing' but due to ministerial intrigue and conspiracy.

The war coalition: caesarism raised

From this point on the features of caesarism strengthened, with Lloyd George assuming the mantle of national saviour, and the power of the state concentrated yet more at its apex. For some of the Unionist collectivists, notably Austen Chamberlain and F. E. Smith (later Lord Birkenhead), the Lloyd George coalition created the type of regime for which the tariff reformers had struggled, and provided the Unionist Party with the means for regeneration. Thus for them continuation of the coalition was imperative though the manner of its creation marked the antithesis of the populist dreams of the tariff reformers. Indeed each successive mobilization of Unionist radicals from 1903 to 1922 articulated a narrower conception of the popular, until vanishing point was reached in the decidedly non-popular, caesarist politics of Austen Chamberlain and Birkenhead.

There were three important shifts in alignment. First, the Milnerites had been among the last of the Unionists to concede that the time for creating a mass movement of the right was over. The formation of the Lloyd George coalition all but put a halt to such aspirations. Following Milner's swift elevation to prominence – he had previously held no political position in any British government – his protégés (Amery among them) stepped sideways into power. Lloyd George's acceptance of the proposal that his secretariat be hugely increased in numbers and significance not only gave jobs to Milner's rising men of talent but also did much to bypass both Parliament and the established civil service. This decisively relocated power closer to the centre of the state apparatus and the person of Lloyd George, much to the frustrated anger of the Liberal press which decried the onset of a new absolutism.

However the conspiracies of the Milnerites were not terminated at one stroke. Their plans for an imperialist workers' movement were finally shelved only with the greatest reluctance. Throughout 1916 and 1917 Milner continued his attempts to build a workers' party along the same lines as the tariff pioneers had attempted in 1903. Milner outlined his project in a letter to Lady Roberts in February 1916:

I am at present trying verý hard, but quietly, to further a purely working-class movement, which I hope will knock out the 'ILP' and start a 'Workers' League' among Trade Unionists, which will make Imperial Unity and Citizen Service 'planks' on its platform. This is confidential.[21]

With encouragement from Milner and cash from Astor a British Workers' National League was in fact founded in 1916. After the February Revolution in Russia there appears to have been a transient intensification of this activity. F. S. Oliver, a Milnerite of long standing, contacted Lloyd George suggesting that he meet with Victor Fisher of the British Workers' League. Later in the year Lloyd George, Milner, Addison and Fisher met at Astor's house, but these schemes came to little. The various reactionary working-class groupings were absorbed by George Barnes's pro-coalition National Democratic Party. This represents the last flush of pre-war Unionist radicalism before its fragments were incorporated in the fascist groupings in the 1920s and 1930s.

The second important shift in the coalition arose from a power struggle between the military chiefs, especially Field-Marshall Sir John Haig and the Chief of the Imperial General Staff, General Sir William Robertson, and the War Cabinet. Lloyd George was determined that ultimate authority must rest with the War Cabinet. The resulting confrontation divided the Unionist ranks and proved the most enduring internal contention during the war. The Conservative minister Lord Derby, Northcliffe, Carson and even George V sided with the war chiefs; Milner and Lloyd George put up every resistance to military diktat. In July 1917 they forced Carson to resign from the Admiralty. In the reshuffle which followed Churchill was at last included in the Cabinet as Minister for Munitions on the grounds that he was safer inside than out, although a majority of Unionists still opposed the appointment. In February 1918 Lloyd George and Milner pressured Derby, at the War Office, into sacking Robertson, whom he favoured, for Sir Henry Wilson, whom he despised but who had been closely associated with Milner during the Ulster mutiny. Two months later Derby himself resigned and Milner sacrificed his seat in the inner War Cabinet to take charge of the War Office. This left Lloyd George in an even stronger position. The last splutter of resistance from the military came in May when General Sir Frederick Maurice, an old ally of Robertson's, accused Lloyd George of lying about troop strength on the Western Front. Asquith seized this opportunity to retaliate, badly bungled the affair in the House of Commons and thus deepened the divide among the Liberals.

The third shift in alignment concerned the labour movement. Arthur Henderson, the Labour representative in the War Cabinet, fought with Lloyd George over his belief that the Labour Party should send delegates to the socialist peace conference. He was also deliberately humiliated by the premier. Henderson resigned and quickly re-established relations with the anti-war Labour Party members. This group of Labour leaders consequently resolved that henceforth Labour's strategy depended on eliminating the Liberal Party. In the long run Henderson's resignation was to prove of far greater importance than Milner's loyalty or the enforced subservience of the military.

The coalition had been formed as an exceptional wartime measure. It was accepted that when the war was over an election would be inevitable. The politicians also realized that it would have to be conducted on a new system of suffrage. The 1918 Representation of the People Act enfranchised all men of 21 and over and women of 30 and over. Many Unionists opposed this influx of new voters – Sir George Younger, the Unionist chairman, only managed to win endorsement from the party organizations by 'a narrow squeak'.[22] In the first reading Carson, defying the party leadership, led a hundred Unionists against the bill. The question of women's suffrage, left to a free vote, was the cause of much recrimination, especially in the House of Lords. However radical these reforms may seem by the numbers enfranchised, they were the most conservative that the government imagined it could squeeze through. Even then, the effects were mitigated by the 1918 Redistribution Act which handed to the Conservative Party at least seventy safe seats in the home counties and other middle-class areas.

Lacking any established party organization Lloyd George was in a shaky position to face an election. In May the coalition Liberals declared themselves an official party grouping. In July they decided with the Unionists to continue the coalition pact after the armistice and enter the forthcoming election as a united force. Bonar Law, the old admirer of Joseph Chamberlain, saw great prospects in this arrangement. In a letter to Balfour he wrote:

Lloyd George . . . would secure a great hold on the rank and file of our Party and he would also be so dependent on that Party after the election that he would permanently be driven into the same attitude towards our Party which Chamberlain was placed in before, with this difference – that he would be the leader of it. That would, however, I am inclined to think not be a bad thing for our Party and a good thing for the Nation. I am perfectly certain, indeed, I do not think anyone can doubt this, that our Party on the old lines will never have any future again in this country.[23]

Bonar Law hoped that the Lloyd George/Unionist axis would form the dominant factor in a permanent realignment of the British political scene.

The election was held in December, shortly after the armistice. Officially accredited 'government' candidates were awarded with what came to be known as 'the coupon' – a joint letter of support from Lloyd George and Bonar Law. This did much to undermine the Asquithian Liberals by giving a quite spurious legitimation to the endorsed candidates. These candidates were predominantly drawn from the Unionists and from the camp followers of Lloyd George. With this fixed electoralism working for them and with by far the lowest turnout this century, the coalition won an impressive majority.

In all 478 coalition candidates were returned (335 of whom were Unionist), to face an opposition of 229 (which included 73 Sinn Fein members who refused to take their seats). In practice government members outnumbered the combined opposition by more than three to one.

Labour and post-war incorporation

The character of the government from 1918 to 1922 was one of unremitting reaction, in which there occurred a momentary fusion of the caesarist elements which had marked political developments in the previous decade.

There was, however, no complete embargo on democratic or material concessions. Unemployment benefit was made comprehensive and a separate Ministry of Health was set up in June 1919 with the ex-Minister of Reconstruction, Christopher Addison, at its head. There were also early experiments in 'industrial democracy' following the establishment of the Whitley Councils in 1917 and 1918, and the National Industrial Conference of February 1919. What lay behind these initiatives was a continuing but modified dedication to the pre-war ideologies of social imperialism. The shared objective was to build a regime uniting all classes, in a single bloc, under the banner of 'one nation'.[24] But there was no attempt to encourage popular mobilization. On the contrary, the object was to integrate the working class vertically into the apparatuses of the state in an effort to tame the labour movement through a process of bureaucratic incorporation. This amounted to a concerted attempt to reorganize the means of representation, to recompose the internal power structure of the state, and to replace the dominance of Parliament by the dominance of corporate institutions. There were precedents in the pre-war system of labour exchanges and in the management of particular industries during the war. After 1918 the success of the strategy depended on the creation and encouragement of an 'official' labour movement. The hope was that labour discipline could be bought in exchange for a system of high wages and industrial representation. It was in this context that Lloyd George condoned the plans for universal schemes of social welfare and for some measure of economic redistribution by the Ministry of Reconstruction. There were clear echoes of earlier collectivist schemes. The significant difference was that after 1918 the predominant means by which these goals were to be attained were administrative rather than populist. In the aftermath of the war the bid to institutionalize the corporate arrangement was perhaps the last moment (until the 1940s) in which a hegemonic project was organized around a conception of 'one nation'. Thereafter more modest objectives were followed, on the understanding that before any greater measure of political consensus could be achieved certain outstanding class issues needed to be settled.

This concern for developing corporate institutions was determined in part by the threat to Parliament from what were perceived as hostile forces. After the expansion of the electorate brought about by the Representation of the People Act, Lloyd George effectively retreated from the parliamentary arena altogether. Only sixty-three Labour MPs were elected in 1918, but the Labour Party won nearly 2.5 million votes compared to the Unionists' 3.5 million. It appeared that before very long the Labour Party would be the largest single party in the House of Commons, a prospect which the Unionist dominated government viewed with alarm.

However, a corporatism could not be sustained as the defining policy of the coalition. There was little enthusiasm from organized workers for government-sponsored schemes for industrial representation. A severe economic crisis and a rapid rise in unemployment put paid to a policy of systematic material concessions. The creation of an 'official' labour movement depended on destroying the labour movement which already existed. Time was short and resistance fierce. One defeat after another was inflicted on the working class. But it was not until the failure of the General Strike nearly eight years after the end of the war that the government was sufficiently powerful to dictate its terms. By then, the full corporate programme, on the Mussolini model, was a dead-end.[25]

Lloyd George's bold attempt to remould the state on a corporatist model moved in parallel with the government's direct confrontation with the labour movement. Whatever the ultimate aim, it appeared to lead Lloyd George back to the conclusion that before anything could be done the power of organized labour needed to be broken. This, the legacy of Chamberlain's failure to build an alternative imperialist movement at an earlier date, became the leitmotif of the coalition.

By 1921 the government had little policy but anti-socialism. Periodic bouts of pure and simple diehardism burnt through the party, touching even those renowned for their 'moderation'. The Bolshevik scare became a permanent reference in the political discourse of the day. The government spent thousands of pounds on anti-socialist propaganda, much of it clandestinely inserted in supposedly independent newspapers and journals. The upper and middle classes were recruited into militaristic and volunteer organizations, often indirectly backed by the state, in order to prepare for strike breaking and the preservation of public order. What might previously have been seen, outside Ireland, as a dubious aristocratic eccentricity now appeared deadly serious. A decade earlier de Broke had drilled his Warwickshire yeomanry; in 1921 Bonar Law placed his hopes for salvation on the vigilance of patriotic stockbrokers. This process of extra-parliamentary mobilization no longer aspired to create 'one nation'; it aimed once and for all to 'teach a lesson' to the working class.

1922

In the absence of effective policies the government could do nothing but retreat into a corner. The impact on the Unionist Party was devastating, nearly submerging the party altogether. From 1920 it was clear that given a system of near universal suffrage and the advance of Labour at the polls, a systematic anti-socialist strategy was required. Only one perspective was clearly articulated, mainly by Birkenhead. He advocated a war of manoeuvre – all-out confrontation against the forces of socialism. For this to be achieved he believed, putting only more forcefully what Bonar Law had proposed in 1918, that the pact with Lloyd George needed to be formalized and made permanent, and that the Unionist Party had to shed its old identity. The intention was to create a new centre party, under the leadership of Lloyd George, as a united anti-socialist party. In January 1920 Birkenhead suggested that 'It may be called a National Party, a Constitutional Party or a People's Party', nomenclatures revealing his unparalleled inspiration for mendacity.[26] Allied to Birkenhead was Austen Chamberlain who in March 1921 was to succeed Bonar Law as party leader and who – with a curious sense of filial duty – deemed it his personal mission to re-unite, after nearly forty years, the Liberals with the Liberal Unionists. However, the one serious attempt at fusion in March 1920 foundered largely as a result of Liberal objections. Lloyd George was keen enough (and so was Churchill), but they were unable to persuade sufficient of their supporters. And although the idea had the full backing of the Unionist leadership (Bonar Law, Balfour, Birkenhead and Chamberlain), the local associations voiced their opposition. The aim was to unify all the anti-socialist forces to guarantee a permanent parliamentary majority, preventing any but minimal representation of Labour in the Commons and effectively organizing a one-party system.

Most opposition to the Birkenhead plan was motivated by personal hostility to Lloyd George, whom many perceived as little more than a liability to the Unionists. But through most of 1920 and 1921 this opposition remained fragmented, unable to produce any convincing alternatives.

In the by-elections of these years a scatter of candidates stood as anti-coalition Conservatives. In October 1920 Oswald Mosley resigned the coalition (Unionist) whip in protest against the state-backed Black and Tan terror in Ireland. Throughout 1920 Lord Robert Cecil (a son of the former Conservative Prime Minister Lord Salisbury, and from the start an opponent of the tariff programme) became disenchanted with the coalition and began to plan a more liberal anti-socialist coalition. He won the support of Arthur Steel-Maitland, a former party chairman, Milnerite and (with Amery) a crucial figure in the emerging Baldwinite constellation. A small coterie of high Anglican Conservatives, including the future Lord Halifax and Robert Cecil's brother, Lord Hugh Cecil, made plain their disgust with the ethical tone of Lloyd George's leadership. An identifiable Tory diehard tendency, led by another of Lord Salisbury's sons (the fourth Marquess of Salisbury) vented a great volume of anger against the coalition leadership which, although somewhat insubstantial, none the less made its impact. From another section of Unionism the Harmsworth brothers, Lords Northcliffe and Rothermere, the progenitors of one flank of the radical right, turned from their previous collectivist attachments and attacked the coalition for its profligacy on an 'Anti-Waste' platform. After an attempt to inaugurate his own National Party in the autumn of 1917, Henry Page Croft assumed once more his role as diehard back-bench inquisitor. Leo Maxse appeared in tow; to him the coalition had been sold out by 'defeatist financiers, international Jews, Labour pacifists for whom Mr Lloyd George has always had a weakness'.[27]

The ideological currents which fed these disaffected groupings were heterogeneous, drawing from the contrary terms of diehardism and 'moderation', individualism and collectivism, with neither one set of oppositions connecting with the other. It was a time of political confusion and fragmentation.

Yet there was a coherence underlying these apparently disparate springs of disaffection. This was the resurgence of a Conservative or Tory, rather than a Unionist, identity. A discourse organized around Conservatism automatically excluded Lloyd George from its structure of reference just as it included the junior ministers and back-benchers who had been all but silenced during the coalition years. The idea of a specifically Tory tradition was one symbolically much more potent than that of Unionism, with a longer history, and providing an ideological ensemble more open to 're-invention' at this critical moment. Strategic clarification did not follow for it was far from certain what this notion of a Conservative tradition meant. Thus as the party assumed the role of the political representative of capital the dispute between those who advocated a free market and those who welcomed state intervention was never resolved. The judgements of both could be legitimated by differing historical readings of the Conservative tradition. Furthermore, by the First World War Tory conceptions of state paternalism had become irretrievably stamped in the image of tariff collectivism.[28]

Whatever the ambiguities in this reaffirmation of Conservatism, it played an important part in dispatching Lloyd George from political leadership, for it provided the primary means by which dissent could cohere. Lloyd George and the coalition leaders were hopelessly remote. They badly miscalculated the mood of the opposition and were convinced that any challenge could only fail as no possible alternative leadership existed. The disdain they felt for their Unionist colleagues was unqualified. The Unionist Party divided without their noticing it, so that by the autumn of 1922 there were in effect two Conservative Parties.

The crisis blew open at the end of September. Lloyd George's Middle Eastern policies pushed Britain and the Dominions alarmingly close to war. At the same time he and the Conservative coalition leaders determined to force the pace of the coming election, planning to hold it before the National

Union of Conservative Associations met in November. Sir George Younger and the vast majority of the Conservatives were appalled. Even at this point, however, the anxiety of the Conservatives was not so much about continuing the coalition but rather about the undesirability of entering the election as a combined force. The reassertion of Conservative identity was accompanied by sound tactical planning. Depending on the outcome of the election, there was probably only a minority who would have advocated no alliance with Lloyd George under any circumstances. But to fight the election as independent forces would have been to expose the vulnerability of Lloyd George. This alone was sufficient to rouse the anger of Austen Chamberlain, the party leader. He proposed a meeting to call his party to order, fixed for 19 October at the Carlton Club. To the last Lloyd George was confident. On the eve of the meeting he boasted:

I have with me the official leader of the Conservative Party in Joseph Chamberlain's worthy son; I have the most distinguished of the elder Conservative statesmen and the only living Conservative ex-Premier in Lord Balfour; I have the most brilliant Conservative figure of modern times in Lord Birkenhead; and as the mouthpiece of the rank and file, the most successful organizer of Tory democracy in Salvidge of Liverpool.[29]

But the high command was not the army.

The scene at the Carlton Club is a favourite set piece of Conservative historians. Chamberlain attempted to reassert his authority by reprimanding the upstarts. Baldwin, in his role as a rather elderly junior minister with years of worthy but undistinguished service behind him and few prospects ahead, condemned with force the moral tone of the coalition, the cynicism of its leaders and their destructive ambitions. He claimed that any further deals could only end in disaster 'until the old Conservative Party is smashed to atoms and lost in ruins'. Bonar Law spoke last. To the end Bonar Law was riven by doubt. Baldwin and Amery pressed him constantly to break his old allegiances. In the event he spoke against the coalition and secured victory for the rebels. Chamberlain immediately resigned the leadership and Lloyd George the premiership. A coup from below was a fitting end to the coalition.

Baldwin

In the general election which followed the Conservative Party won an overall majority, proving the tactical wisdom of those who wanted to go to the polls as an independent party. However the socialist threat did not disappear; the number of Labour MPs more than doubled. Conservative policy remained as incoherent as ever. Bonar Law acceded to the leadership once more, thereby assuming the office of Prime Minister. But he was ailing and in May 1923 was replaced by Stanley Baldwin, the modest hero of the Carlton Club drama. All the while Lloyd George's Unionist allies – Chamberlain, Birkenhead, Balfour and Sir Robert Horne – stood aloof, having neither the desire nor the opportunity to join the government, continuing to regard themselves as the real leadership, and waiting for Bonar Law or Baldwin to blunder. And this is exactly what Baldwin did. In November 1923, after minimal consultation with his colleagues and with all the appearance of a premier in a panic, he announced that an election would be held in December to resolve the long dormant issue of tariffs. The Conservatives promptly lost their majority and nearly a hundred seats, while Labour gained nearly fifty MPs establishing itself for the first time as the second party. For a few frenetic days there was a flurry of plotting when the coalitionists thought that their moment had come again. Yet Baldwin held his ground. In January, however, his government was defeated by a combined Labour and Liberal vote and MacDonald formed his government.

In the immediate aftermath of Baldwin's folly the conditions for a decisively new Conservatism were set. The breakthrough was the discovery that the Labour Party was in fact nothing more than a hamstrung alliance of social democrats and socialists, with the former in dominance. At the beginning of 1924 the prospect of a weak minority Labour government looked markedly less dangerous for the Conservative Party than the return of coalitionism for an unknown period. At the time the decision to let Labour rule seemed to some a gamble as reckless as any devised by Joseph Chamberlain. It appeared to open the House of Commons to the full force of the class struggle, a situation which Lloyd George had strained for six years to prevent.

The strategies which came to dominate in Baldwinite Conservatism depended on a different assessment of the state from the one held by the Lloyd George group. It recognized both the structurally limited role of Parliament in determining and accomplishing political objectives, and it also appreciated the political advantage of being the party to endorse full and free parliamentary representation, 'the principal ideological lynchpin of Western capitalism'.[30] The closing of this circle was Baldwin's achievement. Under his leadership the Conservative Party pragmatically created a moderately popular Conservatism, a task which had eluded Chamberlain. In the process Baldwin formed conditions in which the specific constitutional arrangement revered by 'consensus' politicians of the Rab Butler stamp could evolve. To answer a question posed at the beginning of the chapter, the foremost reason why the Conservative Party survived was because, late in the day and against the odds, the Baldwinites arrived at the unwelcome realization of the necessity to take democracy seriously, if only to discover where concessions could be made and where resistance was vital.

This estimation of the long-term political significance of the Baldwin solution needs to be distinguished from the place which Baldwin himself often assumes in Conservative hagiographies. From May 1923 to November

1926 Baldwin's primary objective remained the continuation, in the field of industrial politics, of a war of class against class. But by the time the Conservative Party took over from Lloyd George as the sole party of government, the bulk of this job – the destruction of the shop stewards' movement, the councils of action and the Triple Alliance – had already been accomplished. This left the Conservatives in a position of sufficient power, thanks to Lloyd George, to be able to carry through a project in which parliamentary representation had a central place, and to reap the electoral benefits.

But it was not only over Lloyd George that the Baldwinites had the advantage. In the critical period of working-class offensives from 1910 to 1922, which included the moment when the majority of working people were first integrated into the political nation, the constitutional system was effectively frozen. The failure of Joseph Chamberlain and the assertiveness of the labour and socialist movement combined to force on the Conservative Party an unmanageable crisis. This in turn fed the impulse to spurn popular politics. The Baldwinites, at the beginning of 1924, had more room for manoeuvre and were able to deploy – strictly within the sphere which they themselves were in the business of defining as 'constitutional' – a more popular politics.

Baldwin's objectives in 1923–4 were modest. He aimed to win consent from the dominant classes for a 'two-nation' strategy, well understanding the difficulties in the immediate future for constructing any grander consensus. But at the same time he set about developing in rudimentary form the ideological work in a war of position – the preparation for a more lasting solution through a broad popular consensus in support of the Conservative project. The organizing principle was the division between constitutional and non-constitutional. The object was to register as unconstitutional all forms of direct action, and to use the parliamentary arena to the advantage of the dominant bloc by neutralizing antagonistic forces – by 'constitutionalizing' them and reducing antagonism to a simple 'difference', a form containable within the tit-for-tat rhetoric of everyday parliamentarianism.

Conclusion

The effect of these Conservative advances partially defused the caesarism of the earlier political era. From 1922 the gradations of caesarism slowly decreased and the imposition of two-party constitutionalism based on universal suffrage looked like a definitive break with the coalition of Lloyd George. This was marked by the desperation in the following fifteen years with which Baldwin did all he could to prevent the return, in any capacity, of the discredited figure himself, Lloyd George.

But the break with Lloyd George should not be exaggerated. Baldwin's Conservative Party was in fact the continuation of coalition by other means. Baldwin was often described as a 'coalition' in his own person. In February

1924 the coalition Conservatives made an ignominious return to Toryism, joined later by Churchill and some of the Lloyd George Liberals. In ensuring that the Conservative Party expanded by absorbing as fully as possible all anti-socialist elements, the leadership did no more than revive the traditional role of Conservatism. Except in moments of crisis, from its formation until the onset of the crisis of the state in the 1970s and 1980s, the Conservative Party has existed as a coalition of anti-socialist or anti-progressive forces, its leaders deliberately discouraging the permanent implantation of rival parties in the political centre.[31] The strength of Baldwinism in the 1920s was that it effectively functioned as a coalition, attracting the broad range of anti-socialist elements, but – critically – operating within a constitutional two-party mould.

After the débâcle of the 1924 Labour government, the dominance of Conservatism was ensured for the following electoral term. After the fall of the second minority Labour government in 1931 the caesarist solution once more became more fully pronounced. This new phase of parliamentary caesarism held until 1945 when a newly formed popular movement generated by the war had the effect of finally breaking, 'from below', the political log-jam and completing the diffusion of coalitionism and caesarism. At this point the 'natural' rotation of political parties at last got going. The route to this point, nominally at least, was no centre party, but the Conservative Party appearing in its guise merely as one force operating in a perfectly balanced two-party system (bar one or two unfortunate contingencies). During the 1920s and 1930s the supreme political force which held this scheme in place, although unable to develop it to its full potential, was Baldwinism. After the defeat of the political project which was inaugurated on 15 May 1903, a new conjuncture and a new historic role opened for the Conservative Party on 19 October 1922 with the arrival of that 'Little Caesar', Stanley Baldwin.

Notes and references

1   Lord Butler, *The Art of the Possible* (Penguin 1973), p. 128.
2   Sir Ian Gilmour, 'Tories, social democracy and the centre', *The Political Quarterly* **54**, no. 3 (1983), p. 267.
3   Brian Harrison, *Peaceable Kingdom. Stability and Change in Modern Britain* (Clarendon Press 1982).
4   For the technical details see Alan Sykes, *Tariff Reform in British Politics, 1903–1913* (Clarendon Press 1979).
5   George Dangerfield, *The Strange Death of Liberal England* (Paladin 1970); E. Halévy, *Imperialism and the Rise of Labour* (Ernest Benn 1961).
6   Quoted in B. Semmel, *Imperialism and Social Reform* (Allen and Unwin 1960), p. 93.
7   N. Blewett, 'Free-fooders, Balfourites, Whole Hoggers: factionalism within the Unionist Party, 1906–1910', *Historical Journal* **11**, no. 1 (1968).

8   Henry Page Croft, *My Life of Strife* (Hutchinson 1948), p. 43.
9   Sykes, p. 238.
10   John Ramsden, *The Age of Balfour and Baldwin* (Longman 1978), p. 85.
11   Leo Amery, *Diaries. Volume I. 1896–1929* (Hutchinson 1980), p. 93.
12   Much has been written recently in an attempt to identify with precision the radical right. These arguments have been reviewed by Alan Sykes, 'The radical right and the crisis of Conservatism before the First World War', *Historical Journal* **26**, no. 3 (1983). Here Sykes makes a distinction between the Milnerites and those whom he sees as the authentic radicals – de Broke, Maxse and George Wyndham; he warns against the view which sees 'Traditional Conservatism almost disappearing in a world already overrun by proto-fascists'; and he argues that the crisis of Conservatism was over by 1914. All these points deserve detailed consideration, but briefly: emphasis may be better placed on the separate issues (rather than attempting to identify individuals) and on discovering on what grounds Unionists after 1910 were prepared to countenance an active popular mobilization – and to exclude the Milnerites takes any meaning from the category of the radical right; second, proto-fascism was marginal but it was none the less formed in this period, and one route to it was via a reworked Tory traditionalism; on the third point, as I argue later, the political dilemmas which disrupted Unionism in these years were not resolved until the arrival of Baldwin as party leader.
13   A. Gramsci, *Prison Notebooks* (Lawrence and Wishart 1970), p. 219.
14   Quoted in A. M. Gollin, *The 'Observer' and J. L. Garvin* (Oxford University Press 1960), p. 131.
15   Quoted in Dangerfield, p. 47.
16   Semmel, *Imperialism and Social Reform*, p. 243.
17   Quoted in R. R. James, *The British Revolution. British Politics, 1880–1939* (Methuen 1978), p. 321.
18   Semmel, *Imperialism and Social Reform*; R. J. Scally, *The Politics of Social Imperialism* (Princeton University Press 1975).
19   A. J. P. Taylor, *Lloyd George: Rise and Fall* (Cambridge University Press 1961), p. 25.
20   Quoted in K. O. Morgan and J. Morgan, *Portrait of a Progressive. The political career of Christopher, Viscount Addison* (Clarendon Press 1980), p. 51.
21   Quoted in J. O. Stubbs, 'Lord Milner and patriotic labour, 1914–1918' *English Historical Review* **87** (1972), p. 728.
22   Quoted in ibid., p. 132.
23   Quoted in Ramsden, p. 109.
24   For comments on this and on 'two nation' strategies, see the remarks in Bob Jessop, *The Capitalist State* (Martin Robertson 1982), pp. 244–7.
25   Keith Middlemas, *Politics in Industrial Society* (Deutsch 1979).
26   Quoted in M. Cowling, *The Impact of Labour* (Cambridge University Press 1971), p. ix.
27   Quoted in ibid., p. 80.
28   It is for this reason that there is a case for including even Mosley as one who adopted in 1920–22 this rediscovered Tory identity.
29   Quoted in H. M. Hyde, *Baldwin* (Hart Davis 1973), p. 114.

30   Perry Anderson, 'The antinomies of Antonio Gramsci' *New Left Review*, no. 100 (1976/7), p. 28.
31   The switch in allegiance of the Duke of Portland from Fox to Pitt in 1794 can be taken as a starting point. In current times, the last manifestation of this process was the defection in 1977 of the Labour MP Reg Prentice – after which Labour renegades stopped midway in their journey, signing up with the Social Democratic Party.

3 Liberalism, state collectivism and the social relations of citizenship*

David Sutton

Three issues are integral to the transformation and influence of liberalism in this period. First is the significance of the protracted extension of the parliamentary franchise and the impact of near universal suffrage on the institutions of party and government. Second is the emergence of a 'social' or 'welfare' politics, where social inequalities were to be counteracted by welfare legislation and the whole populace supported by a 'national minimum' of social provision. Extended democratic representation and welfare politics embodied the first manifestations of social democracy. Third is the role of those who did most to pursue such a strategy. Greater stress will be given here to the writers and journalists – the 'philosophers' and intellectuals of liberalism – and to the civil servants, than to the party politicians. Although the Liberal Party, until the war, most frequently enabled the designs of these intellectuals to be realized – as testified by the social reforms of the Liberal governments of 1906 to 1914 – the new liberal intellectuals were generally impatient with party labels and with the divisive squabbles of everyday parliamentary exchange. They preferred to construct alliances across parties and to draw in strategically placed individuals. Their reach stretched beyond the Liberal Party. Perhaps most important of all, their vision was fixed on something more permanent and of a higher order than everyday party politics.

The terms of citizenship

The title of this chapter refers to the social relations of citizenship. Its purpose is to suggest that the idea of citizenship was the result of competing definitions, of negotiation and struggle, extending beyond formal politics.

In the latter part of the nineteenth century the importance of citizenship for the liberal mentality was not so much that it provided an alternative politics and discourse to class but that, as a notion, it referred to a set of practices designed to mitigate the effects of class divisions. How this could be achieved has been a central theme in liberal and social-democratic ideologies up to this day.

* Thanks to Bill Schwarz for his helpful advice on this chapter.

An early invocation of citizenship appeared in response to the diehard opposition to the Reform Bill in 1867. An influential case was put by A. V. Dicey. In an essay entitled 'The balance of classes' he argued that holders of voting rights would not necessarily act out of class interest. They would view themselves not only as members of a class but as 'citizens' and 'persons'. 'It is highly improbable', he argued, 'that the whole of the poor . . . would act together as one man in opposition to the wishes of those who are not technically working men.'[1] The realization that the idea of citizenship could become an organizing principle in a strategy to secure the political incorporation of the subordinate classes gave the term a wide currency among the more liberal-minded of the governing class. Citizenship, henceforth, became a touchword for the rights and duties with which the new electorate should be inculcated. T. H. Green and the Oxford idealists elaborated a political philosophy of citizenship in which the responsibility of the state to its subjects was a central theme.[2] In philanthropic texts, the popular press and imperialist tracts it was frequently emphasized that any rights bestowed upon the people brought with them the reciprocal duties of citizenship.

• By the 1870s liberal discussions of citizenship revolved around the belief that it could neutralize class consciousness and play a crucial role in integrating the working class into the state. Alfred Marshall's *The Future of the Working Classes*, published in 1873, rejected the conventional wisdom that there were necessary limits to the amelioration of the condition of the working class.

The question is not whether all men will ultimately be equal – *that they certainly will not* – but whether progress may not go on steadily, if slowly, till, by occupation at least, every man is a *gentleman*. I hold that it may, and that it will.[3]

The very term 'citizenship' has been bequeathed by liberalism and social democracy. No alternative conception of citizenship really exists. In the political philosophy of marxism, for example, it is common to find citizenship described as a mechanism by which the dominant classes can break up oppositional class forces by 'individualizing' them. They organize political institutions in such a way that the dominant forms of representation depend on the individual (as in existing parliamentary democracies) rather than on classes. This critique draws attention to the misconceived separation of the political from the economic in liberal and social-democratic theories of citizenship. However it has tended to underestimate the significance of the rights of citizenship.

The notion of citizenship refers to social and political rights of fundamental importance. But our analysis needs to go beyond the liberal conception by establishing the links which hold together class relations and the social relations of citizenship. How do class forces shape, and how are they shaped by, relations of citizenship?

Such questions lead us to inquire how citizens are 'made'. Many of the elements which exist in the constellation of citizenship – the principles of juridical and political rights or of universal provision – came about as a result of struggles 'from below', from oppressed groups. These successes did not, however, bring the full fruits of liberation hoped for by those who fought for them. This failure suggests the need not only to investigate the balance of forces inside the state, but to examine how reforms became compromised and bureaucratized in their legislative form. As those far-sighted liberals of the 1860s and 1870s had supposed, citizenship could also serve as a means of containment.

The apparent apathy felt by working people for the benefits of citizenship derives from their experience of its bureaucratic forms. Reynold's *Seems So! A working-class view of politics*, for example, demonstrates the working-class scepticism felt towards official society and the intrusion of its agents.[4] While qualitative evidence of such scepticism is scarce these lived realities need always to be borne in mind when philosophical and official ideologies of citizenship are discussed.

The municipal precedent

Experiments in municipal socialism in the 1870s and 1880s prefigured the collectivist strategy of the Liberal governments of 1906–14. It was this practice which was theorized by the new liberal and Fabian intellectuals into what J. A. Hobson called 'Liberal statecraft'. According to L. T. Hobhouse, 'the Fabian Society brought Socialism down from heaven and established a contact with practical politics and municipal government'.[5] The attempt to consolidate popular support was particularly important in these early experiments. The specific social grouping to which the municipal reformers appealed was the new *petit bourgeoisie*. This emergent social stratum, increasingly composed of municipal workers, was replacing the 'old' *petit bourgeoisie* of shopkeepers and small businessmen as leaders of the local community in voluntary activities. The traditional *petit bourgeoisie* were commonly excluded as direct beneficiaries – in terms of employment opportunity – by municipalism, but they were placated by tax or rate relief.

The very label 'municipal socialism' marks the beginning of an important debate at the end of the nineteenth century about the connotations of the word 'socialism'. J. T. Bunce, Birmingham's official historian, described the city's achievement as follows: 'a real Socialism, self-imposed, self-governed, conducted with the assent and by the effort of a united community . . . equal to the advantage of its members'.[6] The description 'real Socialism' needs serious qualification. The municipal enterprise instigated by Joseph Chamberlain in the 1870s is more accurately described as municipal collectivism. Chamberlain's 'socialism' was far from concerned with breaking the power of capital or with the systematic redistribution of wealth. In a speech at the end of January 1885 he made his position as clear as he could.

The proposals which I have made are not directed against any class or individual. I have had two objects in view. In the first place I want to see that the burthen of taxation is distributed according to the ability of the taxpayer, and in the second place I want to increase the production of the land and I want to multiply small owners and tenants.

Thus, as John Rae demonstrated in his *Contemporary Socialism*, 'socialism' accreted meanings not only from collectivism but from radical liberalism, as the early career of Chamberlain exemplified.[7] If Chamberlain's schemes did not represent a redistributive socialism they were undoubtedly reformist in intention – even to the material discomfort of certain sections of capital. As mayor between 1873 and 1875 Chamberlain shifted the Birmingham council – previously dominated by a lower middle-class ratepayers' 'economy' lobby – towards major reforms in the management of municipal affairs. With a base in the radical artisanate, he was prepared to take entrepreneurial risks to improve the corporation's institutions. For a time he convinced others of the necessity of accumulating debt in order to sponsor municipal schemes in the 'general' and 'public' interest.

The old *petit-bourgeois* stratum of shopkeepers and small businessmen constantly resisted reforms because of the increase in rates, and the experience taught radical liberal and Fabian collectivists that the influence of this stratum had to be curtailed. The new *petit-bourgeois* state bureaucrats were left to take up the reins as collectivist pacemakers.

Norman McCord argues that ratepayer activity in the 1870–1914 period was crucial because 'local authorities were elected by the ratepayers and this makes for a direct link between the ratepayers and social policy'. He maintains that ratepayers were not socially homogeneous; thus some of the upper sections of the working class were householders, ratepayers and – given the nature of the local government franchise – voters and potential participants too. Also, the fact that collective municipal enterprises were funded locally meant that the ratepayers' lobby felt the payment 'in its own pocket', and were more likely to have direct personal knowledge of the cases. As a result, ratepayers were more likely to be vigilant about any 'abuse' of the rates than 'in a later situation in which most social expenditure is administered relatively anonymously . . . by general national taxation'.[8] It was not only that the ratepayers' lobby became the most active watchdog of the public purse. The 'ratepayer' became the ideological symbol of property-owning democracy. The ratepayer interest was *universalized* and made symbolic of the 'little man's' individualism and reward for personal effort, an effort which collectivism appeared to deny. In the case of housing a moralistic disposition not to help the visibly undeserving brought the classic *petit-bourgeois* response. The ratepayers resisted payments from the rates for collective provision.

C. A. Vince cogently expressed the ratepayers' viewpoint in a pamphlet issued following the appointment of a special housing committee in 1901. In favour of public monopolies for gas and water, he argued that municipal house-building was stilting economic enterprise, increasing the rates for a small return, and harming the poor.

It is found that these well meant schemes have directly discouraged a sort of building from which great benefit had resulted. *They have added to the burden of every poorman, who does not live in a municipal house, by increasing his rates, whilst they have deterred those who were willing and able to supply his requirements.*

The 'greatest of all objections' was that the whole basis of municipal politics was threatened by the existence of municipal house-building which gave tenants a privileged interest denied to other social groups. 'Municipal house-building on any considerable scale introduces the possibility of the most perilous sort of corruption. . . . The "Progressives" of London County Council are virtually plundering the ratepayers to bribe a section of the electorate. . . .'[9] Here Vince appealed to a generalized ratepayer interest – which included sections of the working classes. Municipal house-building threatened to disrupt the traditional arrangement of class and power in the community. Paradoxically, the philosophy of non-sectionalism, of not privileging any social class, was invoked in order to maintain the status quo.

Progressivism and socialism in London

The same conflicts within the lower middle class can be seen at work in London during this period. The widening of the local government franchise opened up new opportunities for popular representatives. In London the Progressives exploited the opportunities afforded by the 1888 Local Government Act and the new apparatuses of the London County Council set up the following year. Although London's reform of municipal enterprise was relatively late compared to Birmingham and Manchester, Progressivism in London quickly learned the lessons of the provinces.

From the first election in January 1889 the Progressives, representing all shades of Liberal, Liberal Unionist and Fabian opinion, dominated the Moderates, who exclusively represented the Conservatives. The Conservatives were weak organizationally, and in the 1892 election the Progressives increased their lead. After this the Conservative forces slowly reorganized, forming the London Municipal Society (LMS) in 1894, and adopting a Chamberlain-style programme of social reform in order to make an effective challenge in the elections of 1895. But at the same time the LMS continued to insist that municipal *trading* was wasteful and uneconomic. The Conservatives thus attempted to present themselves simultaneously as municipal reformers and thrifty managers.

The LMS began to make significant inroads into the Progressive vote when it shifted its attack from a particular argument about municipal trading to a general case against financial mismanagement and the defence of the ratepayer. This emphasis promised greater appeal. In the 1905 and 1906 elections the LMS made definite advances against the Progressives in London. In the 1907 election, after an enormous propaganda campaign alleging financial incompetence, the Conservatives took control of the metropolis.[10]

A contemporary radical liberal, Charles Masterman, noted a crucial factor in the class relations which lay behind the Progressives' failure.

The Progressive Party ended its political career in the Metropolis because it had forgotten the Middle Classes . . . it had forgotten the dimensions and latent power of those enormous suburban peoples which are practically the product of the past half century.

In the eyes of the 'sedentary' lower middle classes, he claimed, the Progressive Party represented the 'epitome of socialism'. Masterman's understanding of this level of class conflict is astute:

The rich despise the Working People; the Middle Classes fear them. Fear, stimulated by every artifice of clever political campaigners, is the motive-power behind each successive uprising. In feverish hordes, the suburbs swarm to the polling booth to vote against a truculent Proletariat. The Middle-Class elector is becoming irritated and indignant against working-class legislation. . . . The vision [is] of a 'Keir Hardie' in caricature – with red tie and defiant beard and cloth cap, and fierce, unquenchable thirst for Middle-Class property. . . .

To the 'suburbans' the threat from below was aggravated by the fact that they thought they were funding their own demise:

The people of the hill are heavily taxed (as he thinks) in order that the people of the plain may enjoy a good education, cheap trains, parks and playgrounds; even (as in the frantic vision of some newspapers) that they may be taught socialism in Sunday schools, with parodies of remembered hymns.[11]

The *Daily Mail*, in particular, stirred the wrath of the lower middle classes. Northcliffe, the *Mail*'s proprietor, was the epitome of a new sort of newspaper owner; like Beaverbrook, he was a campaigning Conservative. The *Mail*'s intervention in the London County Council election was decisive. In 1907 it published a 'Handbook to the London County Council Election. Giving both sides', in which the Progressives were dubbed 'Wastrels'. Captain Jessel, Chairman of the LMS, admitted the Moderate campaign had been 'well served by the Press of London, especially the *Mail*. . . . Their efforts materially helped towards the great victory over the Wastrels in the Borough elections'. Jessel's arguments were similar to those used in Birmingham against municipal levying and expenditure. He concentrated on the 'waste' of the Progressive Party. He contended that municipal trading did not produce profits, that housing schemes were a burden on the rates, and that rates increases were undermining industry and therefore damaging the interests of the poor. He also condemned the Progressives for building up a bureaucracy which bred nepotism. The 'evils of officialdom and centralization' were the products of 'Socialistic dogma'. 'The red hand of Keir Hardie . . . will be pulling the strings of the Progressive puppets.'[12]

The Progressives' policy could not match the populism of the Moderates. Masterman was right that the Progressives had forgotten the so-called 'toiling middle classes'. Indeed the whole collectivist project depended upon the encouragement of one section of the middle class, and the neglect of another.

The development of a national state collectivism

Out of this history of municipal collectivism there appeared the possibility that a unified campaign by radical liberal and Fabian intellectuals could be mounted to translate collectivist measures from the local to the national state. However, this alliance failed to materialize. It is important to examine the reasons for this, not least because it throws light on the differences between the liberal and Fabian ideologies.

The Boer War split radical liberals from Fabian collectivists. While the Fabian majority backed British imperialism, the new liberals were critical of its military adventures. Conflict and controversy over the South African War also divided liberal opinion.

The Rainbow Circle represented all shades of liberalism. Its periodical, the *Progressive Review* by 1895 had become a powerful intellectual organizer of the new radicalism and social reform. The divisions in the Rainbow Circle mirrored the emerging splits in the Liberal Party itself between anti-imperialist, free-trade Liberals and Liberal Imperialists. Lord Rosebery, the former Liberal Prime Minister, came out of retirement in 1902 to try to give a lead to the 'Limps'. Backed by prominent party leaders like Sir Edward Grey, Asquith and Haldane, Rosebery's Liberal League promoted national efficiency through a combined policy of imperialism with social reform. The majority of Fabians, under pressure from Sidney Webb and George Bernard Shaw, supported imperialism as a means of funding social reform at home. A number of prominent executive members, like Ramsay MacDonald, Hobson, Curran and Barnes resigned. This left Webb with an opening to create an alliance with Rosebery's Liberal Imperialists. In two famous articles – 'Lord Rosebery's escape from Houndsditch', and 'Twentieth-century politics: a policy of national efficiency' – Webb lauded Rosebery's abandonment of Gladstonian Liberalism and his advocacy of imperialism. This not only signified a shift in Fabian thinking towards imperialism but also marked the Webbs' rejection of party politics. Webb painted a picture of the twentieth-century citizen uninterested in political and party ideologies and racked by disillusionment:

They are not thinking of Liberalism or Conservatism, or Socialism. What is on their minds is a burning feeling of shame at the 'failure' of England. . . . This sense of shame has yet to be transmuted into political action.[13]

Radical liberal intellectuals who had been active partners with the Fabians in the 1890s recoiled in horror at the reactionary philosophy now proffered by Webb. In response the leading Fabians moved away from the job of trying to permeate political parties with the spirit of collectivism. Instead they set about organizing non-party groupings, aiming to forge a close relationship between administrative experts and leading politicians.

The Fabians followed their co-operation with Rosebery in the Liberal League with participation in the Coefficients in 1902. Unfortunately for the Webbs the politics of social imperialism proved too narrow and to weak a base at this time for the Fabians to realize their domestic policy. This became startlingly clear the following year in the wake of Joseph Chamberlain's founding of the Tariff Reform League.

The League's populist ambitions undercut at one blow the Webbs' tactical manoeuvrings and ended the prospects of the Fabians forming the nucleus of a single 'Efficiency Party'. This fracture within the collectivist forces pushed those who were more liberally inclined back into the Liberal *Party*. This was to have great significance for the development of the welfare legislation in the years before the First World War. By forming an alliance with the Liberal imperialists rather than with the radical liberals, the Webbs had made a strategic miscalculation.

Differences over imperialism and democracy made the sort of co-operation afforded by the umbrella of Progressivism in the 1890s an impossibility after 1900. On the other hand the common collectivist purpose learned in the municipalities left both groups with similar practical goals. In a broader and more long-term sense, both groupings may be characterized as forming a distinct collectivist 'party'.

Despite their relationship to the Liberal Party, the 'radical wedge' of liberal intellectuals and politicans was only a minority grouping in the party. Its subordinate position ensured that Fabian-type tactics – permeation, personal influence, journalistic interventions – were still vital in the attempt to win support inside the party. Thus Hamer is adamant that even after 1905 the traditional Liberal causes – anti-imperialism and militarism, Home Rule for Ireland, temperance, agitation against landowners – remained the life-blood of the party. Moreover:

Social reform was rather the work and the enthusiasm of the great 'outsiders' such as Lloyd George and Winston Churchill – neither of whom fitted comfortably into the *established* order of Liberal politics – plus Fabian socialists and strong-minded civil servants, such as the Webbs and Morant.[14]

The Liberals won their landslide victory in 1906 on traditional issues. There was an uneasy balance of Liberal Imperialists and radicals in the Cabinet, although the latter, like Lloyd George, secured executive positions crucial for instigating social reform. However, most of the strategic ideological preparation was conducted outside the established power centres of party and government. One influential grouping organized around the *Nation* lunch, and included H. W. Massingham, John Hammond, F. W. Hirst, Hobhouse, Hobson, Charles Masterman and H. N. Brailsford.

Despite the similarities between Fabians and new liberals, it is the differences which count most. Historically, Fabianism and liberalism, despite important convergences, remained separate even competing tendencies, their fortunes tied to different parties. Hobhouse articulated the key point of difference most succinctly. 'Liberal socialism', he explained, represented a distinct form of politics separate from the 'mechanical socialism' of the Social Democratic Federation and the 'official socialism' of the Fabians. Giving short shrift to the 'false economic analysis' and 'materialistic Utopia' of marxism, Hobhouse was also critical of former friends. He argued that Fabianism, in its methods and philosophy, was fundamentally undemocratic. He found Fabianism guilty of 'a measure of contempt for average humanity in general' owing to the fact that its conception of community welfare began and ended with 'administrative reforms' directed by a 'class of the elect' or 'master minds'. He rejected the Fabian assumption that social reforms could be implemented without the active involvement of those for whom they catered. In short, the winning of active consent in the country had been abandoned in favour of wheeling and dealing at the centre: 'The socialistic organisation will work in the background, and there will be wheels within wheels, or rather wires pulling wires.' For Hobhouse liberal socialism had two different qualities. One represented democracy; the other, individual liberty.[15] Elaborating these distinctions, P. F. Clarke concludes that the Fabians represented a 'mechanical reformism', the new liberals, a 'moral reformism'.[16] Sidney Webb, for instance, brought to national politics his experience in local government. In his hands policy-making and implementation were more matters of administrative rationale and committee resolution than responses to pressure from the public. In contrast the radical liberal intellectuals saw their role much more as educationalists and moral crusaders. Many of their number – Hobhouse, Hammond, Hobson, Charles Trevelyan, for example – were active journalists. With an eye to the grand traditions of the nineteenth-century Liberal press, they had a far more sensitive understanding of the importance of public opinion and popular consent. The radical liberals sought to mobilize an organic 'general will' with the ambition of promoting and activating a sense of citizenship among 'the people'.

New liberalism as philosophy

The theoretical and philosophical premises of new liberalism differed from those which underpinned Fabianism. The starting point of the new liberalism was a review and reassessment of the nineteenth-century preoccupation with a biologistic view of society governed by naturalistic and evolutionist laws. For Herbert Spencer this biological determinism produced a militant individualism and advocacy of *laissez-faire*. For Hobhouse and Hobson the biological and organic conception of society was retained but, reversing previous logic, the state became the arbiter and insurance of a balanced, regulated society.

In Hobson's writing the analogy between a biological organism and human society is at its clearest. The health of the body politic was consummate only when each and every part was sustained. 'In a body which is in health and functions economically, every cell contributes to the life of the organism according to its powers.'[17] In social terms this meant that every individual had a 'positive' place in the order of things. The task ahead was one of

discovering, educating and utilizing for social purposes the best productive powers with which nature has endowed each member of society . . . (securing) a division of labour, or 'differentiation of functions. . . .' Every failure to put the right man or woman in the right place, with the best faculty of filling that place involves social waste.

However, the efficient allocation of functions, the argument continued, was impeded and blocked among the lower classes of society as a result of material privation. It was necessary, therefore, to provide a national minimum of social security for those individuals unable fully to realize their human potential.

Perhaps the most significant text to come out of the new liberal tradition was Hobson's *The Crisis of Liberalism: New issues in democracy*, published in 1909. As the title suggests, Hobson was acutely aware of the crisis which faced liberalism and he saw the solution as the democratization of society along liberal lines. It was this dimension in new liberalism which, *in the theory*, distinguished it from the statism of either the Unionist collectivists or the 'mechanical' and administrative collectivism of the Fabians. Traditional, liberal, philosophical concern for the delicate balance between individual and community, private and public, civil society and state was carried forward into new liberalism, reworked and integrated at its very core. This intellectual and ethical component was one of the most far-reaching elements in new liberalism. In comparison, the possibilities of what Hobson called a 'practicable' socialism were rather less ambitious and imaginative. In practice the 'socialism' of new liberalism

aims primarily not to abolish the competitive system, to socialise all instruments of production, distribution, and exchange, and to convert all workers into public employees – but rather to supply all workers at cost price with all the economic conditions requisite to the education and employment of their personal powers for their personal advantage and enjoyment.

And, as Freeden notes in a revealing comment, 'This proposed course was probably as radical as one could get within the limits of the existing system.'[18]

In this context Hobhouse insisted on the need for the intervention of the state as 'over-parent' to secure 'the conditions of self-maintenance for the normal healthy citizen'. The justification for state aid, he explained, was to ensure that individual fulfilment would harmonize with the public good.

. . . the function of the State is to secure conditions upon which its citizens are able to win by their own efforts all that is necessary to a full civic efficiency. It is not for the State to feed, house, or clothe them. It is for the State to take care that the economic conditions are such that the normal man who is not defective in mind and body or will can by useful labour feed, house, and clothe himself and his family.[19]

Hobson favoured taxing landowners as a means of economic redistribution. He proposed levying the so-called unearned increment to fund the provision of the national minimum and the 'development of public services'. Hobson was careful to distinguish economic redistribution in this form from other methods, particularly those advocated by the trade union movement. He saw the unions as *unregulated* agents of redistribution (resulting in further inequalities), harmful to the national good (causing strikes) and too closely determined by the particularistic interests of class. By recommending that redistribution should be organized by state agencies Hobson's version of social reform was prescribed as an alternative to trade unionism. This denial of class was central to new liberal ideology. The new liberals always carefully distinguished between their conception of redistribution and that advocated by socialists. Socialists, and their labour theory of value, Hobson complained, failed to recognize 'the actual industrial services rendered by savings and the direction of industry, and the validity of some interest and profit in payment for these services'.[20] Social reform was to be funded by taxing unearned increment. Charles Masterman summed up this point of view, referring to the aims of the Liberal government:

It appears specially anxious to promote legislation which will obviously benefit one section of the community without exciting compensatory anger in any other; a class of legislation, indeed, which all the world has been seeking for a considerable number of centuries.[21]

The Liberal Party

In the middle of the nineteenth century the bulk of the manufacturing classes supported the Liberal Party. But between 1868 and 1886 the Tory Party began to undermine this support. As the century closed the polls suggested that both the traditional *petit bourgeoisie* and the new ranks of white-collar workers were also aligning with the Conservatives.[22] The foundation of the Labour Representation Committee in 1900 meant that the Liberals could no longer rely on the support of the working man. At first the Liberals tried to use organizational measures to stem the rise of independent labour represen-tation. The MacDonald–Gladstone pact of 1903 enabled both parties to avoid a split vote in certain constituencies. Blewett argues that the Liberal victory in 1906 disguised long-term psephological and geographical trends which were already working to erode the Liberal Party's popular support. The victory was built on short-term and ephemeral factors; the Unionist hegemony was broken only temporarily; and the facts of 'electoral region-alism' still obtained.[23]

The ideological projection of new liberalism was a response to this situation. Its proponents were determined to mobilize 'middle opinion' as a countervailing force to the 'extremes' represented by class politics. The most immediate threat came from independent working-class representation. The Liberal welfare programme was motivated in part by a desire to steal the Labour Party's thunder. More importantly, however, these reforms were dedicated to a politics of containment. The male working-class citizen was addressed not as an active agent but as one provided for. Women were addressed in the social field only in so far as they were integrated into the family and followed the appropriate domestic and maternal duties. Political success could only be achieved if the policies did not alienate the middle classes. Thus the most sensitive task was to win a strategic section of the professional middle classes. If those sections could be won, they could become the leading advocates of a radical alliance with a general appeal to the electorate.

In 1908 Lloyd George explained that the goal of Liberal welfare legislation was to provide 'civil equality' among all citizens. 'You will not have estab-lished it in this land until the child of the poorest parent shall have the same opportunity for receiving the best education as the child of the richest.' *This* was the promise the Liberals afforded through the equality of social citizen-ship. The status of citizenship was, however, still subject to *moral* consider-ations which differentiated what the rhetoric claimed to be absolute. The deserving/undeserving criterion was still widely invoked. The ideal citizen was still a member of the skilled and respectable section of the working class.

The Liberal reforms

The welfare legislation enacted during the Liberal government of 1906–14 fell into two broad categories:[24] first, a number of acts intended to alleviate the situation of children and the old; second, legislation affecting unemployment, the labour market and the minimum wage. The first category included the 1907 Education (Administrative Provisions) Bill, which promoted the facility of school medical services, and the 1908 Chil-dren Act. The 1906 Education (Provision of Meals) Act, originating in a Labour MP's private member's bill, gave powers to local authorities to raise a halfpenny rate to feed needy schoolchildren. Although the amount was inadequate the act was significant because it made provision without the traditional view that pauperization relieved by 'charity', ought to be accompanied by loss of citizenship rights of the parents. The Old Age Pensions Bill, however, which became law in August 1908, exhibited a degree of moral selectivity and denial of the principle of universalism. Schemes for providing old age pensions had been mooted from the late 1870s, but controversy about how they should be funded had delayed legislation. However Asquith's utilization of a super-tax in the 1907 and 1908 budgets had generated a surplus and opened the possibility of a non-contributory scheme funded from taxation. When Asquith became Prime Minister in 1908, Lloyd George, as the new chancellor, steered such a recommendation through Parliament. Disqualifications were recommended on both economic and moral grounds. Thus a pension was not forthcoming if a person's annual income had exceeded a certain level. In its original statute a moral proviso could also prevent its receipt; payment was withheld if it could be shown that the pensioner's poverty was the product of feckless and 'undeserving behaviour.

In the second category of legislation the concept of a universal minimum was also peppered with exceptions – again, often deriving from moral criteria. In the 1906 Workmen's Compensation Act the exceptions to compensation for accident or disease were mainly technical, although the act did not provide at all for casual labourers. The Trades Board Act of 1909 was the only legislation which fulfilled the promise of providing a national minimum. Engineered by Winston Churchill at the Board of Trade the act set up trade boards in sweated industries and empowered the boards to fix a minimum wage.

On the other hand the debate on the 1909 Labour Exchanges Bill and the 1911 National Insurance Bill rekindled discussion of moral exceptions to citizenship. William Beveridge originally intended that labour exchanges should be introduced in parallel with a scheme for unemployment insurance. However, inspired by the Bismarkian schemes of social insurance, Lloyd George included unemployment and health insurance in one bill – the 1911 National Insurance Bill. Unlike old age pensions this aspect of social insurance was to be funded on a contributory basis. Given the method of funding, both Churchill and Lloyd George were opposed to any moral exceptions on the grounds of individual irresponsibility. But the civil servant Hubert Llewellyn Smith insisted that those workers sacked for misconduct would not be eligible and this view prevailed.[25]

Despite the fact that citizenship rights were not an absolute, the Liberal reforms undoubtedly established the precedent for a welfare state embodying the principle of a universal minimum. Whether the policies were *popular*, however, is doubtful. Dangerfield forcefully argues that workers as a whole were motivated by the struggle for wages, not for welfare reforms.[26]

The middle class

If the welfare reforms were relatively successful in heading off demands which might otherwise have been exploited by Labour, the People's Budget of 1909 forced the Liberals to attend to the middle classes. It was clear that the middle classes were preparing nationally to oppose the Liberal Party reforms. Organizations such as the Income Tax Reduction Society, the Anti-Socialist League and the British Constitutional Association represented well established bourgeois interests. Even more threatening, however, were those groupings which claimed to represent the hard-pressed lower middle classes – the 'black-coated brigade'.

The careful cultivation of the middle classes can be seen in the tax arrangements which both Asquith and Lloyd George, as successive Chancellors of the Exchequer, employed in their budgets. In 1907 Asquith put into practice the principle of distinguishing between earned and unearned increment. The main source of income subsequently derived from a super-tax on estates valued in excess of £1 million. At the same time this provided sufficient funds to give relief to earned income below £2000. The *Nation* immediately lauded Asquith's solution as welcome relief for 'the laborious middle classes'.[27] The full political rationale behind these financial arrangements became even clearer with the publication of Lloyd George's budget in April 1909. The old age pensions scheme, which was funded from the national exchequer, had exacted a much greater demand on resources than the government had anticipated. Lloyd George was therefore forced to raise funds by imposing a new measure of direct taxation. In the 1909 budget the principles of progressive taxation were applied to income tax as well as real estate. However, it is crucial to note that once more the middling range of incomes was protected: incomes above £5000 became liable to super-tax, incomes below £500 were given an allowance for every child below the age of 16; and incomes below £2000 were to be taxed at a lower rate.[28] The Liberal populism of Lloyd George's budget was based on a familiar formula of mobilizing 'the people versus the aristocracy'. The concessions to the middle strata were aimed at wedding them to a popular coalition against the landed interest.

Although there were substantial differences between Fabians and radical liberals, the collectivist project expressed a common *petit-bourgeois* outlook. This welfare ideology was underpinned by a belief that it was the destiny of the intermediate social sectors to hold the balance between the two warring factions of bourgeoisie and proletariat. They could therefore lay claim to a more valid and authentic conception of community and harmony. For them the key objective was to create the conditions which would encourage equality of opportunity. This was especially welcomed by those sections of the *petit bourgeoisie* which depended, above all, on educational qualification to ensure the maintenance of their social position.

The social relations of citizenship worked ideologically to neutralize class antagonism and create a unity based in common rights and duties. However the practice of welfare provision produced new relations of antagonism and inequality. This further undermined the rhetoric of universalism.

Radical liberals and Fabians were often ambivalent in their approach to the middle class as a whole. Hobhouse condemned the sedentary existence of the lower middle class, their inwardness, their complacence and small mindedness.[29] Similarly, Masterman often expressed his disappointment. For both of them the source of this disappointment lay in the fact that it was the lower middle class who were supposed to be the ideal 'servants of the state'.[30]

The period 1880–1920 saw the expansion of both the private financial sector and the public activities of the state. These developments brought the first build-up of a distinctly new social stratum. Hobsbawm divides the social composition of the Fabians into two sections. The first group, who were prominent in the early organization, were 'members of the traditional middle classes who had developed a social conscience'. These included a 'large bloc of emancipated and presumably middle-class women'. But it was the second group which made the running in terms of the collectivist drive – 'the much more interesting body of self-made professionals (writers, journalists, self-made higher civil servants, professional organisers) elevated from the ranks of white-collar workers'.[31] This group of Fabians became preoccupied with perfecting the machinery of social engineering.

Crucial to this Fabian vision was the transformation of class relations brought about by the forward march of municipalism. The very conception of socialism itself came to be imprinted by the desires and aspirations of the emergent municipal workers and managers. Their greatest asset in the labour market lay in their administrative abilities. This was a group whom Webb and Shaw assiduously courted, hoped to train as experts and remunerate accordingly. In this, the Fabians were at their most instrumental and engaged. They legitimated the creation of this class of administrators who functioned as the personnel of state socialism.

Conclusion

As many liberal intellectuals discovered with a degree of bitterness after 1916 the Liberal Party, under the leadership of Lloyd George, fast turned its back on liberalism. A number of the foremost ideologues of the new liberalism found themselves isolated and unsettled in a post-war world. The hopes of social reconstruction speedily foundered. The persistence of class antagonism between 1916 and 1926 appeared to defy all their objectives.

The new liberals' project had always been conceived as one which would influence the long-term ordering of civil society and its relation to the state. This legacy proved more long-lasting. Most of all, it helped to effect the transformation of classic liberalism into a liberal social democracy. The common element which predominated at both the beginning and the end of

this period was the preoccupation with what Ritchie called the 'moral function of the state'. Increasingly this came to be interpreted as the state
assuming a role which was positive and active. Ironically, the belief in the
moral functions of the state was underpinned by the realization that the state
must also act as the embodiment of 'reason'. The state had to become the
rational organizer which could stand above and regulate contending
sectional interests. Thus it was that these theorists arrived at the conclusion,
as liberals, that they had to countenance the intervention of the state to
guarantee and preserve the conditions of individual liberty and equality of
opportunity within civil society.

Collectivism could mean many different things. One thing which the new
liberal collectivism was not was socialism. It was, rather, the formative
moment of an emergent social democracy which was developing in a parallel
form on the continent. As early as 1890 the *Speaker* had come to the conclusion: 'We must assimilate Socialism; if "Liberal" is not to become a mere
shibboleth . . . we must take from Socialism what is good and reject what is
bad or doubtful.'[32] And it was exactly these 'bad and doubtful'
elements – above all, those to do with class – which were systematically
eliminated from the new liberalism and from the subsequent development of
social democracy.

Notes and references

1   A. V. Dicey, in W. L. Guttsmann (ed.), *A Plea for Democracy. An edited
    selection from the 1867 essays on reform and questions for a revised parliament*
    (MacGibbon and Kee 1967), p. 65.

2   M. Ritcher, *The Politics of Conscience. T. H. Green and his age* (Weidenfeld
    and Nicolson 1964), p. 342.

3   Alfred Marshall, quoted in T. H. Marshall, *Citizenship and Social Class*
    (Cambridge University Press 1950).

4   S. Reynolds, B. and T. Wooley, *Seems So! A working-class view of politics*
    (Macmillan 1911); and see H. Pelling, 'The working class and the origins of the
    welfare state', in his *Popular Politics and Society in Late Victorian Britain*
    (Macmillan 1968).

5   J. A. Hobson, *The Crisis of Liberalism. New issues of democracy* (republished
    Harvester 1974), p. xi. L. T. Hobhouse, *Liberalism* (Oxford University Press
    1964), p. 112.

6   J. T. Bunce, *History of the Corporation of Birmingham*, vol. 2 (Cornish Bros
    1885), p. xxix.

7   J. L. Garvin, *The Life of Joseph Chamberlain*, vol. 1, *Chamberlain and Democ-
    racy. 1836–1885* (Macmillan 1932), pp. 556 and 551; J. Rae, *Contemporary
    Socialism* (Swan Sonnenschen 1907).

8   N. McCord, 'Ratepayers and social policy', in P. Thane (ed.), *The Origins of
    British Social Policy* (Croom Helm 1978), pp. 22 and 27–8.

9   C. A. Vince, *Notes on the Housing Question* (publisher unknown, reprinted
    from the *Birmingham Evening Mail*, 1902), pp. 2–3 and 15–18, emphasis added.

10 K. Young, *Local Politics and the Rise of Party. The London Municipal Society and the Conservative intervention in local elections, 1894–1963* (Leicester University Press 1975), pp. 52, 58, 65–70.

11 C. F. G. Masterman, *The Condition of England* (Methuen 1909), pp. 58–9.

12 Capt. H. M. Jessel, 'A foreword to municipal reformers', in *The Daily Mail and the Fight for London* (Amalgamated Press 1907), pp. 11–12.

13 S. Webb, *Twentieth-Century Politics: a policy of national efficiency* (Fabian Tract, no. 108), 1901, p. 7.

14 D. A. Hamer, *Liberal Politics in the Age of Gladstone and Rosebery. A Study in Leadership and Policy* (Oxford University Press 1972), pp. 326–7.

15 Hobhouse, *Liberalism*, p. 91.

16 P. F. Clarke, *Liberals and Social Democrats* (Cambridge University Press 1978).

17 Hobson, *The Crisis of Liberalism*, p. 81.

18 J. A. Hobson, *The Social Problem* (Nisbet and Co. 1901), p. 10; Hobson, *The crisis of Liberalism*, pp. 172–3; and M. Freeden, *The New Liberalism. An ideology of social reform* (Clarendon Press 1978), p. 47.

19 Hobhouse, *Liberalism*, p. 83.

20 J. A. Hobson, *The Industrial System An Inquiry into earned and unearned income* (Longman 1909), p. 220.

21 C. F. G. Masterman, 'Politics in transition', *Nineteenth Century and After*, January 1908, p. 9.

22 J. Cornford, 'The transformation of Conservatism in the late nineteenth century', *Victorian Studies*, 7 (1963).

23 N. Blewett, *The Peers, the Parties and the People. The General Election of 1910* (Macmillan 1972), pp. 40–2.

24 Details of the legislation are taken from E. Halévy, *The Rule of Democracy 1906–14* (Ernest Benn 1932); B. Gilbert, *The Evolution of National Insurance in Great Britain* (Michael Joseph 1966); D. Fraser, *The Evolution of the British Welfare State* (Macmillan 1973).

25 Fraser, p. 160.

26 G. Dangerfield, *The Strange Death of Liberal England* (MacGibbon and Kee 1966), p. 187.

27 *Nation*, 20 April 1907.

28 Halévy, p. 292; the appeal to the middle classes is detailed in B. K. Murray, *The People's Budget 1909/10: Lloyd George and Liberal Politics* (Clarendon Press 1980).

29 L. T. Hobhouse, *Democracy and Reaction* (T. Fisher and Unwin 1909 edition), pp. 69–72.

30 Masterman, pp. 64–5 and 67.

31 E. J. Hobsbawm, 'The Fabians reconsidered', in his *Labouring Men* (Weidenfeld and Nicolson 1974), pp. 256–7.

32 Quoted in Freeden, p. 51.

4 The corporate economy, 1890–1929

Bill Schwarz

In the period from the late nineteenth century to the 1920s the British economy underwent a profound transformation. This transformation, in the years from the end of the Great Depression of 1873–96 to the world economic crisis of 1929–31, can be identified as the first stage of the transition to monopoly capitalism in Britain. The term monopoly capitalism can refer to an advanced moment in the concentration and centralization of individual capitals; or, more broadly, it can refer to the organization of the corporate economy by a new form of (interventionist) state; or, more widely still, when coupled to the concept of imperialism, it can refer to the whole epoch of modern capitalism. These difficulties of definition are compounded in the British case, for it is commonly assumed that the relative retardation in the growth of the economy also meant that Britain was relatively slow in developing the institutions characteristic of the modern corporate economy.

In this chapter, the concept of monopoly capitalism is used to refer to a variety of economic forms rather than to a specific relation between the state and the economy. The formation of a new kind of state cannot logically be derived from, or fully explained by, economic developments. The purpose of this chapter is to identify the predominant patterns of state intervention and to determine the role of the state in the constitution and reproduction of the relations of production. This involves asking which sites of intervention came to be deemed legitimate and how state regulation was exercised. It is important also to understand the forms of amalgamation and merger in Britain, where, in contrast to the United States, there was no concerted popular anti-trust movement. Moreover, it is impossible, *a priori*, to perceive any general identity of interest between the leading businessmen in the monopoly sectors and Liberal or Conservative politicians. This is not to underestimate the extent of the reorganization of the British economy in this period, nor the scope of state intervention. It is hard to accept that the formation of monopoly capitalism in Britain was massively 'retarded'; the peculiarities of this transition, however, deserve the fullest attention.

In the 1890s pressures imposed by fierce competition, falling prices and diminishing profit margins gave British companies the first big push towards monopoly. The Great Depression itself provided the impetus behind the drive to recovery. Foreign capital was often crucial in stimulating this recovery, and in the longer term the overseas market was of critical importance for British manufacturers. But the influx of foreign investment cannot by itself explain the wide-ranging transformation of the economy.[1]

The 1890s opened with the amalgamation of fifty-three firms to form the United Alkali Company. By the early twentieth century many huge firms had developed, dominating their respective sectors. Capitalization intensified production for the home market creating a new structure of working-class consumption. Brewing was largely controlled by three major giants. Imperial and Wills divided the lucrative market in tobacco. The soap entrepreneur William Lever not only owned a number of plants abroad but also controlled the production of all its raw materials; by 1914 it had become 'the perfect prototype of a multinational'.[2] In the retail business Boots, Liptons and Home and Colonial sprang up, each boasting a chain of outlets. In other sectors a similar expansion can be identified, particularly in the steel armaments and engineering complex which became a labyrinth of interconnected firms. Vickers, Armstrong-Whitworth, GKN, Cammell Laird, Beardmore and Brunner Mond were all powerful companies before the war. According to Leslie Hannah,

Between 1888 and 1914 an average of at least sixty-seven firms disappeared in mergers each year, and in the three peak years of high share prices and intense merger activity between 1898 and 1900 as many as 650 firms valued at a total of £42m were absorbed in 198 separate mergers.[3]

By the early 1900s the foundations of a modern corporate economy were discernible.

In the speculative boom of 1919–20, and in the 1920s as a whole, trends towards centralization were consolidated, and more mergers were conducted in the 1920s than in any period before the 1960s. It is from the 1920s that the contemporary multi-national giants took on their modern institutional form – Unilever, ICI, Courtaulds, Commercial Union, Dunlop, and the motor firms of Morris and Austin. Except for the nationalization and rationalization of two key industries – coal and steel – the structural organization of British manufacturing in 1930 was broadly similar to the period of post-war expansion.

The inter-war slump exposed the weaknesses of Britain's industrial structure. Staple industries – coal, iron and steel, textiles, shipbuilding – were uncompetitive and ravaged by under-capitalization and overcapacity. Even before the war their development had been dogged by chronic under-investment. Yet they remained major contributors to Britain's export trade: as late as 1907 70 per cent of all exports were made up from coal, iron, steel and textiles. This exceedingly narrow industrial base highlights the extent to which the British economy as a whole was still cast by the configuration of the first industrial revolution. The rise of competing industrial nations exposed the vulnerability of a British economy, which was dependent on the fortunes of the world market as never before. This was the cause of the persistent anxieties about Britain's economic performance which cut into every political debate of the period. The traditional power of British capital was always inseparable from its role in the world market. The opening of what Hobsbawm called the 'permanent crisis' of British capitalism was a direct consequence of its new position in a world economy dominated by more powerful national capitals.[4] In the short term successive governments attempted to uphold Britain's place as a leading imperial and world economic and financial power. But the long-term tendencies towards crisis continued to assert their baleful influence, favouring the financial sectors and imposing added burdens on the development of industry.

Many of the companies in the more modern sectors of the economy were unstable. Speculative booms in 1898–1900 and 1919–20 fuelled this instability. Few of the huge firms which had emerged in the 1890s still occupied a predominant place in the league of top firms of the 1920s. Many of the first wave of amalgamations were defensive responses to heightened competition resulting from earlier failures to modernize. In the 1920s the motor companies faced perpetual crisis, and the great engineering and steel combines were crippled by their reluctance to diversify. Even by the late 1920s many of the largest firms were still controlled by single families, delaying the transition to the professional management appropriate to a large corporation. As many observers who have put their emphasis on the 'retardation' of the British economy have demonstrated, the *rate* of growth decelerated in this period. Britain declined both in relation to its mid nineteenth-century position, and in comparison to the more streamlined economies of its metropolitan rivals.

The interconnections between economic crisis and the emergence of new corporate forms are complex. But the general point – the period as the first stage of the transition to monopoly capitalism – still stands. Across the economy as a whole, productivity continued to climb.[5] New technologies, and new industries based on chemical and electrical engineering, developed at a heady rate. In engineering, automatic machine tools – an innovation of the 1890s – were the norm by the end of the 1920s.[6] Between 1895 and 1913 coal production more than doubled, partly as a result of the 'massive dilution' of labour, and partly because mechanization, although minimal before the war, spread rapidly in the 1920s.[7] Evidence suggests that over the period as a whole the intensity of labour in the textile industries was decisively increased.[8] On these grounds the distinctions between 'new' and 'old' industries lose their force. Some new industries evolved directly out of the old. Smiths and Lucas, for example, the component industries for the motor firms, grew from the manufacture respectively of clocks and oil lamps. Morris depended on standardized components from an early stage, placing vast orders with Dunlop, Lucas and Smiths. In the motor industry the production of vehicles doubled between 1923 and 1927, while for Austin it increased tenfold in the four years between 1922 and 1926.[9] The concentration of workers in large factories increased markedly. Even before the war (when the number of those working in 'factories' was seven times greater than those in 'workshops') the modern corporate plant had emerged. The large-scale enterprises established by Westinghouse in Rugby in 1902 and by General Electric in Birmingham and Courtauld in Coventry a year later are key examples. Britain's first industrial estate was established at Trafford Park in Manchester in 1894.

Management functions multipled and managers claimed new status as a salaried profession. (And so too appeared the first suggestions that the division between ownership and control signalled the end of 'capitalism'.)[10] Managerial texts for the conscientious employer, dealing with every aspect of accountancy, production and office work, proliferated. In the 1890s far-sighted managers became involved in cumbersome experiments with complicated bonus-systems, handwritten, individualized worksheets, rational storekeeping and accounting procedures in the hope of systematically calculating and controlling the ratio of input to output. By the end of the period the most advanced managements could rely upon new technologies of flow-production, constructed around the assembly-line in purpose-built factories. The Austin plant at Longbridge was completely overhauled in 1928 and Ford opened its newly built complex at Dagenham in 1931. In company structure and in the very composition of the collective labourer the period from the 1890s to the 1920s was decisive in the emergence of modern forms of industry.

State intervention increasingly extended into new areas of social life. State systems of welfare and the 'expanded' reproduction of labour power contributed to the complexity of the economic transformations of the period. This is most notable in state activity in relation to unemployment which created an unprecedented nexus between economic policy and political management. However, there is very little evidence, apart from in the exceptional conjuncture of war, that the state ever became directly integrated into the productive circuits of capital on any scale, or intervened at all in the private management of business. Nor did the state undertake any sustained measures to assist the monopoly sectors. Thus the notion of a 'state monopoly capitalism' makes no sense for this period. Nor is there sufficient evidence to support the belief, propounded most forcefully by Lenin, that it was necessary for banking and industrial capital to fuse (to form 'finance capital') to stimulate the concentration and centralization of capital. Until the late 1920s a significant monopoly sector developed with very little sign of the classic organization of finance capital. In the decade following the war, however, banking capital was transformed into its present oligopoly structure.

It is impossible to point to a single state strategy for manufacturing industry in this period. State initiatives were generally *ad hoc* responses to specific, conjunctural crises in market relations. Indeed it is important not to underestimate the widespread business opposition to state intervention.

Politicians were reluctant to intervene unless there was some pressing reason, while the belief that the state was bureaucratic and incompetent was part of the common sense of business circles. E. M. H. Lloyd, writing in the aftermath of the war, rightly assessed that 'In the abstract there was an almost universal bias against State interference.'[11] A Gladstonian mentality, influential particularly in the Treasury, survived well into the twentieth century. But to the extent that the state was forced into assuming a new role in the economy, the pressures which determined this shift were not merely contingent or accidental. By safeguarding the general mechanism of market relations – even at the cost of overriding its principles in specific sectors – state regulation secured the conditions in which larger capitals could gobble up smaller capitals and in which the stronger could send the weaker to the wall. In the first stage of monopolization in Britain, from the 1890s to the 1920s, the spontaneous workings of market relations were sufficient to establish the development of a significant monopoly sector with minimal *direct* aid to monopoly companies themselves from the state. The paradox, however, lies in the fact that market forces, left to their own drive, piled up one 'social problem' after another. The alleviation of these resulted in the deepening political regulation of the free sway of the market.

1890–1914

Before the war, the state had two key areas of concern: the armaments industry and the railways. In 1913, 35 per cent of the national budget was devoted to armaments. Despite this enormous expenditure, from the 1880s direct state regulation of the production of armaments was increasingly dismantled. In 1887 half the industry was in private hands; by 1900 this amounted to two-thirds.[12] Yet it was largely in the steel, engineering and munitions sectors that the corporate giants of the future were created. State guaranteed contracts ensured a steady source of super-profits. For example the directors of Armstrong-Whitworth claimed that profits from a single gunboat exceeded those from 6000 motor vehicles. From the late 1890s the naval fleet was virtually rebuilt, encouraging a succession of mergers, take-overs and informal trade and cartel agreements. According to Trebilcock, 'Government contracting seems to have created, in the three decades before 1914, a cadre or élite of firms in any industry touched by the military demand for munitions.'[13] This government sponsored, corporate élite developed wider business interests in chemicals, electrical engineering and motors. When Vickers acquired Wolsley in 1901 their salesmen abroad sold both dreadnoughts and Wolsley cars. New corporate organizations developed, new technical priorities, producing high-speed steel, standardized production and an indispensable dependence on the transferability of skills. All this was stimulated by the power of the state as the nation's largest contractor.

With the railways government controls – on the length of the working day

(1893), on freight charges (1894), and through the conciliation boards (1907) on industrial relations – left the managements little room for manoeuvre in their bid to avert losses. The fourteen largest companies hoped, through secret agreements, to cut competition.[14] However, internal agreements threatened the government's control. Lloyd George and Churchill at the Board of Trade pressed for combination under state supervision. In the Commons Churchill's proposal that 'there is no real economic future . . . for British railways apart from amalgamation of one kind or another' secured a narrow majority in 1909.[15] The rail companies, never entirely won by this arrangement, withdrew their support despite continued attempts by the Board of Trade to push through direct state controls. The rail strike in 1911 increased the bitterness between the companies and the Board, and the former reverted to the well-tried system of secret agreements. The intransigence of the owners and the ambivalence of Parliament scuttled the most concerted pre-war attempt by the state to bring about publicly regulated amalgamation.

State welfare provision reveals a rather more coherent pattern than its economic initiatives. Its attempts to overcome *specific* blockages in the processes of accumulation and circulation, and to ease the pressure and inhibitions on the general conditions for the extraction of surplus value were of critical importance. The discordant forces which combined to produce these legislative and administrative transformations are not easy to disentangle. Although there were voices clamouring for the recomposition of the state in the long-term interests of the advanced sectors of capital, the varied settlements were in every case the result of a protracted, negotiated process. This begins to explain a paradox which runs right through this period. There were plenty of civil servants, social theorists, politicians and journalists who could no longer accept that the market provided its own mechanisms of self-regulation. This view drew these individuals into a range of collectivist groupings. But on the other hand many state initiatives of a distinctly collectivist tenor – especially under Conservative administrations – were justified by contractual individualism and anti-socialism. State intervention frequently proved to be a safer option than facing the political consequences of doing nothing. Successive state measures to introduce and then broaden unemployment insurance provide perhaps the best example of this dilemma. But more than this, the deep ideological resources upon which an individualist rhetoric could draw were not simply illusory. The voluntarist terms of state regulation and the *general* absence of direct state intervention in the private contractual relations of the market gave the language of individualism some substance. The predominant voice of government was individualistic rather than collectivist. In each instance, therefore, the collectivist case had to be argued on its merits.

The main pressure for intervention along collectivist lines, aiming to secure adequate conditions for the accumulation and circulation of capital, came in the first instance from the dynamic at the heart of the accumulation process itself: the resistance by workers to exploitation, especially after the revival of the socialist movement in the 1880s. The first response of the state to this challenge was to set up the Royal Commission on Labour (1891–4) to investigate issues of the most 'practical importance': strikes, the eight-hour day and arbitration. This was followed, in 1896, by the Truck Act and the Conciliation Act. These responses suggest that the civil servants and politicians were moving towards a new perception in which the class struggle itself was to be regulated, constrained and bureaucratized. The state's focus rested on *organized* trade unionism. This was clearly brought out in the Final Report of the Royal Commission:

It must be admitted . . . that strikes are occasionally initiated at the head-quarters of an organization, in furtherance of a general policy adopted by the leaders, which would, perhaps, not have been entered upon had no organization existed, or an organization more loosely knit and less widely extended. It is also true that when both sides in a trade are strongly organized and in possession of considerable financial resources, a trade conflict, when it does occur, may be on a very large scale, very protracted, and very costly. But just as modern war between two great European States, costly though it is, seems to represent a higher stage of civilization than the incessant local fights and border raids which occur in times or places where Governments are less strong and centralized, so, on the whole, an occasional great trade conflict, breaking in upon years of peace, seems to be preferable to continued local bickerings, stoppages of work, and petty conflicts. A large conflict of this kind is usually begun with cool deliberation, turns upon some real and substantial question, is carried out with less bitterness and violence, is probably settled by a regular and well thought out treaty of peace, and does not leave behind it much personal rancour or ill-feeling between individual employers and their workmen.[16]

Collective bargaining precipitated the breakdown of traditional industrial relations, and forced on to the signatories of the Final (majority) Report the recognition of the beneficial effects of a well-ordered trade unionism in negotiating conditions of work. But the report remained sceptical about the capacity of state intervention to contain class struggle:

We desire to say in conclusion that, in our opinion, many of the evils to which our attention has been called are such as cannot be remedied by any legislation, but we may look with confidence to their gradual amendment by natural forces now in operation,

and went on to insist that this could not 'be attained through what are usually known as Socialist or Collectivist methods'.[17]

Unfortunately for the commissioners, 'natural forces' did not prove as reliable as hoped. The quickening tempo of industrial conflict resulted in the creation of machinery for state conciliation which appeared all too collectivist and 'socialist' for the liking of many employers. The establishment of the Labour Department of the Board of Trade (perceived by businessmen as the 'acme of socialist interventionism')[18] and the appointment of George Askwith as Chief Industrial Commissioner in 1911 with a staff of full-time negotiators, were of central importance. A key component in these early measures of state arbitration was that the state was conceived as the representative of the whole community, equally pitted against both the tyranny of labour and the tyranny of capital.

State intervention in economic relations before the war depended on a conception of responsible trade unionism. This was increasingly being urged as a solution to industrial conflict by reforming intellectuals both inside and outside the state. In the decade before the outbreak of war the state took on a number of functions previously associated with the trade unions. For instance, the Trade Boards Act of 1909 introduced compulsory legislation to fix minimum wages and to prevent sweating; in 1906 the state regulated the number of hours worked by the miners, and in 1912 wage levels also came under statutory control. The state also attempted to free the labour market by means of a national system of labour exchanges and to provide unemployment insurance and pensions backed by the state. In addition, growing concern with the *quality* of labour power, and with its general conditions of reproduction, encouraged state administrators to press for the state to adopt wider 'trade union' functions.

The expansion of state intervention led to an increase in state personnel. It also encouraged a greater degree of direct intervention by civil servants in monitoring conditions of work. From the 1890s a professional factory inspectorate emerged which was active if not particularly effective. In 1908, 1201 breaches of the Factory and Workshop Act were recorded, and under the same act two years later, 32,868 contravention notices for unfenced machinery were served. Although in practice the impact of the state may have been slight,[19] the significant point is that the right of the state to intervene to abolish abuses had become widely accepted.

The systematic advance of state intervention carried an administrative logic which could not easily be rolled back. There were set-piece confrontations – over the Lloyd George budget of 1910, over tariff reform – in which the political limits of state intervention were broadly demarcated. But as Whiteside has accurately argued, by 1913 'the state management of labour had become a respectable political doctrine and . . . its advocates were ready to take on the task without any consultation with the parties about the content of their proposals'.[20] By 1914 there were probably few politicians who still put their faith in 'natural forces' or in full-blown *laissez-faire*. All the future Prime Ministers – Lloyd George, Bonar Law, Baldwin and Churchill – served their apprenticeships at the Board of Trade. Apart from those committed to full state intervention, a rather different line of arguments now emerged from the politicians. The Unionist MP Arthur Steel-

Maitland was undoubtedly more in sympathy with the collectivist case than many others in his party. In a letter to Will Thorne he claimed, 'We both of us have given up the old theory that the State should no longer interfere with industry at all. That has been relegated to the rubbish basket.' This was unusually forthright. The key question, however, was on what grounds state intervention could develop. In April 1911, during the first parliamentary debate on a general minimum wage, Steel-Maitland found no objection in principle to the idea so long as it was based on 'real business' foundations.[21] This suggests that despite the persistence of the language of individualism, what was at issue was not so much the reconciliation of collectivism with individualism as the attempt to reconcile collectivism with the principles of sound business.

The war

The war both accelerated and transformed state regulation of the economy. Immediately war was declared the government took over the railways (although nominally they remained in private hands), the Bank of England and finance, overseas trade and the control of labour. By December, for the first time ever, government controls were imposed on overseas investment. But it was not until the following spring, when it became clear that the war was going on for years rather than months, that further significant measures were taken. To the politicians there appeared two overriding problems. The first was in getting sufficient numbers of men to join the army (and the related dilemmas of conscription versus voluntarism); and the second was in ensuring the production of an incessant supply of munitions. Both tasks depended upon the mobilization of the mass of the working population in the armed forces or in the factories, under direct state supervision. This was fundamentally a crisis of labour. By the end of the war more than 5.5 million men were in the army, and the Ministry of Munitions was the largest single employer. In August 1914 the Army Contracts Department had a staff of twenty clerks; by November 1918 the Ministry of Munitions employed an administrative staff of 65,000. By 1918 coal, shipping, rail, finance, food, labour, textiles and rents came within the orbit of state control. Profits for coal and ship owners were guaranteed by the state at their 1913 levels. Apart from the Ministry of Munitions, ministries were organized for labour, food, pensions and reconstruction. According to one authority, Lord Rhondda's objective at the Ministry of Food was to 'suspend the laws of supply and demand'.[22] The same was true for all the other apparatuses of the state concerned directly with the economy.

The issue of conscription has been thoroughly examined by Middlemas.[23] The difficulties in securing a sufficient quantity of skilled labour proved the most intractable domestic problem for the politicians throughout the course of the war. The Treasury Agreement of March 1915 (or to give it its correct name, the agreement on the 'Acceleration of output on government work') was drafted by William Beveridge, Hubert Llewellyn Smith and Arthur Henderson. It aimed to achieve a combination of increased production from a depleted workforce by offering high wages and by penalizing strikes. Two committees were set up to stimulate production: the Committee on Production, headed by Lloyd George, and the rather feeble Armaments Output Committee run by Lord Kitchener. In May 1915, a shortage of shells precipitated a deep political crisis. This was speedily followed by the passing of the Munitions of War Act and the creation of the Ministry of Munitions with Lloyd George as its first minister. The act stipulated:

Any rule, practice or custom not having the force of law which tends to restrict production or employment shall be suspended, and if any person induces or attempts to induce any other person (whether a particular person or generally) to comply with such a rule, practice or custom, that person shall be guilty of an offence under the Act.

This was strong stuff, but a compromise none the less: Beveridge's hopes for a complete system of industrial conscription were dashed. Lloyd George recalled in his memoirs that, 'Two things were essential to the efficiency of the new organizaton for munitions of war – to increase the mobility of labour and to secure the greater subordination of labour to the direct control of the state.'[2]

The Ministry of Munitions followed directly in the traditions of the Labour Department of the Board of Trade but with far greater powers. It concentrated within the single ministry not only many of the prior functions of the Board of Trade, but also the pre-war labour concerns of the Home Office (the Factory Acts) and the Local Government Board (under the Poor Law). It spawned a number of influential subcommittees, notably the Manpower Board and the Welfare Department (directed by Seebohm Rowntree). Under the aegis of the latter the Health of Munitions Workers' Committee was set up which established links with the Medical Research Council and the Department of Scientific and Industrial Research. This agency ultimately pioneered, directly under state auspices, 'human relations' management in Britain. Both in the ministry's concentration on the 'human factor' in munitions production, and in the vastly extended systems for compulsory arbitration, the early initiatives of the state in adopting trade union functions were continued into the years of the war. The new department focused especially on the 'problem' of women's employment in munitions.[25]

The welfare functions of the Ministry of Munitions indicate that civil servants felt it crucial that the state should help preserve and improve the quality of the labour power of the collective labourer. Indeed, the mode of exercising statutory power was itself significant. In his management of the Welfare Department, Rowntree 'set out to educate rather than compel, and he always held his statutory powers in reserve'.[26] The explicitly coercive functions of the Ministry of Munitions were, however, most frequently in dominance. It was primarily through the ministry that the dilution of labour in the metal industries was enforced, securing the conditions of labour often associated with 'Taylorism' or 'scientific management'. Extraordinary powers to deal with working-class militants in particular areas could be sanctioned by the ministry. For example, after the Clyde strikes of December 1915 the Clyde Dilution Commission, in conjunction with the local employers, virtually brought the power of the state on to the shop-floor; and in July 1918, when Churchill was minister, it was through the ministry that strikers were first threatened with military conscription if they refused to return to work.[27] The most comprehensive analysis of the Ministry of Munitions as a directly repressive and anti-working-class apparatus can be found in James Hinton's history of the shop stewards' movement. Hinton confirms Lloyd George's own boastful characterization of the ministry as 'from first to last a businessman's organisation'.[28]

However, this depiction of state regulation as direct and absolutist, dictated by hard-nosed businessmen for their own short-term interest, is not wholly accurate. Perhaps such an end may have been desired by Lloyd George but a number of inhibitions and resistances (apart from overt working-class hostility) prevented its full realization. These resistances were partly technical. The apparatuses of the state were insufficiently developed to plan and supervise a national economic programme. They were also partly political. Antagonisms between the state bureaucrats and the business classes cannot be discounted.

One of the distinctive features of state intervention in economic relations before the war was the attempt to accumulate information about production, to appropriate for the state a range of knowledge in which state practices could be cast. The creation of the Labour Department of the Board of Trade in 1893, and the introduction of the *Labour Gazette*, marked the turning point in the state's role as an appropriator of 'mental labour' in this field. In fact it was largely due to the Board of Trade's superior statistical knowledge that it was able to overtake the Home Office as the pre-eminent economic apparatus of the state. In 1899 the Commercial Intelligence Branch was added to the Board. The establishment of the Census of Production Office in 1906 marked a further, decisive stage in this process, delivering the first ever Census of Production in the UK the following year.

However, when the crisis in production began to bite in the spring of 1915 the lack of an adequate knowledge about the details of production proved a severe handicap. In the dominant political discourse of the day one major blockage to accumulation and to the full mobilization of the nation for the war effort was represented as recalcitrant labour. But the official history of the Ministry of Munitions demonstrates that this was not the only cause. Enrolment began on 24 June 1915 for War Munitions Volunteers. By

September, through the labour exchanges, more than 100,000 volunteers had signed up – hardly suggesting an unwillingness on the part of labour. The problem for the ministry was what to do with them:

Before it could hope to effect an economic distribution of the skilled labour available, knowledge of the actual position of several thousand firms engaged more or less on work of national importance must be built up . . . with information from the Supply Departments concerning the real urgency of each class of war material. It was necessary to investigate the equipment and organization of each workshop in order to discover whether skilled labour was being squandered on machines or by methods of production which were out-of-date and to what extent firms were actually engaged on work of importance for the prosecution of the war.

And the author continued: 'The collection of so vast a body of information and its articulation on a reasoned system of priority required the assembly of a large staff of technical experts and many months of assiduous work.'[29] This problem was connected with the wider field of 'science' and with the need for a nationally organized system of research and development. In July 1915 the Committee for Science and Industrial Research was founded as a permanent state institution. Its first report, published a year later, was proud and hopeful:

The State had thus recognized the necessity for organizing the national brain power in the interests of the nation at peace. The necessity for central control of our machinery for war had been obvious for centuries, but the essential unity of our knowledge which supports both the military and industrial efforts of the country was not generally understood until the present war revealed it in so many directions as to bring it home to all.[30]

The rudimentary possession and organization of this knowledge by the state in the first years of the war imposed a severe handicap on the co-ordinated regulation of the economy as a whole.[31]

A further effect of the limited reach of state regulation raises political questions about the relation between the state and the owners of capital. In the first place the only means by which the state could impose regulation was through the agency of businessmen themselves. This required winning their consent and actively overturning their suspicions and fears of state 'interference'. The difficulties facing both politicians and businessmen were further complicated by the fact that by early 1915, in the munitions sector at least, the free market had collapsed. This initiated a crisis to which the state was forced to respond to guarantee war supplies. It also provided the means by which further controls could be exerted. The most celebrated occasion, which opened this phase of closer intervention, occurred one Saturday in March 1915 when the public authorities appropriated 1.5 million sacks of grain from a private owner, promising to pay a fair market price. Such powers contributed a crucial element in the state's initial entry into the direct regulation of the market:

The Royal Prerogative . . . came to play an essential part in the development of control. It was by virtue of the absolutist theory that the subject had no legal right to compensation against the Crown that the tyranny of market prices was overthrown.[32]

But such unilateral and absolutist state practice was less appropriate as a long-term strategy. The Rowntree formula of, where possible, reserving statutory powers in favour of 'educating' and persuading businessmen proved in the end to be more viable. This required state 'interference' to be seen to work in guaranteeing a steady flow of profits. Attempts to calculate real production costs, price-fixing, the centralization of buying and selling, and the elimination of middle-men could substantially increase profit margins in many sectors of manufacturing. Grants from the Ministry of Munitions for re-equipping plants were welcomed. Thus in many instances the legal powers of the state remained largely formal:

in the great majority of cases, what was lawful and what was not lawful did not much matter; what mattered was the extent to which any measure commanded general support and was applied impartially all round. . . . Measures of State interference, which went beyond what the best opinion in any particular trade regarded as necessary and possible, were practically certain to fail, however valid their legal sanction.[33]

The ideal was for state regulation to operate through representative boards set up in each industry, at one remove from central government itself, balancing state controls with self-government. On the other hand administrators and intellectuals from civil society were directly absorbed into the state. These intellectuals were frequently encouraged to continue work they had been doing beforehand. A dense array of private and semi-private institutions finally emerged through which state organization and regulation were implemented.

It is paradoxical that far-reaching statutory powers coexisted with such a high degree of 'private' or consensual forms in practice. Vacillation on military conscription continued long after huge casualities were first inflicted on the British army.[34] Beveridge's plans for industrial conscription were the dreams of a bureaucrat, not a party politician. Even the powers of the Munitions of War Act – in practice impossible to enforce in every machine-shop in the country – were generally only paraded in response to specific, local crises. When the state dealt with labour the legalism of the rhetoric was rarely just a formality. Furthermore, whenever private organizations were adequately performing a specific task (the celebrated 'voluntary' work of English middle-class women is a good example) then civil servants were content to keep out of the way.[35] The political stress on voluntarism, even at the height of state regulation, was no bluff. It was from this basis, at least in the liberal spectrum of political forces represented in the Lloyd George coalition, that ideologies of reconstruction developed. The aim was to reconcile collectivism with voluntarism. As the end of the war approached the coalition Cabinet was concerned, not with controls or intervention in the abstract, but with a specific ideal of regulation organized around notions of equal representation between capital and labour, citizenship and nation-building.

Decontrols

In a famous essay R. H. Tawney argued that, although the free market had been 'jettisoned wholesale' by 1918, the shift to state intervention had none the less been improvised and pragmatic. 'The most extensive and intricate scheme of State intervention in economic life which the country had seen was brought into existence, without the merits or demerits of State intervention ever being discussed.' Consequently, he continued, the task of dismantling the whole system at the end of the war was relatively easy. 'The arguments used to defend State control in time of war had only to be reversed, to appear, once the crisis was over, convincing arguments against it.'[36] To a large degree Tawney was right: decisions to relax controls could often have been taken as the line of least resistance (mirroring some measures of wartime regulation) rather than as a result of pre-determined principles. However it was not accurate to suggest that they were forced through 'in haste'. This underestimates the extent to which the Treasury needed to win politically its dominant position before it could command a frontal assault against high state expenditure. Even then the evidence suggests that through most of 1919 the Treasury itself resisted a full rush into decontrols.[37] The recomposition of the state and the forms of regulation which emerged in the 1920s cannot be explained in terms of a straightforward opposition between intervention and *laissez-faire*.

In July 1918 a deputation from the National Union of Manufacturers urged Lloyd George to abolish, in one go, all wartime restrictions. This deputation must have been disappointed for in the direct aftermath of the armistice state intervention continued apace. Two new ministries were established in 1919, for health and transport. Sir Eric Geddes, at the Ministry of Transport, attempted to construct an integrated, state-organized transport system, which for its success was dependent on the nationalization of the railways (a measure receiving, as before the war, the vociferous support of Churchill). Only in 1921, when the railways were returned to private hands, did Geddes's plan collapse. The mines remained under public control until March 1921. In 1919 Parliament passed the Seven Hours (Mines) Act. Both Bonar Law and Baldwin, at that date, favoured permanent nationalization. The abandonment of state regulation was only achieved in the teeth of massive resistance from the miners and the breaking of the 1921 strike. The determining factor in the decision to decontrol appears to have been the fear that the state itself might become directly caught up in the bitter fight between coal owners and miners. The Cabinet minutes noted on 27 January

1920 that 'the Government themselves would never be free until they resigned control over the industry'.[38] The Industrial Courts Act of 1919 sought, through a state-financed service, to strengthen the non-mandatory channels for industrial arbitration which had been cultivated before the war. The retention of the Ministry of Labour, despite business hostility, was defended as a further contribution to the regulation of industrial disputes. The establishment of the National Industrial Conference in February 1919 was a further measure to contain burgeoning trade union militancy. These corporate institutions, with direct public backing, were an attempt to generate the conditions for industry to govern itself, thereby allowing the state to draw back from what threatened to be a succession of industrial struggles on a national scale.

Regulation continued with the Housing and Town Planning Bill of March 1919. This placed upon local authorities the duty to provide houses wherever they were needed, and offered state subsidies to the local authorities for securing loans. Desperate measures to make workable the pre-war machinery for the payment of unemployment insurance were passed one after another, effectively establishing a new basis for eligibility. Perhaps most radical of all, within ten days of the signing of the armistice, the Wages (Temporary Regulation) Act was sped through Parliament. This act aimed to avoid the political consequences of a precipitous fall in wages, at first for six months, but later extended to twelve.

Nor did old powers of regulation disappear at one blow. It was not until as late as April 1919 that the first big batch of economic regulations were suspended or revoked. The first major apparatus to go, ominously for many of the collectivist intellectuals, was the Ministry of Reconstruction in the following June. The Ministries of Food, Munitions and Shipping were closed in March 1921. The 1919 Profiteering Act – never of much effect – lapsed in May. The last of the direct wartime controls to go under was the power invested in the Liquor Board, on 17 August 1921.

Thus it was not until the middle of 1919 that the bonfire of regulations began to flare, and the anti-interventionist forces began to cohere as a political force. For many, a general ideological commitment to voluntarism had not wavered during the course of the war. But their arguments were strengthened by a number of post-war developments. First, in the aftermath of the war Britain became a debtor nation. Through the 1920s a huge slice of public expenditure was paid as interest on the war loans – until the National Government finally reneged on its commitments to paying the full sum to the United States. This recharged the anti-interventionist position which received official endorsement from the 1922 Report of the Committee on National Expenditure (commissioned the previous year, and subsequently known as the Geddes Axe). Second, these years were a time of high speculation and inflated profits, prompted by industrial concentration and government acquiescence. Two-thirds of the MPs returned in 1918 were businessmen themselves or directors of companies. Third, collectivism and public regulation (particularly for the mines) increasingly became linked to a socialist programme of nationalization and workers' control, politically polarizing collectivists from 'individualists'.

The most dramatic political expression of renewed neo-liberal hostility to state intervention was Lord Rothermere's Anti-Waste Party. Between 1919–21 Rothermere's party campaigned against 'squandermania' (especially state spending on welfare benefits) and its electoral success exerted formidable pressures on the coalition. It was instrumental in preparing the ideological terrain for the appointment of the Geddes Committee. The combination of these factors produced the conditions for at least a temporary alliance between the Treasury (preoccupied with the national debt) and those sectors of manufacturing industry capable of sustaining high profits without the aid of government controls. The movement away from controls in the post-war period has to be situated within this set of forces rather than interpreted as a general swing against state intervention as such.

The 1920s

The foremost issues for state economic policy in the 1920s were the twin problems of the chronic destabilization of the staple industries, especially coal, and the consequent leap in unemployment which doubled between December 1920 and March 1921. None of the administrations in the 1920s came even close to resolving either issue. So long as the leading politicians remained committed to a strategy of 'sound' finance, the maintenance of the pound at an artificially high rate and reversion to the gold standard they were tied to the logic of deflation. Such a strategy became established as the political common sense of the decade, for Conservative and Labour chancellors alike. But this was not a simple 'capture' of state and manufacturers by the City, nor a straightforward return to *laissez-faire*. On the one hand, on the financial question there existed a broad agreement between the various fractions of capital. On the other, the major political parties had produced their own specific, programmatic conceptions of direct state management. For the Conservatives, this involved an acceptance in principle of a full policy of tariff reform. For Labour it meant nationalization. For the Liberals, guided on unemployment policy by Lloyd George and on economic matters by Keynes, it meant a commitment to a managed economy. The Liberal position evolved from the collectivism of the new liberalism of the pre-war years. It culminated in the publication of *Britain's Industrial Future* (the Yellow Book) in February 1928, deliberately designed as an alternative to the political 'shibboleths' of nationalization and protection.[39] Interventionist programmes made little headway in the 1920s. After the Conservative electoral defeat in 1923, generally attributed to the party's explicit endorsement of protection, tariff reform was not actively pursued for the rest of the decade. When in 1925 representatives from the steel industry applied for protective duties, electoral considerations forced the Conservative government to reject them. Struggles of the labour movement for nationalization of the railways and mines were smashed. And the Liberals were never near enough to government to carry through their policies. Just as before the war, the broad political definitions of state practice were at least partially autonomous from administrative developments. Responses to specific crises consolidated areas of limited but often significant public regulation. The centralization and concentration of capitals continued and indeed accelerated, with very little direct state interference.

One of the key questions about the 1920s is the extent to which banking capital and the City flourished at the direct expense of domestic industrial capital. Some direct financial and trade controls survived the post-war moment, although these were few. Regulations on the export of capital were relaxed but not lifted in March 1919. At the time the Treasury itself instructed that 'The main need now is to protect the foreign exchanges and to conserve capital for development within the United Kingdom.'[40] But the perennial problem of channelling capital into domestic industry was not so easily solved. All statutory powers regulating the export of capital were repealed later that year. From this time onwards it was up to the Bank of England to step in – without any legal sanctions – to impose semi-official embargoes (backed by the Treasury), a state of affairs which continued until November 1925. The purpose of these embargoes was primarily to encourage investment in domestic manufacturing. But, although the export of capital may to some degree have been checked, there is no evidence that British industry was affected. Similarly, the protectionist McKenna duties, first introduced in 1915, were conceived as a means to safeguard vulnerable or strategically important sectors of manufacturing. These forced the first breach in the operations of a strict *laissez-faire*. The motor industry, for example, was protected from its outset. The McKenna duties were also crucial for the protection of the chemical industry, initially to stimulate production for explosives. As a direct result, in 1918, the state helped to set up the British Dyestuffs Corporation, which eight years later was to merge into the vast ICI combine. The Finance Act of 1919 retained the McKenna duties and introduced state powers against dumping (although these were never implemented). This in turn was followed by the Safeguarding of Industry Act of 1921 which was extended to cover new areas in 1925, 1926 and 1928, notwithstanding the government's reluctance to embrace 'protection'. But although extensive formal powers existed for the protection of domestic industry, it was estimated by the Balfour Committee on Industry and Trade that in 1928 only about 5 per cent of manufacturing industry actually benefited. Thus none of these provisions decisively tipped the balance in favour of industrial capital. Under-investment in the staple industries was certainly damaging. But how far it can be claimed that industrial capital was economically subordinated to the City and to what extent the vigour of banking capital can be taken as a causal explanation for the relative decline of British manufacturing is a more complex set of questions than can be answered here.

However it would be wrong to be mesmerized by an apparently fixed antagonism between City and business in these years. The deflation which followed from government financial policy not only provided direct benefits to the financiers but may also have produced the conditions in which the larger manufacturing capitals could thrive by reducing wages and forcing down the general value of labour power. From 1919 wage cuts were imposed industry by industry. Although it is difficult to prove, this would have been likely, at least in some cases, to have discouraged rationalization, for a relatively low organic composition of capital would have helped to secure an adequate rate of profit. It has been argued that domestic political strategies in the 1920s favoured the City. The most common illustration is the return to the gold standard and its consequences for the coal industry leading to the strike of 1926.[41] However, this was as much due to the nature of the *political* alliances of the period and the concessions and compromises sought by industrial capitalists in all sectors in negotiating with the politicians. If the onslaught against the miners could help to force wages down across the board, then there was every reason for industrial capitalists to lend their support. The route to monopolization in Britain was not only characterized in its early stages by the absence, or displacement, of direct state organization. It was also characterized by systematic deflation and wage-cutting. Even in the advanced monopoly sectors, the emergence of policies of planned rationalization integrated to programmes for 'high wages' were, at least for the 1920s, largely mythical.

Paradoxically, despite all Baldwin's protestations about the need for business to be taken out of the hands of politicians, the state frequently crept in through a back entrance. As a general comment on the decade, Pollard claims that, 'A large share of industry and transport was, even in the 1920s, not controlled by private enterprise at all, but by various types of public or non-profit-making organizations and their growth is one of the most significant aspects of the period.'[42] The state was also instrumental in securing amalgamations in rail in 1921, the airways in 1924, and electricity in 1926. When leading manufacturing companies reached a point of collapse, as many did in the 1920s, the government was forced, reluctantly, to take notice. One of the first crises of the decade was the near downfall of the Austin company. By April 1921 it was in the hands of the receiver and it was only saved by the prompt intervention of the Midland Bank. The bankers immediately reorganized the management and appointed a new works director – perhaps the clearest example in the period of banking capital adopting a direct role in the running of manufacturing capital. But when a company the size of Armstrong-Whitworth began to rock in 1925 state pressure was exerted from the outset. From that date the fate of the company was 'entirely in the hands of the Bank of England'. The merger with Vickers two years later was overseen and instigated by the government. To Montagu Norman, the Governor of the Bank of England, the merger was 'essential' and he cajoled Churchill (then Chancellor of the Exchequer), who was none too keen, to give way. Characteristically the Sun Insurance Company acted as a 'screen' for the Bank of England, thereby concealing the full role of the state behind two intermediary organizations.[43]

The most illuminating instance of state intervention in a private company was the government's role in the creation of ICI in 1926. The previous year Reginald McKenna (Chancellor of the Exchequer 1915–16; Chairman of the Midland Bank from 1919; and a decisive figure in propping up Vickers and pushing it on the road to rationalization in 1925) approached Baldwin with a plan to amalgamate the chemical industries. He followed this by a lunch with Sir Harry McGowan, Chairman and Managing Director of Nobel Industries. The significance of this meeting is perceptively recorded by Reader:

One of the original impulses towards the foundation of ICI came from the direction of public policy, via that network of semi-official channels, straddling the frontier between business and politics, through which so much influence flowed in Great Britain between the wars. . . . The proposition he put to McGowan was that Nobel Industries, for reasons of national policy rather than commercial profit, should take over British Dyestuffs Corporation and, with it, responsibility for the British dyestuffs industry: an industry of prime importance if the country went to war.[44]

Four companies were eventually amalgamated, comprising 47,000 workers, making ICI the largest manufacturer in the UK. Its first chairman was Sir Alfred Mond (an ex-Liberal minister, defector to the Conservatives in 1926) and its directors included McKenna himself, and Lords Weir and Birkenhead. As Reader suggests, with perhaps a deliberately ironic understatement: 'Directors of this stamp might, perhaps, be considered informal trustees for the public interest, and they certainly ensured a close connection between ICI and the world of government and politics.'[45]

These altruistic 'informal trustees for the public interest' appear to have proliferated in the 1920s, marking an important shift in the relation between state and capital. Yet earlier patterns of *indirect* state intervention were preserved. This semi-private approach reached its culmination in the last year of the Conservative administration. Baldwin himself had been urging Montagu Norman to organize state intervention in the staple industries through the offices of the Bank of England and by amassing sufficient *private* capital.[46] In January the steel interests of Vickers, Vickers-Armstrong and Cammell Laird were reorganized into the English Steel Corporation. In November the Securities Management Trust was founded, to be followed in early 1930 by the Bankers' Industrial Development Company for the express purpose of rationalizing the staples. State regulation of the economy was mediated through diverse institutions occupying an unstable frontier between business and politics.

Conclusion

The imperatives of the new world crisis from 1929 reshaped the relation between state and capital. According to Samuel Beer it was the National Government 'that laid the foundation of the Managed Economy' by abandoning the gold standard, instituting monetary expansion, and encouraging rationalization behind a protective wall of tariffs.[47] On the eve of introducing the protectionist bill, Neville Chamberlain explained that import curbs would provide the government 'with such a lever as has never been possessed before by any government for inducing or, if you like, forcing industry to set its house in order'.[48] From this date on, opposition to state-regulated collectivism could not carry the conviction of earlier years. Forlorn pleas to the government such as that made by the Federation of British Industries in 1929 'to take a holiday from social legislation' sounded increasingly anachronistic.[49] In a radio talk in 1934 John Hilton could contrast contemporary public enthusiasm for monopolies to the apprehensions of the immediate post-war moment: 'we never for a moment thought of it (monopolization) as something so essential to industrial salvation that we should encourage it and insist upon it'.[50] Ernest Bevin announced to the Macmillan Committee on Finance and Industry in 1930: 'Laissez-faire, as understood before the war, can never be recreated. If for no other reason, the Russian Five Year Plan cuts across the whole thing.'[51] References such as these to the Soviet Union were not merely rhetorical. Commitment to planning – especially to rationalization and to a proto-Keynesian recomposition of consumption – became the central theme of progressive ideologies in the 1930s. They proposed a more *active* role for the state in the mobilization of the 'countervailing tendencies' to halt the tendential decline in the general rate of profit.

The forms of monopolization which developed, and the position of the state in the economy, do not appear to conform to any easily recognizable model. As Lloyd George perceived when he was writing his war memoirs in the 1930s the situation in the war was 'neither Stalin nor Roosevelt'.[52] This was not because the transformation of economic relations suggested by the concept 'monopoly capitalism' did not occur in Britain. Hobsbawm rightly argues that by the time of the Second World War Britain was in all probability one of the most economically concentrated of the metropolitan nations.[53] Clapham identified the problem when he indicated that 'What is notable among British consolidations and associations is not their rarity or weakness so much as their unobtrusiveness.'[54] This can be explained by the unusually mediated role of the state in the transition to the corporate economy.

The depth to which the initial stages were both in reality and in appearance accomplished 'spontaneously' exposed the ambiguities of English 'liberalism' and anti-statism. Collectivism now appeared as the true liberalism. Protectionism edged forward under the slogan of non-intervention. And the monopolists fought in the last ditch for the free market. When Sir Alfred Mond assumed chairmanship of the largest monopoly company in the UK he shifted his political allegiance to Conservatism because it adhered 'to the fundamental principle of individualism'. Five years later, as Lord Melchett, he implored: 'If we had a Five Year Plan for the British Empire and were prepared to pursue it with the determination and self-sacrifice that the Russians have shown, how much more we should achieve!'[55] In Baldwin these paradoxes reached their height. In March 1925 he declared:

What this Government will not do is to attempt to control the industries of this country. . . . By the natural evolution of our industrial life in England, we are confronted today . . . with great consolidations of capital, managed by small concentrated groups . . . and by great organizations of labour led by experienced and responsible leaders. . . . It is little that the Government can do (*sic*): these reforms, these revolutions must come from the people themselves.[56]

In Baldwin's outlook monopoly and voluntarism (in its popular key) become superimposed. Civil society appears as the active agent in this transition, the state as passive. The corporate economy has emerged as if by natural process and by the will of the people.

There was undoubtedly an element of deliberate subterfuge in Baldwin's statement. He knew better than most the deepening links emerging between state and economy. It was remarkable that a bureaucratic and managed economy could be legitimated in this way. The fact that it could may highlight the peculiar forms of the transition to monopoly capitalism in Britain, a transition which required, to borrow from Gramsci,

a particular environment, a particular social structure . . . and a certain type of State. This State is the liberal State, not in the sense of free-trade liberalism or of effective political liberty, but in the more fundamental sense of free initiative and economic individualism which with its own means, on the level of 'civil society', through historical development, itself arrives at a regime of industrial concentration and monopoly.[57]

It would be a mistake to be deceived by these peculiarities and to underestimate the depth of the economic transformation in Britain in this period, and the extent to which the structures of monopoly capitalism were developed.

Notes and references

1 M. Dobb, *Studies in the Development of Capitalism* (Routledge and Kegan Paul 1963), p. 314.

2 C. Wilson, 'Management and policy in large-scale enterprise: Lever Brothers and Unilever, 1918–1938', in B. Supple (ed.), *Essays in British Business History* (Clarendon Press 1977), p. 125; and Walter Rodney, *How Europe Underdeveloped Africa* (Bogle-L'Ouverture 1972), pp. 198–204.

3 L. Hannah, *The Rise of the Corporate Economy* (Methuen 1976), p. 23.

4 This argument has best been put by Andrew Gamble, *Britain in Decline* (Macmillan 1981).

5 D. H. Aldcroft, 'Economic growth in Britain in the inter-war years: a reassessment', *Economic History Review* II, **20**, no. 2 (1967), p. 13; and A. E. Musson, *The Growth of British Industry* (Batsford 1978), pp. 153–5.

6 G. C. Allen, *The Industrial Development of the Black Country 1860–1927* (Cass 1966), p. 322.

7 A. J. Taylor, 'The coal industry', in D. H. Aldcroft (ed.), *The Development of British Industry and Foreign Competition 1875–1914* (Allen and Unwin 1968), p. 68.

8 R. E. Tyson, 'The cotton industry', in Aldcroft, p. 123.

9 R. Church and M. Miller, 'The big three: competition, management, and marketing in the British motor industry, 1922–1939', in Supple, p. 166.

10 Walter Meakin, *The New Industrial Revolution* (Gollancz 1928); and L. Urwick, *The Meaning of Rationalization* (Nisbet 1929).

11 E. M. H. Lloyd, *Experiments in State Control* (Clarendon 1924), pp. 259–60.

12 C. Trebilcock, 'Spin-off in British economic history: armaments and industry 1760–1914', *Economic History Review* II, **22**, no. 3 (1969), p. 479; and J. D. Scott, *Vickers. A History* (Weidenfeld and Nicolson 1962).

13 ibid., p. 485.

14 P. J. Cain, 'Railway combination and the government 1900–14', *Economic History Review* II, **25**, no. 4 (1972), p. 623. According to Cain these companies owned 40,054 miles of track out of a total of 47,091; by 1904 they 'had taken on most of the features associated with a modern corporative enterprise'.

15 Quoted, ibid., p. 636.

16 *Fifth and Final Report of the Royal Commission on Labour* (1894), Part I, para. 92.

17 ibid., paras. 363 and 366.

18 K. Middlemas, *Politics in Industrial Society* (Deutsch 1979), p. 58.

19 On the strains imposed on state intervention by the lack of development of a bureaucracy, see J. Pellew, *The Home Office 1848–1914* (Heinemann 1982), pp. 64–93 and 150–83. And see too Roger Davidson, 'Government administration', in C. Wrigley (ed.), *A History of British Industrial Relations 1875–1914* (Harvester 1982).

20 N. Whiteside, 'Welfare insurance and casual labour. A study of administrative intervention in industrial employment', *Economic History Review* II, **32**, no. 4 (1979), p. 513.

21 Quoted in H. V. Emy, *Liberals, Radicals and Social Politics* (Cambridge University Press 1973), p. 257.

22 Lloyd, p. 31. For a comprehensive survey see Kathleen Burk (ed.), *War and the State. The transformation of British Government, 1914–1919* (Allen and Unwin 1982).
23 See for example Middlemas, pp. 80–4.
24 D. Lloyd George, *War Memoirs* (Odhams 1938), vol. 1, pp. 155–6.
25 Ministry of Munitions Health of Munitions Workers Committee, *Industrial Health and Efficiency. Final Report* (Cd. 9065, 1918) deserves to be read in full in this respect.
26 A. Briggs, *Social Thought and Social Action: A Study of the Work of Seebohm Rowntree* (Longman 1961), p. 120.
27 H. Wolfe, *Labour Supply and Regulation* (Clarendon 1923), p. 143.
28 Lloyd George, vol. 1, p. 147; and see J. Hinton, *The First Shop Stewards' Movement* (Allen and Unwin 1973).
29 Ministry of Munitions, *History of the Ministry of Munitions* (HMSO 1922), vol. 4, pp. 11–12 and p. 15.
30 *First Report of the Committee on Science and Industrial Research* (Cd. 8336, 1915–16), p. 9.
31 For a later attempt to reverse this situation, see Ministry of Reconstruction, *Report of the Machinery of Government Committee* (The 'Haldane' Committee) (Cd. 9230, 1918).
32 Lloyd, p. 52.
33 ibid., p. 64.
34 S. J. Hurwitz, *State Intervention in Great Britain. A study of economic control and social response, 1914–1919* (Cass 1968), p. 104.
35 A. Marwick, *Women at War, 1914–18* (Fontana 1977), pp. 80–1.
36 R. H. Tawney, 'The abolition of economic controls, 1918–1921', in J. Winter (ed.), *History and Society* (Routledge and Kegan Paul 1978), pp. 131, 139, 162.
37 P. B. Johnson, *Land Fit for Heroes: The Planning of British Reconstruction 1916–19* (University of Chicago Press 1968), p. 452.
38 Quoted in M. J. Kirby, 'The politics of state coercion in inter-war Britain: the Mines Department of the Board of Trade, 1920–42', *Historical Journal*, **22**, no. 2 (1979), p. 378.
39 J. M. Keynes, 'The end of laissez-faire', in *Essays in Persuasion*, Collected Works vol. 19 (Macmillan 1972).
40 Quoted in J. Aitken, 'The official regulation of British overseas investment, 1914–31', *Economic History Review* II, **23**, no. 20 (1970), p. 325.
41 See for example Keynes's position: D. E. Moggridge, *Keynes* (Fontana 1976), p. 73; and J. Foster, 'Imperialism and the labour aristocracy', in J. Skelley (ed.), *1926 The General Strike* (Lawrence and Wishart 1976).
42 S. Pollard, *The Development of the British Economy* (Edward Arnold 1975), p. 162.
43 Scott, pp. 161–5.
44 W. J. Reader, 'Imperial Chemical Industries and the state, 1926–1945', in Supple, pp. 227–8. And see G. Werskey, *The Visible College* (Allen Lane 1978), pp. 30–3 on the proto-technocratic intellectuals grouped around the journal *Nature* and for their adulation of I C I as the vanguard in science and technology.
45 ibid., p. 231.
46 And for the joint Baldwin/Steel-Maitland attempt to win the Conservative

cabinet to a corporatist style of representation, see Middlemas, pp. 194–7 and 207–80.

47 S. Beer, *Modern British Politics* (Faber 1969), p. 278.

48 Quoted, ibid., p. 293.

49 Quoted in R. Skidelsky, *Politicians and the Slump* (Penguin 1970), p. 177.

50 J. Hilton, 'Putting industry's house in order', *Listener* (14 March 1934), p. 449.

51 Quoted in A. Bullock, *The Life and Times of Ernest Bevin* (Heinemann 1960), **1**, p. 434.

52 Lloyd George, **2**, p. 1114. James Cronin has recently argued, rightly, for the specificity of the formation of monopoly capitalism in Britain; from the mid 1920s he identifies 'a sort of bastardized liberalism or, perhaps more accurately, a form of corporatism without Keynes, without the state and without the cash'. This depiction, however, needs to distinguish more clearly the periods before and after the break in economic management posed by the 1929 crisis, and the subsequent shifts into 'planning' – what I have suggested here constitute the second formative stage in monopoly capitalism in Britain. J. Cronin, 'Coping with labour', in J. Cronin and J. Schneer (eds.), *Social Conflict and the Political Order in Modern Britain* (Croom Helm 1982), p. 126.

53 E. J. Hobsbawm, *Industry and Empire* (Penguin 1969), p. 214.

54 J. H. Clapham, *An Economic History of Modern Britain* (Cambridge University Press 1951), vol. 3, p. 316. And see A. Marshall, *Industry and Trade* (Macmillan 1919), book 3, ch. 11.

55 A. Mond, *Industry and Politics* (Macmillan 1927), p. 304; and the *Daily Worker*, 25 April 1931.

56 Quoted in K. Middlemas and J. Barnes, *Baldwin. A biography* (Hutchinson 1969), pp. 380–1.

57 A. Gramsci, *Prison Notebooks* (Lawrence and Wishart 1971), p. 293.

5   Reorganizing the labour market: unemployment, the state and the labour movement, 1880-1914*

Mary Langan

The debates and struggles around state intervention in the relief of unemployment and the reorganization of the labour market to reduce its incidence bear directly on the wider 'crisis of authority' of late Victorian and Edwardian society. Much of this is well documented by the historians.[1] What is less easy to grasp is the impact of the labour movement, from below, in shattering the ideologies of pauperism associated with the New Poor Law of 1834. Central in this respect was the new challenge of labour of the 1880s and the changed conditions of the conflict between capital and labour. From this period the struggle between capital and labour became decisively constituted by issues concerned with production and jobs rather than with negotiations about prices for subsistence goods. The last major food riots occurred at the end of the 1860s. By the 1870s the organized working class had come to learn the 'rules of the game' of industrial bargaining.[2] In these struggles a recognizably modern culture of labourism was cast in which possession of a job and a secure place in the labour market, depending on various degrees of skill and dexterity, conferred corresponding degrees of status upon its owner. But although these matters have been the subject of a great deal of debate, the relations between the labour movement in the 1880s and the protracted formation of new state policies on unemployment still need to be pieced together.

One thing, however, is clear from the outset. Even if the labour movement was decisive in overturning the principles of the New Poor Law, the initiative in elaborating new theories and policies was quickly won by intellectuals working inside the state who were formed in the philosophies of new liberalism and who contributed to the making of social democracy. Rationalizing the labour market through a system of labour exchanges, developing the principles of unemployment insurance, and incorporating representatives of labour to administer and manage the new schemes constituted the basis of the 'progressive' solution to the newly defined problem of unemployment. Its advocates were represented in the state bureaucracy at the Board of Trade

---

* Thanks to Michael McMahon, and to John Clarke with whom I worked closely in the early stages of this chapter.

by William Beveridge and Hubert Llewellyn Smith, while the case was argued in Parliament by Lloyd George and Winston Churchill.

The experts and the politicians took advantage of labour movement hostility to the Poor Law system to forge a consensus in favour of a new approach to the problem of unemployment. Indeed it was in the field of unemployment that a close working relationship between the state and the labour movement was first established. Here the various corporate pacts which developed in the twentieth century were first anticipated. Representatives of labour secured consultative positions in the administration of the new policies. The integration of the labour leaders had advantages and dangers. On the one hand, both socialists and trade union leaders were delighted at the setback to the Poor Law authorities and their traditional supporters. On the other hand, the labour politicians came to accept theories of unemployment and policies for dealing with the unemployed that had been developed by liberal bureaucrats with little real sympathy for the working class.

By the time of the First World War the labour movement, alongside the employers and the civil servants, had won a new authority as the putative co-founders of the new consensus, imposing policies designed to mitigate the worst effects of unemployment. But this was an authority won at the cost of successive compromises, a subordination which effectively silenced those more radical proposals, still active in various sections of the labour movement, which took the issue to be the injustice of unemployment itself, not merely its effects.

Let us turn to examine this process in more detail, beginning with the 'problem of labour' that guided the evolution of state policy in the field of unemployment.

The 'problem of labour'

By the end of the nineteenth century economic uncertainties and growing social instability focused attention on the 'problem of labour'. Recurrent economic crises were accompanied by the expansion of pools of jobless workers whose skills and capacity to work appeared to diminish in ever-deepening conditions of poverty and idleness. Rioting by demoralized workers in London and elsewhere from the 1880s onwards shook the Victorian social order. The emergence of socialist organizations which placed the issue of unemployment at the centre of their strategies was perceived as a serious threat. The 'problem of labour' required both a solution to the difficulties of regulating the quality and supply of workers to the labour market and a remedy to the appeal of the prescriptions of socialism.

As the capitalist economy became more closely integrated the effects of periodic crises, previously localized in particular trades or regions, registered on a broader scale. Intermittent dramatic rises in unemployment in whole industries resulted, affecting broad areas of the country.[3] The consequences were twofold. The position of skilled workers became increasingly insecure, their allegiance to the system weakened, and they became a potentially disaffected and volatile force. At the same time, there proliferated a large stratum of unskilled and impoverished workers for whom unemployment became a semi-permanent state.

Data collected by the trade unions suggest that following the Great Depression skilled workers faced greater economic uncertainty, with longer and more frequent spells of unemployment. From the 1870s episodes of slump and unemployment regularly hit the shipbuilding and metal trades.[4] The resources of the trade union and friendly societies (to which workers paid dues while at work and from which they could claim benefits in lean times) became severely strained.[5] By 1898 only 5000 friendly societies had surplus funds and 1200 were in deficit.[6] The advent of widespread unemployment undermined both the prestige of the artisans and the inward, corporate nature of their organizations.

In his seminal *Life and Labour* Charles Booth noted with alarm that it was among the 'highest grades of labour' that 'we find the springs of Socialism and Revolution'.[7] The 'new unions' formed among unskilled workers at the close of the 1880s were strongly influenced by the militant outlook of the revolutionary socialists. In the vast sprawling slums of London there existed a sub-class of workless or casually, often seasonally, employed workers. Irregular and badly paid employment was a feature of the docks and building industries as well as the sweated clothing, furniture and finishing trades which flourished in the capital. The East End 'mob' made its first appearance in the demonstrations and riots during the recession of 1886–7 in which the Social Democratic Federation played a leading role. The spectre of a 'residuum' uniting with the respectable working class began to haunt the bourgeoisie.[8]

State policy towards the working class and the labour market in the nineteenth century was guided by the orthodoxies of classical political economy. 'Unemployment' was not a recognized category, for a balance in the supply and demand for labour was assumed. Those who were out of work were considered to be in transition from one job to another according to the due processes of the labour market or, according to the same mechanisms, to have priced their labour too highly. The rest were simply wilfully idle. Poverty was seen as the natural and inevitable condition of a system of wage labour, a vital incentive to industriousness and good behaviour. Pauperism on the other hand was the result of a defective character and an indolence which bred improvidence, drunkenness and vice. This outlook, codified in the 1834 Poor Law Amendment Act, dominated nineteenth-century social policy. According to the prevailing ideology state intervention in the labour market could only impair the free movement of labour, force wages down and encourage idleness and licentiousness. The Poor Law encouraged workers to rely on wage labour for their livelihood. The economically active working class was subject to the discipline of the free labour market; those who lacked the moral fibre to work were subjected to the tyranny of the workhouse.

The Poor Law was enforced with increased severity from the 1870s onwards in response to the growth of unemployment. The Local Government Board (established in 1871) and the Charity Organisation Society (COS), which was established in 1869 to co-ordinate philanthropic work among the poor, formed an alliance to ensure that the regulations were imposed ruthlessly. 'Outdoor relief' – benefits provided only to those prepared to undergo a stringent means test and often an arduous labour test to prove willingness to work – was highly restricted, provided on the basis of the character and conduct of the applicant. As a result outdoor relief was virtually abolished in some areas and the labour test imposed even more widely; the national incidence of able-bodied outdoor pauperism declined sharply through the 1870s and 1880s despite persistent recession.[9] The problem, however, was that the Poor Law system, and the ideology that sustained it, could no longer cope with the burgeoning masses of the impoverished and workless in the big industrial cities.

At the same time the rising threat from rival imperialist powers provoked a deep anxiety among British capitalists about the quality of British labour power. Concern with the quality of labour power was directly linked to concern about the effect of unemployment on the working class. In 1904 Beveridge used an appropriately military metaphor to underline his anxieties about the impact of unemployment:

Many who are active members of the industrial army . . . are seen falling out of that army and being driven beyond hope of return to it by the pressure of prolonged idleness and starvation. With these families 'chronic' distress is in danger of being created as the result of physical and moral deterioration during a period of 'exceptional' distress.[10]

For Beveridge unemployment was a damaging waste of national resources: 'Involuntary idleness . . . means first and directly a present waste of productive power; secondly and indirectly, a depravation of human material and destruction of productive power for the future.'[11] The message was clear: if Britain were to get the best out of its working-class 'productive power', the nation had to do something about unemployment.

The formulation and implementation of a government policy appropriate to the 'problem of labour' became the goal of a grouping of influential intellectuals. Charles Booth investigated and classified the London poor of the 1880s and 1890s. His massive seventeen-volume *Life and Labour of the People of London* laid the foundations for all subsequent work. Booth distinguished between the 'respectable working class' and 'the residuum', proposing measures of state intervention to deal with both. William

Beveridge was Booth's most important protégé. His proposals for more systematic state intervention in the labour market, expounded in *Unemployment: a problem of industry* in 1909, challenged classical prejudices against state interference. Under the patronage of Liberal leaders Churchill and Lloyd George, Beveridge worked closely with Hubert Llewellyn Smith, a pioneering expert in the problem of labour. At the Board of Trade Llewellyn Smith developed social research, statistical methods, and strategies of conciliation and arbitration in relations between capital and labour. Together Beveridge and Llewellyn Smith forged a policy to manage the unemployment problem, creating a suitable state apparatus to administer it and winning the consent of the forces of both capital and labour for its implementation.

The emergence of unemployment policy

At the turn of the century the government had no 'unemployment policy'. Indeed the term 'unemployment' itself only came into widespread use after 1895.[12] Yet by 1911 the Liberal government had completed a major programme of legislation, establishing labour exchanges and a national scheme of unemployment insurance, both designed specifically to deal with the unemployment problem. This package of measures was based on the theoretical work of Booth and Beveridge.

Booth's researches led to a complete classification of working people. He broke up the old poor/pauper distinction by constructing a continuum of categories of workpeople according to their level of skill, regularity of employment, standard of income and life-style. He identified a residuum consisting of 'savage, semi-criminal loafers, beggars and bullies' and a much larger grouping of very poor, very irregularly employed casual labourers; together these two classes made up almost 10 per cent of the population. Booth also described three categories of the 'respectable' working class, differentiated largely according to skill and regularity of employment, but also according to morality. Between the residuum (Booth's categories A and B) and the respectable (D, E, F) he located a substantial intermediate layer of casual workers with a marked tendency to become 'victims of trade depression' who were also given to 'improvidence and drink'. Booth emphasized the danger of this class C (8 per cent of the population) drifting into the residuum in times of recession and also warned of the risk of classes D and E sliding down the social ladder.[13]

Booth did not abandon the notion of moral culpability for worklessness and poverty so dear to the Poor Law authorities. But he did introduce an important external factor into his analysis of the causation of distress. He thus broke with orthodox political economy by establishing a dynamic relationship between character and environment in which personal weakness could push a worker down the social scale in conditions of economic crisis.

For Booth, unemployment and poverty were broad *social* problems not simply attributable to moral failings.

Booth was especially concerned about the 'residuum' which he identified closely with the prevalence of casual labour and prolonged unemployment. The residuum's condition was dangerous because of its potential ill effects on the classes above as a source of moral contamination.[14] Within the residuum Booth focused on class B, the poorest workers, morally and physically incapable of achieving better: 'Here in class B we have the crux of the social problem. Every other class can take care of itself, or could do so, if class B were out of the way.'[15] Class A could, through straightforward coercion, easily be dispersed, but class B was much larger and capable of infecting wide layers of working people.

Booth's central objective was to restore a clear demarcation between the residuum and the respectable working class. If the residuum were isolated, the discipline of the market could be relied upon to preserve the standards of respectability for the rest. He thus recommended that class B be removed to labour colonies where it would be isolated from the labour market and from the active working population.

Beveridge followed Booth's pioneering work, but concentrated particularly on the labour market. While accepting the proposition that supply and demand were ultimately in equilibrium, Beveridge argued that classical economics ignored the fact that forces which balance in the labour market were constantly disturbed by 'specific imperfections' between supply and demand. These imperfections gave rise to a 'real and considerable problem of unemployment'.[16] Beveridge considered that the demand for labour was always fragmented by specific determinations of place, quality and fluctuation. Supply was equally obstructed by ignorance and custom. What was needed was 'not mere absence of legal obstacles', as advocated by the political economists, 'but organised and informed fluidity of labour'.[17] This led Beveridge to propose systematic state intervention in the labour market.

For Beveridge casual labour was a problem not only of the lower reaches of the labour market but at every level. He found that irregular employment and under-employment afflicted even the most skilled craftsmen. Unemployment was not so much a moral, nor even a social problem:

The inquiry must be essentially an economic one. The evil to be analysed is, in technical language, that of maladjustment between supply of and demand for labour. Second, the inquiry must be one as to unemployment rather than as to the unemployed.

He argued that it was impossible to classify workers according to the causes of their unemployment:

A riverside labourer in Wapping in February 1908 might be suffering at one and the same time from chronic irregularity of employment, from seasonal depression of trade, from exceptional or cyclically caused depression of trade generally, from the permanent shifting of work lower down the river and from his own deficiencies of character or education.

Thus he concluded that the only possible course was 'to classify the causes of the types of unemployment themselves'.[18] He identified three main types: there was unemployment caused first, by various kinds of trade fluctuation (cyclical or seasonal); second, by changes in industrial structure; and third, by the surplus of casual labour throughout the labour market.

Beveridge also refined Booth's concept of the residuum. He rejected the notion of an undifferentiated rabble of 'unemployables', pointing out that the capacity of a worker to find a job depended more on the vagaries of the labour market than on any rigid classification. Beveridge believed there was a hard core of unreformable degenerates, but these he considered were limited to Booth's class A and did not include the residuum as a whole. He thus rejected Booth's proposition that class B should be dispersed to labour colonies. Indeed it was central to his conception of an efficient labour market that it should contain an adequate reserve pool of labour.

The theoretical breakthroughs achieved by Booth and Beveridge guided the formation of government policy on unemployment under the Liberal administration which came to power in 1906. Over the previous twenty years various governments had been obliged, despite their official commitment to the spirit of the Poor Law, to intervene in practice to relieve the extremes of poverty and distress caused by waves of unemployment. Beveridge's proposals emerged through a detailed critique of these *ad hoc* measures and of the various alternative schemes put forward by labour movement leaders and social reformers.

The first significant incursion by the state into Poor Law procedures was the 'Chamberlain circular' in 1886. In response to a sudden increase in unemployment in London which caused widespread distress and disorder, Local Government Board President Joseph Chamberlain authorized local authorities to co-operate with Poor Law guardians to institute schemes of public works. These were created to help able-bodied respectable workers through a brief spell of unemployment: the rest were still expected to go to the workhouse. In fact the schemes were swamped by casual, unskilled workers on the verge of utter destitution. The Chamberlain circular was the first official recognition, at national level, that the state had a responsibility to the unemployed; it was re-issued on several occasions over the next two decades.

In 1904 and 1905 the Local Government Board was forced to endorse further measures as a result of continuing fears about national efficiency and concern about further working-class unrest. Local Government President Walter Long devised a scheme in London through which 'joint committees' representing borough councils, guardians and charities could receive applications for relief and segregate the 'respectable, temporary out of work man' from the 'ordinary pauper'. After a particularly severe winter this 'temporary' scheme was made permanent. Under the terms of the 1905 Unemployed Workmen Act it was extended to other urban areas. Although the Poor Law authorities and the COS were given a central administrative role in the new scheme, in effect the Poor Law system was crumbling. In many areas socialists had been elected to local government office and refused to operate the harsh and restrictive regulations of the Poor Law. In other areas the guardians were simply overwhelmed by the impoverished unemployed.[19] In 1905 the Tory government appointed a Royal Commission to investigate the crisis of the Poor Law system. It soon confirmed that the 1905 act had been no more successful than earlier relief schemes in targeting the respectable working class: all the evidence showed that the schemes were vastly over-subscribed by the urban residuum.

Beveridge's policy proposals followed from a critique of the operation of the 1905 act. For him it had offered simply more of the same. What was required was not more relief works, but organization of the labour market. Behind Beveridge's desire to rationalize the labour market lay the belief that it would make industry more efficient and that society would function more harmoniously. He repudiated the principle of the right to work, which socialists had been advancing since the 1890s, as antithetical to the requirements of capital, considering that 'To give the individual a State guarantee against unemployment is therefore undoubtedly to condone inferiority and to weaken the incentive to industry.' Nor did he approve of direct state employment of the reserve army. What was required was organization of the labour market by the state to ensure national mobility of labour; the classification, matching and redirection of labour power according to the perceived changing needs of industry; the creation of an efficient and mobile reserve army of labour; and the maintenance of a prepared body of reserve labour power fit and ready to re-enter the labour market. The solution lay in a combined system of labour exchanges and unemployment insurance. Labour exchanges were introduced under the 1909 Labour Exchanges Act and unemployment insurance was brought in, together with sickness benefit, under the 1911 National Insurance Act. Beveridge drafted the 1909 act and played a key role, together with Llewellyn Smith, in drawing up the 1911 legislation.

The Labour Exchanges Act established a nationally financed system of labour exchanges, administered by the Labour Department of the Board of Trade. The aim of the exchanges was to allow the classification of the unemployed according to their suitability for particular sorts of work, acting as 'a human sorting house'.[20] Workers registered voluntarily and were assessed according to their training, working experience, work record and personal habits. Applicants were recommended for jobs on the grounds of qualification, competence and suitability. Labour exchanges were designed to promote greater labour mobility, not to cater for the needs of the unemployed. Applicants were required to prove 'willingness to work' and 'genuine employability'. Through unemployment insurance the state for the first time guaranteed to certain male workers, under specified conditions, a basic income while they were unemployed. Benefits were to be made up largely from contributions made by the employer and the worker during employment, but also subsidized by the state.[21]

The central target of the unemployment insurance legislation was the respectable unemployed worker, temporarily out of a job as a result of cyclical depression of trade. The harsh discipline of the Poor Law was preserved to deal with the 'residuum'. 'Military discipline is right for the "submerged" but democracy is the only hope for labour in general.'[22] The scheme was initially introduced to cover selected industries, notably those with a high proportion of skilled workers and with a tendency to periodic crises: shipbuilding, engineering and the building trades. Industries recognized to be in decline and those characterized by high levels of casual, seasonal and women's employment were excluded. The scheme was compulsory for all workers in the selected industries.

The unemployment insurance scheme included significant disciplinary measures. It aimed to encourage regular employment and to discourage recourse to benefits. Thus maximum benefits were kept low and contributions high. The idea was to encourage self-reliance and thrift, while not allowing labour power to degenerate. It was hoped that significant concessions to the workers involved would win popular approval for the new scheme. Benefits were provided at a flat rate and the hated means test of the Poor Law system was abandoned. Unemployment benefit did not carry the stigma of charity but, in theory, was conceived as a social right and workers in receipt of benefits were not deprived of civil or political rights. Indeed, so far as those who created the scheme were concerned, the good work habits which unemployment insurance were meant to cultivate contributed to the making of responsible and mature citizens. The political hopes inscribed in this project were made explicit by Churchill, for whom insurance was an antidote to socialism:

The idea is to increase the stability of our institutions by giving the mass of industrial workers a direct interest in maintaining them. With a 'stake in the country' in the form of insurance against evil days these workers will pay no attention to the vague promises of revolutionary socialism. . . . It will make him a better citizen, a more efficient worker, and a happier man.[23]

The implementation of unemployment policy

Booth and Beveridge were responsible for the formulation of unemployment as a concept and proposed measures to deal with the problem. However, the detailed formulation of government policy and the creation of an appropriate administrative machinery through which this policy could be implemented was the work of Hubert Llewellyn Smith. In 1893 Llewellyn Smith was appointed the first Labour Commissioner at the newly established Labour Department of the Board of Trade, and quickly became involved in compiling statistics on industrial relations and in arbitrating in strikes and disputes. By 1903 he was Comptroller-General at the Board of Trade and became its Permanent Secretary in 1907 – an office he held until after the First World War. He established the first reliable index of unemployment levels and published the results in the department's regular *Labour Gazette*, which was distributed freely – especially among trade unionists with whom he cultivated close relations. To assist the role of the Labour Department as mediator in industrial disputes, Llewellyn Smith recruited the services of numerous former trade union officials – another major innovation.

The Labour Department took an active interest in unemployment, hitherto the preserve of the Local Government Board and the COS. It rapidly tended to displace the old agencies from their position of authority in a field over which they had lost control and direction. When the labour exchange legislation was introduced in 1909 the Labour Department was expanded and in 1910 a Labour Exchange branch was set up within it under the directorship of Beveridge. When the 1911 act was passed a new Labour Exchange and Unemployment Insurance Department was created, still within the Board of Trade: Beveridge automatically became its chief. Thus the state apparatus was itself expanded and transformed at a phenomenal rate in the process of pushing through policies required to reorganize the labour market and integrate the labour movement.

The administration of the labour exchange and unemployment insurance provisions through the new central state department followed the principles established in the Labour Department's attempts to arbitrate and conciliate in industrial disputes. The Labour Department presented itself as impartial, its aim to create 'a perfectly colourless, soul-less piece of commercial mechanism. It is not intended to twist to one side or the other one inch in the commercial course of events, only to remove friction'.[24] Central control was exerted through the dominant 'industrial intelligence department' which established firm financial and administrative guidelines which were to be carried out by a clearly identified hierarchy.

Gaining consent

The success of labour exchanges and unemployment insurance depended on the state winning a degree of consent to the new schemes from the representatives of both capital and labour. Beveridge and Llewellyn Smith had to take account of the attitudes of different fractions of the capitalist class to their proposals, drawing support from 'informed' public opinion as relayed by groups like the Fabians and the new liberals. At the same time they had to negotiate the diverse outlooks of different sections of the labour movement, and in this they succeeded by integrating the trade union bureaucracy into the new schemes and by skilfully marginalizing opposition from the socialist flank of the movement.

From the late nineteenth century traditional capitalist hostility to government interference in the labour market began to fracture. Progressive employers were affected by the growing recognition of the 'problem of labour': unemployment and poverty, the deteriorating quality of labour power, declining competitiveness and class antagonism all took their toll. By the early years of the twentieth century some employers' organizations were beginning to call for increased state intervention in economic and labour affairs. The local chambers of commerce expressed the demands of the more progressive employers. In 1905 the Birmingham Chamber of Commerce called on the Board of Trade to establish a system of 'labour registries' and to give the chambers of commerce a role in running them.

Before any real practical attempt can be made to prepare a national scheme – and only a national scheme can be deemed satisfactory – for dealing with the unemployed on sound lines, it is essential that permanent machinery be constructed for obtaining reliable information as to the number of . . . bona fide unemployed . . . men who, through some cause over which they have no control, are temporarily out of work – men who will work when they have it to do. These men are assets of the nation, and it devolves on the nation to see that they are not allowed to become pauperised. With regard to the other class, the unemployable, the wastrel and the loafer, the sternest measures are necessary. . . . It is desirable that they should be sifted out and then it would not be difficult to adopt measures for dealing with them.

We believe that the only possible way of obtaining the information which is necessary is to inaugurate a permanent system of labour registries under the control of the Board of Trade, and the bodies which naturally suggest themselves for the kind of work are the Chambers of Commerce.[25]

The Board of Trade had little enthusiasm for giving the chambers of commerce control over labour exchanges for fear of alienating the labour movement. However it was receptive to the spirit of the Birmingham proposals which closely corresponded to the lines along which the Labour Department was moving. The officials at the Board of Trade, working alongside and advising their political chief Churchill, sought to promote such expressions of the employers' sympathies for the new measures. As modern observers have commented, they 'possessed the motivation and specialist knowledge to exploit the growing consensus among the managerial and political élites in favour of state intervention in the labour market'.[26]

The German experience – invoked by the Birmingham Chamber of Commerce – was influential among several sections of capital. From the 1890s a group of Liberal businessmen led by Sir John Brunner, a chemicals manufacturer strongly influenced by Bismark's approach, had been insisting that British competitiveness could only be improved if the state took more responsibility for the economic infrastructure and for technical education.[27] As labour movement pressure mounted more and more employers looked to welfare reforms as an alternative to socialism. The Board of Trade encouraged this admiration for the German experience, and commissioned an investigation into the German system in order to help convince British businessmen.[28]

Between 1909 and 1911 Churchill, Llewellyn Smith and Beveridge carried on regular negotiations with representatives of employers' associations, particularly those in engineering and shipbuilding. While the leaders of one employers' delegation were broadly sympathetic to state welfare reforms, they had a number of reservations about the Board of Trade proposals. They were concerned about the cost of the new schemes; they feared that labour exchanges might become centres of industrial discontent; and they wanted assurances that the incentive to work would not be weakened and that the malingerer would be dealt with harshly. Some were reluctant to allow direct trade union representation in the administration of the schemes and others – notably the shipbuilding magnates – were worried that cutting back on casual labour would undermine efficiency and discipline.[29]

The Board of Trade representatives reassured the employers, point by point. They argued that on cost the 'tax on industry' would be more than compensated by a more efficient workforce, that they could pass on the cost to workers and consumers, and that the new scheme was cheaper than charity. Llewellyn Smith and Beveridge insisted that the strict and impartial discipline imposed by the labour exchange would prevent trade unionists from putting pressure on unorganized workers during industrial disputes. At the same time they succeeded in convincing the employers that the Board of Trade could not allow labour exchanges to be used systematically to provide scab labour during strikes, which would so alienate trade union support as to destroy the whole scheme. While employers were persuaded to accept trade union participation they were also reassured that workers other than trade unionists would be represented in the administration of the schemes. The Board of Trade officials intimated that if the unions were not drawn into the state scheme then they would preserve their own insurance schemes – and would perhaps use their reserve funds to finance strikes. Employers of casual labour – shipbuilders especially – were urged to swap the chaotic discipline of large reserves of the impoverished semi-employed for the discipline of a properly organized pool of labour. And finally, the Board of Trade officials emphasized the elaborate measures in both labour exchanges and unemployment insurance calculated to maintain discipline and punish the malingerer.

While Llewellyn Smith and Beveridge did much of the backroom negotiating with the employers' associations, Churchill guided the reforms through Parliament. On the Tory backbenches there was a strong, diehard, pro-Poor Law element, although to counter it there also emerged a 'social reform group' of progressive Tories. Liberal free-traders welcomed the new unemployment provisions as an alternative to tariff reform as the solution for unemployment. New liberals approved the provisions with their emphasis on the collectivist and educative role of the state and on individual and mutual responsibility.

The real casualties of the new order of 1909–11 were the Poor Law authorities. By the turn of the century deepening social turmoil forced the Local Government Board to concede to official incursion into Poor Law procedures and to endorse measures designed to relieve the 'respectable unemployed'. These measures – in particular the Unemployed Workmen Act – threatened the positions of the Poor Law guardians and the COS, particularly as they implied an increasing degree of central state control. Together the Poor Law authorities and the COS fought any incursion into their control over the provision of relief and they resisted further central state intervention at every stage. Their campaign was based on the continual reassertion of the traditional principles of 1834. Indeed the Local Government Board blamed the poverty crisis on the *relaxation* of the Poor Law regulations under pressure from the labour movement, believing the removal of the discipline of the workhouse and the labour test had *encouraged* pauperism. The Local Government Board demanded stricter controls on relief – not more state provision.[30]

However, by the middle of the first decade of the century, the approach of the Local Government Board and the COS was widely regarded as out of date and inadequate. Many commentators have observed how the contrast between the scrupulous scientific objectivity of Llewellyn Smith and Beveridge and the prejudiced generalizations of the Poor Law apologists told against the latter in the councils of state.[31] Moreover, the whole notion of total moral responsibility to which the Local Government Board clung was increasingly recognized as obsolete and of little use in framing policies to deal with unemployment.

The Liberal unemployment reforms put the Board of Trade at the centre of state social policy and squeezed the Poor Law authorities from their predominant position in the regulation of poverty. The Local Government Board continued to supervise the treatment of the 'residuum', and the COS continued to co-ordinate charitable and voluntary social work effort. But the Board of Trade now became the state agency responsible for the 'deserving poor' – the respectable temporarily unemployed.

One other consequence of the demise of the Poor Law system was that radical and socialist local government representatives were also deprived of any influence in the new system. Clearly a figure such as Beveridge was not at all unhappy about this. Indeed, he disapproved of all popular representation: 'it is dangerous to allow recipients of public relief to elect its dispensers'.[32]

The administration of the new unemployment provisions meant a shift in the balance of power from local representatives, whether reactionary or progressive, in favour of a state bureaucracy staffed by 'experts'.

The labour movement

Perhaps the greatest achievement of the Board of Trade representatives was their success in accommodating the labour movement to their policies. They achieved this by identifying two distinct trends in the emerging labour movement and using one against the other. First were the trade union leaders and the expanding stratum of officials that their organizations sponsored. For thirty years the state had extended legal recognition and protection to trade unions, encouraging the emergence of a conservative layer at the bureaucratic head of the unions which could mediate between capital and labour and contain rank and file militancy. For ten years the Board of Trade had played a central role in assisting the consolidation of this bureaucracy as a prime agent of representation in the labour movement. Now it sought to use the labour bureaucracy to integrate the working class *as a whole* around the new unemployment measures.

Second were the swelling ranks of socialists, organized in the Independent Labour Party and the Social Democratic Federation. Their increasing influence on all sections of the working class was viewed with panic by the dominant classes. Local links between the ILP and the SDF proliferated, especially on the issues of unemployment and the demand for work. Strikes and demonstrations displayed a militant challenge both to the established order and to the authority of the trade union leaders over the working class. The recognition extended to the labour leaders by the state authorities helped to enhance their status in the working-class movement. The new machinery for dealing with unemployment gave the labour bureaucrats a greater stake in the system. The whole scheme also gave them something to show the rank and file as an example of what could be achieved through the methods of collaboration. The state intellectuals also won wider influence over the working class by their success in defining the terms of the public debate on unemployment. By establishing an ideological hegemony on the issue of unemployment, over not only the trade-union leaders but more significantly over many socialists, the liberal experts helped to undermine the potential rank and file challenge to the state and the bureaucracy.

The Liberal politicians appreciated the importance of establishing firm links with the union leaders. Churchill declared that he wanted 'to cooperate in the closest and frankest terms' over labour exchanges;[33] and on unemployment insurance he considered that 'no such novel departure . . . could possibly be taken without much further consultation and negotiation with the trade unions'.[34] Sidney Buxton, who succeeded Churchill at the Board of Trade, also acknowledged this when he reassured trade unions on their continued full involvement in unemployment provision as a means of catering to 'the susceptibilities of the trade unionists', and he appealed for their 'benevolent sympathy' for the unemployment schemes.[35] The direct involvement of trade unionists in the Board of Trade machine increased dramatically after 1906. Between 1906 and 1912, 117 were appointed and a further 124 received positions connected with unemployment insurance.[36] In response the TUC gave increasing attention to ministerial deputations, which soon became of greater significance for the TUC than its attempts to influence policy through Parliament.[37]

The Board of Trade's direct approach to the TUC helped aggravate the division between the trade unions and the Labour Party. This clearly suited the TUC and enhanced its status. Once the Board of Trade negotiations had established close links with the TUC, and once the TUC had set up a standing committee to advise the Labour Department on labour exchanges, Churchill and Lloyd George invited Labour leader Arthur Henderson and Fabian Sidney Webb to join their discussions. Similarly, on the issue of unemployment insurance, the Board of Trade drew Labour Party representatives into the later stages of its joint negotiations with the TUC. In this way the Board of Trade used its ties with the TUC to organize the rest of the movement around its unemployment proposals. One aspect of this propaganda campaign was a study trip to Germany for trade unionists sponsored by the Board of Trade to investigate the operation of Bismarck's labour exchange and national insurance systems. The delegation returned greatly impressed. 'The introduction of state insurance of workmen against sickness, invalidity and old age had in no way exercised an injurious effect upon the Trade Unions of the country.'[38] In March 1909 a special conference of trade union delegates was organized by the parliamentary committee of the TUC to discuss the merits of labour exchanges and passed a resolution in their favour. At the TUC conference in September a resolution was successfully proposed in favour of state unemployment insurance.[39]

There were, however, a number of anxieties within the trade union movement about the proposed schemes, many of which were voiced at these conferences. The trade union leaders were concerned about the possible use of labour exchanges to promote scabbing during industrial disputes and to undercut wage levels. Organizers of dockers and other workers who relied on casual labour were worried that measures of decasualization might produce an *increase* in unemployment among their members,[40] and many union leaders were reluctant to relinquish the limited controls they had already established over the labour market through their own unemployed lists and union-sponsored benefit schemes. Some union leaders expressed a narrowly sectional viewpoint in their desire to restrict the schemes to the 'superior' workmen already organized in trade unions, fearing that 'Otherwise . . . parasites on their more industrious fellows . . . will be the first to avail themselves of the funds the Bill provides.'[41]

Churchill presided over a series of discussions between the Board of Trade and the trade unions. The Board of Trade officials made assurances that trade union rights and wage levels would be adequately protected if labour exchanges publicized trade disputes and allowed unions to advertise standard rates within the exchanges, and these were accepted. At the insistence of the union leaders Churchill added a clause to the legislation guaranteeing that no worker would be penalized for refusing to work during a strike or at less than the going rate.[42] The key controversy, however, surrounded questions of trade union control and monopoly.

Beveridge and Llewellyn Smith had always appreciated that 'trade union jealousy' would need to be disarmed and compensations offered for the invasion of the 'unions' previous monopoly'.[43] This was one of the reasons why they insisted on contributions from both the state and employers. They also anticipated that the trade unions would argue that unemployment insurance would mean that regular and efficient workmen were supporting the irregular and inefficient. This injustice, Beveridge believed, was cancelled out by the contributions of employers and the state. In the negotiations with the parliamentary committee of the TUC and the shipbuilding and engineering unions in 1909 Churchill added that insurance would give unions additional protection by gradually expelling inferior and cut-price labour from the labour market. At the same time the government allowed unions to continue their own insurance schemes, and even offered cash subsidies to support them.[44]

Most importantly the Board of Trade negotiations offered to involve labour representatives in the operation of the state schemes at every level. Advisory committees were promised containing equal numbers of employers and labour representatives, locally and nationally. Even though the advisory committees were to have no executive function, they were considered to be a concession to the trade unions, for representation conferred considerable public status on the trade union leaders: they became one side of a triangular body representing the nation.

Other objections to the Board of Trade proposals came from the leaders of the general, unskilled unions. Some complained at the narrow focus of the initial unemployment insurance scheme and demanded that it be broadened to cover their members.[45] Others – especially the gasworkers – objected to the unfairness of the flat-rate contribution and benefits for the low paid.[46] Although insurance was gradually extended to cover most trade unionists, the flat-rate contribution was maintained. Beveridge denied that low paid workers could not afford to pay, insisting – with patrician aloofness – that they spent as much on luxuries 'with which they could well dispense'.[47] The claim for non-contributory benefits became a cause for some of the general unions and their socialist supporters – a cause that became welded to the campaign for the implementation of Beatrice Webb's Minority Report on the Poor Laws.

Churchill, Beveridge and Llewellyn Smith cultivated the moderate union leaders and used them as a lever against the more radical sections of the labour movement. As the leadership of the organized working class agreed to co-operate with state regulation of the labour market, the Labour Party – heavily reliant on the unions – fell in behind. During 1908–9 the TUC was central in neutralizing militant agitation on unemployment organized in the campaign for the 'right to work'. Between 1905 and 1909 left-wing Labour MPs, the ILP and the Social Democratic Party (the SDF adopted this new title in 1907) had co-operated in committees which co-ordinated combative campaigns to secure the right to work or maintenance for the unemployed. When the SDP joined the ILP on the Joint London Right to Work Committee in 1908 the unions withdrew their support and the campaign lost momentum. Through Ramsay MacDonald the trade union leaders pulled the more left-wing Labour parliamentarians – notably Keir Hardie – away from radical action. In 1909 the National Right to Work Council was dissolved as a direct result of the TUC and the Labour Party endorsing the Board of Trade policies. To clinch the acquiescence of the Parliamentary Labour Party, the Liberals offered to introduce payment for MPs – a long-cherished goal of impecunious labour representatives – in return for Labour support for the Insurance Bill. It was a deal.

The Board of Trade's manoeuvrings undermined the demands of radical sections of the labour movement, particularly the Right to Work Campaign. However, there already existed ambiguities and contradictions within these more radical strategies which themselves contributed to the disintegration of the Right to Work Campaign and which had implications for subsequent struggles over unemployment and poverty. These contradictions were already apparent in the terms of the Right to Work Bill which the Labour Party introduced, with some Liberal support, in the House of Commons in July 1907. Despite its radical right to work clause, and despite the fact that the left had run a united and often very militant campaign outside Parliament to support it, the bill was none the less constrained in its very premises. It was framed by an acceptance of the definition of unemployment which converged with the theorizations of the state 'experts'. Thus the bill called for the management of unemployment by state experts on the Board of Trade model, and endorsed punitive methods for dealing with the 'residuum'.

Another shared assumption between the terms of the bill and dominant, statist preconceptions concerned the position of women. The unemployment experts, in their desire to organize the labour market, hoped that state intervention would ensure the withdrawal of married women with children from the labour force, while single women would be confined to 'women's work'. Thus although in practice few women were covered by unemployment insurance, even in principle they received a lower rate of benefit than men and they relinquished their contributions on marriage, with no surrender value. In labour exchanges women were classified according to special categories of 'women's' work. The Right to Work Bill reproduced these prejudices, its terms enforcing the subordinate and dependent position of women on men: it was largely designed to ensure a *man's* right to work.

Furthermore, the campaign failed adequately to distinguish its own proposals from the provision of public work. The Right to Work Bill was the most ambitious statement of Labour's policy on unemployment, expressing the ultimate aims of the working-class movement. The right to work clause potentially threatened the 'free contract' between capital and labour and undermined the discipline that unemployment imposed upon the entire working class. However this coexisted in the labour movement with proposals for nationally planned public works for the unemployed which in turn frequently overlapped with advocacy of labour colonies. Following Booth, radical liberals, Fabians and charitable bodies encouraged the foundation of colonies in which casual 'loafing' workers could be isolated in the country where they would no longer contaminate the respectable working class.[48] They also proposed less punitive colonies in which less degenerate workers could be reformed in self-sustaining communities. Trade union leaders gave some support to proposals for self-sustaining farm colonies as a means of encouraging rural labour to stay in the countryside and for urban labour to migrate, thus reducing competition from the unemployed.[49] Some socialists, notably Keir Hardie and Will Crooks, argued that the state should establish farm colonies to retrain urban workers in rural skills.[50] On the other hand, the more radical George Lansbury advocated rural labour colonies as Utopian socialist experiments in co-operative agricultural work and life.

The labour colonies experiment was significant for two reasons. First, it indicated the emphasis in the policies of reforming groups towards state regulation of the labour market, not only to isolate and discipline the residuum, but also to attempt to retrain and reintegrate respectable workers, thus reproducing in policy measures Booth's deeply conservative distinction between the residuum and the respectable. Second, it showed a considerable convergence between these strategies and some socialist approaches to unemployment. Bourgeois philanthropists and social reformers advocated colonies virtually as a penal measure, while labour movement representatives presented them as potential islands of socialism. But in content they looked much the same. Lansbury accepted current thinking on the problems of casual labour and the need to regularize the labour market at the expense of the residuum.[51] Farm colonies were to provide for the self-improvement and moral elevation of the unemployed; penal labour colonies were to discipline the loafers who were alleged to contaminate the ranks of the genuinely unemployed.

The debate about colonies indicated that by the end of the first decade of the century discussion on unemployment was about the nature and scope of state intervention and the place of the labour movement in such developments: it was no longer about whether or not state intervention was justified.

Conclusion

In the thirty years before the First World War state activity on unemployment had shifted dramatically. Nineteenth-century attitudes embodied in local Poor Law procedures had given way to new central state powers to intervene in the labour market and mitigate the effects of unemployment. Labour exchanges and unemployment insurance drastically extended the bureaucracy and power of the state. Henceforth the state assumed a responsibility for organizing the labour market and for managing the struggle between classes.

How far were the measures introduced by the 1906 Liberal Government successful in dealing with 'the problem of labour'? In terms of their effect on unemployment, or even on the wider issue of working-class unrest, the answer must be very little. Up to the First World War the gross imbalances of the labour market remained a major source of social tension. Attempts by the state to decasualize labour met bitter resistance from workers in Birkenhead, Glasgow and South Wales in 1911 and 1912.[52] The war economy proved a much more effective means of absorbing the massive reserve army of labour. But scarcely had the war ended and a brief post-war boom run out of steam than unemployment returned with a vengeance, at three times the level of the pre-war years.[53] Over the next twenty years the system designed by Beveridge and the rest proved bitterly inadequate. It could neither provide an efficient means of allocating labour, nor advance social justice, nor even, in its own terms, prevent the chronically unemployed from becoming demoralized and disaffected. The hunger marches of the 1920s and 1930s testified that the problem of labour remained as unresolved as ever. Indeed it required another world war and a historically unprecedented period of capitalist expansion to create temporarily the full employment economy of which Beveridge dreamed forty years earlier. In the inter-war years, in an attempt to manage unemployment and contain class tensions, unemployment benefit regulations were amended time and again, undermining the actuarial principles of insurance so carefully constructed by Beveridge and Llewellyn Smith.

However, in the inter-war years the state was drawn more closely into managing unemployment. During the period of 'relaxation' of insurance principles the power of centralized state officialdom was increased through the introduction of the 'genuinely seeking work' clause. In the absence of strict actuarial principles, receipt of unemployment benefit became ever more dependent on the discretion of the state bureaucrat,[54] such that a crucial object of class struggle became the regulations and procedures for administering unemployment benefit. But although the insurance principle was in practice breached, the departures were always legitimated as 'exceptional': the insurance *principle*, as invented by the pre-war unemployment experts, remained the desired state of affairs. The 1934 Unemployment Act restored this to the very heart of unemployment maintenance provision, where it still remains.

Notes and references

1 See especially the work of José Harris and Roger Davidson, whose major contributions are cited below. Their interpretations dominate the field, and there are sections in this chapter in which I draw extensively from their work.

2 See E. J. Hobsbawm, *Labouring Men* (Weidenfeld and Nicolson 1964); E. P. Thompson, 'Time, work-discipline and industrial capitalism', *Past and Present*, no. 38 (1967); and J. Cronin, 'Strikes', in C. Wrigley (ed.), *A History of British Industrial Relations 1875-1914* (Harvester 1982).

3 Unemployment statistics for the period should be treated with some caution. They were largely based on trade union returns and thus did not cover all workers. See W. R. Garside, *The Measurement of Unemployment* (Blackwell 1980), ch. 1. Nevertheless the available data suggests more frequent and intensive periods of unemployment from the late 1870s; see W. H. Beveridge, *Unemployment: A Problem of Industry* (Longman Green 1909), pp. 39–45.

4 Beveridge, pp. 39–40; J. Harris, *Unemployment and Politics: a study of English social policy, 1886-1914* (Clarendon Press 1972), p. 273.

5 Harris, p. 52.

6 B. Gilbert, 'The decay of nineteenth-century provident institutions and the coming of old age pensions', *Economic History Review* II, 17 (1964), pp. 551–63.

7 C. Booth, *Life and Labour of the People of London*, vol. 1 (Macmillan 1904), p. 308.

8 G. Stedman Jones, *Outcast London, A Study in the Relationship between Classes in Victorian Society* (Penguin 1971).

9 Harris, p. 53.

10 W. Beveridge and H. R. Maynard, 'The unemployed: lessons of the Mansion House fund', *The Contemporary Review*, no. 86 (1904), pp. 629–38.

11 W. Beveridge, 'The problem of the unemployed', *Sociological Papers*, no. 111 (1906), pp. 323–41.

12 T. W. Hutchinson, *A Review of Economic Doctrines 1870-1929* (Oxford University Press 1953), p. 409.

13 Booth, vol. 1, pp. 24–7, 37–8, 44–50 and 176; vol. 2, pp. 20–1.

14 See Stedman Jones.

15 Booth, vol. 1, p. 162.

16 Beveridge, *Unemployment*, p. 14.

17 ibid., p. 216.

18 ibid., p. 3.

19 Harris, p. 84.

20 P. Thane, *The Foundations of the Welfare State* (Longman 1982), p. 90, quoting the *Minority Report of the Royal Commission on the Poor Laws*.

21 Under the scheme workers and employers paid two and a half pence per week and the state paid one and two-thirds pence. Benefits were paid weekly at a rate of seven shillings up to maximum of fifteen weeks. Initially 2.5 million male workers were covered by the scheme; see Gilbert, *The Evolution of National Insurance in Britain* (Michael Joseph 1973), p. 286.

22 R. Davidson, *Sir Hubert Llewellyn Smith and Labour Policy 1886-1916* (unpublished PhD thesis, University of Cambridge 1971), p. 227, quoting Llewellyn Smith papers.

23   Quoted by Harris, p. 365.

24   Harris, p. 294.

25   R. Hay, 'Employers and social policy in Britain: the evolution of welfare legislation, 1905–14', *Social History*, no. 4 (1977), p. 444.

26   R. Davidson and R. Lowe, 'Bureaucracy and innovation in British welfare policy 1870–1945', in W. J. Mommsen (ed.), *The Emergence of the Welfare State in Britain and Germany* (Croom Helm 1981).

27   Harris, p. 217.

28   R. Davidson, 'Llewellyn Smith, the Labour Department and government growth, 1886–1909', in G. Sutherland (ed.), *Studies in the Growth of Nineteenth Century Government* (Routledge and Kegan Paul 1972), pp. 256–7; Hay, 'The British business community, social insurance and the German example', in Mommsen (ed.), *The Emergence of the Welfare State*.

29   Harris, pp. 330–1.

30   M. Bruce, *The Coming of the Welfare State* (Batsford 1974), pp. 101, 107, 127, 201 and 205. The COS became less rigid in its commitment to traditional principles and reluctantly conceded that respectable workers could be assisted through relief works, as well as through casework, but under charitable and local control. It still opposed central state intervention. See Harris, pp. 108–9.

31   Davidson, 'Llewellyn Smith and the Labour Department', pp. 254–6.

32   W. Beveridge, 'The question of disenfranchisement', *Toynbee Record* (March 1905).

33   Quoted in H. A. Clegg, A. Fox and A. F. Thompson, *A History of British Trade Unions since 1889*, vol. 1, 1889–1910 (Clarendon Press 1964), p. 402.

34   W. S. Churchill, *Liberalism and the Social Problem* (Hodder and Stoughton 1909), p. 271–2.

35   Quoted in R. Martin, *TUC: The Growth of a Pressure Group 1868–1976* (Clarendon Press 1980), p. 100.

36   ibid., p. 105.

37   ibid., p. 109.

38   Quoted in Gilbert, *Evolution of National Insurance*, p. 256.

39   Harris, pp. 289–90; and Gilbert, *Evolution of National Insurance*, p. 256.

40   K. D. Brown, *Labour and Unemployment 1900–1914* (David and Charles 1971), pp. 126–7.

41   Quoted in Harris, pp. 317–18.

42   ibid., p. 291.

43   ibid., p. 307.

44   ibid., p. 315.

45   Brown, p. 145.

46   ibid., p. 148; and Harris, p. 317.

47   Quoted in Harris, p. 308.

48   Stedman Jones, pp. 332–3.

49   Brown, pp. 16–17.

50   F. Reid, *Keir Hardie: The Making of a Socialist* (Croom Helm 1978), p. 166.

51   P. A. Ryan, 'Poplarism 1894–1930', in P. Thane (ed.), *The Origins of British Social Policy* (Croom Helm 1978), pp. 59–64.

52   N. Whiteside, 'Welfare insurance and casual labour: a study of administrative

intervention in industrial employment 1906–26', *Economic History Review* **II**, vol. 32 (1979), pp. 518–19.

53 W. H. Beveridge, *Full Employment in a Free Society* (Allen and Unwin 1944), p. 72.

54 Thane, p. 174; J. Brown, 'Social control and the modernisation of social policy, 1890–1929, in Thane (ed.), *Origins of British Social Policy*, pp. 140–6.

6 'A safe and sane labourism': socialism and the state 1910–24*

Bill Schwarz and
Martin Durham

One of the major themes of this book is the contribution which the popular movements made to the formation of state institutions and to the political crises of the period. Our case studies look closely at the labour movement and at feminist demands and strategies in relation to particular areas of state intervention. But these *particular* histories were part of a much larger over-arching set of changes: the emergence of the Labour Party, and alongside it, movements of the political left – especially the Communist Party – which comprised a minority opposition. This chapter addresses this major change and some of the implications which the rise of Labour had for other political agencies, especially for marxist and left-socialist groupings. In retrospect, the crucial development of these years was the emergence of Labour as a fundamentally constitutionalist force, committed to an almost exclusive stress on Parliament as a means to political change, and suspicious of alternative strategies, especially all those summed up at the time as 'direct action'. This chapter looks at the process by which Labour's parliamentarism was made.

When the Labour Representation Committee was formed in 1900 the strategy of extending the struggles of the labour movement into Parliament appeared to a whole spectrum of opinion within the labour movement as a viable, realistic and necessary political choice. The success of popular Liberalism had long depended on such a commitment from working people. Before 1900 any independent working-class politics had been extra-parliamentary. But in the long term, the reconstruction of the political field which resulted from the reform bills of 1867 and 1884 presented new opportunities for the independent representation of labour. On this most socialists and non-socialists within the labour movement were agreed. Membership of the LRC included representatives from the parliamentary committee of the Trade Union Congress, the Fabians, the socialist Independent Labour Party and the marxist Social Democratic Federation. Not all these groups, by any means, shared a single conception of how this new political space could be worked, nor was there even consensus on what goals

---

* This is a shortened version of a CCCS Occasional Paper published in February 1984.

should be followed, the basic conflict being between the majority of the trade unionists whose tone was fundamentally ameliorative, aspiring to serve 'the direct interests of labour', and the explicitly anti-capitalist demands of the socialists. It was this opposition – forming the classic parameters of 'labourism' – which accounted for the amalgam of currents within the LRC. What was at issue for the majority of socialists and marxists at the turn of the century was not the extension of the struggle into Parliament, as a strategic perspective, but the *forms and conditions* of that extension.

The major defining feature of the period 1910 to 1924 was the mass transformation in the political allegiance of the working class from Liberal to Labour, a transformation without parallel in modern British history. Politics in these years, including socialist politics, were in deep flux. The term socialism itself carried many and varied meanings. It was only by the end of this period that definitions of socialism – 'reformist' or 'revolutionary' – which seem today so much part of the permanent inventory of left politics, hardened into organizing principles. The force of this antagonism crucially depended on the apparent possibilities for a parliamentary route to socialism. The pressures for a fracture between reformists and revolutionaries began to develop from the early 1900s. After only one year the SDF pulled out of the Labour Representation Committee. From 1910 the gap between a gradualist, constitutional strategy and a militant industrial politics rapidly widened. The process of socialist definition finally culminated in the formation of the Communist Party on the Bolshevik model, and the emergence of the Labour Party as a constitutional party of government. These two parties were divided by their antagonistic conceptions of strategies adequate for a constitutional and formally democratic nation. However, our understanding of the *making* of this division is complicated by the fact that the line demarcating constitutional from non-constitutional was not fixed, nor was it generally agreed where it should be drawn. Indeed, it became a primary *object* of struggle from 1910 until the General Strike.

Similarly within the lived conditions of working-class experience no hard and fast distinction could be established between tactical, ameliorative gains and a long-term strategy aiming for collective ownership. The range of demands included within a trade union perspective could be very wide indeed. The National Union of Gas Workers and General Labourers – albeit an unusually militant union – illustrates this. The Union's rules drawn up in 1894 included demands for the eight-hour day, equal pay for women, the abolition of piecework and of unpaid overtime, the enforcement of the Truck Act and 'legislation for the betterment of the lives of the working class'. These objectives were to be secured by 'the return of members of the union to vestries, school boards, boards of guardians, municipal bodies, and to Parliament, provided such candidates are pledged to the collective ownership of the means of production, distribution and exchange'.[1] By the turn of the century, commitment to the independent representation of the working class by a Labour Party tended to blur and disrupt distinctions between immediate and long-term demands to an even greater extent than hitherto. So too did the extension of the state. It was around all these ambiguities that various currents met in the formation of a 'Labour socialism'. This refers to the combination of socialist and social-democratic elements which cohered in the post-war Labour Party.[2]

The extension of the state

In the dominant discourse of the day the increase in municipal and state ownership and control of utilities, the unprecedented regulatory functions of the state and the financing of national welfare schemes by progressive taxation came to be called 'socialism', as a synonym for collectivism.[3] It became clear after the Liberal administration of 1906 that significant social reforms *could* be secured through the state. A conception of state-guaranteed social rights, such as the right to a 'national minimum' wage, was shared by a number of Liberals and (at least as an immediate demand) by the majority of socialists. This was a broad commitment to a *social* democracy, and it is significant that until the war all socialists and marxists considered themselves social democrats. For some, the Liberal reforms actually provided a model for future socialist practice. For others they were understood as consolidating the drift towards the repressive statism of the 'Servile State'.[4]

Socialists were continually confronted with new choices about the extent to which they could or should intervene politically, or organize inside the state. Apart from the possibilities of independent representation in Parliament, there were a number of local bodies – borough councils, boards of guardians, education boards – which could be taken under socialist control. Growing state intervention in industrial disputes following the establishment of the Labour Department of the Board of Trade in 1893 and the Conciliation Act of 1896, led to direct negotiations between trade unionists and state officials. Trade unions were integrated into the apparatuses of the state to assist with the organization of trade boards, national insurance and labour exchanges. Key members of the labour movement were given the opportunity to occupy posts within the state due to their 'expertise' on industrial matters or as representatives of the larger movement, as the 'voice' of labour.

It is not surprising, therefore, that the predominant currents within the socialist movement became more and more preoccupied with the state. To summarize a complex pattern of events we can suggest that three particular issues appeared in a new light. First was the question of participation in the *representative* apparatuses of the state. The hold of abstentionism – a position of principled opposition to parliamentary activity – was traditionally very weak in Britain. As a result political dispute centred not on whether but on how to participate. For the most part, from the 1910s, this effectively meant deciding what to do about the Labour Party. There were moments when it seemed possible to create a specifically proletarian means of representation as an alternative to the parliamentarianism of Labour. This option appeared viable particularly when Labour's electoral machine was itself locked into immobilization during the coalition years of the First World War. For many, this was the ultimate promise of the shop stewards' movement and the embryonic workers' councils. But when these movements – generated by an industrial politics often of a distinctly insurrectionary temper – began to falter, or when they were unable to overcome the constraints of sectionalism, the Labour Party continued to develop into a significant national organization. Even in the adverse conditions of the Coupon Election of 1918 nearly 2.5 million people voted Labour. From then until 1931 the Labour Party's share of the percentage of the total vote continued to grow steadily.

Second was the question of the state as an agent for reform and collectivism – the *interventionist* properties of the state. From the 1880s it was recognized in a whole range of debate that in all aspects of economic and social life market forces could be regulated by state action. From the 1890s proposals for progressive taxation envisaged the possibilities for the redistribution of the social wealth, organized through state fiscal policy. By the beginning of the twentieth century there existed a significant body of opinion, self-consciously socialist, which extended these objectives to include the state as the primary means by which the socialization of 'production, distribution and exchange' could be achieved. The extent to which *in practice* these objectives could overlap is striking. Before the 1920s the distinctions between those who subsequently emerged as social democrats and socialists, or between new liberals and Labour, were often very fine. The case for 'collectivism' and even for 'socialism' could cut right across party boundaries, springing up in some unlikely places. Apart from the outright statist aspirations of the Unionists, most other conceptions of collectivism (with the important exception of the Fabians) believed democratic control to be integral to collective control. Whether adequate democratic controls could be secured inside the existing apparatuses of the state was another matter.

The third question directly hinged on the problem of democratic control. What should be the ultimate objectives of the socialist movement in relation to the state? This sharply raised the problem of the democratic potential of the (existing) state and the question of its limits as an agent for collective control.

The late nineteenth century

Stephen Yeo has recently argued that this drift towards an identification with the state entailed a severe loss for the socialist movement. It broke up older, more co-operative and spontaneous forms of working-class self-activity, marginalizing and driving undergound a vigorous radical culture. He considers that the breadth and generosity of the socialist vision shrivelled into something altogether more utilitarian.[5] Yeo's argument is at its strongest when it highlights the connection between socialism and sexual politics. The socialism of the 1880s and 1890s was perhaps less dogmatic than its immediate successors (although, as the political fortunes of William Morris remind us, this can be exaggerated). A significant number of traditionally-formed intellectuals found in the socialist movement a natural ally in their revolt against high Victorianism. The socialism of the late nineteenth century may indeed have developed a more coherent conception of cultural transformation than in the later period. In general there was probably a greater openness to feminism, while in particular, certain extremely influential individuals within the socialist movement actively thought of their socialism in terms of sexual politics.[6] There was little comparable to this in the 1910s and 1920s, when a commitment to sexual politics, as a primary concern, was confined to the libertarian margins of the movement. In this sense it is right to suggest that this earlier model of socialist activity lost its immediate hold, and the political costs involved may have been very significant indeed.

In other respects, there may be room for more scepticism. After the employers' counter-attack of the 1890s, there was not, as Yeo claims, a sharp break in which the Labour Party, its head crammed with state socialism, simply stepped into the vacuum and completed the defeat of a popular spirit of socialist co-operation. Such a claim ignores both the *process* by which alternatives were rendered subordinate and the deep ambiguities which ran right through both labourism and the ideals of Labour Party collectivism. (Indeed it is paradoxical that some of the worst aspects of a bureaucratic Labour mentality could happily nestle in the older discourse of the 'religion of socialism'.) Nor, on the other hand, is it possible to trace any abrupt discontinuities in the language of socialism, although one significant shift was the greater energy invested by socialists in rationalist and secular societies. Individual militants still overwhelmingly identified with the socialist and cultural critics of the nineteenth century, devouring their writings and treasuring the breadth of their vision. The memoirs of working-class socialists in this period repeatedly indicate the cultural dislocation following the moment of 'conversion'. Socialist consciousness dawned 'with the force of an irresistible revelation'[7] and led to a *total* commitment.

There were gains as well as losses. The energies of the feminists were concentrated in the suffrage movement and in winning entry into the public sphere. Although the relations between the socialist and suffrage movements were far from harmonious, the eventual inclusion of women in the political nation was of fundamental importance for socialism. Through the work of women's organizations – such as the Women's Co-operative Guild and the Fabian Women's Group – feminist concerns began to touch the labour movement. From the 1900s the direction of feminism shifted in a way not dissimilar to socialism, and in the process new issues were opened as points of possible political intervention. The living conditions of working-class women in the family, especially the appalling burden of maternity, is the most notable example. The conflicts between a eugenist-influenced campaign for state endowment for motherhood – tying women into the home and encouraging procreation for national efficiency – and the experiences and aspirations of women themselves reflect a more general process. Pressures for reform and welfare, from below, were vulnerable to bureaucratization as they came nearer to realization.[8] The superimposition of collectivism and socialism could clearly invite such outcomes. There can be no doubt that within the mainstream of the labour movement the very conception of social reforms intersected *at every point* with dominant definitions of the 'social problem'.

The Labour Party's attempts to formulate a programme of reforms which would abolish the 'social problem' was highly contradictory. It challenged the power of capital, forcing the state to construct new solutions. Yet it also reproduced elements of a corporate and subordinate political culture. The contradictions and conflicts contained in the social and political programme of the Labour Party could be resolved one way or another only through a process of struggle, a struggle which had to be pitched both inside and outside the Party.

Syndicalism and proto-syndicalism

In *The Miners' Next Step*, a document produced by the unofficial committee of the South Wales Miners' Federation at the beginning of 1912, the statement on policy opened by declaring: '1: The old policy of identity of interest between employers and ourselves be abolished, and a policy of open hostility be installed.'[9] This is scarcely typical of British trade unionism, but it conveys with clarity the temper of industrial politics in the years before the First World War. The industrial battles of 1910–12 were of critical importance – not only in South Wales – in the disintegration of a popular Liberalism.

The dimensions of these struggles before the war are staggering. Trade union membership shot up from 2 million in 1910 to more than double that number by the outbreak of war. Forty million working days were lost as a result of strikes in 1912 alone. The labour threat took hold of the minds of the governing classes, who were repeatedly confronted with a rash of strikes commonly articulated in a language so insurrectionary it made genteel blood curdle in fear.[10] It was the apparent irrationality of these conflicts which so perplexed employers and politicians.

Most of the strikes in this period were unofficial, fuelled by rank and file discontent. On the occasions when the strikes were official, as in South Wales in 1910, the union leaderships came under vehement attack. The

growth and amalgamation of unions encouraged a system of national negotiations between employers and trade union leaders which often silenced the
voice of the union branches. From the beginning of the century a permanent
suspicion of Parliament and the judiciary had developed in response to a
string of anti-labour legislation. The effects of the Taff Vale judgement had
been overturned by the Trade Disputes Act of 1906, which also gave unions
unprecedented legal immunities. But the detail of legislation could seem
irrelevant to those workers fighting employers hell-bent on getting a wage cut
or imposing a lock-out. And for militants, the trade union leaders could be as
much a liability as the high court judges. Thus Richard Bell, the leader of
the Railway Servants, welcomed Taff Vale – a judgement against his own
union – as 'a useful influence in solidifying the forces of trade unionism and
in subjecting them to wholesome discipline'.[11] After the defeat of the
Cambrian strike, militants found it necessary to create an alternative structure at branch level, in order to break the official South Wales Miners'
Federation policy of conciliation. One motivation in the strike movement
was an attempt to win back popular control of the trade unions.

In almost every case the formal objectives of the pre-war strikes were
compatible with orthodox trade unionism – recognition, wages, conditions.
However, this does not explain the combative spirit of rank and file workers,
and the widespread desire to 'abolish' class conciliation. It was largely
between the Dock Strike of 1889 and the conflicts of 1910–14 that modern
trade unionism was formed. The unionization of non-skilled and women's
labour was the most visible shift. But also the right to tolerable conditions at
work, to some free time, and to a living wage became generalized in this
period as social rights, appropriate for all working people.

From the 1890s progressive employers began to urge a more rational
consumption of labour power and to invest more in its cultivation. Board of
Trade officials more readily intervened to discipline backward capitalists
and, with the Home Office, to attempt to broaden and make effective the
system of the factory inspectorate. Liberal politicians were quick to see the
dangers of enfranchised workers experiencing a system of apartheid in
economic life. Ethical, economic and political considerations converged in
the minds of the dominant classes in response to the socialist revival of the
1880s. The Liberal concern for a national minimum cannot be separated
from working-class pressure and from some of the most bitter industrial
struggles of the period. But this commitment to a living wage and to social
rights injected into the strike movement of 1910–14 the politics of the 'ultimatum' which so baffled liberal commentators. The national miners' strike
of 1912, aiming to secure a national minimum wage guaranteed by the state,
was the most forceful example of this transformation. This confrontationist
approach defined the new trade unionism of this period, and contributed a
further strand to the making of social democracy and socialism.

The trade union branch was temporarily transformed into a strong

nucleus for workers' representation. The critical determinant of this transformation was the feebleness of alternative forms of representation. A
combination of a severe drop in living standards and the decline of Liberalism forced workers to adopt 'direct action' methods to achieve their objectives. Strikes were underpinned by a commitment to basic economic rights,
advocacy of direct industrial representation, a determination to shift the
balance of forces in industry and by perceptions of shared class experience –
of class *solidarity*. All these factors did not necessarily add up to support for
the revolutionary overthrow of capitalism. However, these strikes were
expressions of a proto-syndicalism, to borrow Holton's term, a fierce,
embattled resistance to the injustices endured by labour.[12]

In his lucid account of syndicalism Holton warns against an exaggerated
assessment of the socialist potential of these years. He suggests that there did
not even occur 'a universal shift towards industrial disaffection and aggres-
sion'. Rather, the significance of the period lay in 'a polarisation between
militancy and Labourism, that is, a commitment to gradualist reform within
the liberal capitalist framework'.[13] To indicate a polarization between
constitutional Labour politics and industrial struggles informed by an alternative conception of socialism is a useful approach.

The syndicalist perspective on politics contained conflicting currents. In
its most negative form it was straightforwardly economistic. But on the other
hand, as a critique of dominant political forms, it expressed ideas which were
immensely valuable for socialism. First, it exposed the inadequacy of existing
forms of parliamentary democracy, emphasizing the processes of indivi-
dualization at work in the abstract act of marking the ballot paper. Second, it
raised the possibility of organizing an alternative state founded on a principle of workplace control. Third, it stressed the self-activity of the working
class, with the implication that the working class must become the *ruling*
class and assume the role of a conscious force in the historical process. These
ideas were often embryonic, only to be developed under new conditions at a
later date. But the similarities with some of Lenin's subsequent formulations
on the nature of the proletarian state, and with Gramsci's earliest writings,
should not be overlooked.[14]

In syndicalist ideology parliamentary democracy and capitalism were
viewed as a necessary unity. Ben Tillett's address to the Annual Conference
of the Dockers' Union in the summer of 1912 expressed the anti-
parliamentary fervour:

The class war is the most brutal of wars and the most pitiless. The lesson is that, in
future strikes, the strikers must protect against the use of arms, with arms; protect
against violence, with violence. . . . The other lesson is that Parliament is a farce and
a sham, the rich man's Duma, the Employers' Tammany, the Thieves' Kitchen and
the working man's despot. . . . Capitalism is capitalism as a tiger is a tiger; and both
are savage and pitiless towards the weak.[15]

Even though the speech was delivered in a moment of defeat Tillett's tone and critique were consistent with much that he had been saying in previous years.[16] Coercion, repression and militarism were all that could be expected from the state.

This could be extended to a critique of 'state capitalism'. The Liberal welfare legislation provided plenty of ammunition in this respect. The syndicalist-influenced Birmingham branch of the newly formed British Socialist Party drafted a denunciation of the National Insurance Bill:

The present Government – backed up by their friends and cousins the Opposition and ardently supported by the official 'Labour' Party . . . is now engaged in engineering measures like the national insurance bill aimed at the official regulation of wage slavery, the stereotyping by law of the social subjection of all non-propertied persons, measures that are doubtless in the near future to be fortified by such installations of State Capitalism as may suit the book of the exploiting interests.[17]

And as the reference to the Labour Party suggests, an attack on the collectivism of 'state capitalism' could easily swing round to an attack on the collectivism of 'state socialism'.

The Labour Party

Miliband's analysis of the failures of the pre-war Labour Party in Parliament is well known.[18] Labour MPs were few; many were not socialists; and the tactical alliances with the Liberals provided almost no chance for Labour to push through even the most mild measures of its own policy. For many of the most militant sections of the labour movement deep disillusionment set in, not only with the Labour Party, but with its whole political approach.

In 1906 the Labour Representation Committee became a political party in its own right, the Labour Party. But with the disintegration of the Unionist forces in Parliament, the rifts between Liberal and Labour, and within Labour itself, grew more pronounced. In 1907 Arthur Henderson replaced Keir Hardie as chairman of the party, and from the very start he was at loggerheads with the ILP. The ILP Members of Parliament were frustrated by the Labour Party's continuing failure to achieve significant reforms. For the next two years they were in a state of almost continuous revolt, and more than once came to the point of threatening secession. The main matter of contention for the ILP members was whether working as a constituent element in the Labour Party within Parliament held any hope. However, it is significant that there was no concerted attempt to remedy this failure by mobilizing socialist forces outside Parliament.

A central figure in this conflict was Ramsay MacDonald. He had been secretary to the LRC from its formation, first becoming an MP in 1906. He was a socialist and a member of the ILP. MacDonald's socialism was frequently proclaimed in terms perceived as extreme by some moderate trade unionists in the Labour Party. Yet he was never seen by them as a real danger, partly because he always maintained excellent relations with the Liberals. Even after the Labour Party asserted its independence, he still favoured an alliance with the Liberals to forge a progressive anti-Unionist bloc. Like many ILP members, he was profoundly influenced by new liberalism, most particularly by J. A. Hobson. The starting point for his socialist theory was collectivism and the regulation of the market, a process which he understood as already having begun with the advent of the new monopolies. His approach placed socialism *above* class, transmuting its meaning into a term which referred to a 'quality' of society, almost to an evolutionary stage. Thus, he claimed, socialism was a matter of belief, not of class. It was as concerned with the reorganization of intellectual and moral factors as with the economy: 'Socialism marks the growth of society, not the uprising of a class.'[19]

MacDonald did much to shape the socialism of the ILP even though his relations with the ILP were often strained. From the beginning of 1908 he demonstrated his increasing impatience with ILP leftists and with their threats to secede from the Labour Party. Indeed it was partly through his skills that the revolt was contained and the ILP and Labour remained united. In 1911 he became chairman of the Labour Party and Henderson secretary. This began an uneasy twenty-year alliance which marked a new phase in the consolidation of the Labour Party as a broadly based political formation. From this moment, MacDonald seems also to have entertained the idea that the Labour Party might achieve political maturity and responsibility by entering a coalition, either with the Liberals, or by securing a rearrangement of the forces inside the power bloc. In 1911 he recorded in his diary a meeting with Lloyd George: '22nd October. Breakfasted with the Chancellor of Exchequer. He sounded me out on coalition Government: "not just yet" '.[20] According to David Marquand, MacDonald's biographer, there is some evidence that in the same year MacDonald contemplated joining a coalition with Lloyd George and Balfour, to oust Asquith. This may be far-fetched. But none the less in 1912, and again in 1914, the overtures between MacDonald and Lloyd George continued.[21]

In response to the increasing attacks on the Labour Party from within the labour movement itself, socialists and intellectuals committed to a parliamentary Labour Party attempted to fashion a new 'common sense' of socialism. This task fell primarily to MacDonald and Philip Snowden. In assembling the elements of Labour socialism, the central tension which had to be resolved was the balance between class and community. In a speech in the House of Commons in 1912, MacDonald provided one of the clearest illustrations of this conception of community, one which was to recur in Labour socialism throughout the 1920s:

We are too fond of imagining there are two sides only to a dispute . . . there is the side of capital, there is the side of labour; and there is the side of the general community; and the general community has no business to allow capital and labour, fighting their battles themselves, to elbow them out of consideration.[22]

Formulations of this sort were to prove critical in determining the attitude of Labour Party politicians towards the state.

The most sustained defence of the Labour Party and its relation to the state was Snowden's *Socialism and Syndicalism*, written in 1913 in which he rejected the notion of class war, and put forward three major, alternative propositions. First, in a curious mirroring of syndicalism, he insisted that the Labour Party aimed for the 'conquest' not of political but of economic power – in other words, the regulation of trusts and monopolies. Second, political power was to be 'acquired', or as Snowden put it with a large degree of wishful thinking,

nowadays not even the loudest voiced Revolutionary Socialist thinks that the Social Revolution will be achieved in any other way than by the gradual acquisition of political power by democracy and the gradual transformation of the capitalist system into a co-operative commonwealth.[23]

And lastly, he argued that just as anarchism was an off-shoot from the main body of socialism in the nineteenth century, so syndicalism was an off-shoot of contemporary socialism. Socialism, he concluded, by definition accepted the beneficence of the state.

There was not much here to convince the likes of Tillett or Tom Mann, whose hopes stuck firmly to the syndicalists. They could argue, with justification, that the Labour Party had provided pitifully little for working people, whereas direct industrial action had won some notable victories. But proto-syndicalism was more unstable than the militant leaders imagined. It could fluctuate between sudden angry outbursts and a more accommodative stance. It lacked the resources to sustain continual set-piece confrontations with the state, yet localized pockets of intransigent anarcho-syndicalism continued to exist. This is not to say that within the collective memory of the working-class movement, and within specific organizational forms, the critique of statism was lost, or the embryonic shifts towards conceptions of workers' control halted. But with the onset of the war, and then later during the period when massive defeats were inflicted on the labour movement, the grip of social democracy on the minds of the mass of the working class was much greater than the syndicalist leaders had bargained for.

The war and the Labour Party

The outbreak of the First World War had a cataclysmic effect on the European socialist movement, virtually destroying the Second International and splintering party after party. From 1914 developments within European socialism had direct repercussions on the configuration of the socialist parties within the British Isles.

However the immediate impact on the Labour Party was relatively muted. Ramsay MacDonald's pacifist opposition to the war drew him back into the political orbit of the ILP and opened a breach with the official Labour Party, forcing him to resign as party chairman. His power and influence within the Labour Party rapidly diminished. He lost his seat in the 1918 election, largely as a result of his anti-war stand. It was not until 1922 that he was re-elected chairman after regaining his parliamentary seat. During the war, his position in the party depended upon the amount of support he could gather, and upon the decisions of Arthur Henderson.

Henderson's response to the war was in keeping with his trade union background and commitment. He was instrumental in setting up the War Emergency Committee with the prime objective of defending working-class interests for the duration of the war. The committee was chaired by Henderson himself, and composed of representatives of the Labour Party executive and the trade unions. The WEC gave Henderson enormous powers at a time when other Labour leaders who opposed the war were marginalized. It was clear that the war provided unrivalled opportunities for the accredited leaders of the labour movement to win legitimacy in national politics. It also became apparent to the government that before long there would have to be centralized and state supervised bargaining with the representatives of the working class, especially over the conflicts arising from the production of munitions. Henderson and Lloyd George were instrumental in drawing up the Treasury Agreement between government and unions in March 1915. Two months later Henderson was invited to join Asquith's coalition government, reaching unprecedented heights for a Labour politician.

In December 1916 Henderson was admitted into Lloyd George's new War Cabinet of five ministers. In the following year he was delegated by the government to visit Russia and assess the military and political situation. While in Russia, reversing his earlier position, he swung round in support of the proposed socialist peace conference. On his return he recommended British representation to Lloyd George; the latter rejected this advice and in August 1917 Henderson resigned from the government. With Henderson virtually sacked, and certainly disillusioned with Lloyd George, a regroupment occurred involving as the key figures Henderson himself, MacDonald and Sidney Webb. The prospect of the Labour Party cashing in on the growing opposition to the Lloyd George coalition healed the breach between the pro- and anti-war factions inside the party. A fundamental transformation took place: no longer did Labour's leading trio seek to build a progressive alliance with the Liberals. On the contrary, they set about turning Labour into an independent political force, as a potential party of government in its own right. This seriously shifted the balance of forces within the power bloc, for above all else the immediate strategy of the Labour Party needed to prevent a possible post-war revival of the Liberals. For those who were responsible for instigating this new policy, it was imperative that the Labour Party should build itself in the image of the Liberal Party it planned to oust. This appeared to be the way to enter the constitutional conflict as a serious contender.

Within a month of his resignation Henderson was drafting the plans for the reconstruction of the Labour Party, drawn up in the conviction that the government would shortly have little option but to enfranchise the vast majority of working people. Henderson's long memorandum proposed extending the membership of the Labour Party, extending and strengthening the local constituency parties, increasing the number of parliamentary candidates, and producing a full party programme. In the course of the discussions which followed this memorandum three new principles emerged. First, the party was to be opened to individual membership. As Henderson wrote at the time in a letter to C. P. Scott, his policy 'was to enlarge the bounds of the Labour Party and bring in the intellectuals as candidates. The Labour Party has been too short on brains'.[24] This dispiriting conclusion not only disparaged the potentialities of the working-class membership, but also assumed that the intellectuals organic to the Labour Party had to be recruited from outside rather than created from within. However, this objective squared exactly with the process by which new liberal and Fabian definitions of the 'social problem' were channelled into the Labour Party. Second, the national executive was to be elected by the full party conference. This boosted the power of the union block votes, installing an institutional and corporate power inside the party apparatus. This hit hardest at the ILP. Third, for the first time in its history, the official objective of the Labour Party was to be the attainment of socialism.

The Representation of the People Bill passed through the House of Commons in December 1917, while these negotiations inside the Labour Party were in progress. The bill provided for the enfranchisement of all the male population aged 21 and over. After a free vote in the House of Commons, women aged 30 and above were also to be enfranchised. According to Ross McKibbon, this was the most cautious and conservative bill the coalition government thought it could possibly get away with.[25] However, the bill enfranchised more than all the previous reforms bills put together, amounting to some 80 per cent of the new voting population. It 'transformed the conditions under which Labour grew'.[26] It was of critical importance in shifting the allegiance of the working class from Liberal to Labour.

Early in 1918 Henderson's plans were put to the party conference and accepted. In June of the same year the Representation of the People Bill was accepted by the Lords and became law. The reorganization of the Labour Party at the end of the First World War was intimately connected with the extension of the franchise. By the time of the armistice at the end of the year the Labour Party was poised to enter future elections as a potential party of government, awaiting only its constitutional mandate from the electorate.

The formation of the Communist Party

By the time the Communist Party was founded in the summer of 1920 the situation had already became bleak for socialists. The shop stewards' movement had collapsed. The Forty Hour Strike in Glasgow in January 1919 was defeated despite its great hopes. Unrest in the armed forces had died down and police strikers had been sacked. In March 1920 a motion at the TUC demanding strike action to secure the nationalization of the mines was lost. By the summer, unemployment began to bite and this proved decisive in rolling back militancy. In the spring of the following year the bitter failure of the three-month-long miners' strike signalled a defeat for the labour movement as a whole. From that moment struggles became desperate and defensive. The early years of the party were characterized in its slogan, 'Stop the retreat'.

The most positive feature of 1920 was a significant political reorientation. In August local councils of action were set up to co-ordinate opposition to British intervention in Russia. These were based on local trades and Labour councils, which at the time comprised the local constituency Labour parties. Both the Parliamentary Labour Party and the parliamentary committee of the TUC were sufficiently pressured to lend their official support. In the following months approximately 288 councils of action were formed many emerging from trades and Labour councils. According to John Foster, 139 councils of action passed resolutions in defiance of the national leadership and backed calls for political strikes to end the economic sanctions on Russia and to force withdrawal of troops from Ireland.[27] This combination of both constitutional and direct action, drawing on support from the Labour Party and marxists in the Communist Party, formed a *political* force which had few precedents.

After extensive negotiation the groups which united to form the Communist Party (predominantly the British Socialist Party and a minority of the Socialist Labour Party) resolved to run candidates for Parliament and to apply for affiliation to the Labour Party. This latter decision was only narrowly passed, and excluded from the Communist Party a significant number of marxists who had no intention of ever having anything to do with the Labour Party. Initial approaches by the CP to the Labour Party lacked urgency. When the Labour Party first refused affiliation the *Communist* replied: 'So be it. It is their funeral, not ours.'[28] After the CP's first few bouts of militant bravado the Communist International made it clear to the British comrades that they should take the issue of affiliation more seriously. The early 1920s were punctuated by further applications and further rebuffs.

The unifying factors among the marxist groupings which eventually formed the Communist Party were support for soviets, the dictatorship of the proletariat and the Communist Third International. In no European country (with the possible exception of Bulgaria) was a Communist Party formed without drastic upheaval, multiple splits and protracted regroupments. There were various reasons for this. Of crucial importance was that simultaneously to the struggles between socialists and communists there also developed critical points of antagonism between socialists and social democrats. In this respect events in Britain closely followed the European pattern. One unintended effect of the Comintern hostility to reformism was that it encompassed socialists and social democrats alike so long as they refused to support soviets and the dictatorship of the proletariat. As a result the Comintern neutralized these points of conflict between socialists and social democrats. This operated as a strategic closure, forcing socialists back into an alliance with social democracy. This encouraged the construction of a new explicitly anti-Bolshevik political bloc with formidable staying-power.

Throughout 1920 the transformed situation in Europe and the strategic response of the Comintern threw the British communists into confusion. By the beginning of the year it was becoming clear to the majority of European marxists that there no longer existed the chance for achieving a straight repetition of the Bolshevik Revolution in the west. An overpowering factor in this analysis was the allegiance of an increasing number of working people to social-democratic parties. The response in Moscow was clear. In *Left Wing Communism – An Infantile Disorder*, written in May, Lenin advocated the need for Communists to create tactical alliances with the social-democratic parties. A copy of this pamphlet was issued to each delegate at the Second Congress of the Comintern, held two months later. From this Congress emerged the Twenty-One Conditions outlining the membership terms for the International. This document was of historic importance in codifying the organizational division between socialists and Communists. But the Comintern also recognized the hold of social democracy in the west and the necessity for Communist Parties to be *mass* parties. By the end of the year this strategy was instituted as the United Front. The newly formed Communist Parties were directed to ally with social democrats to expose the treachery of reformist leadership and the fallacies of parliamentary socialism.

In Britain, opposition to the Labour Party ran deep in the marxist groupings and many most active in their support of the Comintern had arrived at their position through a critique of the Labour Party. In the very moment of its foundation the Communist Party was ordered to affiliate with Labour. For this to be achieved an immense amount of pressure, argument and cajoling from Lenin and the Comintern was required. It was mainly through the Comintern pressure that the marxist sects fused and created in Britain a new type of marxist party which sought mass membership and an organic connection to the mainstream of the labour movement. However, even in theory the strategy of the United Front severely underestimated the penetration of social democracy into the labour movement. Onslaughts against the leadership of the Labour Party and the TUC and clear revolutionary principles made little impact. In practice, espousal of the strategy was cautious. But increasingly socialists were forced to make a choice between social democracy and Leninism.

Constitutional versus direct action

In effect the reconstruction of the Labour Party in 1918 and the formation of the Communist Party in 1920 separated socialists and social democrats, on the one hand, from marxists on the other. While this division now seems familiar it is important to emphasize the points regarding the conditions in which it emerged. First, the political situation in the period from 1918 to 1924 was highly volatile and the subsequent ascendancy of Labourism over Communism was by no means guaranteed from the start. Second, the Labour Party was only won to a position of constitutional gradualism as a result of a number of decisive struggles which were fought both inside and outside the Labour Party, determining the limits of constitutionalism itself. The question which then emerges is what were the political and ideological conditions which effected the division between socialists and marxists?

In May 1920 John MacLean, with characteristic insight, declared that the Lloyd George government was about 'to clear the ground for a safe and sane Labourism'.[29] But whatever the perceptiveness of this statement, its tactical grasp was at best partial. MacLean failed to distinguish conflicting strategies inside the power bloc which, by early 1920, were far from settled. Indeed, the dominant strategies represented by the coalitionists scarcely pinned their hopes on letting any kind of 'Labourism' on to the state scene. In addition, he underestimated the continuing struggles within the Labour Party, especially the antagonism over direct action between social democrats and socialists. In fact the success of a Labour socialism subordinated to MacDonald and Henderson was all but secured as a result of the shattering defeat inflicted on the miners in 1921. Furthermore, as McKibbon demonstrates, the centre of gravity of the Labour Party remained extra-parliamentary until as late as 1922. The significance of MacLean's view is not, however, simply one of timing. Rather it indicates the opinion, endorsed by the vast majority of marxists of the period, that representative democracy was in diametrical opposition to direct democracy (a belief shared by MacDonald). Thus when the very frontiers of constitutionalism were most open and when (from 1918) the Labour Party occupied a strategic place in determining the possibilities for expanding a democratic politics, those drawn to the Communist Party were excluded from effectively intervening.

At the Leeds Convention in June 1917 resolutions were passed supporting the establishment of soviets and workers' and soldiers' councils in Britain.

Despite the deep differences which separated the participants the discourse of direct action and of direct democracy spread across the whole spectrum of radical and socialist opinion. In an excess of enthusiasm generated by events in Russia and in Britain the divide between constitutional and non-constitutional politics hardly appeared.

However, after the reconstruction of the Labour Party as a potential party of government, constitutional politics were reasserted from *inside* the labour movement by the leadership of the party. At the Annual Conference in June 1919 this had become the most contentious issue. As Miliband notes:

The opponents of direct action . . . sought to defeat the Left by narrowing the alternatives open to the Labour movement to constitutional, meaning parliamentary, action on the one hand, and revolution and civil war on the other.[30]

The confrontation inside the Labour Party, however, cannot be reduced to a straightforward conflict between a bureaucratic leadership and a belligerent and activist rank and file. The leadership broke the power of the direct actionists not only by utilizing their organizational control of the party but also by winning a measure of consensus for their constitutionalist aims.

The crucial factor in the strategic analysis of the constitutionalists was the perpetual anxiety that a political backlash would occur, engineered by the radical right. Alternatively the coalition government might be able to achieve a sufficient degree of stabilization, on an explicitly anti-Labour and anti-socialist ticket, to exclude Labour from office for the foreseeable future. Such assessments of the political situation were not unfounded. To those who argued most forcefully for the constitutional position within the party, political backlash and the erosion of welfare rights could only be prevented by the consolidation of the Labour Party's role as a constitutionally accredited party of government. Indeed, this reasoning took hold of the party through the 1920s. Marquand concludes his biography of MacDonald by emphasizing: 'As MacDonald pointed out ad nauseam, the ground which the Labour Party gained between 1918 and 1922 was vulnerable to counter-attack.'[31]

The fear of social disintegration, as on the continent, or of the reversal of Britain's historic 'liberal' route by the forces of the right provided the conditions on which the Labour representatives could present themselves as the historical guarantors of Britain's constitutional traditions. The political break which made this possible, and which gave an unprecedented ideological credibility to the constitutionalist camp within the party, was the extension of the suffrage and the passing of the Representation of the People Bill in 1918. Defence of the British democratic system could now be given a specifically Labour articulation. In the eyes of many of the leading figures in the Labour Party the rules of the political game had been transformed. Unparalleled opportunites existed for the labour movement, and this was no time for a political recklessness which could destroy everything which had been so painstakingly constructed.

The forms and conditions of the extension into Parliament

In shaping the passage of the Labour Party to government, some key moments and determinations can be identified: the reorganization of the party in 1918, the Representation of the People Act and the codification of Comintern's policies in the Twenty-One Conditions in July 1920. The break-up of the coalition government in October 1922 opened up prospects for a renewed two-party parliamentary system. All the while the defeat, weakening and exhaustion of the shop stewards' and rank and file movements after 1921 was critical.

To many conservatives it seemed as if the Representation of the People Act threatened the very constitution itself. A simple majority of socialists in the lower house could at one blow sweep away all the institutions of British democracy. But at the same time, to some more liberal and far-sighted politicians, it also provided the conditions for the taming and 'constitutionalization' of the Labour Party. Labour could now be integrated into the political system as the (second) party of government. Thus from 1918 to 1924-6, the preoccupation of power-bloc politics rested on riding this contradiction, and on ensuring that the constitutional limits were preserved.

The more the Liberal Party was sold down the river by Lloyd George's commitment to coalition government, and the more the two-party alternative gathered pace as a strategic option, the more the aims of the constitutionalist perspective inside the Labour Party converged with the Baldwinite forces in the power bloc. According to Marquand, after the break-up of the coalition MacDonald's first objective 'was to ensure, if possible, that politics revolved around a struggle between the Conservative and Labour parties in which the Liberals could be dismissed as irrelevant'. MacDonald perceived that Labour's advance depended on victory in Parliament: 'If the Party fails in Parliament, it fails in the country, and the dream of a Labour Government will vanish for a generation.'[32] After 1922 a common political vocabulary emerged between what were fast becoming two of the key sections in the power bloc: the Baldwin faction and the MacDonald faction.

This convergence in language derived from a convergence in immediate political aims: the installation of two-party constitutionalism built around Labour and Conservative. The creation of the universal democratic subject of the Representation of the People Act effectively *disorganized* the socialist movement. It fractured it down the middle, deepening the split between the adherents of representative democracy on the one hand, and direct democracy on the other. In other words, the political effects of the introduction of a system of (near) universal suffrage served ultimately to compound the divisions which were being generated from inside the labour movement itself.

Out of this double movement – the recomposition of the power bloc and the divide within the labour movement – emerged, in its fully formed state, modern Labour socialism.

Fears of backlash, loss of real democratic gains, and the threat of the state being permanently occupied by an anti-socialist bloc all had a real pertinence. That no radical right venture materialized as a decisive political force must also be recognized. The new means of representation for the working class – the Labour Party, the trade unions and the TUC – shifted the political terrain. At least for those organized in the mainstream of the labour movement, these developments resulted in some important material gains. The constitutionalists in the Labour Party were right in their assessment that to break the caesarism of the Lloyd George coalition required the rotation of parliamentary parties with the Labour Party itself integrated into the dominant structure.

However, Labour socialism was chronically deficient in that it aimed to set the constitutional wheel in motion – extending the movement into Parliament – on exactly the same terms as before, creating Labour in the image of the Liberals before them. There were alternative strategies which did not eschew parliamentary politics altogether, but attempted to link electioneering with direct action. Of course, to do this Labour would have had to brave the condemnation of Conservatives and risk charges of Bolshevism. But if it had adopted such a perspective it would have been in the business of redefining the forms and criteria of legality, the definitions of what counted as 'politics'. Paradoxically, at the very moment when political rights seemed to be definitely won (through the extension of the suffrage at the end of the war) it was necessary immediately to raise the level of political demands and to extend the very notion of rights.

Of course, in historical context, the dilemmas were much more pressing than this analysis implies. The legacy of the late nineteenth-century democratic reforms, and the insertion of Labour into the centre of the parliamentary arena both precluded the likelihood of a long-term authoritarian solution (as MacDonald and others insisted) and provided the means for the internal recomposition of the power bloc. But it was on this dilemma that Labour socialism was caught. While on the one hand it aimed to defend and implement the results of the previous struggles against a potential political backlash, on the other the very terms of this defence was one which spurned a strategy which could construct a mass popular democratic movement. And without such a popular basis from below, from which to generate its *own* political strength, the leadership was led time and again into 'betrayals' – or rather, the structural reproduction of class corporatism inside the state itself. A radical, assertive intransigence was called for to prevent the extension into Parliament and the renewed rotation of parties reproducing a passive and immobilizing relationship between representatives and represented. The creativity of class and popular struggles – councils of action, rent strikes, the politics of the unemployed – needed to be harnessed, not disciplined, and the party itself needed to carry out its own programme of political education. For those who set the course of the Labour Party, the 'constitution' was taken as the *definer* of the possibilities of political action, whereas in fact (as Baldwin himself understood much more acutely) this was what the struggle was about.[33]

The paradox of the Labour socialist solution was that, in dismantling the caesarism of Lloyd George but negating the strength of its own popular constituency, the break with a caesarist structure of politics could only be partial. Gramsci's fleeting comments on MacDonald are not as arbitrary as they might first appear:

A Caesarist solution can exist even without a Caesar, without any great, heroic and representative personality. The parliamentary system has also provided a mechanism for such compromise solutions. The 'Labour' governments of MacDonald were *to a certain degree* solutions of this kind; and the degree of Caesarism increased when the government was formed which had MacDonald as its head and a Conservative majority.[34]

MacDonald's caesarism can be understood in terms of the concentration of his politics on the power bloc, the consequent hobbling and constraining of the popular activism within his own party, the convergence in immediate aims with the Baldwinite faction, and the setting in motion of two-party constitutionalism at its most cautious and gradual pace. And when, in 1931, the rotation of parties again collapsed there was a continuing logic to his position: nation, community and constitution took precedence over the 'sectional' interests of labour. In this sense, the alliance with Baldwin had had a covert existence for a number of years prior to 1931.

The relation of the Labour Party to the state, as expressed in constitutionalist perspective, had its parallel in the Labour Party's commitment to an abstract collectivism. Given the ambivalent connotations attributed to 'collectivism' and 'socialism' in the pre-war years, state ownership could easily become *identified* with socialism.[35] The rationality of collectivizing the mining industry or the railways, for example, could be perceived from well outside a socialist framework. In the immediate aftermath of the war a number of the most inveterate right-wingers were advocating nationalization of specific industries. It was only later (by 1920 or 1921), when demands for nationalization and workers' control became part of a socialist discourse, that the anti-nationalization position of the Conservatives became entrenched. Debates on collectivization were articulated to the imperatives of the reconstruction of the state itself. The effects (if not the ideologies themselves) of new liberalism and Fabianism were to suffuse conceptions of collectivism in a rhetoric of statism.[36] At a critical moment in the ideological formation of the Labour Party these theories had a decisive influence on leading Labour intellectuals. This merging of an undifferentiated collectivism with the socialist project was a crucial step in the developing *statism* of the Labour Party. It played a wider role in the reconstruction of the British state along the lines of a 'passive' revolution. This reconstruction was largely confined to the internal and administrative recomposition of the apparatuses of the state.

The containment of a rank and file activism in the labour movement by 1921, the rapid constitutionalization of the Labour Party which itself contributed to the 'passive' regeneration of the state, were all factors which had a decisive influence on the key class conflicts in the 1920s. For the working class these struggles were primarily defensive, and localized or sectional. They had three major focuses: resistance to the dismantling of the staple industries, resistance to unemployment, and resistance to the disciplinary and coercive core of the state system of welfare. Cumulative struggles over these issues at times overcame a narrow constitutionalism and, by following a much broader definition of the general democratic tasks of the labour movement, raised corporate issues to a more popular level. Although, in the older vocabulary, the movements which grew up around these struggles in the 1920s were firmly 'direct actionist', negative attitudes to the institutions of representative democracy ran far less deep. Indeed, many of the fiercest struggles were concentrated within and against the apparatuses of the local state.

We have argued that between 1918 and 1924 a central object of the struggle between the major classes was the issue of constitutionalism. The showdown during the General Strike finally secured for Baldwin his victory against the forces of direct action. However, for a number of years before 1926 the focus of class struggle had begun to shift. It is ironic that the predominant initiatives intended to regulate and restructure the working class through state practices in the 1920s had precious little to do with a constitutional form of politics. The characteristic mode was administrative. Thus, for example, a memorandum or directive from the Ministry of Health could have devastating effects on those receiving unemployment benefit. 'Profligate' local councils were placed under the controls of non-elected auditors, carrying unprecedented financial powers. Similarly, appointed government committees, although only advisory, could wield enormous power – especially when representatives of labour added their signatures. The most infamous occasion was the Blanesburgh Committee of 1927 which advised the reduction of unemployment payments and the tightening up of the 'genuinely seeking work' clause. The final report was signed by three trade union representatives, including Margaret Bondfield, a member of the TUC and future Minister of Labour in the 1929 government. The incorporation of Labour and trade union representatives at the very highest levels of the state could mean that socialists in various localities might find themselves pitched in struggle against their own representatives.[37]

Evidence from accounts of the 'Little Moscows', of the unemployed struggles, and of Poplarism suggests that on specific issues the constitutional/ non-constitutional distinction was simply inoperative at the local level.[38] Perhaps the primary determination for this was that, as a result of the remorseless administrative logic of the bureaucratic machine, rights which had come to be regarded as social rights came increasingly under threat. This was partly a product of economic considerations but was also due to concerted moves by the central state to curb the constitutional and democratic routes by which forces perceived as hostile could win command of various apparatuses of the local state. Rights which were seen as constitutionally guaranteed were systematically pared down in the 1920s. Conflict with the state was exacerbated by the fact that it was the state itself which was decisive in regulating the distribution of what was increasingly becoming a 'social' wage. Collective, anti-state resistances were thus integral to the politics of the labour movement in the 1920s – even when only apparently economic issues were in dispute. But far from remaining defensive, at their most developed, anti-state struggles of this type could be raised to the offensive. The building of popular alliances in specific communities against the vindictiveness of petty officialdom could be extended to a movement *for* the deepening of democratic rights to secure the substance, as well as the form, of social rights. The unemployed struggles organized by the National Unemployed Workers' Movement were particularly assertive in this respect. They engaged in dramatic, symbolic actions against the coercive and regulatory functions of the local welfare apparatuses of the state. The objectives of the NUWM were to smash the bureaucratic dominance of the welfare system and expand into the state itself a representative structure which could encourage real popular controls. The greater the purpose of these resistances, the greater the conflicts with the boards of guardians, the Ministry of Health, the police and Cabinet and party representatives. Similarly, Poplarism illustrates the significance of struggles within the state. The electoral success of the Poplar councillors against Labour Party bureaucratism of the Morrison type, the possibilities for the redistribution of wealth through the local apparatuses of the state, and the popular mobilization behind the Poplar action all showed that legitimacy could be won for an intransigently 'unconstitutional' campaign.

At best, official Labour Party support for such actions remained dilatory. At worst it was overtly hostile and obstructive. The effects of these anti-state struggles were necessarily undercut by the ambivalent response of official Labourism and by the structural constraints of its insertion into the power bloc on the constitutionalist ground which had been staked out between 1918 and 1924. By disciplining and hobbling its own base, the possibilities for Labour members to exert a strategic and assertive political presence, transcending the passive recomposition of the state, correspondingly looked weaker and weaker.

Notes and references

1   S. Webb and B. Webb, *Industrial Democracy* (Longmans 1902), pp. 147–8.
2   We take this term from Stuart Macintyre, *A Proletarian Science. Marxism in Britain 1917–33* (Cambridge University Press 1980).
3   In the 1880s the Fabians defined the two strands of socialism as 'Collectivist' and 'Anarchist', but found it too early to decide which would be the dominant trend in Britain. Given the broad connotations of 'collectivist' and 'anarchist', it was a pertinent analysis. *What Socialism Is* (Fabian Tract, no. 4, 1886).
4   For one of the earliest commentaries, typical apart from its date, see the discussion of Theodore Rothstein's article of 1901 by Bill Baker, *The Social Democratic Federation and the Boer War, Our History*, no. 59 (1974), p. 12. Rothstein noted the onset of imperialism, regulation superseding *laissez-faire*, the accentuation of nationalism and the tightening of the links between class and state.
5   Stephen Yeo, 'A new life: the religion of socialism in Britain 1883–1896', *History Workshop Journal*, no. 4 (1977). See also the correspondence by Sheila Rowbotham, Royden Harrison and Stephen Yeo in *History Workshop Journal*, nos. 5–7 (1978–9). A rather similar perspective, although differing in conclusion and chronology, is suggested by Stanley Pierson, *Marxism and the Origins of British Socialism* (Cornell University Press 1973) and *British Socialists. The Journey from Fantasy to Politics* (Harvard University Press 1979). Yeo's analysis of the shift in this period from co-operative to capitalized and state insurance is more compelling, 'Working-class association, private capital and the state', in N. Parry *et al.* (eds.), *Social Work, Welfare and the State* (Edward Arnold 1979).
6   See especially S. Rowbotham and J. Weeks, *Socialism and the New Life* (Pluto Press 1977).
7   T. A. Jackson, *Solo Trumpet* (Lawrence and Wishart 1953), p. 49.
8   For the latter, see M. Llewelyn Davies (ed.), *Maternity. Letters from working women* (Virago 1978; first published 1915); and for statism and motherhood, Jane Lewis, *The Politics of Motherhood. Child and maternal welfare in England 1900–1939* (Croom Helm 1980) as well as Caroline Rowan's chapter in this volume.
9   Unofficial Reform Committee, *The Miners' Next Step* (Pluto Press 1973), p. 29. For the historical location, H. Francis and D. Smith, *The Fed. A history of the South Wales miners in the twentieth century* (Lawrence and Wishart 1980) cannot be bettered.
10   The best account is given by the Board of Trade troubleshooter, G. Askwith, *Industrial Problems and Disputes* (John Murray 1920). Despite his faith in the powers of conciliation, and even though he exerted a measure of control, the anxiety is still communicated through these pages.
11   H. A. Clegg, A. Fox and A. F. Thompson, *A History of British Trade Unionism Since 1899, vol. 1, 1889–1910* (Clarendon Press 1964), p. 319.
12   The term is introduced by Bob Holton, *British Syndicalism 1910–1914* (Pluto Press 1976). He sees it referring to 'forms of social action which lie between revolt and clear-cut revolutionary action', p. 76. We understand it more as a specific form of revolt, which carried its own *self-imposed* limitations.

13 Holton, p. 77.
14 Both Lenin and Gramsci were to acknowledge the influence of Daniel de Leon, and recognize his contribution to a theory of soviet power; and Lenin, in *State and Revolution*, defended Pannekoek's 'anarcho-syndicalism' against Kautsky's 'statism'.
15 Quoted in Alan Bullock, *The Life and Times of Ernest Bevin*, vol. 1 (Heinemann 1960), p. 35.
16 R. Miliband, *Parliamentary Socialism* (Merlin 1973), p. 28.
17 Holton, p. 179.
18 Miliband, *Parliamentary Socialism*.
19 David Marquand, *Ramsay MacDonald* (Cape 1977), p. 90.
20 ibid., p. 142.
21 ibid., pp. 143, 150 and 159–60.
22 ibid., p. 146. For a classic example of this reasoning which a) privileges 'community' over 'producers', b) posits 'community' against both private monopolies and labour organizations, and c) advocates the 'channelling' and education of 'syndicalism' to these ends, see Emil Davies, *The Collectivist State in the Making* (G. Bell 1914).
23 P. Snowden, *Socialism and Syndicalism* (Collins 1913), p. 133.
24 Quoted in R. McKibbon, *The Evolution of the Labour Party* (Oxford University Press 1974), p. 94.
25 ibid., p. 237.
26 ibid., p. xv.
27 This paragraph relies on John Foster, 'British imperialism and the labour aristocracy', in J. Skelley (ed.), *1926. The General Strike* (Lawrence and Wishart 1976), pp. 28–9. Differing figures can be found in Alan Clinton, *The Trade Union Rank and File: Trades Councils 1900–1940* (Manchester University Press 1977), and Stephen White, *Britain and the Bolshevik Revolution* (Macmillan 1979).
28 16 September 1920.
29 Quoted in Nan Milton, *John MacLean* (Pluto Press 1973), p. 230.
30 See Miliband, ch. 3; and also Noreen Branson, *Poplarism* (Lawrence and Wishart 1979), pp. 54–7.
31 Marquand, p. 793.
32 Quoted in Marquand, pp. 289 and 290.
33 One of the most famous examples is still the most revealing. J. C. C. Davidson was Chief Civil Commissioner in the 1923 Conservative administration, with responsibility for preparing secret contingency plans for the threatened general strike. He recorded in his diary the coming of the new Labour Government:

> I handed over as Chancellor to an old friend, Josh Wedgwood, who had been a pacifist before the War, but who had fought most gallantly in it. I told him that, whoever was in power, it was his duty to protect the Constitution against a Bolshevik-inspired General Strike. . . . I begged him not to destroy all that I had done and not to inform his Cabinet of it. This did not concern party but was a national matter. Josh said that he could not continue to build my organisation, but he promised not to interfere with the work we had done. On my return I found that Josh had been as good as his word. . . .

> J. C. C. Davidson, *Memoirs of a Conservative* (Weidenfeld and Nicolson 1969), p. 180.

34 A. Gramsci, *The Prison Notebooks* (Lawrence and Wishart 1971), p. 220, emphasis added.

35 To see how this is reproduced in the historiography, see Robert Skidelsky, *Politicians and the Slump* (Penguin 1970).

36 A telling cameo is the confrontation between the two brothers-in-law, Beveridge and Tawney, in their evidence to the Sankey Commission: Beveridge, representing the Board of Trade, stressed the need for a statist collectivization along nationalization lines; Tawney, representing the miners, for a strong injection of popular controls.

37 Perhaps the clearest case was the conflict between George Lansbury and the Poplar councillors, and Herbert Morrison. Morrison's views on local government were unequivocal: 'A machine without high principles is à machine of no real value. And high principles without an efficient machine constitutes but a voice crying in the wilderness. We have to make an efficient machine for a high moral purpose' – a prime example, as it turned out, of an abstract faith in 'collectivism'. Clement Attlee's response to Morrison over the Poplar confrontation deserves note: 'I have always been a constitutionalist but the time has come when it is necessary to kick', Branson, pp. 56 and 80.

38 Stuart Macintyre, *Little Moscows* (Croom Helm 1980); Wal Hannington, *Unemployed Struggles* (Lawrence and Wishart 1977); and Branson.

7 Imperialism in crisis: the 'Irish dimension'

Robin Wilson

We were beset by an accumulation of grave crises – rapidly becoming graver. . . . It was becoming evident to discerning eyes that the Party and Parliamentary system was unequal to coping with them. . . . The shadow of unemployment was rising over the horizon. Our international rivals were forging ahead at a great rate and jeopardizing our hold on the great markets of the world. . . . Our working population . . . were becoming sullen with discontent. . . . The Irish controversy was poisoning our relations with the United States of America. A great Constitutional struggle over the House of Lords threatened revolution at home, another threatened civil war at our doors in Ireland   (*Lloyd George, recalling the situation in 1910*).[1]

Throughout the whole period covered by this book the crisis of Ireland was a central, integral factor in the crises of Westminster governments and the British state. More than anything it was under the impact of events in Ireland that the mid Victorian constitutional system disintegrated. In these years the configuration of political struggle in Britain was persistently refracted through the Irish issue.

In 1886 Gladstone had tied the fortunes of the Liberal Party to a policy of Home Rule, provoking a major split in the party itself. The combined power of the Conservatives and the Liberal Unionists defeated Gladstone's Home Rule Bill, and the Liberals were speedily ejected from office as a result. In his next administration Gladstone made a second attempt: this time, in 1893, the bill was rejected by the House of Lords, and the following year Gladstone resigned for the last time the leadership of his party. It was with this uncompleted historic project that the Liberals assumed office in 1905. By this date there were many prominent figures in the party who – if they could have so chosen – would have unobtrusively pushed the whole issue to one side.

Events in Ireland itself were to force the Liberal government to adopt a more positive strategy, taking up once more the cause of Home Rule and for the third time putting a bill before Parliament. The vast Liberal majority of 1906 was lost in the January election of 1910 and the Liberal Party became dependent in the House of Commons on the Labour and Irish minorities. This dependence meant that the Liberals were committed to Home Rule as an immediate policy. It also provoked a militant backlash from the Unionists in the north of Ireland who were desperate to resist at all costs the end of their union with the United Kingdom. In Britain the Home Rule issue mobilized the Conservative Party around a single, radical and unifying cause. The threat of treason, armed rebellion and civil war made 1910 a year of profound political crisis, the magnitude of which threatened not just particular party policies but the foundations of the political institutions themselves. The force of the Home Rule crisis pulled together previously irreconcilable leaders from each party in bizarre convergences of opposites. Out of this crisis emerged a peculiarly modern, cross-party or 'coalitionist' means by which the Westminster parties came to deal with the seemingly intractable issue of Ireland.

To unravel this complicated process three broad strategic perspectives can be identified, drawing from and modifying some of the formulations to be found in Gramsci's work. The first can be called transformist. This refers to the attempts by the Liberal Party to make a certain number of concessions to the nationalist forces, through negotiations with the Irish Parliamentary Party under the leadership of first Charles Stewart Parnell and then John Redmond. Characteristic of transformism is the attempt to broaden the ruling bloc by gradually absorbing contending and potentially hostile forces and incorporating representative leaders. By 1910 this strategy, at least in its pure form, was impracticable.

Second is the militant populism of the Ulster and British Unionists, a politics which was essentially extra-parliamentary and which looked for some 'catastrophic' resolution to the impasse on Ireland. It was this which led to the mobilization of the Ulster protestants and parallel groups in Britain, and which carried with it the threat of devastating civil conflict. The purpose was not, as in transformist solutions, to ride out social antagonisms and to neutralize them through a process of compromise. It aimed rather to heighten antagonism, to eliminate once and for all the opposition and thereby to rearrange the basic elements of the political situation. This conception was accepted by the radical right in the British Conservative Party and by the followers of Sir Edward Carson in Ulster. This alliance determined to win the working class to the cause of Union and empire and thus decisively break Liberal hegemony.

Third is the emergence of the inter-party, coalitionist or 'caesarist' strategy. This first appeared in the midst of the crisis of 1910 (it was tentatively proposed by Churchill and Lloyd George) and gathered force over the next decade. The coalitionist strategy depended on neutralizing both the antagonistic forces in Ireland (the nationalists and the Ulster radicals) and substituting a pragmatic for a historical or political solution. The object was to insulate as far as possible the British state from the Irish conflicts. In sum, the aim was not to rebuild a new hegemony but to contrive a situation in which bourgeois domination could be secured, based on the barest minimum of 'consensus'.

At no single moment were specific strategies ever spelt out in these terms. Nor did there occur a straightforward sequence in which one policy followed another: indeed, nowhere was confusion more rife than on Ireland. But it is important to trace how, within and between parties, these strategies came to coexist and combine in various moments in the years between the Liberal victory of 1905 and the signing of the treaty in 1921.

The failure of the Liberal renewal

By 1906 two key developments had ensured that Home Rule was no longer an overwhelming issue for the Liberal leadership. The first was the Conservative resolution of the land grievance in Ireland through the successive land purchase legislation (a process finally completed under Liberal auspices in 1909). The second was the emergence of an imperialist faction *inside* the Liberal Party, the Liberal Imperialists (the so-called Limps) who held no great commitment to Home Rule and who were becoming increasingly influential in the party. The compromise elaborated between the traditional Gladstonians and the Limps became known as the 'step-by-step' policy. As the future Liberal leader, Asquith, argued in 1902, Home Rule should not be included in the Liberal programme. While it was still an objective, it could 'only be attained by methods which will carry with them, step by step, the sanction and sympathy of British opinion'.[2] The subsequent Liberal landslide in December 1905 broke Liberal dependence on the Irish Parliamentary Party (IPP) and seemed to remove the final obstacle to the success of radical social reform. It also allowed the party to pursue a 'historic' project other than Home Rule, with all its manifold dangers.

Measures to do with Ireland were introduced cautiously and hesitantly. The Irish Council Bill of 1907 – a 'modest, shy, humble effort' as Campbell-Bannerman described it[3] – was, in line with this overall approach, a limited measure of devolution. Yet it was here that the Liberal strategy began to come unstuck. The IPP leadership vacillated at first. Both its organization in Ireland, the United Irish League and the Catholic Church gave the bill a hostile reception. This led to a temporary resurgence of Sinn Fein.

The dominance of the IPP within Ireland was further challenged by the emergence of Larkinism as a proletarian force. Militant trade union organizer Jim Larkin claimed three strike victories in 1908 and founded the Irish Transport Workers Union a year later.

The 1908 University Act removed the last remaining grievance of the church, which consequently no longer had any interest in the Liberal alliance. And the alliance with the Liberals – on which the IPP as a parliamentary force had been totally dependent since the party had split in 1890 on the issue of Parnell's leadership – was placed under further strain by the 1909 budget. The drink trade (a significant component of the IPP's political base) mobilized popular opposition against increased taxation.

In the face of the progressive disintegration of the historic bloc which it had constructed, the IPP became increasingly isolated. It was forced to adopt a more aggressive and independent position on the national question. But the national question did not itself precipitate the crisis of Liberal strategy. It was rather the fusion of the issue of Home Rule with the explosive struggles around the budget and the Lords' veto that did the damage. By 1908 the Liberal parliamentary majority was declining as a result of a series of Labour Party by-election victories. Labour's successes led to growing pressure from the radical Liberals for a more progressive social programme. But this required an assault on the Lords to counter resistance to social reform from the upper chamber. When he assumed the Liberal leadership in 1908 Asquith insisted that the party treat the Lords' veto as 'the dominating issue in politics'.[4] The problem for the Liberals was that this objective required the support of the IPP. After the election of January 1910, the Liberals were once more dependent on the IPP to secure a parliamentary majority. In return, the IPP demanded Home Rule – which the removal of the Lords' veto would for the first time make possible. To secure IPP support, and to maintain the support in Ireland they needed for the construction of a new *Pax Hibernica*, the Liberals could not but accept.

The conjunction of social reform and Home Rule was to cause the collapse of the Liberal strategy. It made the possibility of social reform conditional upon the success of Home Rule – precisely what the earlier Liberal strategy had set out to avoid. The intractability of the Home Rule issue led to the political paralysis of the Liberal government. In Britain the popularity of Home Rule was minimal. A report from Joseph Pease's constituency in January 1913 noted 'complete apathy with regard to Home Rule. Among all the workmen I have heard no one mention the fireworks of Sir Edward Carson'.[5] To make matters worse, the 'fireworks' pushed the Liberals' social concerns into the background. The Secretary of the Central Land and Housing Council, referring to the party's land campaign, told Lloyd George in May that 'the campaign in the boroughs has been disappointing. . . . Public attention has been so occupied with gun-running, army revolts . . . that it has been difficult to arouse interest in Land and Housing'.[6] Once the two issues of Home Rule and supremacy of the House of Commons had become fused the Liberals could no longer afford to drop Home Rule. At the end of May 1914 the Yorkshire Liberal Association reported that 'if Home Rule is not settled without a general election we are all wasting our time on land and housing'. Unless the Government showed that the Parliament Act would be used to defeat Conservative opposition, 'the working people will drop us for a long time to come'.[7] In July, junior minister Charles Trevelyan reported anxiously to Walter Runciman on a meeting of Liberals from his Yorkshire constituency:

They were entirely faithful men. They did not use violent language. But they say that the whole of the Liberal working-class is on the point of revolt; that the prestige of the government is gone, and that the great mass of working-men think that the government is funking. They have never approved of leaving Carson alone, they were more angry about the gun-running, and the[y] are quite furious about the [Buckingham Palace] Conference. There is *no one at all* in favour of it. I have never seen such unanimity. . . . The Government has got to show itself top dog *now*, or the Liberal Party will disintegrate, even in the West Riding.[8]

The populist alternative

The Liberal strategy attempted to recompose bourgeois rule in part by challenging the Lords' veto in a concession to popular-democratic aspirations. The Unionist (Conservative) counter-offensive was a populist redefinition of popular-democratic concerns in aggressively nationalist terms. The Conservative Party too was in a thoroughgoing crisis by 1911. Despite having established its status as the 'natural party of government', after 1886 it had subsequently failed to win three successive elections. It was crippled by division over tariff reform and had failed to stem the attack on the Lords or defeat the budget. 'Pacifism' and 'socialism' appeared to be in the ascendant. The failure of the tariff reformers to win the party to a united pro-tariff position meant that 'in the autumn of 1911 the party had thus passed the point where it could be rallied without a new focus of loyalty'.[9] Ireland provided the required new focus. As Stubbs argues, Ireland was 'an important, if not the most important catalyst for the reunification and regeneration of the party after the shambles of the period 1906 to 1911'.[10]

Only an appreciation of the breadth of this crisis can explain the intensity of the Tory revolt and the resort to extra-parliamentary, populist politics. Buckland correctly points out that Conservatives believed, irrespective of the merits of the Ulster case, that Home Rule would lead to the break-up of empire, encouraging nationalist revolts elsewhere in more prized possessions, most especially in India.[11]

The Tory right-wingers were not motivated merely by patriotic bigotry and prejudice. They actively sought to secure bourgeois rule on a new basis. This can be seen from their early and wholehearted support for the full *political* programme of the Tariff Reform League. They were prepared to resort to novel means to secure their position, as the outriders of a populist movement and as the nucleus of support for Ulster militarism in Britain. Thus, as Phillips and Searle argue, the diehards are better understood as radical rightists.[12] For them the issue of Ireland was inextricably bound up in an 'accumulation of crises'. The peers' campaign embraced tariff reform, hostility to the budget, and control of the House of Commons – as well as hostility to Home Rule.

Lord Selborne was clear that the threat was not just Home Rule, but the 'Home-Rule, pro-Boer, Little-England-Socialist party'.[13] By the time the diehards had organized themselves in the Halsbury Club, Milner had proposed a comprehensive policy on which they should unite, including tariff reform, imperial unity, defence, 'social uplifting', the constitution, and 'A real United Kingdom'.[14] Home Rule was one of a whole series of folk devils conjured up in diehard 'nationalist-populist' ideology, part and parcel of the 'enemy within'. Just as they attacked 'Cobden Millionaires' and 'Radical Plutocrats', so they also lashed 'Domestic Germanophiles' and 'Cosmopolitan Jews'. When Redmond returned from a fund-raising tour for the I P P in America they dubbed him the 'Dollar Dictator'. The 'German Menace' was a particular diehard phobia. Many diehards had served in the army or navy and had been activists in the National Service League and the Imperial Maritime League. The possibility of German exploitation of a civil war in Ulster became a favourite theme.

But it was the Parliament Bill – opening the door to Home Rule – which unified the diehards as a political force. The exhaustion of the tactic of resisting Home Rule by relying on the formal, constitutional powers of the Lords led to a shift from a rhetorical to an *organized* populism. After 1911 this achieved a greater resonance in the Conservative Party under Bonar Law's leadership.

After the Parliament Bill was passed, the language became altogether more strident and the struggle moved from the debating chambers of Parliament to the streets and the barracks. The Liberal Government was now presented, as Bonar Law put it at Blenheim in July 1912, as 'a Revolutionary Committee which seized by fraud upon despotic power'.[15] The 'revolutionary committee' was anti-popular, in Conservative ideology, because it had been founded against the will of the people. Bonar Law claimed that with the constitution abrogated, Home Rule could only be achieved by 'tyranny, naked and unashamed'. Home Rule, he told a rally at Balmoral in April 1912, was 'a conspiracy as treacherous as had ever been formed against the life of a great nation'.[16]

Ironically, the Liberal reaction to the Tory revolt operated within a strikingly similar discourse. In September 1911 the *Nation* attacked 'Robespierre-Carson' for inciting Ulster to 'sedition and outrage'. In February 1912 it denounced the opponents to Churchill's Belfast visit as 'anarchists'.[17] Asquith attacked Bonar Law's Blenheim speech as 'an absolute end to Parliamentary Government' and 'a complete grammar of anarchy'.[18] But it was Churchill, a fervent, anti-populist at this stage in his political career, who took the strongest line. He described the Ulster Volunteer Force as a 'treasonable conspiracy'. In Bradford in 1914 he declared: 'we stand for law and order, and must see that the nation is not held up by a few malcontents'.[19]

But Conservative support for Ulster was not merely opportunism. There were close parallels on a wide range of issues between Ulster Unionism and the British Unionists, particularly the diehards. Ulster Unionist ideology was formed in the mould of 'social-imperialism', except that the 'socialism' (or collectivism) of British social-imperialist discourse was replaced by – or rather, subordinated to and defined in terms of – nationalism. As Gibbon presents the Unionist argument:

The Ulsterman, by virtue of his imperial citizenship, shared the most advanced privileges and liberties in the world; the threat of home rule was a threat to them, just as in classical social-imperialist ideology the threat of socialism occupied a similar position.[20]

This was related to – though not reducible to – the dependence of northern industry on the imperial connection for raw materials and export markets. The Unionist bourgeoisie, heavily concentrated in engineering, shipbuilding and textiles, keenly supported tariff reform. The Ulster Covenant of 1912 provides a clear expression of Unionist allegiance to British imperialist ideology:

Being convinced in our consciences that Home Rule would be disastrous to the material well-being of Ulster as well as the whole of Ireland, subversive of our civil and religious freedom, destructive of our citizenship, and perilous to the unity of the Empire, we . . . pledge ourselves . . . to stand by one another in defending for ourselves and our children our cherished position of equal citizenship in the United Kingdom.[21]

The Covenant was signed by 218,206 men, and an even greater number of women signed a declaration in support of 'their men'. After labouring in the wilderness in groups like the National Service League, and after the failure of tariff reform as a political and popular movement, the Covenant appeared to the imperialists in Britain a significant breakthrough. Lord Milner and Leo Amery, two prominent Unionists, were quick to follow this example. They organized a British Covenant which, from March to July 1914, acquired – it was alleged – some 2 million signatures.

Masculinism was to the fore in this ideology. The attributes of staunchness, sobriety, determination and discipline were held to reside in the Ulster*man*. Sir Edward Carson once described Ulster Unionist resistance to Home Rule as an effort to 'assert the manhood of our race'.[22] Blanch points out how a key feature of imperialist ideology in this period was 'its strikingly connotatively male character. Its militaristic and leadership models were essentially patriarchal.'[23]

Moreover, the displacement of the Cecil patriciate of Salisbury and Balfour by Bonar Law supplied a leadership for British Conservatives with more affinity for the Ulster Unionist movement. Bonar Law was impressed by a meeting he addressed in Belfast in late 1913:

That meeting consisted of practically the whole business community of Belfast. They are the very class which hates disorder, which knows that disorder injures their business, perhaps ruins their business, yet this class showed an enthusiasm which equalled, if not surpassed, the enthusiasm of the workers in the shipyards.[24]

A willingness to bypass existing political structures in favour of a populist strategy was common both to the Tory rebels and to Ulster Unionism. The supporters of Carson and Milner overlapped in organizations like the Unionist Social Reform Committee, the Tariff Reform League and the British Workers National League.

To British Unionists, Ulster offered a ready means to link popular-democratic ideological concerns to a stridently populist right-wing assault on the custodians of the state. As Gamble puts it,

The Ulster Volunteer movement . . . became a model for what many of the right wanted. Its military organisation, its patriotic ethos, and its inclusion of men from all classes provided a political vehicle for the right outside the constitutional political market. Many Unionists now found this preferable to parliamentary games at Westminster.[25]

At this point we can compare the competing political strategies of Liberalism and Unionist populism. The Liberal strategy was transformist, yet although the populist strategy was counterposed to this there were significant similarities. Both invoked 'the people' against the rich and powerful. Both the 'peer' of Liberal propaganda and the 'Dollar Dictator' for the Tories were presented as having undeserved wealth and illegitimate authority. Both strategies involved some concessions to popular-democratic politics, and thus reflected increasing awareness inside the ruling bloc of the need to win popular consent. The key difference was this. Liberal transformism attempted to defuse the potentially antagonistic relation between popular democracy and the state by absorbing representatives of subordinate groups into the power bloc of dominant political forces. Unionist populism, on the other hand, attempted to channel popular-democratic aspirations, not against the state as such, but against the faction currently in charge. The object was that the dissident grouping of Unionist leaders would ride to power on the back of a campaign fought outside Parliament, 'with the people'.

As the Tory counter-offensive mounted, the Liberal strategy more or less retreated into a simple and ineffectual anti-populist opposition. No longer able to manage the changing equilibrium of forces, the Liberals could only react in a defensive fashion. Thus as early as February 1912, Asquith told the King that the government felt free to 'make such changes in the [Home Rule] Bill as fresh evidence of facts, or the pressure of British opinion, may render expedient' in terms of 'special treatment' for the Ulster counties.[26] Indeed Asquith even suggested that the government might not press the bill within the terms of the Parliament Act.

Why was Conservative populism able to force the Liberal government into such an ignominious retreat? The latter-day Gladstonian Liberal ideologue Robert Kee puts it down to 'failure of the Liberal nerve', and Dangerfield takes a similar view. But the fact is that the Conservative strategy was *active* and *transformative*, aiming to reconstruct the power bloc and recompose its hegemony. A characteristic feature of this was the way in which imperialist ideology was able to penetrate deeply into civil society through a plethora of public and private organizations. As Blanch comments:

If to the formal and informal aspects of schooling and to the youth organisations we add the popularity of the display and spectacle of military and nationalistic events, the daily reproduction of imperialist slogans in the press . . . the early impact of media like film and the fact that popular forms of amusement, like music hall, were saturated with similar sentiments, we obtain some idea of the sheer weight and pervasiveness of the nationalist mood.[27]

By contrast, the Liberals really had no strategy at all. As the Liberal alliance was eroded by the growth of various forms of non-parliamentary direct action, on the one hand, and by the loss of capitalist confidence on the other, the government was reduced to an increasingly passive and non-interventionist stance. It was unable to redefine the political terrain in favour of its own party. In sum, while the Conservatives sought to 'lead', the Liberal government attempted merely to 'dominate'. It is thus not surprising that the more adventurist elements in the Liberal camp attempted to build an alternative strategy which, if necessary, would look beyond the very boundaries of the Liberal Party itself.

The government's position finally collapsed when gun-running and the Curragh Mutiny of 1914 achieved the objective of the diehards to 'paralyse the arm' of the state, as Milner had once expressed it to Carson.[28]

Caesarism

The Liberal commitment to Home Rule and the Tory revolt should not obscure the fact that in this period there were formidable pressures on the members of both the major parties for political realignment. The eventual development of a 'consensus' can only be understood as the outcome of these pressures. On the Conservative side, there were a number of tariff reformers who were relatively indifferent to the maintenance of the Union. They were prepared to engineer a compromise on this rather than some other issue. Thus 'For Chamberlain it was a distraction from the real problems of British politics.'[29] A prominent tariff reformer in the City warned Balfour in 1907:

I have noticed in recent years a class has grown up, and it has its reflex largely in our organisations, of men who are lukewarm or indifferent on questions that twenty years ago used to hold the first place in our affections. . . . Even in such matters as the unity of the empire, the more material or commercial aspects of the question appeal to them more strongly than the aspects which called forth the outburst of opposition to home rule in Ireland.[30]

This view of the secondary importance of the question of Irish Home Rule lay behind the proposal for an alliance between tariff reformers and the IPP made by the right-wing *Morning Post* in 1908. At the time this went against the grain of both orthodox and militant Conservatism. At the opening of the 1909 parliamentary session there was a heated controversy in the Shadow Cabinet which resulted in the subordination of the Irish issue to the question of tariff reform. For the first time the Unionist amendment referred specifically to Ireland as a beneficiary of tariff reform. Balfour told Lord Lansdowne in January 1910 that some tariff reformers were even 'urging an arrangement with the Irish on the basis of sacrificing the union (more or less completely) in the interests of tariff reform'.[31] Balfour did not mince words in expressing his view of any alliance with the IPP. It would be tantamount to 'eating dirt', he told J. L. Garvin, the great Unionist journalist.[32]

Two alternative political strategies evolved in the Conservative camp. On the one hand, the populist revolt, but on the other, a new sentiment appeared in the party. As Sandars commented in the midst of the crisis of 1910, there was emerging,

a restless movement of the young men who are anxious to rid themselves of the shackles of the old party traditions . . . [who] will not allow their big ideals of empire, defence, trade and social reforms to be sacrificed in the matter of an old creed.[33]

As Balfour told Garvin in October 'Many of the best of our young men are moving towards federalism.'[34] They were looking for a solution along federal lines in Ireland which could balance the contending forces and extricate the party from the deteriorating situation. Garvin was himself one of the 'restless young men'. He became aware much earlier than most Conservatives of the possibility that imperialism and Ulster Unionism might emerge as conflicting causes. In early 1909 he told St Loe Strachey, the editor of the *Spectator*, that the *Observer* would not fight from the 'narrower Ulster point of view . . . and identify it with mere class interests and sectarian rancour. The question of imperial integrity and power is and always has been decisive for me'.[35] Moreover, Garvin was acutely aware of the danger of political collapse resulting from the divisions in the power bloc manifested in 1910. On the one hand he feared that if the IPP were allowed to exploit those divisions then other forces would follow in their wake. The result might unleash such demons as the disestablishment of the Welsh Church and a Right to Work Bill. He thus gave every support to the 1910 inter-party conference on Ireland, hoping that it would unite the 'responsible statesmen' against the 'irresponsible, almost anarchic elements' like the socialists and the Irish.[36] In this context Garvin became increasingly fearful of the effects of Carsonite populism. In February 1911, he warned that if civil war ensued in Ireland it would have the 'almost inevitable reflex of Labour Anarchy in Britain'. The following September he said that Carson provided an 'example of violence to every subversive movement of the future'.[37] Thus for Garvin the general threat of disorder arising from Ulster Unionist militancy was simply too great a risk. The reason for this – in his mind – was the challenge which might be posed by the socialist forces on both sides of the Irish sea.

On the Liberal side, the Lloyd George/Churchill wing shared the conviction of Unionists such as Garvin that Ireland should not force its way on to the centre of the political stage. To Lloyd George Ireland was 'a small chip on the imperial board', yet its domination of the political arena was obstructing the various attempts to hold back the challenge of labour.[38] This explains why Liberal radicals like Lloyd George and Churchill – whose political strategies were most directly threatened by the socialists – were most interested in a coalition. Lloyd George's comments on Ireland in his 'Criccieth memorandum' of 1910 gave first formal expression to this view. Here Ireland was only broached in a brief footnote under the general rubric of imperial affairs, as an issue which should not need to excite party controversy. This marks the origins of a recognizably modern bourgeois position on Ireland. Here in embryo is the 'bipartisan approach' so consistently invoked in the present crisis. And here also is the associated analysis, pitting British 'moderation' against the 'extremists of both sides': 'The advantages of a non-party treatment of this vexed problem are obvious. Parties might deal with it without being subject to the embarrassing dictation of extreme partisans whether from Nationalist or Orangeman.'[39] Lloyd George told F. E. Smith in October 1913 that the differences between the parties – on Home Rule especially – were 'very artifical', not touching the 'realities'.[40] And as he explained to assembled visitors at Criccieth in September, Ireland should be treated as a subsidiary of imperial defence, in which the primary concern was the 'German menace'.

The implication of the Lloyd George approach was some form of special treatment for Ulster, breaking the pledge to the IPP. As early as April 1910, Lloyd George and Churchill expressed their hostility to Redmond at a Cabinet meeting. This was all the more significant because they were the only Liberals who were seriously concerned about the Ulster problem during the preparation of the Home Rule Bill. And it was Lloyd George and Churchill who first proposed partition in Cabinet in February 1912.

Lloyd George's project bore some similarity to the strategy of the Liberal imperialists, for whom the former Liberal Prime Minister Lord Rosebery played the role of prospective 'caesar'. Like Lloyd George, the Liberal imperialists originated as radicals and land reformers in the 1880s. Their emergence as a distinctively *imperialist* tendency came about in the wake of the defeat of the second Home Rule Bill. They sought to replace Home Rule with imperialism as the organizing principle by which to hold together the Liberal party:

A new Liberal approach to the Irish question was regarded by Liberal Imperialists as essential. Their strategy of party reconstruction depended on substantial Liberal

Unionist defections, and Ireland was an obvious barrier to these. The success of social reform depended on the availability of parliamentary time for legislation, and in 1892–5 the Irish question had severely restricted this. The Liberal Imperialists saw the Gladstonian form of Home Rule as a principal agent in causing an increase in inter-party bitterness and hence in breaking up the politics of the centre which they favoured.[41]

However, the Limps suffered from an irreconcilable internal division between Rosebery on the one hand, and Asquith, Grey and Haldane on the other. Rosebery's policy of the 'clean slate' meant erasing Home Rule altogether from Liberal policy. The more tactical policy of the Asquith/Grey/Haldane group favoured the 'step by step' approach.

Lloyd George was most hopeful of a positive response to his proposal for a 'coalitionist' solution to Ireland from the tariff reformers, especially Garvin and Milner. The latter were by no means committed to a traditionalist Unionist position and they were even prepared to countenance an attempt to draw the IPP into an anti-socialist bloc. Garvin was playing a characteristically complex game. He thought that if the Limps could be inveigled into confounding Redmond and the IPP then the Conservatives could move in and 'exchange views' with the IPP and win their support for tariff reform and other issues. Milner attempted to persuade Balfour that some concession of 'provincial' rather than 'national' Home Rule might ensure some such alliance. He believed the IPP to be 'a conservative force in United Kingdom politics standing for Tariff and private property – as against collectivism'.[42] This was hardly a vain hope in the light of the IPP's hostility to the budget and the popularity this stance had won in Ireland. This, too, pointed towards a federalist solution in the context of a federal reorganization of the whole of the United Kingdom.

Behind the scenes in the inter-party negotiations, the Round Table group of imperialists played a key organizational role. This set of young and ambitious intellectuals, particularly F. S. Oliver, advocated active imperial regeneration. They were concerned primarily with the issue of imperial union, proposing a separate Imperial Parliament, above day-to-day party conflict and without the normal congestion of parliamentary business. This would concentrate exclusively on imperial affairs and eventually include representatives from the Dominions. Some members of the Round Table, in particular Milner, were keen that Unionism should not be sacrificed in this bid to realize a 'greater' imperialism. Others, especially Oliver, took the view that the primary cause of empire could only be advanced by an undivided ruling bloc at Westminster. They implied that certain limited concessions on Home Rule would in the long-run maintain the fundamental unity of the United Kingdom and empire.

In September 1910 Oliver wrote to Balfour arguing in true caesarist style that the inter-party Constitutional Conference was 'the natural safety valve of popular government'. He recommended that the Unionists could 'honourably surrender [on some measure of Home Rule] . . . for the sake of ending a long and dangerous controversy, and also for the sake of bringing the hope of Imperial Union a stage nearer'.[43] The Round Table advocates of federalism were unable to shift the Unionist leadership in 1910. Yet they kept pressing as the crisis over the Home Rule Bill deepened, advocating a 'non-party' national convention to resolve the Irish issue and prevent party conflict breaking out into open warfare. However it was not until the war, when they were drawn into the Lloyd George administration, that they were able to make an impact on practical affairs. Yet their influence before 1914 should not be underestimated. Oliver's 'Home Rule All Round' position found support among some of the younger tariff reformers, and Lloyd George elaborated some of the Criccieth proposals with a view to winning the federalists in the Conservative Party. By 1912 Churchill had become convinced by the Round Table and both he and Lloyd George pressed – to little avail – for a federalist position during the preparation of the Home Rule Bill. By early 1914, Lloyd George had reached preliminary agreement on a federal scheme with Churchill, Garvin, Oliver and Waldorf Astor.

Both the populist and cross-party or caesarist strategies were responses to the crisis of 1910. Both were advocated by imperialists, and both contained, to varying degrees, elements of social-imperialism. Both were extra-parliamentary in their primary form. These common aspects help to explain two apparent paradoxes. First, the Round Table group contained within it proponents of both coalitionism and populism, and elements of each subsequently came together in the Lloyd George coalition. Second, certain figures vacillated between the two positions – in particular Milner and F. E. Smith. Both the populist and coalitionist bids are best understood as responses to the growing appreciation by the politicians that the existing party boundaries were no longer adequate.

The coalitionist strategy of compromise created its own difficulties. The cross-party alignments around Lloyd George, Smith and Churchill were blocked by the adherence of the party leaderships to traditional party positions. This led to the failure of Lloyd George's 1910 bid: while the Unionists were prepared to concede Commons control on money issues (the budget), they were not prepared to concede on constitutional issues, especially Home Rule. In the crisis of 1910 and its aftermath the pressures for compromise were too weak to allow a full cross-party solution. Asquith, as Liberal leader, resisted concessions till the last possible moment, while Bonar Law had to take account of the strength of the Southern Unionists who were implacably opposed to partition.

In the summer of 1914 the divisions inside the power bloc were once more as severe as in 1910 and the consequences were regarded as extremely dangerous. As Asquith informed the Cabinet in July: 'The issues so far [are] reaching not only civil war, but interests in India, [the] industrial world and throughout [the] empire might be broken up by catastrophe in Ireland.'[44]

Lionel Curtis, in a report written in 1917 recalled the pre-war situation in even more graphic terms:

The naked fact is that the country, the mother of free institutions, was four years ago on the brink of civil war. And if the Germans had not saved us the struggle would have raged not only between Catholic and Protestant Ireland but throughout Great Britain between class and class. The Irish difficulty would have been, not the cause, but only the occasion of conflict.[45]

Curtis was correct to describe Ireland as 'occasion', not 'cause'. As Churchill put it, the issues involved in Ireland in the summer of 1914 were in themselves 'inconceivably petty'. Yet 'the political future of Great Britain turned upon the disposition of clusters of humble parishes'[46] in Tyrone and Fermanagh.

War and the triumph of caesarism

The situation in 1914 was of the sort described by Gramsci 'in which the forces in conflict balance each other in a catastrophic manner' and make a caesarist intervention possible. But it was only the outbreak of war – and Asquith's handling of it – that provided the necessary change in the wider conjuncture to allow a 'third force' to 'intervene from outside' and 'subjugate' what was left of the party system. The Lloyd George coalition represented just such a 'third force', although it did not come completely 'from outside'. For coalitions, Gramsci pointed out, are only the first stage of caesarism. The formation of a 'single united party', as canvassed in the later days of Lloyd George's rule, would have completed the project. As it was, however, 'party' still had its sway, albeit suppressed in a coalition which, from December 1916 under Lloyd George's command, was a Conservative-dominated affair.

Two questions arise. First, given the relative subjugation of party – the biggest single obstacle to the resolution of the Irish question before the war – why was the 1921 'solution', treaty and partition, so long in coming? And second, given the balance of forces inside the coalition, why did such a dramatic rift open up between British Conservatives and their former Ulster Unionist allies?

Curtis was close to the mark when he claimed that the war had saved the British state. When the very survival of British imperialism was at stake, civil war over the 'inconceivably petty' issues involved in the Irish question could hardly be countenanced. However the Easter Rising came to exploit the Anglo-German antagonism at its most explosive.

It was through the prism of this conflict that the Rising was represented in Britain – essentially as a German plot. The effect of this equation, 'advanced nationalism' equals German imperialism, was the repression which in turn provoked the recomposition and expansion of Sinn Fein.

The Rising precipitated the final collapse of British hegemony in Ireland. As Asquith announced in May: 'The Government has come to the conclusion that the system under which Ireland has been governed has completely broken down'.[47] Asquith and others saw the need to construct a local power centre in the form of 'devolved government'. This in turn implied an orientation by the British state, not towards winning agreement between the parties in Britain, but towards forging a 'consensus' among the *Irish* political forces. Asquith continued his statement:

The only satisfactory alternative, in . . . [the Government's] judgment, is the creation, at the earliest possible moment, of an Irish Government responsible to the Irish people. The Government has determined, therefore, to address itself forthwith to the task of endeavouring to make such arrangements as will enable it, by agreement between different parties in Ireland, to put the Government of Ireland Act into operation at the earliest practicable moment.

The urgent tone of this statement – 'earliest possible moment . . . forthwith . . . earliest practicable moment' – stands in stark contrast to the discussions of the Home Rule Bill in 1911.

What had changed? First, a rebellion in Britain's backyard, instigated, so it seemed, by Germany, was a serious threat to the successful prosecution of the war effort. Second, the collapse of British hegemony in Ireland had to be stemmed. Third, the Easter Rising and the events which it set in train introduced a new inter-imperialist contradiction between Britain and America. This new conjuncture provided the conditions for the emergence and realization of the 'non-party' solution first advocated by Lloyd George in 1910. This solution aimed to avoid the 'embarrassing dictation of extreme partisans whether . . . Nationalist or Orangeman'.

The Irish Convention of 1917–18 marked the realization of a 'bipartisan policy' on Ireland. But it also marked the limit of consensual 'political initiatives'. The Convention recognized the continuing decline of British hegemony in that the whole emphasis now rested on the achievement of 'substantial agreement' among representatives of 'all leading interests, classes, creeds and phases of thought in Ireland'. The arbitrating role of the British state was much reduced.[48] The idea for the Convention was, as McDowell points out, 'a last minute addendum' to a new proposal which Lloyd George had conceived.[49] Lloyd George himself described it as 'a last resort'.[50] It is generally believed that the Convention was set up primarily as a result of American pressure. But, once more, hopes for a speedy resolution soon ran aground.

The drift to coercion became inevitable after the Convention failed to reach 'substantial agreement', especially as the exigencies of the war effort threatened conscription in Ireland. Conscription was a major factor in the eclipse of the IPP by Sinn Fein, a shift which had already been evident from the early days of the Convention.

The rift between the British and Ulster Unionists

A growing split between Conservatism and its former Ulster allies also became evident during the Convention. The Easter Rising had sharpened this contradiction. In May 1915 Garvin argued 'Home Rule will undoubtedly conduce to the greater moral integrity and practical security of the United Kingdom and to the strength and welfare of the Empire as a whole.'[51] Just so. Before the war the Ulster Unionist position had seemed to imperialists in Britain as a cause which symbolized their own aspirations. However the outbreak of war, the entry of the United States, and the breakdown of British hegemony in the south had completely turned the tables.

The Ulster Unionists increasingly appeared to British Unionists to be pursuing a 'sectional' demand. They seemed to be prepared to undermine the greater imperial interest by refusing to accommodate the new balance of forces in the south and in the wider empire. A realignment was already becoming evident in the failure of Sir Edward Carson's revolt against Bonar Law's leadership of the Unionist Party in November 1916, and in Bonar Law's eventual prominence over Carson in the Lloyd George coalition.

By 1918 a number of influential Conservatives – including Austen Chamberlain – supported a federal solution, which received a new, if temporary, lease of life. Leo Amery, who before the war had been an instigator of the British Covenant, now argued that a bill 'definitely dividing Ireland in two would be misunderstood abroad and is fundamentally unacceptable to Irish national sentiment'.[52] The following year, in response to Carson's threat once more to 'call out the Ulster Unionists', one Conservative MP went so far as to say: 'every man who cares for his empire should dissociate himself from that Ulster view'.[53]

Most of the press opposed the Government of Ireland Bill of 1920 which proposed the establishment of two states in Ireland. *The Times* detected 'the selfishness of big business interests' behind the acceptance of the bill by the Ulster Unionists.[54] In November 1921 the *Birmingham Post* noted: 'Whether we like it or not, Ireland has become the centre of gravity in our relations not only with other members of the Empire, but with the whole English-speaking world.' It concluded that if Ulster resisted a settlement issuing from the negotiations with Sinn Fein 'she will do the greatest disservice it is possible to imagine to the Empire she professes to love'.[55] The *Daily Express* went further, claiming that Ulster would be 'guilty of the greatest political crime in history'.[56] This is worth emphasizing because nationalist historians have consistently reduced the relations of this particular moment to the simple opposition of 'British imperialism' to the 'Irish nation'. Thus Farrell tells us bluntly: 'The [Ulster] Unionists had the fullest backing from the Conservative Party and the British military establishment.'[57] But this was not the case, either in the pre-war period, or afterwards when the shift in Conservative opinion assumed decisive importance. The autonomy of Ulster Unionism from British Conservatism is amply demonstrated in the failure of successive efforts by the coalition to get the Ulster Unionists to accept some form of all-Ireland settlement.

The American connection

American influence was of crucial importance in producing a sense of urgency inside the power bloc that a solution had to be found. Again it was the Easter Rising, and particularly the subsequent repression which began to create a real crisis. In May 1916 the British Ambassador in Washington wrote to Lord Grey, the Foreign Secretary, saying:

the events in Ireland are exciting a great deal of hostile comment in the American press. . . . It is true that the rebellion has miserably failed. But the military executions which have been its consequence have raised the victims to the status of martyrs . . . the sorrows of Ireland now fill the front page.[58]

In October, Reginald McKenna, the Chancellor of the Exchequer, warned the Cabinet what financial dependence on America meant:

If things go on as at present, I venture to say with certainty that by next June or earlier the President of the American Republic will be in a position, if he so wishes, to dictate his own terms to us.[59]

But it was Britain's military dependence on the United States that really forced the government to take seriously American concern about Ireland. In January 1917 President Wilson addressed Congress on the principles of American participation in the war. In effect the US government sought a new inter-imperialist arrangement in return for involvement in Europe. The concession it demanded in return for US intervention was support for the principle of the right of nations to self-determination. This was potentially embarrassing to the allies who retained colonial empires even though they were supposedly fighting in defence of Belgium and the rights of 'small nations'. As Wilson told Congress, 'every people should be left free to determine its own polity, its own way of development, unhindered, unthreatened, unafraid, the little along with the great and powerful'.[60] Thus in April 1917, when America entered the war, Wilson wrote to the American ambassador in London saying:

only one circumstance now appears to stand in the way of perfect co-operation with Great Britain. All Americans, who are not immediately connected with Germany by blood ties, find their one difficulty in the failure of Great Britain so far to establish a satisfactory form of self-government in Ireland. In the recent debates in Congress on the War Resolution, this sentiment was especially manifest. . . . If the American people were once convinced that there was a likelihood that the Irish question would soon be settled, great enthusiasm and satisfaction would result and it would also strengthen the co-operation would we are now about to organize between the United States and Great Britain. Say this in unofficial terms to Mr. Lloyd George but impress upon him its great significance.[61]

And later Wilson feared that conscription would 'accentuate the whole Irish and Catholic intrigue which has gone hand in hand in some quarters in the country with German intrigue'.[62] The American connection played a signifi-cant role in 1921 in the decision to negotiate with Sinn Fein. Even such a hard-liner as Churchill was swayed. Arguing for a truce in cabinet in May that year, he said: 'we are getting an odious reputation; poisoning our rela-tions with the United States'.[63] And, speaking in Dundee in September, while describing negotiations with Sinn Fein as 'repugnant', he nevertheless argued that

we must cheer ourselves by remembering that a lasting settlement with Ireland would not only be a blessing in itself but with it would also be removed the greatest obstacle to Anglo-American unity and that far across the ocean we should reap a harvest sown in the Emerald Isle.[64]

'Bolshevism', anti-colonialism and coercion

After the First World War British Unionists took up an increasingly coercive stance against Irish republicanism. The coalition position in the election of December 1918 was that while Home Rule – possibly on a federal basis – was an ultimate solution, law and order had first to be restored. Thus began the pursuit of the chimera of the military solution.

The intransigence of the British government in the face of the rise of Sinn Fein derived from a perception of an international threat from Bolshevism and anti-colonialism. Sinn Fein thus quickly acquired all the connotations of 'Bolshevism'. The Lloyd George coalition was obsessed by Bolshevism. As Lloyd George put it to the Peace Conference: 'In a short time we might have three-quarters of Europe converted to Bolshevism'. Britain, he said, might find itself standing alone 'for social order and common sense against anarchy'.[65]

In the van of anti-Bolshevism was Carson who became transfixed by an alleged 'Sinn Fein-Bolshevik conspiracy'. In 1918, in an attempt to rally working-class opposition to this danger, he set up the Ulster Unionist Labour Association, while in Britain he headed the British Empire Union. Formed by a group of Conservative peers, the Union proudly described itself as 'strictly non-party'.[66] In 1920 the BEU promoted a book called *Red Terror and Green* by one Richard Dawson, who claimed:

While Sinn Fein was thus preparing for armed rebellion in anticipation of a great labour upheaval in Great Britain, the left wing of the Republican party was busily engaged in cementing the Bolshevik alliance at Berne, promoting British industrial unrest through its agents in England and Scotland, and promoting serious labour troubles in Belfast, both as an embarrassment to the Irish government and as an encouragement to the revolutionaries on the other side of the Channel.[67]

Although Carson was by this stage isolated from the political mainstream on this issue, Lloyd George nevertheless sympathized with his frustrations. Thus after Carson's resignation Lloyd George wrote to him complaining of Dublin Castle's failure to 'suppress these Bolsheviks'.[68]

The identification of Sinn Fein with anti-colonialism was a consistent theme in Cabinet discussions of Ireland during the war of independence. In the more paranoid versions, as in the War Office's response to the defence cuts imposed by the 'Geddes axe', Sinn Fein was perceived as part of a 'world-wide conspiracy fomented by all the elements most hostile to British interests – Sinn Feiners and Socialists at our own doors, Russian Bolsheviks, Turkish and Egyptian Nationalists, and Indian Seditionists.'[69]

In this context Ireland was seen as of central strategic significance. If Ireland were 'lost', so the theory went, then it would be only the first 'domino' to fall. As Lloyd George expressed it in the Cabinet in September 1921:

supposing we gave it to them. It will lower the prestige and dignity of this country and reduce British authority to a low point in Ireland itself. It will give the impression that we have lost grip, that the Empire has no further force and will have an effect on India and throughout Europe.[70]

The centrifugal tendencies in the empire were becoming all too clear. Anti-British movements were growing month by month. Persia was abandoned and various degrees of self-government granted to Egypt, Transjordan and Iraq. The pressures towards imperial fragmentation proved difficult to stem, partly because of the force and confidence of many of the anti-colonial movements themselves. In addition British military forces were badly over-stretched and popular opinion at home imposed definite limits on the government's ability to pursue repression overseas.

Fears of disintegration of the empire were also related to the balance of forces among the imperialist powers. British military chiefs were afraid that an independent Ireland could become a base or ally for a hostile power. As the Chief of the Imperial General Staff, Wilson, observed in March 1921: 'a hostile Ireland . . . is just as fatal to the continued existence of the British Empire as a hostile England was, is, and will be to the growth and existence of a German Empire'.[71]

The collapse – conciliation and extrication

If the government's perception of the wider international conjuncture militated in favour of coercion in Ireland, the broader impact of the coalition strategy came to place increasing constraints on its room for manoeuvre. In July 1920, Thomas Jones, the Assistant Cabinet Secretary, argued that Churchill's policy was 'disastrous because of its repercussions at home'. 'Violent opposition' would result if repression were pursued without restraint or any offer to compromise with Sinn Fein. And he noted significantly: 'Throughout the consideration of policy the industrial situation here must be borne in mind.'[72] In the same month a special TUC conference called to deal with the munitions strike in Ireland – the Irish railwaymen were NUR members – passed a resolution condemning the military occupation.

Fears of popular resistance to military adventures, and the government's concern to present the conflict as one of 'law and order' led to a military strategy which Lloyd George called 'police war'. To assuage critics at home and abroad the police – including the Black and Tans – were placed in the forefront, rather than the army.

But this strategy ultimately rebounded, for Black and Tan atrocities were a key issue on which opposition in Britain began to mobilize. From the time of the Balbriggan reprisal in September 1920, domestic opposition broadened beyond Asquithian Liberal and Labour circles, as the coalition bloc began to weaken. The Conservative press articulated a growing concern. Four Conservative MPs crossed the floor in February 1921. The 'Peace with Ireland Council' drew together such diverse figures as the Bishops of Winchester and Lichfield, Ramsay MacDonald, Sir John Simon, Oswald Mosley and Cavendish-Bentinck (two of the Conservative dissidents), the Webbs, Shaw, Hobhouse, and other figures from the liberal establishment. *The Times* attacked reprisals on the basis that the government were 'trustees' of the 'reputation of England', a responsibility which the government had 'defiled'.[73] And, it argued later:

Deeds have unquestionably been done by them in Ireland which have lastingly disgraced the name of Britain in that country. British processes of justice which for centuries have commanded the admiration of the world have been supplanted by those of lynch law.[74]

Eventually *The Times* came to describe government policy as 'utterly irreconcilable with the ideals of this Christian country'.[75]

In January 1921 a Parliamentary Labour Party commission toured Ireland, reporting in the same month:

every institution of which we as British citizens are so proud – a free press, freedom of speech, liberty of the subject and trial by jury – are things of the past in a large part of Ireland, and rule by military force, which we sought to destroy when resorted to by Germany is an established fact in South and South-West Ireland today. These facts are fatal to our reputation for national good faith, and cannot fail to prejudice our national standing in the eyes of our Self-Governing Dominions and the Dependencies.[76]

The Labour Commission of Enquiry led to a massive campaign; five hundred meetings were organized within the month, and twenty thousand copies of the report were sold.

The opposition to the coalition's Irish policy was symptomatic of the fragmentation of the coalition bloc in the face of two alternative positions. It was faced on the one hand with calls for the renewal of populist diehardism, and on the other with demands for a *new* caesarist or coalitionist arrangement.

One bid to make concessions to the government's liberal critics and reconstruct the coalition as a new government of 'national unity', ditching on the way those most deeply committed to military victory, came from Robert Cecil. He recognized, as did the coalition leaders, that 'the war has shattered the prestige of the European governing classes'.[77] Yet while the coalitionists concluded that what was needed was a united front against the socialist 'threat', Cecil drew the opposite conclusion. He feared that the government's tendency to 'incite the possessing classes to band themselves together under their leadership for a fight against Labour'[78] involved, like the Tariff Reform League, the narrow pursuit of the corporate economic interests of capital at the expense of the overall hegemony of the power bloc: 'I was brought up to think that a class war, whether the class attacked be landowners or Labour, is the most insidious form of national disintegration.'[79] So the 'aristocratic' old guard's distance from the dominant bourgeois fractions allowed it to pursue an apparently more cohesive 'national' strategy. It could still play a historic role in a new coalition including 'some of the old landowning Tories' and 'some of the best of the Liberal and Labour people' under Grey's leadership.[80] Cecil's position on Ireland followed directly from this political assessment. Reprisals, he argued, would have a 'disastrous . . . effect . . . on revolutionaries in England and . . . other parts of the Empire'.[81] Cecil won the support of former Conservative Party chairman, Steel-Maitland, of Cavendish-Bentinck, and, at different times, of the new Lords Rothermere and Northcliffe. Cecil also made overtures to Arthur Henderson in the hope of incorporating 'responsible' Labour representatives in this new bloc. In June 1921 Cecil's coalition bid took shape in discussions with Grey, and various prominent Asquithians gave their support. By July Asquith believed it was only a matter of days before it would get off the ground. But this attempt to build a new coalition was blocked by the eventual success of the treaty negotiations. However, as a dissident faction inside the Conservative Party, the Cecil wing was to contribute, along with some diehards, to the return to party politics in 1922.

By 1921 it was increasingly realized within the coalition that it would be impossible ever to achieve a clear military victory over the IRA. This was evident in terms of the military balance of forces. But behind the military matters lay the political questions. Concerns about sending more forces to Ireland were activated by fears for the security of the empire and the government's ability to resist working-class struggles in Britain.

At the end of 1919 the public were 'sick and tired of Ireland', according to Riddell. This was an obstacle to victory over the IRA (which, given the measure of repression involved, would have required at least a modicum of popular legitimacy at home). It was also equally unlikely to lead to a mass oppositional movement. Thus in June 1921 Macready had warned that full martial law could only be carried through on the basis that 'Great Britain should be behind them, not only in passive acceptance but also in active approval'.[82] These harsh political and military realities all pointed in one direction – towards negotiation with Sinn Fein, despite the resistance this would invoke from the Unionist diehards.

The diehards continued the populist thrust of the pre-war revolt, taking the view that 'The people's "better nature" wanted national solidarity and patriotic endeavour of the sort Carson had given Ulster.'[83] For the diehards 'civilization' had to be defended against 'barbarism'. But for them it wasn't the reprisals which were 'barbaric' – it was Sinn Fein. The diehard faction moved a motion of censure at the 1921 Tory conference. But their assault on the Conservative coalitionists was unsuccessful, because their position implied a renewal of war in Ireland, which by this date had fallen outside the realm of practical politics. Nevertheless, Ireland did bring new adherents into the diehard camp. For example, Salisbury claimed in November that Bonar Law had expressed 'fury' with the government for 'throwing over Ulster'.[84] At the conference itself, the leadership won its position only because Austen Chamberlain made it an issue of confidence, and by renewed pledges to Ulster.

The final solution

Lloyd George's July 1921 proposals to De Valera, who negotiated for the Irish, represented the most developed government policy on Ireland in this period. He proposed Dominion Home Rule, qualified by naval facilities, rights of recruiting, restrictions on the size of Irish armed forces, free trade, and a financial contribution to the war debt. The prevalence of 'security' concerns is notable. This demonstrates the significance, in the ideology of the ruling bloc, of the wider imperial ramifications.

Thus while the question of Ulster was of only tactical importance in the treaty negotiations, the oath of allegiance to the monarchy was central. A British note to the Irish delegation explained the significance of the crown: 'the crown is the symbol of all that keeps the nations of the Empire together. It is the keystone of the arch in law as well as in sentiment'.[85] The acceptance of Dominion status, however qualified, constituted a recognition, even among imperialists, of the centrifugal tendencies in the empire. Through Curtis's role as secretary to the British delegation, and the role of his advisers Philip Kerr and Edward Grigg as secretaries to Lloyd George at this time, the

Round Table group had direct access to government. Having come to accept in principle limited self-government for India, and the formal equality of Britain and the Dominions, they were now prepared to concede Dominion status for Ireland. This acceptance of the need for Westminster to extricate itself from Ireland was clearly related to the collapse of British hegemony in Ireland. It was also connected to the more long-standing concern about the effects of the Irish question in preventing a recomposition of the ruling bloc in Britain. After all, the power bloc had more urgent considerations. As Cowling comments:

With the signature of the Irish Treaty, the leaders of the Coalition thought they could now talk chiefly about the thing that interested them most. Ireland, it is clear, interested none of them. By the time the treaty was signed, they all hoped that Craig would give in or go away or make some other unspecified disappearance as a major problem. What they wanted to discuss was resistance to Socialism.[86]

It also became increasingly apparent that only a local ruling bloc in the south would be able to defeat the republicans. As Birkenhead (as F. E. Smith was now titled) told the Lords in the debate on the ratification of the treaty:

you have in Southern Ireland men who have hitherto been organized against us now . . . honestly attempting to . . . put down this movement in the South of Ireland . . . I would far rather that they were undertaking the task than that we were.[87]

This desire for a degree of autonomy in relation to the Irish situation led to a permissive attitude to Irish unification. Thus the 1920 Government of Ireland Act had set up two symmetrical local states in Ireland – that in the south, of course, never functioning. And the significance of the 'reserved' powers defined in the act was that these services were to be placed under the auspices of a Council of Ireland with a view to transferring them to an all-Ireland Parliament should the latter materialize out of the experience of co-operation.[88] Transfer of these powers would reduce the extent of British responsibility.

But the attitude to unification was only permissive; it was not a positive objective as such. For the latter would have required *greater* British intervention, not less, with the danger of the spillover effects on British politics which the government did all it could to avoid. This was made clear by Lloyd George during the treaty negotiations. In an exasperated reply to a charge by Arthur Griffith of the Irish delegation that Britain was supporting the Unionists in Ireland, he said:

We are only behind them to this extent that we cannot allow civil war to take place at our doors which would embroil our own people. It would be bad enough if we could bring down a fire curtain between us. There is nothing we would like better than that they should unite with you.[89]

The proposals which Lloyd George had put to De Valera in July demonstrate clearly the two sides of the Lloyd George position:

the settlement must allow for full recognition of the existing powers and privileges of the Parliament of Northern Ireland, which cannot be abrogated except by their own consent. For their part, the British Government entertain an earnest hope that the necessity of harmonious co-operation amongst Irishmen of all classes and creeds will be recognised throughout Ireland, and they will welcome the day when by those means unity is achieved. But no such common action can be secured by force. . . . There can, in fact, be no settlement on terms involving, on the one side or the other, that bitter appeal to bloodshed and violence which all men of goodwill [as against the 'men of violence'] are longing to terminate. The British Government will undertake to give effect, so far as that depends on them, to any terms in this respect on which all Ireland unites. But in no conditions can they consent to any proposals which would kindle civil war in Ireland. Such a war would not touch Ireland alone for partisans would flock to either side from Great Britain, the Empire, and elsewhere, with consequences more devastating to the welfare both of Ireland and the Empire than the conflict to which a truce has been called.[90]

Conclusion

At one level the treaty that was finally negotiated was a triumph for Lloyd George. Yet it also gave a number of concessions to Sinn Fein. Throughout the period from 1910 to 1922 Lloyd George's preferred solution was federalism, which would have maintained the south much more closely within the orbit of empire than eventually occurred. Over and over again, as crisis succeeded crisis, he tried to play the federalist card. Its significance was not primarily in terms of resolving the Irish question, but the role it played in his domestic ambitions. For only the federalist proposal could have hoped to win sufficient Conservative support, ultimately, for fusion between the Lloyd George Liberals and the Conservatives. But time and again federalism was defeated by party resistance from the Unionists. On this issue, more than any other, the coalition remained precisely that – an alliance of distinct parties – rather than the unified social-imperialist political force that Lloyd George sought to construct.

Yet the Irish question stubbornly refused to go away, returning in ever more intractable forms, blocking the process of realignment and throwing up new pressures and new opposition. And in turn, the failure of fusion left the coalition weak in the face of the forces directed against it. Thus Savage claims: 'the decline and fall of Lloyd George can be dated from the signing of the Irish treaty'. And he concludes:

Lloyd George throughout his career tried to play a similar role [to Chamberlain]. His search was for a centrist position in the flux of parties and issues, the hallmark of which would be national patriotism and the requisite social reforms to rejuvenate the nation. The centre party of Lloyd George's ambitions would be free from the pacifist internationalism of radicals and labour, the centrifugal force of Irish nationalism and the outdated attitudes associated with the aristocratic tradition. Above all it would be free from the ideologies which characterised all three. A federal solution to the Irish question was the only one which fitted well with these larger political designs, but . . . it was one which was wholly dependent upon the creation of this centre political force. The failure of the one consistently spelt the failure of the other.[91]

Yet however inadequate the solution was to be from this wider standpoint of bourgeois politics, the Lloyd George treaty proposals have a decisively modern, 'bi-partisan' ring. Or to put it the other way round, the modern character of Lloyd George's position reflects the failure of the British state to develop any new strategic persectives from the 1920s until the 1960s. At one level this can be understood in the durability of a fatalistic common sense about Ireland as the locus of eternal and unchangeable tribal or religious disputations.

Historically decisive however was the relationship established between Westminster and the north in the years immediately following partition. That relationship, based on the principle of minimization of British intervention, furnished the fire-curtain to 'insulate' the state in Britain from the combustible material across the water.[92] That 'insulation' did not, however, characterize only the relations between the two states. Frozen, too, was the thinking of those who still seek an alternative to bi-partisanship in a bid to return to the 'unfinished business' of the 1920s.

Notes and references

1   Quoted in R. J. Scally, *The Origins of the Lloyd George Coalition* (Princeton University Press 1975), pp. 188–9.
2   Quoted in N. Mansergh, *The Irish Question, 1840–1921* (Allen and Unwin 1975), p. 195.
3   Quoted in G. Dangerfield, *The Damnable Question* (Constable 1977), p. 55.
4   Quoted in W. L. Arnstein, 'Edwardian politics: turbulent spring or Indian summer?', in A. O'Day (ed.), *The Edwardian Age* (Macmillan 1979), p. 68.
5   Quoted in P. Jalland, *The Liberals and Ireland* (Harvester 1980), p. 123.
6   Quoted in H. V. Emy, *Liberals, Radicals and Social Politics* (Cambridge University Press 1973), p. 230.
7   Quoted in Jalland, p. 257.
8   Quoted in R. Douglas, *The History of the Liberal Party* (Sidgwick and Jackson 1971), p. 60.
9   J. Ramsden, *The Age of Balfour and Baldwin* (Longman 1978), p. 41.
10   J. Stubbs, 'The impact of the Great War on the Conservative Party', in G. Peele and C. Cook (eds.), *The Politics of Reappraisal* (Macmillan 1975), p. 16.
11   P. Buckland, *Ulster Unionism and the Origins of Northern Ireland* (Gill and Macmillan 1973), pp. 41–2.
12   G. D. Searle, 'Critics of Edwardian society', in O'Day.
13   Quoted in G. D. Phillips, *The Diehards* (Harvard University Press 1979), p. 137.
14   Quoted in ibid., p. 145.
15   Quoted in Mansergh, p. 220.

16   Quoted in R. Kee, *The Bold Fenian Men* (Quartet 1976), pp. 172–3.
17   Quoted in Jalland, pp. 57 and 62.
18   Quoted in Dangerfield, *The Strange Death of Liberal England* (Constable 1936), p. 102.
19   Quoted in Jalland, p. 218.
20   P. Gibbon, *The Origins of Ulster Unionism* (Manchester University Press 1975), pp. 136–7.
21   Quoted in A. T. Q. Stewart, *The Ulster Crisis* (Faber and Faber 1967), p. 62.
22   Quoted in ibid., p. 223.
23   M. Blanch, 'Imperialism, nationalism and organized youth', in J. Clarke, C. Critcher and R. Johnson (eds.), *Working Class Culture* (Hutchinson 1979), p. 117.
24   Quoted in Ramsden, p. 93.
25   A. Gamble, *The Conservative Nation* (Routledge and Kegan Paul 1974), p. 23.
26   Quoted in Jalland, p. 63.
27   Blanch, p. 118.
28   Quoted in Stewart, p. 131.
29   R. Shannon, *The Crisis of Imperialism* (Paladin 1974), p. 235.
30   Quoted in J. R. Fanning, 'The Unionist Party and Ireland, 1906–10', *Irish Historical Studies*, 15 (1966–7), p. 160.
31   Quoted in ibid., p. 161.
32   Quoted in J. D. Fair, *British Interparty Conferences* (Clarendon 1980), p. 80.
33   Quoted in Fanning, p. 164.
34   Quoted in ibid., p. 168.
35   Quoted in P. Kennedy, *The Rise of Anglo-German Antagonism* (Allen and Unwin 1980), p. 387.
36   Quoted in Scally, pp. 179–80.
37   Quoted in ibid., pp. 230 and 236.
38   ibid., p. 241.
39   Quoted in ibid., p. 386.
40   Quoted in ibid., p. 240.
41   H. C. G. Matthew, *The Liberal Imperialists* (Oxford University Press 1973), p. 263.
42   Quoted in Scally, p. 164.
43   Quoted in J. E. Kendle, 'The Round Table movement and "Home Rule all round" ', *The Historical Journal*, 11, no. 2 (1968), p. 341.
44   Quoted in Jalland, p. 253.
45   Quoted in Scally, p. 350.
46   Quoted in Mansergh, p. 294.
47   Quoted in F. Gallagher, *The Indivisible Island* (Gollancz 1957), p. 111.
48   Quoted in R. B. McDowell, *The Irish Convention* (Routledge and Kegan Paul 1970), p. 77.
49   ibid., p. 76.
50   Quoted in ibid., p. 76.
51   Quoted in D. G. Boyce, *Englishmen and Irish Troubles* (Cape 1972), p. 33.
52   Quoted in Boyce, 'British Conservative opinion, the Ulster Question, and the partition of Ireland, 1912–21', *Irish Historical Studies*, 17 (1970–1), p. 96.
53   Quoted in ibid., p. 98.

54 Quoted in Boyce, *Englishmen*, p. 113.
55 Quoted in ibid., p. 162.
56 Quoted in Buckland, *A History of Northern Ireland* (Gill and Macmillan 1981), p. 38.
57 M. Farrell, *The Orange State* (Pluto Press 1976), p. 19.
58 Quoted in Dangerfield, *Damnable Question*, p. 224.
59 Quoted in Scally, p. 344.
60 Quoted in D. Macardle, *The Irish Republic* (Gollancz 1938), p. 215.
61 Quoted in Mansergh, p. 299.
62 Quoted and E. M. Carroll, *American Opinion and the Irish Question* (Gill and Macmillan), p. 108.
63 T. Jones, *Whitehall Diary, vol. III: Ireland*, ed. K. Middlemas (Oxford University Press 1971), p. 69.
64 Quoted in Macardle, pp. 541–2.
65 Quoted in K. O. Morgan, *Consensus and Disunity: The Lloyd George coalition government* (Clarendon 1979), pp. 77–8.
66 BEU policy declaration, quoted in H. Patterson, *Class Conflict and Sectarianism* (Blackstaff, Belfast 1980), p. 127.
67 Quoted in ibid., pp. 126–7.
68 Quoted in Dangerfield, *Damnable Question*, p. 257.
69 Quoted in Morgan, p. 289.
70 Jones, p. 109.
71 Quoted in C. Townshend, *The British Campaign in Ireland, 1919–21* (Oxford University Press 1975), p. 36.
72 Jones, p. 32.
73 Quoted in C. L. Mowat, 'The Irish question in British politics, 1916–22', in T. D. Williams (ed.), *The Irish Struggle* (Routledge and Kegan Paul 1966), p. 148.
74 Quoted in Gallagher, p. 147.
75 Quoted in F. Pakenham, *Peace by Ordeal* (New English Library 1967), p. 59.
76 Quoted in *Ireland Socialist Review*, no. 3 (1978), p. 10.
77 Quoted in M. Cowling, *The Impact of Labour* (Cambridge University Press 1971), p. 61.
78 Quoted in ibid., p. 65.
79 Quoted in ibid., p. 60.
80 Quoted in ibid., p. 64.
81 Quoted in ibid., p. 62.
82 Quoted in Boyce, *Englishmen*, p. 135.
83 Cowling, p. 84.
84 Quoted in Morgan, p. 246.
85 Quoted in Pakenham, p. 157.
86 Cowling, p. 131.
87 Quoted in Macardle, pp. 716 and 694.
88 The act defined three sorts of powers: 1 'excepted' – these were the decisive policy matters to be retained under the control of the imperial parliament relating to the crown and declaration of war; 2 'transferred' – these were the devolved powers; 3 'reserved' – which could be devolved in the future at the imperial parliament's discretion. This tripartite structure is still a standard feature of modern devolution bills.

89   Quoted in Jones, p. 129.
90   Quoted in Macardle, pp. 502–3.
91   D. W. Savage, ' "The Parnell of Wales has become the Chamberlain of England": Lloyd George and the Irish question', *Journal of British Studies*, **12**, no. 1 (1972), pp. 107–8.
92   P. Bew, P. Gibbon and H. Paterson, *The State in Northern Ireland* (Manchester University Press 1979), p. 176.

8   Suffrage and after: feminism in the early twentieth century*

Martin Durham

Feminism was a major factor in the transformation of the state in the period from the 1880s. The women's movement was crucial in activating the disintegration of nineteenth-century liberalism and played an important role in the realignment of British politics during and after the First World War. Even though feminism continued to be expressed most frequently in the language of radical liberalism, as a movement it spanned and cut across the full range of existing political forces. The purpose of this chapter is to outline, if only provisionally, the different trajectories of the suffrage movement during and after the war, and to examine both the relationship between the feminist and socialist movements, and the role of those men who actively supported the enfranchisement of women. The entry of women into the public sphere of the political nation permanently shifted the relations between state and civil society.

At the beginning of the twentieth century women were excluded from the parliamentary franchise, despite a long-standing campaign to reverse this situation by means of private members' bills. In 1903 a radical grouping, the Women's Social and Political Union (WSPU), emerged within the Independent Labour Party. In its earliest public actions members raised the question of women's suffrage at Liberal public meetings and were forcibly removed; such tactics were successful in securing publicity and in attracting converts to the movement. In the years that followed the WSPU grew steadily in numbers and gradually moved away from its socialist roots. Its imaginative methods of direct action ensured that it became the most visible and important section of a renascent suffrage movement. The older constitutionalist suffrage organization, the National Union of Women's Suffrage Societies (NUWSS), also grew in this period. The autocratic style and increasingly militant tactics of WSPU leaders Emmeline and Christabel Pankhurst resulted in several breakaways. The first major split resulted in the formation of the Women's Freedom League (WFL) in 1907. In 1912 leading WSPU figures Emmeline and Frederick Pethick-Lawrence left the

* I would like to thank Lucy Bland, Mary Langan, Caroline Rowan and Bill Schwarz for their comments on drafts of this chapter.

organization, and two years later Sylvia Pankhurst departed to found the East London Federation of the Suffragettes (ELFS). There were numerous other suffrage organizations.

Although the suffrage movement grew in strength and influence the vote for women of 30 and over was not granted until 1918 and was then affected only indirectly by the pressures of the women's movement. A great deal has been written on both the complexities of parliamentary affairs before 1914 and on how these hindered the attainment of women's suffrage.[1] Certain crucial factors stand out. First was the controversy over the extent to which the franchise should be broadened. Both parties were divided on this issue. Leading Conservatives who were sympathetic to women's claim to citizenship were frequently unwilling to press their parliamentary supporters to adopt a similar view. Liberals were concerned that a limited extension of the vote would add several hundred thousand middle-class female votes to the right-wing camp. If there was to be any extension at all, Liberals wanted it to be massive to ensure that men and women of the lower classes would outnumber and outvote the wealthy.

The second obstacle to votes for women was the deep strength of a simple, intransigent anti-suffragism, a view held by prominent members of both major parties. Some Liberals – notably Asquith – were strongly opposed in principle to women's suffrage, while many Conservatives, although able to calculate that the extension of the franchise might strengthen both party and state, believed that women's rightful place in the domestic sphere precluded their political mobilization. Anti-suffragism did not vanish from political life after women had gained the vote.

Socialists and suffrage

The left was divided on the question of votes for women. Over a third of the adult male population was voteless. As a result a bitter dispute raged between the women's suffrage movement and adult suffragists as to how the vote could be gained. Feminists argued that a campaign to win universal adult suffrage immediately was impractical. They argued that a bill to grant the vote to all adults could and would easily be amended to extend voting rights to more males and keep women disenfranchised. Adult suffragists, on the other hand, argued that the extension of the vote on a limited basis would reinforce the power of the upper classes while maintaining the voteless and subordinate position of the mass of working women.

The Labour Party shifted its position over the years.[2] In 1904 the Labour Representation Committee's annual conference decided to support a limited women's suffrage bill. However the following year, and on several subsequent occasions, conference rejected the idea of such a bill and supported instead full adult suffrage. After the 1912 conference, however, relations between the Labour Party and a section of the women's suffrage movement improved. Although adult suffrage was approved by conference yet again, delegates decided that the party would oppose any franchise bill that merely gave the vote to more men and continued to exclude women. As a consequence, the NUWSS set up a special election fighting fund to help Labour candidates in by-elections.

The Labour women's organization, the Women's Labour League (WLL) was, according to Rowbotham, affected by 'the feminist consciousness which was growing outside' but was itself unconcerned with developing a socialist feminism.[3] Accounts of the WLL show the tensions generated in its ranks by the militancy developing outside (and to some extent inside) the organization. At the 1908 WLL conference, a Halifax delegate was criticized by the chairperson for supporting the WSPU despite its non-party stance and its declared opposition to working with the Labour Party. Such tensions led some prominent activists, such as Ethel Snowden and Theresa Billington-Greig, to resign. Others, such as Charlotte Despard, belonged to both the WLL and the WSPU and openly criticized the WLL's opposition to a limited franchise bill.[4]

The Labour left, as represented by the Independent Labour Party (ILP), was more sympathetic to feminism.[5] Since its inception in the 1890s many women had been members of the party. But, as Liddington and Norris remark, 'its support for women's claims could never be relied on without question'.[6] This failure was undoubtedly accentuated by the events of 1907 when leading members of the WSPU resigned from the ILP, preferring instead to wage a straight anti-government campaign. Locally the breach between the ILP and the WSPU was often avoided. Jessie Stephen was involved in the pre-war period in both the ILP and the WSPU in Glasgow, and another ILP suffragette, Hannah Mitchell, gives numerous examples in her autobiography of the ties between socialists and suffragettes in the north of England.[7]

There was no uniform policy among revolutionary socialists, and their attitudes ranged from misogyny to strong support for the suffragette campaign. E. Belfort Bax, a leading member of the main marxist group, the Social Democratic Federation (SDF) was the most extreme opponent of the demands and methods of the WSPU and an active campaigner against women's suffrage. However, marxists generally followed the view of women espoused by Marx, Engels and August Bebel, arguing that women's oppression would end with the widespread entry of women into industry and the full enfranchisement of the working class. Ultimately women's liberation was to be achieved through social revolution. Rather than oppose women's equality, to which they were formally committed, British revolutionaries argued instead against WSPU strategy and its supposed class-interests.

The common belief that the WSPU was pursuing a 'votes for ladies' campaign reinforced the marxist tendency which both underestimated the importance of feminism, and which attempted to explain the existence of social movements solely by economic factors. The SDF opposed any demand for the vote which fell short of universal adult suffrage.

The smaller marxist group, the Socialist Labour Party (SLP), published a pamphlet on women's rights in 1909, which denounced all reform movements as bourgeois and advocated adult suffrage.[8] Some of the material which appeared in the SLP journal, the *Socialist*, was bitterly hostile to the suffragettes. One letter claimed that the 'pseudo-revolutionary movement of the Suffragettes represents the economic interests of the big landowners frightened at Lloyd George finance and of the big capitalists in mortal fear of the labour unrest'.[9] Often this 'class' response to the suffragettes was suffused with blatant sexism.

In both the SDF (which in 1911 became the BSP) and the SLP arguments raged over the issue of women's rights and some members resigned from the BSP because of its anti-feminism. Although both organizations were formally committed to adult suffrage neither showed much energy or verve in struggling to attain it. The BSP took part in some activity for adult suffrage while the SLP kept its distance from practical involvement. Among the dissidents on this issue, one is of particular interest. An SLP member, J. C. Matheson, although at best half-hearted on the question of an autonomous women's movement, did at least recognize that socialists should involve themselves in the women's suffrage movement. While criticizing 'all that is erroneous, all that is bourgeois' in the women's movement, socialists should approach that movement 'not as enemies but as friends and helpers'. Only in this way could they aid 'those elements in the Woman Movement who are struggling to a solid democratic proletarian basis of action'.[10] But even this condescending view never became the majority view of any revolutionary organization. For most of the British revolutionary left, the tide of feminist militancy passed them by.

The general belief of marxists of the time was that the essential contradiction in society was between the working class and the capitalist class. The movement for women's suffrage was commonly seen as a bourgeois movement to which some working-class women had unfortunately been recruited. Socialists, it was argued, should fight for the enfranchisement of all workers, and not get involved in the existing women's suffrage movement. Yet this understanding of the women's movement as an essentially bourgeois movement ignored crucial gender divisions in the working class.

Men and the suffrage movement

One aspect which has received little attention in the history of the suffrage movement is perhaps the most controversial of all: the role of sympathetic men.[11] While women played the leading role in the campaign, men played a significant auxiliary role. One of their most important contributions was the interruption of Liberal speakers at public meetings. The Liberal Party's exclusion of women from their public meetings in 1908 failed to stop WSPU disruptions, not only because suffragettes gained access to the gatherings, but, as Christabel Pankhurst wrote,

To keep the votes-for-women question out of meetings would have necessitated the barring of men as well as women and speaking to empty seats. Many brave men, from that day, risked insult and broken heads, and even their livelihood, by challenging delinquent Liberal leaders on the issue of votes for women.[12]

Interrupting Liberal meetings was only one of the tasks that male supporters carried out. In her memoirs, leading suffragette Annie Kenney writes that they 'were thrown out of meetings, went to prison, some of them were forcibly fed; they helped in our processions, spoke at meetings, worked in our secret organization. . .'.[13] Another suffragette, Mary Richardson, records another function served by sympathetic men for the WSPU:

The Men's Political Union rendered good service behind the scenes in various unusual ways. One way . . . was in supplying 'husbands' for Suffragettes who wished to make use of an invitation card sent to them by friends or sympathizers. Such invitations to government and social functions were inevitably made out to Mr and Mrs — or to Sir and Lady —. Of necessity, in order to attend these affairs, a Suffragette had to have a husband.[14]

On one occasion, she recalled, a suffragette successfully infiltrated a Foreign Office reception.[15] After the inevitable incident, the FO unsuccessfully attempted to trace her male companion. 'The "husband" she had appropriated for the evening had vanished – which, for him, was just as well.'[16]

A number of men were imprisoned for their part in the suffrage struggle. Some went on hunger-strike and were forcibly fed. The best known were George Lansbury and Frederick Pethick-Lawrence. Others included Victor Duval, the founder of the Men's Political Union, and Hugh Franklin, the nephew of a government minister.[17] There were at least seven different men's organizations. There were also men in some of the women's suffrage organizations and regardless of whether they excluded men or not, suffrage organizations deliberately tried to appeal to men as well as to women. The WSPU called for both men and women to help it 'rush' the Houses of Parliament.[18] The NUWSS in 1914 organized a mass meeting of male supporters in the Albert Hall, a meeting so well attended that many men had to be turned away.[19]

Notions of chivalry and 'fair play' often underlaid the motivations of male sympathizers with women's suffrage. Even in the suffrage camp Edwardian men could still maintain their patriarchal assumptions. But none the less the feminists of the period found ways of working with men without losing control of their struggle. This was summed up in Christabel Pankhurst's phrase, 'The help of men was welcomed but a women's movement must be led by women.'[20] For some sympathetic men the experience of a women-defined struggle was a distressing one. Thus one Labour activist noted in his autobiography that although he had admired the dedication and commitment of suffrage women activists he also found them to be 'wilful beyond belief. It became with them almost a point of principle not to accept advice from a man'.[21] Other men, however, understood that their role could only be an auxiliary one, and respected the autonomy of the women's movement.[22]

The image of advice proffered and rebuffed is indicative of the tensions between men and women within the suffrage camp. Men, accustomed to command, could not suppress their desire to try to direct the campaign in the way that they saw fit. Yet some male support could be retained even though its 'advice' might be rejected. This suggests that the women's movement had found ways to create an alliance which strengthened its effectiveness.

Different roads

Very little has been written on the decline of the suffrage movement after 1914. Jane Lewis's article, 'Beyond suffrage: English feminism in the 1920s'[23] discusses the National Union of Societies for Equal Citizenship (NUSEC), the successor to the NUWSS, which continued to pursue female equality in the post-war period, and was concerned to extend the franchise beyond those who won the vote in 1918. It also campaigned on matters such as equal pay and divorce, and, later, on birth control and family allowances. The WFL also continued after the war and new organizations emerged, such as the Six Point Group and the Open Door Council, formed in 1926 to campaign against protective legislation.[24] Yet we still know relatively little about feminism between the wars.

Further research would no doubt bring to light many points of contact between the post-war feminist movement and other movements and groups. The links between feminism and other 'progressive' currents had been an important feature of the pre-war period. After 1918 the decline of Liberalism and rise of Labour socialism changed the constellation of forces in the 'progressive' camp. The meteoric growth of Labour Party women's sections, first formed in 1918, drew partly on a hitherto untouched female constituency. But the Labour Party also won the active support of many women who had participated in the pre-war suffragette movement.[25] Earlier, in 1915, suffrage activists from different organizations were instrumental in the formation of the pacifist Women's International League for Peace and Freedom, which is still in existence to this day.[26] Other former suffragists became involved in bodies like the League of Nations Union and the women's organization of the Liberal Party. However, there were also developments that undermine any assumption that feminism *per se* was inflected to the left.

It is well known that on the outbreak of war the WSPU declared a truce with the government and threw itself into the war effort. Less well known are developments that occurred later in the war and in its immediate aftermath. In 1917 Emmeline and Christabel Pankhurst and their two lieutenants, Annie Kenney and Flora Drummond, turned the WSPU into the Women's Party. In the 1918 General Election Christabel Pankhurst ran unsuccessfully as its candidate in Smethwick. Although some aspects of the programme and activities of the Women's Party were highly progressive, it combined these demands with an ultra-patriotic anti-union policy that placed it firmly to the right of Conservatism.[27] The Women's Party did not last long, and its leaders went their separate ways. Annie Kenney and Christabel Pankhurst threw themselves into religion and both remained anti-socialist. Emmeline Pankhurst joined the Conservative Party. Flora Drummond formed the Women's Guild of Empire (WGE), which pioneered the idea that women should be mobilized against the trade unions and which, in April 1926, organized a march of thousands of working women which demanded an end to strikes.[28]

The Women's Party and the WGE were the most obviously right-wing developments of the pre-war suffragette movement, but they were not the only examples. In the 1930s at least three WSPU militants were involved in the Women's Section of Moseley's British Union of Fascists, and a fourth joined shortly before its suppression by the Government in 1940.[29] Indeed, Mosley himself declared in 1936 that he was proud that his organization included former suffragettes in its ranks.[30] This drift to the right, also evident among feminists elsewhere, has been interpreted by a minority of modern socialists as evidence, or even proof, that feminism – emphasizing sisterhood of women across class divisions and the achievement of equal rights with men within existing society – is at best reformist, and, in a situation of crisis, downright reactionary.[31] But to generalize from these specific situations is to misuse the historical evidence. Unlike sections of the women's movement on the Continent, feminists were active in opposing fascism.[32] The WSPU's ultra-patriotic response to the outbreak of the First World War was unrepresentative of the suffrage movement as a whole. In the NUWSS several officials and ten members of the national executive resigned in 1915 because they opposed the war, and in 1918 three 'Patriotic' members of the WFL leadership resigned because they felt their beliefs to be out of sympathy with the policies of the League.[33] Important sections of the WSPU broke away. Some joined the East London Federation. Others formed new organizations which continued the work of the WSPU, such as the Suffragettes of the WSPU and the Independent WSPU.[34]

Sylvia Pankhurst's East London Federation of the Suffragettes was the organization in the women's suffrage movement most resistant to the lures of patriotism. Sylvia's resolute anti-war campaign and her shift to the left demonstrates a very different feminism from that represented by the other prominent members of the Pankhurst family. In 1912 she determined to work among the working women of the East End. In her words:

I regarded the rousing of the East End as of utmost importance. . . . The creation of a women's movement in that great abyss of poverty would be a call and a rallying cry to the rise of similar movements in all parts of the country.

But she was not only concerned with the vote:

the existence of a strong self-reliant movement amongst working women would be the greatest aid in safeguarding their rights on the day of settlement. Moreover, I was looking to the future: I wanted to rouse these women of the submerged mass to be, not merely the argument of more fortunate people, but to be fighters on their own account . . . demanding for themselves and their families a full share in the benefits of civilization and progress.[35]

Sylvia Pankhurst was expelled from the WSPU for addressing a socialist public meeting, for having a democratic constitution in the East London Federation, and for relying on working women. All this was incompatible with Christabel Pankhurst's belief in an army of 'picked' women, pursuing a single aim independently of other political forces. The Federation subsequently spread beyond East London and became a mixed organization with a general socialist programme. The Federation tried to tackle women's issues in a prefigurative way, through such measures as setting up a crèche, a cost-price restaurant and a factory run by the women who worked in it.[36] But after the 1917 events, Sylvia Pankhurst moved away from this form of activity, regarding it as merely alleviating rather than ending the oppression of the East End poor. Her feminism became submerged by concern for the liberation of the working class as a whole, male and female. There had been intimations of this shift earlier. When her organization changed its name in 1916, from the East London Federation of the Suffragettes to the Workers' Suffrage Federation, Pankhurst's paper the *Woman's Dreadnought* published a letter from a woman who greeted the new name as marking a shift in the Federation's position, from aspiring to the salvation of only a section of humanity to a new concern for the salvation of all humankind, men and women together.[37] The *Dreadnought* gave very little space to issues of women's oppression after 1917. There was no longer any developed sense of the need for a mass women's movement. When, for instance, it was proposed in 1917 that the Labour Party should set up women's sections Pankhurst criticized the idea as divisive.[38] As a Communist she appreciated more than most the need to organize among women – in 1920 she argued for housewives' soviets.[39] But her idea of a mass working-class women's movement, and her socialist feminism, had fallen by the wayside, replaced by an unproblematic unity of working-class men and women.[40]

Conclusion

The contrast between Sylvia Pankhurst's radical shift and Emmeline Pankhurst's embrace of reaction has led some to argue that the communist movement provided the only way forward for post-war feminism.[41] But the continued existence of other forms of feminism demonstrates that the choices for the British women's movement after the outbreak of war were less circumscribed than this. There were other options to the bleak alternatives of a shift to the right or a marxism that subordinated the fight against women's oppression to a gender-blind, class politics. Before the war, revolutionary socialists had been unwilling to pursue a genuine alliance with the women's movement. The subsequent decline of organized feminism made such an alliance even more remote. Other forms of feminism persisted, sometimes connected with Liberalism or Labour socialism, but could not find a way to make their concerns once more a matter of mass politics. It would be decades before a new generation and a new movement would emerge to take up the struggle that the suffrage movement had pioneered. This new movement would come up against the problems that early twentieth-century feminism had debated – arguments about the relation of the women's movement to the labour movement and to marxism, about tactics of lobbying, demonstration, and direct action. It would also have to confront issues arising from the relation between the women's movement and sympathetic men, and tread the uneasy borderline between negotiating an alliance from a position of strength and losing a vital autonomy.

Much of this chapter has concentrated on the ties and antagonisms which emerged in this period between the feminist and socialist movements. In this discussion I have been keen to demonstrate the heterogeneity of the women's movement and at least to point to the various ways in which feminist demands were differentially constructed, and became allied to (and partially re-formed) a number of existing political forces. However, I suggested that the feminism of these years was most deeply fashioned by the traditions of radical liberalism. The arguments of the day were largely conducted in terms of the natural rights of women and the consequent right to citizenship. In the aftermath of war with the dramatic subsiding of an autonomous feminist movement and the granting of enfranchisement, those women who found themselves in the currents of either revolutionary socialism or of the radical right were in a distinct minority. The predominant development and transformation of feminist politics after 1918 was its reconstitution and distillation in the social relations of citizenship. But the critical factor is that the breadth of the feminist demands of the period became channelled almost exclusively into the political subject of 'the voter'. It was in this development that all the contradictions were compressed.

The eventual constitutional settlement for women was the outcome of a number of factors. Britain at war put unprecedented demands on national unity. The government was a coalition in which Liberal and Conservative suffrage supporters co-operated more closely than before. The Prime Minister himself supported suffrage. Women's suffrage was presented as part of a package of franchise changes and any opposition to part of this package could have scuttled the lot, leaving the politicians to face the hostility of all the reform groups and parties. Not least the fear of a revival of militancy was at high pitch. Organized anti-suffrage sentiment inside the power bloc was not eliminated, but it was defeated.

In Sylvia Pankhurst's opinion women received the vote because of ruling-class fears of revolution.[42] This assessment exaggerated both the revolutionary threat and the conspiratorial single-mindedness of the ruling group. It also underestimated the extent to which, in the initial moment, the major political parties were forced to address their potential women supporters, if only to win their votes. Thus in the coalition election manifesto of December 1918 there appeared above the signatures of Lloyd George and Bonar Law the promise: 'It will be the duty of the new Government to remove all existing inequalities of the law as between men and women.' Labour's 'Call to the People', under the heading 'The Real Women's Party', declared:

Labour has always stood for equal rights for both sexes. . . . In politics the Labour Party stands for complete adult suffrage, in industry for equal pay and the organization of men and women workers in one trade union movement. . . . Better pay and pensions for the workman or soldier mean better conditions for his wife and family. There must be no sex party: the Labour Party *is* the Woman's Party. Woman is the Chancellor of the Exchequer of the home.[43]

Such promises and appeals were unprecedented and attest to the newly-won presence of women as a force within the political nation.

But in another sense Pankhurst's view does touch on an important dimension of women's enfranchisement. The franchise bill was passed in a moment of quiescence among women, when the fissures created inside the state by an insurgent feminist movement had markedly decreased. This had very different political implications from granting the vote as a 'capitulation' to extra-parliamentary pressure. The suffrage movement before the war had been a force pitched against the dominant parties, generating a breadth of demands beyond that merely of enfranchisement. It expanded and reconstituted the very concept of 'citizenship' in order to address the problems of the cultural specificities of gender and sexuality. The success of 1918 was achieved at the cost of many of the specifically feminist aspects of these demands being drained away, with the residue squeezed into the programmes of the established parties. Labour's conception of women as 'the Chancellor of the Exchequer of the home' captures this with dreadful clarity. The rights of citizenship which women had won were in the very process of being pared down to their most legalistic and abstract forms. The contradictions of liberalism as 'philosophy' and the discursive ambiguities of citizenship took their toll. Once women received the vote they could be constituted in political discourse like any other legal subject, regardless of gender. This lay at the basis of Labour's claim to be the woman's party. Before the war the movement for women's suffrage had embodied an active if volatile means of representation for women. But after 1918 the forms in which women were passively *represented* by the political parties – condensed in the political ideologies of the time in a universal, but legalistic and often genderless notion of citizen – effectively contained much that was so crucial to the pre-war feminists.

Notes and references

1   D. Morgan, *Suffragists and Liberals. The politics of women's suffrage in England* (Basil Blackwell 1975); M. Pugh, *Women's Suffrage in Britain 1867-1928* (Historical Association 1980); H. Rosen, *Rise Up Women! The militant campaign of the Women's Social and Political Union 1903-1914* (Routledge and Kegan Paul 1974); C. Rover, *Women's Suffrage and Party Politics in Britain 1866-1914* (Routledge and Kegan Paul 1967).

2   J. Liddington and J. Norris, *One Hand Tied Behind Us. The rise of the women's suffrage movement* (Virago 1978); M. Ramelson, *The Petticoat Rebellion* (Lawrence and Wishart 1972), pp. 153-61; M. Rendel, 'The contribution of the Women's Labour League to the winning of the franchise', in L. Middleton (ed.), *Women in the Labour Movement: The British experience* (Croom Helm 1977), pp. 57-83.

3   S. Rowbotham, *Hidden From History. 300 years of women's oppression and the fight against it* (Pluto 1974), p. 94.

4   Rendel, p. 63; Liddington and Norris, p. 236.

5   Rowbotham, pp. 94-5.

6   Liddington and Norris, p. 131.

7   H. Mitchell, *The Hard Way Up* (Virago 1977); *Spare Rib* (February 1975).

8   L. Gair Wilkinson, *Revolutionary Socialism and the Women's Movement* (S L P 1909).

9   *Socialist*, March 1913.

10 *Socialist*, January 1913. The writer used the initials J. C. M. I am unsure whether this stood for Jane or John Carstairs Matheson, both of whom were critical of SLP sectarianism. Although Jane Matheson is the more likely candidate, since she wrote extensively on the subject of women's oppression in the *Socialist*, it is noteworthy that 'Mr Matheson' was criticized by a fellow member of the SLP for attaching too much 'importance to the question of Woman's Suffrage'. This was attributed to his class position as an intellectual! *Socialist*, September 1914.

11 For some interesting remarks on the question, see B. Harrison, 'Men on women's side', *Times Literary Supplement*, 27 January 1978. Sylvia Strauss, *'Traitors to the Masculine Cause.' The Men's Campaign for Women's Rights* (Greenwood Press 1982), raises the question of the contribution of 'male feminists' and has brought to light interesting material. But it both overstates men's role in the development of feminism and appears unaware of the problems feminists found in working with male sympathizers.

12 C. Pankhurst, *Unshackled! The Story of How We Won the Vote* (Hutchinson 1959), pp. 117-18.

13   A. Kenney, *Memories of a Militant* (Edward Arnold 1924), p. 218.
14   M. R. Richardson, *Laugh a Defiance* (Weidenfeld and Nicolson 1953), p. 148.
15   Richardson, pp. 148–50.
16   ibid., p. 150.
17   For Lansbury, see E. S. Pankhurst, *The Suffragette Movement* (Virago 1977), p. 489; for Pethick-Lawrence, see E. Pankhurst, *My Own Story* (Virago 1979), p. 255; for Duval, see E. S. Pankhurst, p. 340; for Franklin, see E. S. Pankhurst, pp. 345, 435.
18   E. S. Pankhurst, *The Suffragette* (Gay and Hancock 1911), p. 262.
19   *NUWSS Annual Report 1914*, pp. 4–6.
20   C. Pankhurst, p. 183.
21   Lord Snell, *Men, Movements and Myself* (Dent 1938), p. 184.
22   See, for example, L. Housman, *The Unexpected Years* (Jonathan Cape 1937), p. 275.
23   *Maryland Historian* (Spring 1975).
24   See e.g. A. Linklater, *An Unhusbanded Life* (Hutchinson 1980), pp. 243–52 and 258–9; S. Boston, *Women Workers and the Trade Union Movement* (Davis-Poynter 1980), p. 180.
25   *Workers' Dreadnought*, 2 November 1918.
26   G. Bussey and M. Tims, *Pioneers for Peace: Women's International League for Peace and Freedom 1915–1965* (Allen and Unwin 1965). For former suffrage activists and the peace movement, see also M. Ceadel, *Pacifism in Britain 1914–1945: The defining of a faith* (Clarendon Press 1980), pp. 93, 239.
27   M. Mackenzie, *Shoulder to Shoulder* (Penguin 1975), pp. 316–7
28   D. Mitchell, *The Fighting Pankhursts* (Jonathan Cape 1967), pp. 163–6, 169–70.
29   C. Cross, *The Fascists in Britain* (Barrie and Rockliff 1961), pp. 98, 179–80; R. Benewick, *The Fascist Movement in Britain* (Allen Lane 1972), p. 95.
30   *Action*, 28 November 1936.
31   'The Pankhursts: suffrage and socialism', *Women and Revolution* (Summer 1976); 'Sylvia Pankhurst and the workers movement', *Women and Revolution* (Summer 1978); 'From Weimar to Hitler: feminism and fascism', *Women and Revolution* (Spring 1981); 'Women's oppression under capitalism', *Revolutionary Communist* (November 1976), pp. 34–7; 'From suffrage to soviets', *Workers Power* (March 1979); 'The suffragette', *Women's Fight* (July 1977); 'Sylvia Pankhurst: From feminism to left communism', two parts, *World Revolution* (October–November 1980, December 1980–January 1981).
32   There is at present no systematic study of the subject but see e.g. B. Harrison, *Separate Spheres* (Croom Helm 1978), p. 233; 'Women and the National Front', *Red Rag* (August 1980), pp. 29–30.
33   Morgan, p. 136; R. Strachey, *The Cause* (Virago 1978), p. 351; Jo Vellacott Newberry, 'Anti-war suffragists', *History* (October 1977); Taylor, p. 56.
34   Rosen, pp. 252–4.
35   E. S. Pankhurst, *Suffragette Movement*, pp. 416–17.
36   See e.g. Rowbotham, pp. 114–16; G. Richman, *Fly a Flag for Poplar* (Liberation Films 1975), pp. 116–18; and above all, E. S. Pankhurst, *The Home Front*.
37   The change of the name of the paper in mid-1917, from *Woman's* to *Workers' Dreadnought*, also symbolized Pankhurst's shift. Arrested for sedition late in

1920, she declared at her trial that her attempts to alleviate the burdens of the East End poor had proved to her that such efforts were doomed and that the only answer was Communism. *Workers' Dreadnought*, 6 November 1920.

38 *Workers' Dreadnought* (27 October 1917).

39 *Workers' Dreadnought* (27 March, 19 June 1920).

40 Here I concur with Rowbotham, p. 160 and J. Ash, 'Sylvia Pankhurst: The suffragette who went to the East End', *Workers' Action* (3 March 1976), and dissent from D. Widgery, 'Sylvia Pankhurst', *Radical America* (May–June 1979), pp. 36–8.

41 See footnote 31.

42 *Workers' Dreadnought* (2 November 1918).

43 F. W. S. Craig, *British General Election Manifestos 1900–1974* (Macmillan 1975), pp. 30 and 32.

9 'Cleansing the portals of life': the venereal disease campaign in the early twentieth century*

Lucy Bland

Let us not be deceived. It is no light or small task that the medical profession today are calling on the nation to undertake. It will be laborious; it will be expensive. But it is worthwhile: for it is nothing less 'than the cleansing of the portals of life'.[1]

It may seem strange to devote a chapter to venereal disease in a book about the British state at the turn of the century. Yet the book considers the political crisis of the period. The moral panic about venereal disease in the years around the First World War can be related to this experience of crisis. For many, venereal disease stood as a metaphor signifying and condensing fears of the period. There was widespread concern about national efficiency and the physical and mental 'deterioration' or 'degeneracy' of civilians and troops. Venereal disease was believed to be an important factor in this 'deterioration'. There was also alarm at the falling British birth-rate, which was regarded by many as heralding a downward slide towards 'race suicide'. Venereal disease was widely blamed for causing sterility and infant mortality.[2]

The venereal disease rate was also read as an index of the nation's sexual immorality. It was known that venereal disease was contracted primarily through 'promiscuous sex', and that it was unpleasant and potentially deforming. Yet it was still surrounded by ignorance and taboo. Venereal disease represented a lurking, undefined threat to stability, the family, the British race and empire. An imaginary scenario was constructed, heightened by war imagery, in which the family and the nation were portrayed as the prey of these lethal invading diseases. For many feminists, moreover, venereal disease indicated not simply the 'perils of promiscuity' and the extent of prostitution ('the social evil') but also the horrific consequences of male moral hypocrisy. They argued that numerous chaste women were the unsuspecting victims of venereal disease, caught from their licentious husbands. The feminist focus on venereal disease became a way of 'speaking out' about sexual immorality and male double-standards.

---

* Many thanks to Martin Durham, Joan Austoker, Jane Lewis, Richard Johnson and Bill Schwarz for their helpful comments and encouragement.

There is a further reason for focusing on venereal disease. A number of chapters in this book indicate increasing state intervention at the turn of the century. However, when we come to look at the issue of venereal disease, state activity does not appear to fit this pattern. Between 1864 and 1886 the state regulated prostitution through the Contagious Diseases Acts. (These allowed the coercive detention and medical examination of any woman suspected of being a prostitute in certain sea-ports and garrison towns).[3] Yet in the late nineteenth and early twentieth centuries the state adopted a *'laissez-faire'* approach towards the control of venereal disease.

In the couple of years preceding the First World War, however, there was a growing demand for state action. As *The Times* expressed it: 'The state has a compelling duty to perform. It is under a deep responsibility to itself and to future generations.'[4] During the war, two contrasting strategies for the management of venereal disease were implemented. The first, a combination of medical treatment and moral guidance, continued into the inter-war years. The second, the brief reintroduction of repressive control through the regulations of the Defence of the Realm Act (DORA) effectively lasted only for the duration of the war. The former strategy was state funded, although it was not administered solely through state bodies and there was no enforcement of compulsory treatment. Central government financed 75 per cent of local authority medical provision and the state made an annual grant to the National Council for Combating Venereal Disease (NCCVD). The moralizing work of the NCCVD, which enjoined individuals to lead chaste sexual lives, encouraged a form of self-regulation. Individuals were encouraged to subordinate their private activities to the wider concerns of race and nation. Self-regulation was a prevalent theme in the teaching of all aspects of health and hygiene in this period. However, although this 'self-development' strategy developed prior to the First World War, it did not come to fruition until the inter-war years.

A close examination of the debates and conflicts over the control of venereal disease during the First World War clearly demonstrates the absence of a cohesive or unified state strategy. Indeed, it illustrates the difficulty in speaking either of one overarching state 'view', or of the state itself as a unitary body. The state's 'view' was fragmented in its expression at different levels of the state apparatus. The 'view' was a composite of parliamentary and Cabinet debates and the positions of various ministries. The state's 'view' also had to take account of the proposals of a host of official and semi-official committees and commissions directly and indirectly concerned with venereal disease. The outcome of debate, in the sense of the official policy formulated, was the end-product of diverse arguments and pressures. Many pressures came from outside the state 'proper' – from doctors, moralists and feminists, and during the war, from leaders of the allied forces. However, to characterize the official policy as an end-product is somewhat misleading. State policy continued to be opposed, negotiated and changed in the course of its implementation. Thus policy was in no straightforward sense necessarily 'realized'.

According to the vantage point from which the question of venereal disease was viewed, the 'problem' appeared in different forms. The existence of venereal diseases in themselves neither neutrally constitutes nor gives any unitary definition of what the problem actually is. After all, venereal diseases had long been labelled 'moral' diseases because they were thought to be caught through prostitution and 'promiscuous' sex. This chapter examines the differing and frequently conflicting objectives and strategies of the main groups involved in campaigning against venereal disease. It considers the conditions of existence of these strategies, and the ways in which certain strategies informed state policy, while others – in particular the main feminist definition of the problem – became marginalized.

Feminist 'speaking out'

Throughout the nineteenth century public reference to venereal disease was taboo. However, the turn of the century saw the gradual 'speaking out' on the subject, and the build-up of a moral panic. This culminated in 1913 in a widespread demand for action and the subsequent establishment of a royal commission. Although the medical profession stood at the forefront of the call for a government inquiry into venereal disease, the demand for breaking the conspiracy of silence on the subject and the wider public agitation were initiated by the women's movement.[5] In the early years of the twentieth century feminists campaigned against venereal disease, transferring the blame for it away from the prostitute and on to her male client. They claimed that male lust was the cause of prostitution and thus of venereal disease.

In the 1870s and 1880s feminists had indirectly raised the issue of venereal disease in their campaign against men's use of prostitutes and their demand for the repeal of the Contagious Diseases Acts. Yet their concern had been not so much with the effects of *disease* as the effects of state regulation on prostitutes and suspected prostitutes. But in 1895 Sarah Grand, one of the 'new woman' writers of the late nineteenth century, had published *The Heavenly Twins*, which, according to Kersley 'was the first to attack male sexuality both within and outside marriage. . .'.[6] One of its themes was the problem of venereal disease. It became an immediate bestseller. In Grand's obituary in 1943, Letitia Fairfield remarked that she 'was the real pioneer of public enlightenment on venereal disease. Participants in the Ministry of Health's campaign today can only guess dimly how much courage this took fifty years ago.'[7] *The Heavenly Twins* was one of several feminist literary works dealing with venereal disease at the turn of the century.[8] However, it was not until 1908 that feminists presented the venereal disease issue in a factual tract as opposed to a fictional form, and it was clear that most of them were well aware of the current medical debates on the question.

Widespread concern with questions of national health and hygiene was not simply a by-product of the fear that Britain was under threat economically, politically and imperially. By the early twentieth century medical definitions of a wide variety of social issues were influential in many government debates and investigations. Feminists were not unresponsive to this rise of medical hegemony. A number of feminists were themselves doctors; and the vast majority of feminists were often well-versed in medical matters and attentive to current medical debates. In 1908, on commission from the National Union of Women Suffrage Societies (NUWSS), Louisa Martindale, herself a doctor of medicine, wrote a book entitled *Under the Surface*.[9] She carefully detailed various horrific physical effects of venereal disease and quoted eminent doctors on the harmlessness of male chastity. She opened her treatise by arguing that 'the Women's Suffrage Movement is a moral movement' whose aims included 'a desire to purify, by means of good laws, the social life of the people'. She also linked prostitution and venereal disease with the demand for the vote. If the demand for prostitution was rooted in male 'addiction', she argued, the supply of prostitutes was due to economic necessity – the inability of many women to earn a living wage. The 'cure' for prostitution, she declared, lay in granting the vote to women, for only then could women hope to gain the economic independence necessary to rid the world of prostitution. The book 'was the occasion for a furious onslaught on the National Union in the House of Commons by a member, who held it to be injurious to morals. This proved a great advertisement'. The NUWSS responded by sending the book to every member of both Houses of Parliament.[10]

White slavery was also a concern of many feminists – as it had been from the 1880s. Once the 1912 White Slave Traffic Bill was enacted many of the feminists involved in its promotion shifted their focus to the venereal disease campaign. As one historian has rightly suggested, it was at this point that the Women's Social and Political Union (WSPU) 'moved the issue of man as abductor to man as polluter'.[11] In contrast to the issue of white slavery, which laid the blame on a relatively small number of procurors, the venereal disease campaign appeared to many feminists to implicate virtually all men. It struck simultaneously at men and at male–female sexual relations inside *and* outside the home.

But if the 'health risks' of marriage were at issue, so too was the very notion of health itself. Feminists' concern with questions of health and disease took place in the context of a general *moralizing* of medicine. Feminists played a central role in this moralizing process. In 1915, the feminist organization committed to the abolition of the state regulation of prostitution changed its name to the Association for Moral and Social Hygiene (AMSH). Abolitionists claimed to have rescued 'hygiene' from its equation with the purely 'physical'. The categories 'health/ill-health' now overlaid those of 'virtue/vice'. Further, it was *women* who were seen as crucial in the acquisition of such moral hygiene. As one commentator expressed it, in a discussion of nursing, 'the woman of the future will be far more than a nurse . . . she will have a positive religion to realise. She will be a hygienist or priestess of health'.[12] Writing in 1912 in the *Freewoman* of the 'unspeakable' – namely veneral disease – Ellen Gaskell followed through the logic of the general call on women to be more attentive to hygiene: 'It will simply become impossible for any man to face a woman without a positive assurance of a good bill of health.' This was a measure which she, like many eugenists, [13] would have liked to have seen made law.

The most (in)famous of feminist tracts on venereal disease was Christabel Pankhurst's *The Great Scourge and How to End It*. This was published as a book in 1913, having first appeared as a series of articles in the *Suffragette*. Drawing on medical statistics Pankhurst claimed that 75–80 per cent of men were infected with gonorrhoea and 'a considerable per cent' with syphilis. Although they accused Pankhurst of great exaggeration, doctors were themselves presenting similar figures.[14] The effects of the prevalence of venereal disease were, Pankhurst claimed, horrendous: 'the sexual diseases are the great cause of physical, mental and moral degeneracy and of race suicide . . . ravaging the community. . .'.

For Pankhurst sexual disease was due to the doctrine 'that women are created primarily for the sex gratification of men and secondly for the bearing of children', and she criticized rhetoric founded upon 'the idea that women exist only for race and sex purposes'. If 'the cause of sexual disease is the subjection of women . . . to destroy one we must destroy the other'. Therefore, to do away with venereal disease, she argued, women must have the vote. For 'when they are citizens women will feel a greater respect for themselves and will have the power to secure the enactment of laws for their protection and to strengthen their economic position'. But to remove prostitution, and with it venereal disease, it was also necessary that *men* change. She presented an ultimatum: 'syphilis and gonorrhoea can be eliminated in two ways. One is that men shall lead chaste lives. If they refuse, then the other way . . . is by exterminating the race itself'. She warned that until men reformed and women were no longer subordinate women would refuse (and were already refusing) to marry and cater sexually to men. The two elements of her argument were drawn together in her catchy slogan: 'Votes for Women, Chastity for Men'.[15]

The response to Pankhurst's campaign was mixed. The WSPU and a number of influential feminists supported the argument. However, not all were so enthusiastic. The *Shield*, for example, although finding the book 'courageous', believed her claims to be misleading. It disliked both the implication that all men were bad and all women good, as well as the tone of what they took to be 'sexual antagonism'.[16] Louise Creighton, a social-purity feminist, similarly took exception to the 'spirit of antagonism against men'.[17] She upheld women's suffrage because it 'would do away with the idea that women exist for the pleasure and use of men'. But she also urged that sex be thought and spoken of as little as possible:

For most people the wisest and safest plan is to concern themselves as little as possible with the things of the body. . . . the sensual desires, the flesh, are what have to be kept in subjection, and to do this the wisest plan is to think . . . and speak about them as little as possible.

Men's 'weakness and wrongdoing' were 'clearly the cause of the degradation of numberless women'. Yet Creighton urged readers to remember that 'chastity is more difficult for men than women. . .'. She suggested that women should help men in this respect, not condemn them. Pankhurst's demands on *men* to reform their sexual behaviour were replaced by Creighton with the age-old demand on *women* to be pure and chaste themselves.

Feminists who sought sexual equality with men, not through demands for purity, but for sexual freedom on the same terms as men were also critical of Christabel's campaign. In her acidic response to the *Suffragette* articles Rebecca West commented: 'I say that her remarks are utterly valueless and likely to discredit the cause in which we believe'. Further, 'this scolding attitude . . . is also a positive incentive to keep these diseases the secret, spreading things they are.'[18]

Medical pressure

Although feminists were the first to 'speak out' on venereal disease it was the medical profession which instigated the campaign for a government inquiry. The doctors' claim that venereal disease was first and foremost a *medically manageable* condition informed their pronouncements on the issue.

At the end of the nineteenth century the British Medical Association failed to persuade the government to set up an inquiry into venereal disease, although in the years that followed official bodies began to show an increasing interest in the question. What eventually pushed the government into setting up a royal commission in 1913 was the combination of three medical initiatives. The first was a report on venereal disease commissioned by the Local Government Board which proposed extensive provision of medical facilities for its diagnosis and treatment.[19] Second, a medical manifesto was published in the *Morning Post* on 22 July, signed by thirty-eight prominent doctors, requesting a royal commission to be composed largely of members of the medical profession, to consider what means were necessary to deal with venereal disease. The manifesto was backed by an editorial which reported that of 276 MPs who had received a copy of the manifesto, all but two had supported it. The third medical pronouncement in 1913 came from the International Medical Congress, held in London in August, which discussed 'Syphilis, its dangers to the community and the question of public control'.

In response to this concerted medical pressure the government acquiesced and in October set up a royal commission composed of a combination of doctors, clerics and moralists. The eighty-five witnesses, however, were nearly all in some way engaged in the medical profession. Its terms of reference were also strictly medical:

To inquire into the prevalence of venereal diseases in the United Kingdom, their effects upon the health of the community, and the means by which those effects can be alleviated or prevented, it being understood that no return to the policy or provisions of the Contagious Diseases Acts of 1864, 1866 or 1869 is to be regarded as falling within the scope of the inquiry.[20]

The Commission's report, published in 1916, noted that although a consideration of the policy of the CD Acts was not within the terms of reference of the Commission, it wished to express the view that no advantage would accrue from such a return. A similar statement had been made in the Local Government Board report, and indeed by nearly every speaker at the 1913 International Medical Congress. It is crucial to consider what lay behind medical denunciations of the CD Acts.

The move away from state regulation

The CD Acts had been introduced as military reforms, linked to the policy of creating a professional bachelor army and navy and as an answer to the rising rate of venereal disease among troops. The acts stood squarely within the framework of Victorian public health policy. The sanitary movement had equated public order and public health; control of prostitutes as a source of moral and physical pollution represented a logical extension of this approach. It corresponded to the broader concern of social policy to control the casual poor – the 'residuum'.[21] The pressures for legislation were thus initiated by the military, but also strongly backed by the medical profession. The regulationists argued that prostitution was a *permanent* feature of society and that venereal disease could be controlled only through the control of prostitutes. The acts faced increasing opposition, in which feminists played a central part. The abolitionists opposed the acts on a number of grounds: they condemned the state sanctioning of vice, the interference with civil liberty, and the great discomfort and humiliation for those forcibly examined. Feminists further argued that the acts were the apotheosis of the double standard and they pointed to the absurdity of hoping to restrict venereal disease through focusing on only one partner. The abolitionists managed to win the repeal of the acts in 1886. Their final success was due largely to their strength and persistence, aided by the failure of the acts permanently to reduce the rate of venereal disease.

On the repeal of the acts, the *Shield* (the organ of the feminist abolitionist group) closed its pages and declared its work done. However, in 1897 it sprang back into existence in opposition to proposals to introduce legislation similar to the CD Acts in relation to the British army in India. Debate in Parliament revealed a desire from some quarters to revive the CD Acts in Britain as well. Doctors too declared that 'England must learn from Europe and regulate prostitution'.[23]

However, at the turn of the century a critical shift was underway. At the First and Second International Congresses on the Prevention of Venereal Disease, in 1899 and 1902, many leading doctors admitted that state regulation of prostitution had failed. For the first time the medical profession was considering the need for a *moral* solution to the problem of prostitution and its related diseases. There appear to be several reasons for this volte-face of the medical profession, formerly staunch supporters of state regulation. First, venereal disease among the military had been falling rapidly since the repeal of the CD Acts in 1886.[24] Second, it was now being viewed primarily as a *civilian* rather than a military problem, and as such, a regulationist strategy was deemed by many to be impracticable. Since venereal disease was not compulsorily notifiable (despite the fact that many other contagious and infectious diseases such as smallpox, cholera and typhoid had recently been made so) there were no figures on its prevalence among the civilian population. Available statistics were limited and unreliable. Although the Registrar-General's figures on the number of deaths due to syphilis indicated a fall, such deaths were believed to be greatly under-registered.

Many doctors and infant and child-welfare workers believed that venereal disease was greatly contributing both to the falling birth-rate and to infant mortality and morbidity. Gonorrhoea was said to be the commonest cause of sterility in women – 50 per cent of all cases according to an estimate of the Royal Commission on Venereal Disease. In 1914 *opthalmia neonatorum* was made compulsorily notifiable. This was gonorroccal infection of infants' eyes at birth, which led to blindness if untreated.

Yet the failure of the CD Acts and the redefinition of venereal disease as a civilian problem are not in themselves sufficient to explain fully the medical profession's rejection of the regulationist strategy. It is important to recognize that between the period of the CD Acts and the Edwardian era there developed fundamental shifts in the medical definition of venereal disease. The development in 1906 of the Wasserman test for accurate diagnosis, and in 1909–10 of Ehrlich's salvarsan treatment of syphilis brought venereal disease more and more firmly under the medical 'gaze'. According to the 1913 medical manifesto medicine was now in a 'new era'. Initially there was great enthusiasm that salvarsan (an arsenic derivative) was the 'perfect specific', and that gonorrhoea rather than syphilis would come to represent the greater danger in the future.[25] Whereas in the nineteenth century syphilis could only be diagnosed and treated through attention to various bodily 'clues' it was now believed to be detectable and curable by science. For the treatment of venereal diseases to fall within the net of official medicine, it was essential that the grip of the numerous 'quack' remedies for the diseases be loosened. This could partly be achieved by legal means, by the clamping down on the advertisement, display and sale of such remedies, for example. But venereal disease also needed to become less of a taboo subject, to an extent which would allow those afflicted but unable to afford the services of a private practitioner to seek out the medical services of hospitals and clinics. The public also needed to have more information so that people themselves could detect early signs of the diseases, enabling treatment to be sought in time to guarantee full cure. If the medical profession was to advance against yet another virulent disease it had to win public co-operation – and public funds.

The moralizing of medicine

The views of the medical profession on the control of venereal disease were not just narrowly medical and instrumental, for medicine itself had also become moralized. In the early twentieth century the 'social hygiene' movement blended medicine and morality. The language and concerns of social purity, deriving from religious conceptions of self-control, will-power and morality, united with the medical redefinition of 'hygiene' to form a *holistic* view of health. The individual was addressed in his/her entirety – physically, morally and genetically. On the one hand doctors claimed moral foundations for the 'laws' of health. On the other hand social purists, including many feminists, claimed scientific and medical 'facts' as confirmation of certain moral positions. Groups and organizations drawn from the fields of morality and medicine came together to address a wide set of issues related to the family, marriage and sexual morality. Individuals of different political persuasions could be found working together in new organizations in this medico-moral coalition. Further, a number of feminists, erstwhile opponents of the medical profession in the struggle against the CD Acts, now saw doctors as their allies. For example in 1913 the feminist journal the *Shield*, in reference to the control of venereal disease, declared: 'We and our former antagonists can work cordially together.'[26] The National Council for Public Morals (NCPM), formed in 1910, claimed a membership ranging from clerics and moralists (including a few social purity feminists), through to doctors, eugenists, new liberals and Fabians. A similar pattern could be observed in the membership of the National Council for Combating Venereal Disease (NCCVD), set up late in 1914. This medical and moral coalition came into its own in the venereal disease debate.

However, not all doctors fell under the embrace of this moralizing influence. During the inter-war years, many doctors opposed the medico-moral strategy with the alternative 'solution' of medical prophylaxis (prevention). Although division of opinion within the medical profession took place largely beyond the period under discussion here it is worth considering the basis of disagreement, since this was already in evidence during the war years.

The issue at stake was the question of whether medical prophylaxis would encourage promiscuous sex. Some doctors favoured moral prevention and curative medical treatment (the medico-moral strategy), while others advocated medical prevention and cure. But the dispute also revealed a wider ambivalence over the question of preventive medicine. In this period the sphere of public health was extended to incorporate preventive medicine. In turn the scope of preventive medicine was widened to include issues of heredity, social, moral, racial and sexual hygiene – 'hygiene of the body'.

Through *education* in hygiene the individual was to become an active agent in the acquisition and maintenance of his/her own health and that of the nation. This focus on the body in its physical and moral capacities demanded forms of *self*-regulation. The reconstitution of preventive medicine entailed a medicalization of the concerns about personal morality, self-restraint – in sexual matters in particular – and the liberal emphasis on free will, individual responsibility and choice. Added to this, however, was the focus on the individual's responsibility to the nation, the community and to the race to avoid ill-health. But this stress on the individual as active agent in health prevention had, potentially, uncomfortable implications for the medical profession. It raised the possibility that the controlling voice in matters of health could be wrested from medical practitioners and relocated in a lay constituency. The attempt to redefine certain issues as not simply *medical* concerns but concerns necessitating skilled and trained medical supervision and treatment was a theme which surfaced in the dispute over prophylaxis in the early 1920s.[27]

The militarization of venereal disease

By the beginning of the war there were two main groupings waging campaigns against venereal disease. On the one hand was a medico-moral coalition, dominated by doctors, and on the other, a loose-knit grouping of feminists united in their opposition to the double-standard and to venereal disease as one of its key effects, but divided in their opinions as to the best means of securing their removal.

Although the different groupings had different definitions of the problem, there did exist certain common concerns which provided the basis for at least a fragile alliance. In addition to the expanded definition of hygiene which was held in common, and the stress on a 'conspiracy of silence' surrounding venereal disease, both groupings tended to view the issue as a civilian problem, and conceptualized this in terms of 'race', 'nation' and 'protection of the innocent'. During the war, however, the enormous rise in cases of venereal disease among troops revived the focus on it as a *military* problem. At one stroke, the Royal Commission's primary focus on venereal disease as a civilian matter was rendered marginal.

In November 1914 Sir Thomas Barlow (President of the Royal College of Physicians and executive member of the newly-formed NCCVD) made a surprise move. He suggested to the Home Office that legislation was required to empower police to remove or exclude prostitutes from military areas. Sir Ernley Blackwell (Assistant Under-Secretary to the Home Office) refused, largely because he feared that removal of prostitutes might lead both to a rise in homosexuality among the troops and to an increase in venereal disease. If professional prostitutes were excluded from military areas, he argued, the floodgates would be open for young 'amateur' prostitutes. These were believed by many to be the 'true' spreaders of venereal disease – 'a great army of girls . . . over whom the police have no control'.[28]

The term 'amateur prostitute' or simply 'amateur' entered the debate almost overnight.[29] Despite the ambiguities of the term there was general agreement that it applied to a young woman engaging in promiscuous sex for 'free'. That she was referred to as an amateur *prostitute* indicated the contemporary equation of female promiscuity with prostitution. Yet it was her distinction *from* the professional prostitute which was of most concern. The 'amateur' indulged in gratuitous sex and was believed to be drawn from all classes (unlike the working-class professional),[30] and to be younger than most professionals.[31] But the most important difference was that the amateur was thought to take no precautions against venereal disease. She was thus seen as 'the real centre of infection'[32] and thereby highly dangerous.[33] Not surprisingly, given the contemporary ideas on women's sexuality, commentators had difficulty in understanding the amateur's motives. Dr Otto May (an active member of NCCVD) patronizingly suggested that some of the 'amateurs' were willing to 'go with soldiers . . . for a mistaken feeling that they were "doing their bit" by confronting the loneliness of a few poor soldier-boys'.[34] More frequently, though, the explanation lay in women's transition from the 'pure' pole of female sexuality (women as innocent and sexually passive) to the 'impure' pole (women as corrupted and fallen, and henceforth themselves sexually *corrupting*). Feminists often saw this as the fault of men. For example, to Dr Helen Wilson: 'Many of the unscrupulous "harpies" of today were merely irresponsible flappers a year ago – and the transformation wouldn't have been effected without the help of evil men.'[35]

Why was focus put upon the 'amateur' as the human agent responsible for the spread of venereal disease, rather than the troops themselves? Obviously, the persistence of the double-standard of morality and the notion of woman as temptress contributed to the blaming of women. But why did the powerful pre-war feminist critique of male sexuality have so little resonance in the debate? The marginalization of the feminist definition related in part to the fact that it was now British and allied troops, rather than civilians, who were held to be most at risk from venereal disease. The urgency for 'fit' men to win the war, the patriotic praise widely heaped upon 'our heroes' fighting in dire conditions in 'foreign parts', and the exceptional circumstances of wartime all contributed to a widespread view that the 'needs' of 'our boys' deserved to be met rather than denied. Such 'needs' included sexual 'needs', and if, as many authoritative figures obviously believed, troops should be sexually serviced – for reasons of morale if nothing else – such 'services' ought ideally be as disease-free as possible.

Meanwhile the British government, under pressure to introduce some national form of regulation of prostitution, introduced regulation 13a of the Defence of the Realm Act (DORA). This allowed military authorities to prohibit anyone previously convicted of soliciting from residing in, or frequenting, the vicinity of stationed troops. But the government was soon to admit the failure of this regulation. Part of the problem, as they saw it, was that it left the 'amateur' untouched and failed to prevent the soldiers themselves seeking out women.[36]

Under further pressure from both the Colonial Office and the War Office, the Home Office introduced a new Criminal Law Amendment Bill in February 1917. As one historian has pointed out, the bill was a confused mixture of liberal clauses for the *protection* of young girls, *repressive* clauses against prostitutes, and *medical* clauses penalizing the transmission of venereal disease.[37] One clause stipulated that sexual intercourse, or its solicitation or invitation, was a crime for anyone with venereal disease; conviction carried a sentence of six months' to two years' imprisonment. Another clause imposed a month's imprisonment on a second conviction for soliciting or loitering. The first of these clauses was condemned from all sides. To those wanting a return to the CD Acts, it represented 'a pill to cure an earthquake', and was believed to be unenforceable.[38] Numerous women's groups sent resolutions objecting to both the clauses.[39]

Despite debates on this bill pressure for further action continued and on 22 March 1918 DORA 40d was introduced. Its objective was clear: 'no woman who is suffering from venereal disease shall have sexual intercourse with any member of HM Forces, or solicit or invite any member to have sexual intercourse with her. . .'. A woman so charged should be required 'to be remanded for not less than a week for medical examination. . .'.[40] The inclusion of women *having* sexual intercourse obviously allowed for the 'amateur'. Immediate widespread protest followed, spearheaded by the feminist organizations the Women's Freedom League and the Association for Moral and Social Hygiene.[41] A large number of newspapers and journals also expressed their opposition,[42] and the TUC protested that '40d was the most disgusting of the government's interference with liberty'.[43] The *Lancet* also objected to 40d, although more for its inadequacy as a public health measure than on grounds of sexual discrimination and harassment. DORA 40d found opponents in Parliament as well.

Meanwhile the Criminal Law Amendment Bill had been reintroduced in

Parliament, close behind Lord Beauchamp's Sex Offences Bill which covered many of the same concerns. The infamous clause banning sex for anybody with venereal disease was still present in the government bill. Lord Beauchamp's bill went further by defining such offences as 'actual bodily harm' if venereal disease was communicated *wilfully* (and thereby punishable with at least five years penal servitude). Feminist protest was widespread and insistent.

However there were divisions in the ranks of those opposed to the repressive clauses over what their response to the bills should be. Certain groups, although against the clauses as drafted, felt that with amendments the bills could be acceptable, even desirable. Most feminists agreed with aspects of the bills, particularly the raising of the age of consent in cases of indecent assault. Feminists certainly tended to think that when venereal disease was acquired through promiscuous sex people should be made *accountable* for the transmission of the disease. However, most baulked at the proposal that accountability be imposed through *criminal* law. Feminists suspected that in the administration of the law it would always be the *woman* who would be charged and convicted. Rather than women's protection, they feared their victimization.[44] This undermined feminist support for the bills. Many feminists, following a basic tenet of the medico-moral definition of the venereal disease problem, held that infection through promiscuous sexual intercourse belonged to the sphere of public health rather than private or criminal injury. Social-purity feminists wanted the state to act in its 'public-health' capacity as a *moralizing* agency – to discourage promiscuity and encourage responsible sexual relations through moral education. This was a theme that was to become dominant in the inter-war years.

On 28 August the War Cabinet was sufficiently disturbed by the claim of Lord Robert Cecil (Foreign Under-Secretary) that agitation against 40d 'was very strong and in the event of a general election considerable pressure would be put on candidates' for it to back Cecil's recommendation for a commission to be set up to assess amendments to 40d. Protest meetings against 40d continued until November when, with the armistice, DORA, including 40d, was revoked.

Moral prophylaxis: another strategy

I have so far omitted any reference to the details of the report of the Royal Commission on Venereal Disease, which appeared mid-way through the war. The Commission had been orginally set up to examine the disease as a civilian problem, and to the extent that its recommendations addressed the question of civilian rather than military health they were found inadequate for the protection of the troops. Nevertheless, two of the report's recommendations were immediately enacted, and other of its proposals were taken up once the war was over. In the inter-war years, the report's 'medico-moral' solution became the dominant strategy.

The Commission concluded that venereal disease was not exclusively a threat to the military and the residuum, but a broader danger to wide sections of the population. This vindicated the feminist argument. The Commission recommended a national scheme of free diagnosis and treatment. (This was enacted in the Public Health (Venereal Disease) Regulations Act, 1916.) It further recommended that compulsory treatment was to apply only to those in 'closed' populations: poor law patients, prisoners, and so on, with the detention of any troops still infected. It advised against compulsory notification, fearing that this would deter those seeking treatment, but recommended prohibition of advertisements for venereal disease remedies. This was part of the attempt by the medical profession to curb 'quackery'. Although the report noted that the Commission's terms of reference precluded consideration of moral aspects, it argued the need for moral instruction, with NCCVD as the authoritative administering body.

Many feminists did not necessarily disagree with the report's conclusions and proposals, but they felt uneasy at its omissions. Thus, for example, the AMSH agreed with most of the report but very much regretted that its terms of reference had precluded any examination of the *social causes* of venereal disease. It argued that the study of preventive medicine had shown that eradication of any widespread malady necessitated 'the removal of unwholesome conditions of life'.[45] But it was Juliette Heale (of the small breakaway group, 'Suffragettes of the WSPU') who most violently attacked the report – seeing it as 'a sinister menace to womanhood' in its focus on cure – 'treatment, treatment all the way' – rather than on *prevention*. She accused the Commission of trying to 'level-up' between the sexes 'the guilt of racial poisoning – so that an ignorant reader would imagine infection of a spouse and offspring to be as frequent by wife as husband'. But, as she gruesomely expressed it: 'the woman is periodically re-poisoned by the untouched, unsuspected death-distributor at her own hearth'.[46]

If Juliette Heale stressed prevention rather than cure, so too did the NCCVD as it expanded its educative work across the country. The immediate post-war years saw a protracted wrangle between two societies – the NCCVD and the Society for the Prevention of Venereal Disease – over the question of whether the forms of prophylaxis should be primarily medical or moral. I have already pointed to the basis of this split among doctors in their general ambivalence towards the question of preventive medicine. The NCCVD, the only society with government backing, held out against medical prophylaxis, both for moral reasons – that provision would be seen as sanctioning sexual vice – and medical reasons, though it was not so much the medical effectiveness, as the removal of treatment from the hands of the doctors into those of the individual in his self-application of preventives, which was of concern. (And I say *his* self-application advisedly since only male medical prophylaxis was considered.)

In the inter-war years the threat of venereal disease lay at the heart of most sex-education material. Feminist writings on sex education were also much in evidence. A number of feminists had joined or become affiliated to the NCCVD and many followed up their concern with sexual morality by writing moralizing sex-education tracts. Although the demand for an equal moral standard was usually present in some form, the biting feminist attack on male sexuality of the pre-war years was largely absent. This was probably related in part to the widely-held belief that as the vote had been gained much of the battle had been won. The feminist voice tended to become marginalized within the NCCVD campaign, and the critique of the double-standard was pushed into the background. The marginalization was compounded by the continued ambivalence felt by many feminists about the question of active female sexuality. Two concepts in particular – responsibility and protection – were centrally developed by feminists and non-feminists alike in discussion of the regulation of women's sexuality, and both were open to many different readings. As we have seen, the 'amateur' was viewed as irresponsible in her sexual behaviour, responsible for the transmission of disease, and in need of 'protection'. But unlike 'protection' for the troops, such 'protection' for women tended to take the form of surveillance rather than the offer of medical prophylaxis.

Venereal disease became a focus of concern for different groups, for different reasons. But in the immediate pre-war years the venereal 'problem' was briefly *collectively* defined as a national and civilian problem, affecting a wide cross-section of the population, including the 'innocent', and having dire consequences for the health of 'race' and 'nation'. The 'solution' to venereal disease was widely held to necessitate a combination of moral prevention and medical treatment (what I have termed the 'medico-moral' strategy) rather than any direct return to state regulation. The highly vocal feminist presence in the campaign was an important element in pushing for *moral* prevention.

The government appeared receptive to this 'medico-moral' strategy, as witnessed in the terms of the Royal Commission, and in the government's subsequent support for the NCCVD. However, once war was declared, venereal disease became defined fundamentally as a military rather than a civilian problem, and under pressure above all from the allied forces, the government capitulated to the demand for some form of state regulation.

Before the war debates about venereal disease had centred both on a narrowly medical cause (certain bacilli) and on the feminist condemnation of human *male* agency. However in the war the central subject to appear in the discourse on venereal disease was the 'amateur' prostitute, to whom responsibility for the transmission of the disease was attributed. The feminist definition and solution to the problem of venereal disease was thereby marginalized. Although this feminist perspective regained some of its strength in the post-war years, as the dominant educative and moralizing forces gathered pace the critique of the man's role in transmitting venereal disease was effectively lost.

Notes and references

1 Dr White, *Eugenics Review* 5, October 1913, p. 270.

2 See Anna Davin, 'Imperialism and motherhood', *History Workshop Journal*, no. 5 (1978); Jane Lewis, *The Politics of Motherhood* (Croom Helm 1980); R. A. Solloway, *Birth Control and the Population Question in England, 1877–1930* (Chapel Hill 1982).

3 The Contagious Diseases Acts of 1864, 1866 and 1868 addressed the dual problems of venereal disease and prostitution. Under their schedules a woman suspected of being a common prostitute could be taken to a certified hospital for medical inspection. If the woman was found to be suffering from venereal infection she could be detained for up to three months and subjected to a hospital regime of education and moral reform. The regulations and the medical discourse surrounding the acts identified active female sexuality as both a moral danger and a physical threat to the nation's health.

4 *The Times*, 6 October 1913.

5 See the feminist Committee of Inquiry, *The State and Sexual Morality* (Allen and Unwin 1920).

6 Gillian Kersley, *Darling Madame: Sarah Grand and Devoted Friend* (Virago 1983), p. 74.

7 ibid., p. 15.

8 See, for example, Ellis Ethelmer, *Woman Free* (Women's Emancipation Union 1893), pp. 100–1.

9 Louisa Martindale, *Under the Surface* (Southern Publishing Co., Brighton, 1908).

10 Committee of Inquiry.

11 Edward Bristow, *Vice and Vigilance* (Gill and Macmillan 1977), p. 193.

12 Frank Gould in *Shield*, June 1917.

13 Ellen Gaskell in *Freewoman*, 18 January 1912, p. 176. Note the evidence of eugenist doctors to the *Royal Commission on Divorce and Matrimonial Causes* (Cd. 6478, 1912).

14 Haynes in *Freewoman*, January 1914. See the attack on Pankhurst's book in the *British Medical Journal*, 4 April 1914, p. 768.

15 Christabel Pankhurst, *The Great Scourge* (E. Pankhurst 1913), pp. 36, 19–20, 110, viii, 24, 26 and 78–9. And for a view supporting the belief that 'innocent' wives were at the mercy of their infected husbands, see Dr Bloxham's evidence to the *Royal Commission on Divorce*, p. 393.

16 *Shield*, April 1914.

17 Louise Creighton, *The Social Disease and How To Fight It: A Rejoinder* (Longman, Green and Co. 1914), pp. 79, 74, 12, 13. Although her 'rejoinder' is not explicitly a response to Pankhurst's *The Great Scourge* it is clear that she has the tract in mind.

18 See Lucy Bland, 'Purity, motherhood, pleasure or threat? Definitions of female sexuality 1900s–1970s', in Sue Cartledge and Joanna Ryan (eds.), *Sex and Love* (Women's Press 1983); Rebecca West in the *Clarion*, 26 September 1913; reprinted in Jane Marcus (ed.), *The Young Rebecca* (Macmillan 1982).

19 Dr R. W. Johnstone, *Report on Venereal Diseases* (Cd. 7029, 1913).

20 *Royal Commission on Venereal Disease, Final Report* (Cd. 8189, 1916).

21 See Judith Walkowitz, *Prostitution and Victorian Society* (Cambridge University Press 1980); Paul McHugh, *Prostitution and Victorian Social Reform* (Croom Helm 1980).
22 See Walkowitz.
23 *Lancet*, 30 January 1897.
24 See, for example, the Advisory Board for the Army Medical Services, 1904; and the *Report of the Royal Commission on Venereal Diseases*, giving the ratios per 1000 admissions for the home army as 275 (in 1885), 86 (in 1900), a slight rise to 110 (in 1902) and dropping to 51 (in 1913).
25 See Morris's evidence to *Joint Select Committee of both Houses on the Criminal Law Amendment Bill and the Sexual Offences Bill* (1918).
26 *Shield*, October 1913.
27 See Bridget Towers, 'Health education policy 1916–26: venereal disease and the prophylaxis dilemma', *Medical History*, no. 24 (1980).
28 Sir Ernley Blackwell's evidence to *Joint Committee*, p. 187.
29 Although this term had been around for many years: see *Shield*, December 1899.
30 See Lucy Bland, ' "Guardians of the race" or "Vampires upon the nation's health"?: Female sexuality and its regulation in early twentieth century Britain', in Elizabeth Whitelegg *et al.*, *The Changing Experience of Women* (Martin Roberston 1982).
31 See Alison Neilans in *Shield*, February 1915, and Lady Barrett's evidence to National Council for Public Morals, *Special Committee on Venereal Disease* (1921).
32 Neilans in *Shield*, February 1915.
33 See e.g. A. Corbett-Smith, *The Problem of the Nations* (Bale 1914), and numerous witnesses to *Joint Committee*.
34 Dr Otto May, *The Prevention of Venereal Disease* (Oxford Medical Publications 1918).
35 Dr H. Wilson, *The Times*, 19 February 1917.
36 See evidence of Sir Ernley Blackwell, *Joint Committee*.
37 Helen Ware, 'The recruitment, regulation and role of prostitution in Britain from the middle of the nineteenth century to the present day' (unpublished PhD thesis, London University 1969).
38 *Parliamentary Debate*, HC XC (1917), 1118 and 1125.
39 See *The Times*, 22 February 1917; *Shield*, March 1917; *Vote*, 9 March 1917 for details of the Medical Women's Federation's opposition.
40 *Statutory Rules and Orders* (1918), pp. 331–2.
41 See issues of *Vote* and *Shield*, April–November 1918.
42 See *Vote*, 23 August 1918.
43 Quoted in *Vote*, 13 September 1918.
44 See AMSH's manifesto on the two bills *Shield*, July 1918, and evidence of Mrs Gordon (President of NUWW) to the *Joint Committee*.
45 *Shield* April 1916.
46 Juliette Heale, *The Woman Pays* (publisher unknown, 1916).

10 Purity, feminism and the state: sexuality and moral politics, 1880–1914

Frank Mort

In July 1885 the Salvation Army launched a nationwide purity campaign, a report of which appeared in *The Times*.[1] In a period of less than three weeks the Army had gathered nearly 4000 signatures for a petition demanding a new Criminal Law Amendment Act to raise the age of consent to eighteen and to give the police increased powers to search and arrest brothel-keepers. The petition was presented to the House of Commons in a dramatic demonstration which was part of a series of campaigns and rallies that took place in the summer of 1885 as an immediate response to the *Pall Mall Gazette's* revelations of the horrors of juvenile prostitution. In early July, W. T. Stead, the paper's editor, had published 'The Maiden Tribute to Modern Babylon',[2] articles which exposed the underlying depravity within aristocratic and fashionable London society and traced the network of vice which linked procuresses and brothel-keepers with the best houses in the West End. He used the language of moral condemnation and evangelical outrage to fuel the campaign for law reform.

Stead's exposé and the Salvation Army spectacle were part of a carefully orchestrated campaign by purity workers and feminists to press the Liberal government to pass the Criminal Law Amendment Bill, which in one form or another had been before Parliament since 1883. The outcome of this campaign was the formation of the National Vigilance Association, whose membership included leaders of women's organizations and prominent feminists. The constitution of the new Association contained feminist demands for the reform of male sexuality together with purity calls for a more coercive policy of sexual regulation. Its main objectives were the enforcement and improvement of the laws for the repression of criminal vice and public immorality.[3] The traditional stress on preventive and rescue work was now linked to campaigns to secure adequate legislation preventing obscenity, indecency and the foreign traffic in young girls.

The purity movement's emphasis on using the state to promote morality marked an important shift away from the traditional strategies of private philanthropy and rescue work which had formed the dominant mid Victorian solution to the problem of prostitution. In contrast the NVA saw the criminal law as an instrument which could improve public morals, and have a positively educative rather than simply repressive role. Legal regulation could be used in conjunction with preventive work. As William Coote, the Association's secretary put it: 'The law becomes schoolmaster to the whole community'. It could exercise 'not merely a preventive and coercive but a didactic influence over opinion and practice'.[4] Legislation was 'the reflex of public opinion, the moral thermometer of the community'. This was a quite new perception of the state's capacity for transforming sexual and moral behaviour. In the thirty years before the First World War purists and feminists consistently argued that criminal legislation was the key to improving sexual morality. The Criminal Law Amendment Act, eventually passed in 1885 as a result of the pressure exerted by private purity organizations, marked the introduction of a new, more coercive system of state intervention into the domain of sexuality. A whole series of acts and statutes followed addressing familiar areas such as prostitution and brothel-keeping and proscribing new practices like male homosexuality and incest.

In an immediate sense purity campaigns for more stringent legislation against immorality were part of the renewed panic about the threat of the urban poor in the 1880s. Purity demands for legislation against prostitution, brothel-keeping and other acts of immorality often explicitly addressed the problems posed by the culture of the urban poor and the difficulties of keeping public order in working-class areas. Agitation may have spoken of *national* morality, but it was clear that the working class was to be the real target of purity action. Many prominent figures in debates over urban poverty were also active in campaigns for legislation against immorality. At the inaugural meeting of the NVA in August 1885 delegates argued that if purity work was to have any chance of success, new criminal laws needed to go hand in hand with state intervention to improve the environment of the urban poor.

Yet the particular role adopted by the state in response to purity demands defies any simple explanation of increased state intervention into sexuality in the late nineteenth and early twentieth centuries. The state was rarely the initiator in the move to criminalize immoralities. There was no expansion of government departments in this area, no recruitment of intellectuals into the state apparatuses. Although the criminal law became increasingly important in moral regulation before 1914 the impetus did not generally come from state agencies. There was no aggressive statist moves towards criminalizing immoralities. The state was a relatively subordinate and often passive partner in the dialogue with purists and feminists. It articulated the various political forces within civil society. Purity groups remained central to the enactment of criminal law legislation – organizing, investigating and petitioning the state to act. In the field of sexuality there was no major shift away from these private, voluntary initiatives, whereas in other areas voluntary organizations were partially eclipsed in this period by new forms of state expertise. Moreover, there was constant and often acrimonious dialogue between purity organizations and state agencies. This was especially so in the case of feminist pressure for law reform.

Feminism and social purity

Feminists were actively involved in the purity campaigns for more coercive state regulation. In the 1880s and 1890s women like Dr Elizabeth Blackwell, Ellice Hopkins, Laura Ormiston-Chant, Millicent Fawcett and Mrs Bramwell Booth argued that the law was central to curbing male immorality and implementing feminist demands around sexuality. Their protests gained renewed impetus in the suffrage struggles immediately before the First World War. A massive campaign was launched by women against the double-standard and its enshrinement in law. The immediate contrast with earlier feminist involvement in sexual politics could not have been sharper. Behind purity feminism lay the legacy of the resistance to the Contagious Diseases Acts.

The repeal movement had been spearheaded by an anti-statist alliance of feminists and radical liberals. Women like Josephine Butler insisted that private voluntary initiatives involving women could do more for moral reform than male-dominated state medicine or the criminal law. Yet a number of prominent repealers, including some feminists, sat on the first executive council of the NVA and threw themselves wholeheartedly into purity work. Recent historians have explained this feminist participation in different ways: either depicting purity women as intrinsically prudish and bigoted, or seeing them as 'seduced' by the conservative aims of the new movement, or stressing that purity was a landmark in the feminist offensive against male sexuality and playing down the contradictory nature of the campaigns.[5] What needs reaffirming here is the complex interrelation between moral languages, often derived from the culture of evangelical religion, and the history of nineteenth-century middle-class feminism.

Religious and ethical morality provided women, quite literally, with a means of representation in the male-defined world of public political debate and with a language which enabled them to develop a feminist critique of male power and domination. This ethical approach often led women to endorse coercive moral regulation. Yet to present the history of late nineteenth-century feminist sexual politics as a 'seduction' by the conservative purity movement is to ignore the much longer contradictory history of middle-class women's involvement in philanthropy and charity work, which dated back at least as far as the evangelical revival in the early nineteenth century.

Ellice Hopkins (1836–1904) displayed many of these contradictions. A central figure in the feminist agitation for criminal law legislation in the 1880s, her rise to prominence in these campaigns was the culmination of a career which combined a feminist commitment to challenging male sexual behaviour with a traditional belief in moralizing philanthropy. Hopkins was clear about the dual strategy of the new purity movement. It needed to be directed to the reform of male sexuality *and* to the improvement of working-class morals. On both issues she acknowledged the importance of the 'women's movement' in promoting reform, noting 'the ever increasing activity in all agencies for the elevation of women . . . above all that new sense of a common *esprit de corps* . . . which is now beginning to bind all our efforts together'.[6] The reform of male sexuality was central both to women's progress and to the evolution of civilization. For Hopkins feminism meant bringing the private sphere of bourgeois womanhood to bear on the public work of social and moral problems.

Hopkins argued that women needed to play a decisive role in public debate on the regulation of the nation's morals precisely because it was women above all who were concerned with sexuality. She was militant and uncompromising about the source of moral evil – *male sexuality* was the fundamental problem. Prostitution was the direct result of men's immorality. It created an outcast class of women and was tacitly approved by church and state.[7] In Hopkins's view all programmes of sexual reform would prove useless unless there was a radical change in men's attitudes. Hopkins, with many other women in the purity movement, increasingly looked to criminal law to enact feminist demands around sexuality. This is the key to understanding social-purity feminists' commitment to coercive legislation in the 1880s. They approved the use of the law to 'protect' women and children from male immorality, to educate men in self-control and chastity, and to reform working-class morals. Men's immorality not only enslaved women but also threatened the stability of the family. In the end it posed a danger to the foundations of good government. It was therefore imperative that the state should intervene to preserve the higher life and progress of the nation.[8]

That the ethical and moral state had an obligation to protect the weak, to promote moral conduct and to encourage the evolution of human development were ideologies particular to the late nineteenth century. These purity ideas resembled the philosophical conceptions of the ethical state outlined by T. H. Green and slightly later by new liberal theorists like Hobson and Hobhouse. Such definitions involved a fusion of Darwin's concept of evolution with older moral and religious traditions. Darwin's *Descent of Man* (1871) had stressed that the growth of moral faculties was central to human evolution. Self-control, combined with love and altruism, were key elements in the progress towards a higher moral culture. Darwin had predicted that these virtuous habits would, in the long term, probably become 'fixed by inheritance'.[9] But purists believed that state intervention could be used to further evolutionary progress. For Hopkins the state could be used to embody the moral law, which was God's law now verified by evolutionary science.[10]

Yet the feminist campaigns for legislation in the later part of the century remained centrally concerned with regulating working-class behaviour. Hopkins emphasized that middle-class women needed to unite with their working-class sisters if male immorality was to be effectively challenged. But the dialogue which purists envisaged between women of different classes was still the traditional bond of philanthropy; the middle-class donor relating to her working-class recipient through notions of moral and material charity. Hopkins appealed to working-class women in the name of 'the common dignity . . . of our womanhood'.[11] Yet working-class women were often seen to be lacking in the moral responsibility which middle-class women could provide for them. Such ambiguities existed in the heart of the feminist dedication to the purity movement. Yet at other times Hopkins herself displayed a much greater awareness of the class basis of the new movement. She understood that purity workers needed a great sensitivity to the class power they wielded. This consciousness sometimes developed into a sustained critique of middle-class morality, with its hypercritical stress on female purity. As Hopkins pointed out, the refinement and sheltered grace of middle-class women had been bought at the price of other women's toil and suffering.[12]

The men at the Home Office

The contradictions in the purity feminist position, and the government's own difficulties in coming to terms with the new movement came to the fore in the debates over the 1885 Criminal Law Amendment Bill. In the early 1880s purists fixed on the perceived growth in child prostitution and the so-called 'white slave trade' to the Continent as the major focuses for their attack. In her address to the White Cross League in 1883 Ellice Hopkins insisted that the 'modest silence' which surrounded the subject had landed England in 'child harlotry'.[13] The only remedy was to 'speak out', getting rid of the vague and horrible air of mystery by carefully defining the extent of the problem. In 1881, in the face of mounting pressure, the British government set up a Lords Select Committee to examine the extent of juvenile prostitution. Its recommendations advocated widespread changes in the criminal law, proposing raising the age of consent from 13 to 16 and extending the provisions of the Industrial Schools Amendment Act. Most controversially, it recommended stronger police powers to search and arrest brothel-keepers and made soliciting in the streets illegal.[14] Much of the political pressure for these last two proposals came from the police themselves.

At the same time women's purity organizations began petitioning the Home Office for a new bill, calling for immediate legislation to raise the age of consent to 18 and to increase police powers to protect children and young girls and to remove girls from brothels.[15] The Home Office response was cautious. It made public declarations supporting the work of the purity movement, insisting that child prostitution was one of the 'burning issues of the day'. But in private it held reservations about the benefits of fresh legislation.[16] In January 1883 Henry Thring, the Attorney-General, had drawn up a draft bill under the Liberal Home Secretary, Sir Vernon Harcourt's direction which incorporated the main recommendations of the Lords Committee, but despite apparent government support a number of ministers objected to the proposals. They were reluctant for police powers to be increased or for the state to become further involved in regulating sexuality. Lord Hartington, the War Secretary, objected to the proposals because of the potential powers the bill gave to 'fanatical local authorities'.[17] Like a number of other senior ministers, he was ambivalent about purists' efforts to reform immorality. The discourse of the purity feminists and evangelicals ran against official Home Office ideology, with its deeply embedded male attitudes towards immorality and its implicit strategy of moral toleration. Hartington confided that he did not really believe that prostitution could ever be removed and that fresh legislation would only drive it into some more objectionable form. The Town Clerk of Hereford, in a letter to the Home Office, felt that the bill actively discriminated against men by ignoring the innate immorality of many women and young girls.[18]

The Attorney-General was also against the proposed increase in police powers, but for different reasons. He felt that the new powers of search and arrest would be used against poor women and that the public attention given to prosecutions would act to *incite* immorality rather than diminish it. He also objected to the proposal to raise the age of consent to 16 viewing it as a device to impress middle-class moral standards on working-class communities.

Outside the state apparatuses influential public opinion was becoming increasingly divided over the contentious issue of greater police powers. Opposition from the anti-statist Vigilance Association and from parliamentary Liberals like Hopwood and Henry Broadhurst, the trade union leader, focused on the threat to personal liberty and the implicit offensive against the poor. It was pointed out that police powers had dangerously increased in recent years while their accountability had diminished. The remedy for immorality was not a centralized state system of surveillance but a co-ordinated network of voluntary efforts directed towards moral education and rescue work.

The purity movement was itself divided over the new proposals, the sticking point being the balance to be struck between police powers and voluntary efforts. Many of them supported the move to recruit the law into the plans for moral reform, but they did not wish to see their own efforts wholly replaced by police powers. The radical liberal, James Stuart, approved of the bill in principle, but wanted amendments which laid the burden of prosecution on private individuals rather than on the state. Anna Wilkes, who ran a rescue home in Poplar, in her evidence to the Lords Committee outlined a form of regulation in which purity workers shared responsibility with the police and the courts, preserving the delicate balance between voluntary bodies and state institutions.[19] It was this solution which was incorporated into the working of the 1885 act in its final form, when the new Conservative government dropped the contentious clauses extending police powers of search and arrest.

The compromise solution

In the early years purity groups received little or no help from the state in implementing the 1885 act. It soon became disappointingly clear to the NVA that what had been conceived as a two-way process between voluntary bodies and the state in practice placed the burden of day-to-day regulation heavily on private initiatives. A number of factors influenced this highly cautious approach by government, local authorities, the police and the courts. Some arose from the practical difficulties of sexual regulation, others from the fact that the courts, the police and local councils were ill-equipped to initiate the type of prosecutions for which the purity groups were pressing. In the months after the act was passed the Home Office was inundated with letters from local police chiefs and magistrates demanding clarification on the extent of the new police powers of prosecution.

The compromise between state regulation and private vigilance often meant that neither side took the initiative. The police did not possess the necessary administrative machinery to root out types of immorality which often necessitated detailed and painstaking investigative work. In addition, as Coote acknowledged, in the early years magistrates were often hostile to the aims and methods of the purity groups and were loathe to convict, especially in cases which seemed to contradict the principles of common law.[20]

However, vacillation over state involvement was more than just a problem of administration and bureaucracy. The political and ideological legacy of the Contagious Diseases Acts also played a part. Successive Liberal and Conservative administrations had lost the battle for the state-medical regulation of female sexuality largely as a result of feminist opposition. It was clear that ministers did not relish a repetition of the humiliating defeat they had sustained over the suspension (1883) and repeal (1886) of the Contagious Diseases Acts.

Influential judges and lawyers and senior ministers of both parties were deeply suspicious of purity groups. Hartington was not untypical in regarding their members as evangelical faddists and fanatics who needed to be restrained. However it was evident that evangelicals like Samuel Smith and Henry Wilson were beginning to transform Liberal opinion. The 1880s witnessed a renewed nonconformist assault on the Liberal Party. When a prominent Liberal like Sir Charles Dilke and the Irish nationalist leader Charles Parnell became involved in divorce scandals, W. T. Stead, among others, was instrumental in politically destroying them. Nevertheless, many senior politicians regarded the purity movement as beyond the pale. A number of the new purity leaders, like Coote and Alfred Dyer, came from respectable working-class or petit-bourgeois backgrounds. Their moralistic style of campaigning differed from the measured, middle-class radicalism of the repealers, and their evangelical tones jarred with the dominant language of high politics. It was also clear that feminist involvement in the purity movement had much to do with the opposition from men within the state apparatuses. 'Faddism' and 'fanaticism' were the terms used by middle-class and aristocratic men to express contempt for feminism. The antagonism between the purity groups and the state representatives was particularly intense over feminist issues. This tension pointed to a deep split within the male-dominated power bloc arising from divergent views on sexual and moral behaviour.

Moreover, the late nineteenth century witnessed the crystallization of the two-party parliamentary system, the growing strength of the organized working class and the gradual decline of the big single-issue movements which had been such a central feature of the mid Victorian political scene. The 'political' was itself redefined. Successive governments from the 1880s hesitated to introduce fresh legislation on immorality because the issue was seen to lie outside politics. It was thus not the concern of national administrations. Liberal Home Secretaries like Reginald McKenna and Herbert Gladstone consistently refused to pledge their government to support a new Criminal Law Amendment Bill in Parliament. Coote pointed out that both men were privately committed to the legislation, but felt that they could not involve the government on the issue.[21]

A pragmatic compromise between state and private organizations formed the dominant strategy of regulation between 1890 and 1910. In the early years the executive committee of the NVA, angry about the cautious approach of the Home Office, the police and the courts, decided to initiate prosecutions themselves. But in an 1887 test case the Home Office had ruled that vigilance associations could not recover their costs for prosecutions from government funds. The NVA faced similar problems in its efforts to press successive governments to introduce fresh legislation. As early as 1886 the Association's legal sub-committee had drawn up a series of amendments to the criminal law that it wanted to see on the statute book. These included, among other measures, raising the age of consent to 18, the abolition of the notorious 'escape clause' (allowing male defendants in assault cases to claim that they believed the girl to be over 16), the extension of the time limit for prosecutions, and legislation criminalizing incest and male importuning. By 1922 all these measures had been enacted. But the impetus and pressure still came largely from feminist and purity organizations and only rarely from the government.

In the 1890s purity groups began to make some headway at a local level by persuading the police and the courts to support their programme. A number of local police chiefs became members of the Association, like the Chief Constable of Birmingham and the notorious Inspector Burroughs in Manchester. A two-way system of regulation began to be established, whereby purity groups either presented information to the police or the local authorities, or the police referred cases to the purists themselves. Co-operation of this kind was most effective in the provincial cities of the north, with their strongly nonconformist councils.

Incest was another area which revealed the growing convergence of opinion between purists, women's groups, the police and the Home Office. The offence was not covered by any effective punishment under law. In the early 1890s the NVA began to pass on evidence of cases to the Home Office, pointing out the difficulties of prosecuting under existing legislation. In 1894 the Ladies' National Association, the feminist veterans of the repeal movement, mounted a campaign to amend the 1885 act to criminalize incest. Though no progress was made when Henry Wilson introduced a bill in 1896 there was growing support for legislation from the police.[22] When the Incest Act was finally passed in 1908 purity feminists claimed it as a triumph.

But it was prostitution which increasingly preoccupied purity workers at a local level. This problem was examined in the 1908 Royal Commission on the Metropolitan Police, and the commissioners concluded that they were well satisfied with police conduct over street prostitution. William Coote, the NVA secretary, however, did object to the double standard enshrined in police practice, and recommended that the existing law should also be used to prosecute *male clients*.[23] The report countered this by insisting on the fundamental difference between occasional solicitation by a man ('addressed to a woman who does not resent it') and the prostitute's immoral business, which was offensive to public decency. Besides, it was argued that prosecutions against male clients would not be acceptable to 'the community at large'.[24] Despite this setback, Coote pronounced himself well pleased with the state of the streets in the metropolis. Men like Coote bothered little about the effects of their work on the prostitutes themselves. They were much more intent on maintaining public order. What was needed was more of the same – intensified police action backed by the ever watchful vigilance of the purity movement.

Suffrage and sexuality: 1908–14

Sexuality became a major issue in the suffrage movement. As Lucy Bland has shown in the previous chapter, alongside the struggle for the vote emerged demands for legislation to curb immorality and to 'protect' women and children. Many feminists in the Women's Social and Political Union, the National Union of Women's Suffrage Societies and the Women's Freedom League formed alliances with purity groups like the NVA, and shared their trenchant critique of male sexuality. The purity position on sexuality became hegemonic within the early women's movement, though it did not go unchallenged. Many feminists looked to the state to enact their demands in the moral as well as the political sphere. They identified a common interest with the purity movement in pressing for reforming legislation.

There was extensive overlapping membership among the purity and vigilance organizations and the various suffrage groups and women's organizations. In the period immediately before the First World War the growing political militancy of groups like the WSPU radicalized the older, more traditional women's organizations. Feminist books and pamphlets incorporated the languages of social purity, religion, medicine and mysticism in a sustained attack on men's sexual attitudes and behaviour. In particular, feminists fought a protracted ideological campaign over Darwinist and eugenist theories and their application to women. Christabel Pankhurst and Frances Swiney drew heavily on racial and evolutionary discourses in their denunciation of male sexuality. Christabel Pankhurst argued that sexuality had been given in trust for the perpetuation of the race but men chose to squander it in degeneracy and debauchery.[25] Swiney's polemic went much further. She claimed women's innate biological, mental and 'racial' superiority and argued that both Darwin and Spencer had been wrong to claim that women were in a state of arrested evolutionary development. It was *men* who were the prime cause of racial decay – through their immorality, their lack of social responsibility and above all by spreading venereal disease:

No female animal has been so ruthlessly, so brutally, so generally mercilessly exploited by the male as woman. . . . She stands as the martyr of an organized and systematic sexual wrong-doing on the part of the man. . . . Vices, however, like curses, come home to roost. In his own enfeebled frame, in his diseased tissue, in his weak will, his gibbering idiocy, his raving insanity and hideous criminality, he reaps the fruits of a dishonoured motherhood.[26]

Many feminists argued that celibacy was a positive step in women's self-advancement. Cicely Hamilton's *Marriage as a Trade* (1909) was a superb polemic in favour of celibacy, arguing that marriage represented a narrowing of women's hopes and ambitions, and that through the sex act men secured women's continuing subordination by cutting off 'every avenue of escape from the gratification of their desire', denying female sexuality any outlet other than compulsory heterosexuality.[27] Men hated and despised spinsters, Hamilton claimed, precisely because the 'perpetual virgin' was a witness to the fact that the sex act was not 'an absolute necessity for women'.[28]

In arguing for celibacy, and spinsterhood, feminists were resisting the growing *sexualization* of women in orthodox medicine and psychology. They also rejected the work of male sexual radicals like Havelock Ellis and

Edward Carpenter and challenged the idea that sexuality lay at the heart of women's personality. Many women mobilized around a quasi-religious or theosophical language to envisage a new, spiritualized form of the sex relation, free of male control. Pankhurst believed that in the future evolution of society, under women's guidance, sex would be raised to a higher plane, where physical passion would be transmuted into human love.[29]

Petitioning the state

As the suffrage struggle intensified many feminists began to insist that the campaign for women's citizenship and the demand for legislation to curb male immorality were interlinked. The vote was perceived as bringing both political and *moral* benefits to women. Christabel Pankhurst argued that 'when women are citizens they will have the power to secure the enactment of laws for their protection'.[30] Militant feminists pointed out that sexual antagonism lay at the heart of the suffrage struggle and could never be resolved within the discourse of political liberalism. Lucy Re-Bartlett, closely associated with the WSPU, argued that sexuality was the underlying issue in the feminist movement:

The public roughly seems to be divided between people who deny the struggle any sexual significance at all, and those who, seeing the significance, attribute it to sexual morbidity and hysteria. The situation with which we are face to face represents indeed a sex war. . . . It is a war which signifies vitality, not decadence.[31]

Feminists saw the state as a tool to circumscribe male power in the political as in the moral sphere. Hamilton pointed out that 'in ordinary life it is the strong arm of the law and not the strong arm of the individual husband which secures women from hurt or molestation'.[32]

The state-orientated strategy adopted by many feminists was clearly related to their affiliations with social purity. But it also had much to do with the overwhelmingly middle-class and aristocratic composition of the feminist movement. Many women came to feminism from social backgrounds in which the state was perceived as an instrument for enacting their own class specific demands through notions of liberal and beneficent paternalism. But many others rapidly became aware that the state itself was patriarchal and needed transformation if women were to be fully represented in the nation's political and moral life. As Christabel Pankhurst argued, the state was composed of men who not only denied women the vote but also tacitly condoned male immorality and sexual violence to women. Men had all the power in the state and therefore not only made its laws but also its morality.[33] As women intensified the campaign of militant action in 1912 and 1913 they became acutely aware that male attitudes and traditions, deeply embedded in the legal profession, the police and the courts, sustained not only men's formal *political* power but also the sexual oppression of women.

Many of the suffrage papers began to carry reports of cases of sexual harassment and male sexual violence towards women in an attempt to raise consciousness and sustain the pressure for law reform. The *Vote* reported one incident of child assault in Surrey, where a man was sentenced to only four months hard labour. Feminists organized a local campaign over the issue at election time, returning a woman to the municipal council on the specific platform of curbing male immorality. The *Common Cause*, reporting a case of wrongful arrest of a woman for alleged prostitution, commented that the suspect was 'taken to a man's court, tried and sentenced by men under men's laws for a fault she cannot commit alone.'[34]

The National Union of Women Workers (NUWW) and the LNA had long been campaigning for legislation to raise the age of consent to 18 and to enforce more stringent penalties against procurers and brothel-keepers. In 1912 their efforts were joined by other women's groups to press the Liberal government to enact the White Slave Traffic Bill, which had been before Parliament in one form or another since 1909. The government's attitude to the proposals, and its relation to feminist and purity pressure groups, displayed all the hesitations and ambiguities which had characterized similar debates in the 1880s and 1890s. Deeply entrenched male sexual attitudes among senior politicians and civil servants revealed themselves in suspicion of feminist aims and intentions, and often in outbursts of explicit anti-feminism and misogyny. Behind the doors of the Home Office, feminist pressure for moral reform, combined with the growing militancy of the suffrage campaign, were challenging the accepted codes and conventions embedded in state administration. Home Office records for the period reveal how politicians and senior civil servants negotiated feminist demands with a mixture of amused contempt and double-dealing. While pledging themselves publicly to moral reform, they worked privately to block many of the attempts to secure new legislation.

A new Criminal Law Amendment Bill had been drawn up in 1909, as a result of pressure on the Home Secretary by the Jewish Association for the Protection of Girls and Women and the NVA. When an influential purity deputation went to the Home Office, Herbert Samuel, then the Under-Secretary of State, declared himself personally committed to legislation in the interests of 'national honour', yet, as Coote noted, he refused to pledge the government to introduce the proposals in Parliament, or even to support them publicly.[35] The outcome of the meeting was the usual compromise. The government kept aloof, if not deliberately obstructive, for official hesitation continued on the question of whether legislation on immorality was a proper area for state intervention. In response to parliamentary questions demanding that the government introduce its own bill, rather than relying on private members' initiatives, the Home Office made its position clear: 'We strongly support the proposed Bill . . . but do not see how it is possible for the Government to undertake legislation.'[36]

Meanwhile, purity groups and feminist organizations intensified their pressure on the government in a nationwide campaign. A special Pass the Bill Committee was formed and the Home Office was inundated with letters and memorials from suffrage societies. The LNA forwarded to Asquith nearly 300 resolutions in favour of the bill with over seventy from feminist organizations. By this stage, Asquith himself was worried by government inactivity, and he wrote to McKenna expressing concern about the continued obstruction, insisting that the Home Office should speed up its progress.[37]

The bill became law in December 1912. But in its final committee stages the clauses giving greater police powers of search and arrest were revised, rendering them almost useless. Though the original clauses were eventually restored, feminists involved in the campaign to pass the bill were deeply split on the question of increased police powers. There were those in the LNA, the NUWW and the women members of the NVA who argued that a more coercive approach by the police was essential for the protection of 'innocent women and children'.[38] Purity feminist support for the bill reflected acceptance of the traditional polarities of 'pure' and 'impure' women; prostitutes were to be pitied but they did not deserve special protection.[39] The NUWSS, however, warned that although the bill deserved general support, the clauses extending police powers needed careful monitoring 'lest they should lead to further harrying of the unfortunate women'.[40] The *Common Cause* argued that coercive legislation was no substitute for tackling the more fundamental problems of poverty and male immorality which stimulated the prostitution trade.[41]

These feminist differences surfaced in a more extreme form in the months after the passing of the act. The LNA saw the new measures as only a beginning. The *Shield* insisted that there was enough conviction and enthusiasm among women to carry further legislation, despite the blatant obstruction from men at the Home Office and in Parliament.[42] The Pankhurst-led WSPU made the twin issues of male immorality and white slavery central to its campaign in 1913, as part of its increasingly militant offensive. The *Suffragette* argued that the new act did not go far enough in curbing male immorality. When Emmeline Pankhurst was tried at the Old Bailey in April 1913, she made the white slavery issue central to her demand for female suffrage. Women, she claimed, 'believed that the horrible evils . . . ravaging our civilization will never be removed until women get the vote'.[43]

But not all feminists approved of these tactics. Teresa Billington-Grieg of the Women's Freedom League condemned the strategy of coercion and the assumptions implicit in the new act. She believed that the law and police had long been shown to have little or no educative or preventive power and that the only way forward was a changed moral outlook and gradual reorganization of economic and social conditions. She went further and accused Christabel and Emmeline Pankhurst and the misplaced moralists of the

LNA and other purity groups as 'dabblers in debauchery'. They had set middle-class women on the rampage against an evil they knew nothing about, 'feeding and flattering a sexual ideology which juxtaposed the moral perfection of women against the bestiality of men'. Nothing had been done for the women who were exploited by prostitution, except to introduce a more punitive regime. Meanwhile the cause of sex reform had been set back by the 'whitewashing of women and the doctrine of the uncleanness of men'.[44] Sylvia Pankhurst's *Women's Dreadnought* developed a similar line of argument. From a very different perspective the *Freewoman*, a radical individualist feminist weekly committed to the 'new morality' based on 'free-unions' also criticized the purity lobby and the coercive consequences of its campaigning. But purity feminists were quick to counter-attack. The *Freewoman* received a spate of letters defending the act. Contributors argued that purity *was* a positive advance for women and that the paper's editors should 'declare themselves to be on the side of reverence and self-control'. Others pointed out that the so-called toleration of the new moralists would merely lead to licentiousness and hinder the sexual freedom of women.[45]

Conclusion

The differences which surfaced over the Criminal Law Amendment Act were symptomatic of deeper divisions within the women's movement about representations of female sexuality and about the role of the state. The new act represented a high point for purity feminism; in the post-war period its politics were increasingly under attack, both from those who stressed the importance of female heterosexual pleasure and from anti-feminists. The growing centrality of the criminal law as a mode of sexual regulation and as the focal point of feminist politics forces us to reassess accounts of 'modern sexuality', such as Foucault's, which stress the subordination of legal controls and the growth of more complex discursive forms of power organized through multiple social practices and knowledge.[46] In legislative terms the reverse occurs in this period: the law dominates the field, but it does not operate through the simple mechanisms of censorship and repression. The law is itself *productive*: seeking out and redefining forms of dangerous or 'deviant' sexuality (the 'fallen woman', the adolescent, the 'pervert'), organizing the cultural and social experience (and the pleasures and desires) of dominated groups and stimulating political demands. There is no simple distinction between juridical and discursive forms of power as Foucault seems to suggest.

Moreover, this emphasis on the law was not the product of some internal shift in the 'technologies of power'; it was the outcome of protracted political struggles. Purity groups, and in particular purity feminists, were both 'inside' and 'outside' the state. They provided a continuing source of private, voluntary regulation in an area where the Home Office and other apparatuses remained cautious about direct intervention. But they also mounted an effective feminist challenge to male sexual power. The feminist campaigns around the state effectively unmasked the 'unofficial' masculine culture of the legislators and administrators, with its deeply ambivalent attitudes to women, which formed the hidden element in policy-making.

The moral discourses of purity feminism were neither a reactionary barrier to feminist progress, nor were they the passive vehicle for conveying an emergent feminist consciousness on sexuality. They were the battleground on which conflicting aims and intentions struggled for space. The class and gender contradictions which confronted these feminists were not merely the result of unfortunate political alliances but of the much longer history of middle-class women's involvement in the field of 'social' regulation. Rescue work, philanthropy and purity crusades were class-specific formations concerned with the moral disciplining of the working class, but they also provided women with space to develop knowledge and feminist strategies to challenge the power of male experts and professionals.

Notes and references

1   *The Times*, 31 July 1885.
2   'The Maiden Tribute to Modern Babylon', *Pall Mall Gazette*, 6, 7, 8, 10 July 1885.
3   National Vigilance Association, *Constitution and Rules of the National Vigilance Association for the Repression of Criminal Vice and Public Immorality* (1885), p. 3.
4   William Coote, 'Law and morality', in James Marchant (ed.), *Public Morals* (Morgan and Scott 1902), p. 45.
5   See Edward Bristow, *Vice and Vigilance*, especially ch. 5; Jeffrey Weeks, *Sex, Politics and Society*, ch. 5; Judith Walkowitz, 'Male vice and feminist virtue: feminism and the politics of prostitution in nineteenth-century Britain', in *History Workshop* 13 (spring 1982), pp. 79–93; Sheila Jeffries, 'Free from all uninvited touch of man: women's campaigns around sexuality, 1880–1914', in *Women's Studies International Forum*, 5 no. 6 (1982), pp. 629–45.
6   E. Hopkins, *The Power of Womanhood; or mothers and sons* (Wells Gardner and Co. 1899), p. 2.
7   E. Hopkins, *Work in Brighton* (Hatchards 1877), p. 60.
8   Hopkins, *The Power of Womanhood*, p. 160.
9   Charles Darwin, *The Descent of Man* in M. Bates and P. Humphrey (eds.), *The Darwin Reader* (Macmillan 1957), pp. 284–93.
10 Hopkins, *The Power of Womanhood*, p. 213.
11 Hopkins, *Work in Brighton*, p. 82.
12 ibid., p. 23.
13 E. Hopkins, *The White Cross Army, A Statement of the Bishop of Durham's Movement* (Hatchards 1883), p. 4.
14 *Report from the Select Committee of the House of Lords on the Law Relating to*

the Protection of Young Girls; Together with the Proceedings of the Committee, Minutes of Evidence and Appendix, 1882; GBPP, 1822, XIII, p. 823.

15   Bath Preventive Mission and Ladies Association for the Care of Friendless Girls to Sir Vernon Harcourt (23 February 1884), PRO HO 45/9546/59343 G; London Women's Christian Association to W. E. Gladstone (22 February 1884), PRO HO 45/9546/59343 G.

16   See Home Office Memo by Lord Kinnaird in response to a letter from the Young Women's Christian Association (1884), PRO HO 45/9546/59343 G.

17   Hartington to Rosebery (30 May 1883), PRO HO 45/9546/593343 G.

18   Town Clerk of Hereford to Rt. Hon. Sir R. A. Cross, Under-Secretary of State Home Office (29 September 1885), PRO HO 45/9656/A40683. See also Home Office Memo on 'Present state of the criminal law' and 'on Proposals to introduce a new bill' (3 January 1883).

19   Evidence of Mrs Anna Wilkes, *Lords Select Committee* (1882), pp. 872–4.

20   W. Coote, *A Romance of Philanthropy. Being a record of the work of the National Vigilance Association* (National Vigilance Association 1916), p. 27.

21   Coote, *A Romance*, pp. 156–60.

22   See: NVA, *16th Annual Report* (1901), p. 27; PRO HO 45/A57406/1 quoted in Victor Bailey and Sheila Blackburn, 'The Punishment of Incest Act 1908: a case study of criminal law creation', *Criminal Law Review* (November 1979).

23   *Report of the Royal Commission upon the Duties of the Metropolitan Police together with Appendices*, 1908; GBPP, 1908, L, p. 135.

24   ibid.

25   Christabel Pankhurst, *The Great Scourge* (Edition Pankhurst 1913), p. 61; and p. 98.

26   Francis Swiney, *The Bar of Isis; or, the Law of the Mother* (Open Road Publishing Co. 1907), p. 38.

27   Cicely Hamilton, *Marriage as a Trade* (Chapman and Hall 1909), pp. 37–8.

28   ibid., p. 38.

29   Pankhurst, p. 128.

30   ibid., p. viii.

31   Lucy Re-Bartlett, *Sex and Sanctity* (Longman and Co. 1912), p. 28.

32   Hamilton, *Marriage*, p. 135.

33   Pankhurst, pp. 118–19; see also Hamilton, *Marriage*, p. 135.

34   'A wronged woman', *Common Cause*, 9 November 1911, p. 530.

35   Coote, *A Romance*, pp. 159–60; also the report in *Common Cause*, 2 May 1912, p. 53.

36   See Home Office memo, undated, in response to parliamentary question from Mr France on the Criminal Law Amendment Bill (8 May 1912), in PRO HO 45/10576/178486.

37   Asquith to Home Office (7 May 1912), PRO HO 45/10576/178486.

38   See, for example, 'A mutilating amendment', *Shield*, August 1912, p. 137.

39   'Debate on the Criminal Law Amendment Bill', NUWW Annual Conference, 1912; NUWW, *Handbook and Report* (1912–13).

40   'White Slave Traffic Bill', *Common Cause*, 13 June 1912.

41   ibid.

42   'The next step', *Shield*, January 1913.

43   'Mrs Pankhurst's speech at the Old Bailey', *Suffragette*, 11 April 1913.

44 Teresa Billington Grieg, 'The truth about white slavery', *English Review*, June 1913, pp. 428, 445 and 446.

45 See, among many, Gertrude Slater, 'Champions of morality', *Freewoman*, 13 June 1912.

46 M. Foucault, *The History of Sexuality* (Penguin 1980).

11 Child welfare and the working-class family

Caroline Rowan

This chapter discusses early welfare legislation as it affected the working-class family in general and working-class mothers in particular. The early twentieth century witnessed a new national concern with the education of working-class mothers in housewifery and childcare and the creation of new norms of working-class domesticity and motherhood. Although other factors, in particular the education system, contributed to this process this discussion concentrates on welfare policy, since it is here that the contra-dictory nature of social reforms, in relation to both class and gender, was most apparent. I shall examine the extent to which social reform not only improved working-class health and reduced infant mortality, but also contained a strategy for the construction of a new kind of working-class family, home-centred like its middle-class counterpart, and a source both of future labour power and social stability.

As we show in Chapter 5, in the late nineteen century it had become increasingly evident that poverty was threatening large sections of the respectable working class, and that if they were not to lapse into permanent pauperism, state aid outside the Poor Law system was not only justified but essential. The involvement of the state with working-class health was influenced by concern for the quality of labour power. In this context of height-ened imperial rivalry, however, the crisis was perceived as one of soldier power as well as of labour power. General Maurice's revelations in the press about the poor physique of recruits for the Boer War caused a public outcry. He claimed a direct correlation between inferior physique in adulthood and poor childhood conditions. The Interdepartmental Committee on Physical Deterioration[1] was set up to investigate these allegations, and while it found no evidence for 'progressive race deterioration' it did acknowledge wide-spread poverty. Many of its recommendations focused on the conditions of childbearing and rearing, giving pride of place to proposed reforms for the domestic education of mothers. With the exception of school meals and medical inspection few of the committee's recommendations were imple-mented. However, with its stress on infancy and childhood and the problem of maternal ignorance it provided the terms of reference for the major debates about child welfare in the future.

It is significant that Maurice stressed the national dimension of the problem. It was not enough to encourage the fittest to join up; the health of the nation as a whole must be improved. This imperial project linked child health with the ideology of national efficiency, an ideology which stressed above all 'racial efficiency'. As Lord Rosebery, a leading exponent of national efficiency, wrote to *The Times*:

An Empire such as ours requires as its first condition an imperial race – a race vigorous and industrious and intrepid. Health of mind and body exalt a nation in the competition of the universe. The survival of the fittest is an absolute truth in the conditions of the modern world.[2]

By linking questions of imperial superiority to that of the imperial race, the discourse of national efficiency placed the national physique at the centre of debate and made the question of working-class health a matter for state concern. The falling birth-rate, a high infant mortality rate and the poor physique of children who survived infancy forced state administrators to intervene in family life to improve the conditions of procreation and child-rearing.

Ideological transformations

At the beginning of the twentieth century there was still very strong opposition to family welfare. The provision of school meals, for example, aroused exceptional hostility as it violated not only the principles of *laissez-faire* but also of parental responsibility. The success of the child welfare movement therefore depended on its ability to rearticulate older ideologies to a new principle of welfare reform, in terms both of the national interest and of popular demand. The new discourse in favour of child welfare was carefully constructed around three themes: the organic community, the rights of the child and national efficiency.

The concept of the organic community provided the legitimation for many of the arguments in favour of state intervention in the family. For example the Fabian Medical Officer of Health, G. F. McCleary, stressed the interdependence of the community and its individual members:

The movement for the protection of children had also been inspired by a growing sense of social solidarity which regards the welfare of the community as depending upon the welfare of the children so intimately that any injury inflicted upon the children is transmitted to the whole community.

He went on to argue that the state intervened to reinforce rather than supplant parental responsibility:

It has not lightened the load of the responsibility which should properly fall on the parent; on the contrary it has fixed upon the parent new obligations for which it holds him responsible under pain of penalty.[3]

The second justification was the protection of the child. This was a relatively new idea since children had previously been seen as little more than the legal property of their parents. In this period, however, developments in physiology, nutritional science and psychology all stressed the specificity of the child's needs. The concept of the child as a legal subject and citizen entitled to state protection was a logical consequence of the emergence of a scientific understanding of the child's needs. School meals campaigner John Gorst summed up the new view of state responsibility for children's welfare:

It is one of the duties of civilized society to protect the rights of every citizen, big and little, and to secure the performance of the corresponding duty. But in the case of default by the parents, the child has a further right of recourse to the state and a right to be maintained at public expense. This is not 'socialism'. It is a description of the law of the land.[4]

However, it was the child's value as future citizen that provided the link between the two main arguments for state intervention. The child's rights and the priority of the community over the parent fused in the notion of the child as a national asset or social investment, within the discourse of national efficiency. Gorst himself invariably linked the two arguments:

The child, it must be remembered, has a legal right to have all things necessary for its health, in default of their being provided for it by its parents, furnished at public expense, and even if it had no such legal right, it would be generally good economics for the state to provide such necessaries now, in order to save greater expenditure hereafter.[5]

These beliefs formed the basis of the new ideology underlying child welfare reform. It was a contradictory ideology and delivered at best a fragile solution with many powerful groups remaining resistant or unconvinced. The Charity Organization Society (COS), for example, continued to regard child welfare as a form of unconditional relief which, lacking the deterrent stigma of the Poor Law, would remove the incentive for parental self-improvement. In connection with school meals, Sir Arthur Clay, a COS official, wrote:

To feed a child is to give relief to its parents, and the effect must be to undermine their independence and self-reliance, and to give their children an object-lesson in the evasion of responsibility which . . . will bear fruit when they in their turn become parents.[6]

The absence of a strong consensus in favour of child welfare measures meant that legislation could not be binding on local authorities. This enabled the COS to exert a strong influence at local level. In London, for example, COS workers threw themselves wholeheartedly into the organization of the children's care committees set up by the London County Council to supervise the relief of schoolchildren.

Other influential voluntary groupings, such as eugenists and social Darwinists were divided over the issue of infant welfare. Some argued that state intervention aimed at reducing the infant mortality rate interfered with natural selection; others, that environmental improvement by the state was necessary because natural selection had already been disturbed by industrialization. More generally the issue of child welfare cut across political parties, from the Lab/Lib John Burns to the Tory John Gorst, and the movement was supported by collectivists of many shades, including the national efficiency movement, Fabians and new liberals. But child welfare never became a popular issue. Support from the labour movement and from working people was decidedly muted. This lack of popular enthusiasm had far-reaching effects on the form in which child welfare measures were eventually implemented.

The labour movement

Feminist and labour movement activity was conspicuously absent from the campaign, especially in the pre-war years. However, in the struggle for the vote the Fabian Women's Group made explicit links between suffrage and motherhood and campaigned for family allowances.

In the labour movement there developed a few isolated local campaigns. However, not until the First World War, when the War Emergency Workers' National Committee took up the issues of maternal and child care, did the labour movement give much active support to campaigns for child welfare.

This was due to a combination of class and patriarchal issues. As a class, working people might reasonably fear the increased state regulation and imposition of middle-class norms which would be likely to accompany any new benefits. Indeed, there is ample evidence of the eagerness of legislators to organize working-class lives according to middle-class habits. In relation to child-rearing, middle-class culture centred on the segregation of children from adults and the maintenance of a long period of child dependence for educational purposes. Working-class families did not conform to such notions. Until the mid nineteenth century the role of children in contributing to the family's subsistence had been unquestioned. In our period they still contributed to the domestic economy, and often played a substantial role in the widespread practice of homeworking. This lack of segregation, which led to early maturity and a short period of child dependence, was particularly deplored by middle-class reformers.

While they might have welcomed milk or blankets for their children, the working classes resisted attempts to undermine the communal solidarity of working-class family life. It was the *nature* of the advice, rather than the fact of intrusion into the home, which working-class men found threatening. Visitors who advised their wives on childrearing not only attempted to impose middle-class norms, but appeared as rivals to the father's authority over his family.

The labour movement was deeply divided on the question of the relationship between the family and the state. The Social Democratic Federation (SDF) favoured collective and communal childcare or state maintenance. But the majority of men and women in the labour movement regarded the family as compatible with the socialist ideal and state intervention as at best a palliative, at worst a gross violation of family privacy. These divisions prevented a concerted mobilization in favour of child welfare reforms.

Problems of the relationship between family and state were reflected in the discussions of the Women's Labour League. Most labour women, with the exception of the Fabians, endorsed the ideology which ascribed specific roles to the male as breadwinner and to the female as homemaker. The League had no objection to maternity and child welfare facilities and supported continuous medical supervision for all children under school age provided it included treatment as well as advice. However, with the exception of its own successful clinic in North Kensington, its members initiated few campaigns. The League did little to influence its male comrades to support maternity and child welfare reform.[7]

The Women's Co-operative Guild, however, fought for maternity and child welfare reforms with energy and success. The Guild, the most autonomous organization of working-class women, developed a clear view of women's rights to economic independence, intellectual stimulation and freedom from drudgery. Its campaign made a priority of the welfare of the mother rather than of abstract duties of mother to child or nation. In 1913, in opposition to Labour MPs, the Guild secured the payment of maternity benefit directly to the mother. With the help of its widely read book *Maternity: letters from working women* (published in 1915), the Guild campaigned for a comprehensive system of maternity services, organized by a Ministry of Health and local authorities rather than voluntary organizations. Many of its demands constituted the basis of the reforms subsequently implemented in the early years of the Ministry of Health.

Child welfare work before the war

The main impetus for child welfare came from medical officers of health. This was a professional movement, but one which was locally based and concerned with environmental improvement and preventive medicine. Before 1907, neither initiatives nor funds came from central government, and the movement was initially heavily dependent on voluntary organizations, such as infant health societies.

In 1907, due to the efforts of its Permanent Secretary, R. L. Morant, the Board of Education acquired a medical department. The Board authorities hoped that this would enable them to circumvent the inactive Local Government Board. Morant's wording of the 1907 Education (Administrative Provisions) Bill ensured that the new medical department had powers well beyond its sponsors' original intentions. These included the power to allocate Exchequer grants to schools for mothers.

Medical officers of health influenced the development of welfare policy in several important respects. The medical profession's response to the problem of infant mortality in terms of educating the individual mother was a crucial starting point. The concern of medical officers of health with sanitary conditions gave them access to the working-class home, and as local authority employees they had freedom of action in their own areas. They could set up comprehensive infant welfare schemes in a number of cities and attempt to force central government to take more concerted action. The medical officers of health also enjoyed access to central government through their allies in the Medical Departments of the Board of Education and the Local Government Board. Before 1914, however, they won nothing more than moral support from these central state agencies.

They also exercised a strong influence over voluntary organizations. At a local level this operated through joint schemes, and by getting medical and financial assistance. At a national level the National Association for the Prevention of Infant Mortality was the main umbrella organization. And as state professionals themselves they championed the adoption of proper medical 'expertise' and, more discreetly, the replacement of the voluntary worker by the trained midwife and health visitor.

The combination of municipal and voluntary activity established the basic pattern of infant welfare services. This framework, with the later addition of trained midwifery and ante-natal care, was taken over by the Ministry of Health in 1919. The fundamental aim was the individual instruction of the mother at infant consultations, weighing centres and schools for mothers, combined with home visiting by health visitors.

In practice, individual instruction bore only a tenuous relationship to the real causes of infant mortality and was in any case often impractical in working-class homes. Instruction was more immediately related to reinforcing traditional notions of domesticity, and was imbued with middle-class prejudice; for example, condemning women's paid employment.

The infant welfare movement constantly stressed the importance of breastfeeding which meant that early attention needed to be given to women's health. Dr Eric Sykes, for example, of the St Pancras School for Mothers (founded in 1907) recognized that poverty prevented breastfeeding and provided dinners for expectant and nursing mothers on condition that they breastfed. By 1913, fifty institutions were providing cheap or free dinners for mothers. The main function of both infant consultations and schools for mothers was again to educate the mother. Schools for mothers provided class teaching, which from 1907 was subsidized by the Board of Education. However these classes were not generally a success. In practice both schools for mothers and infant consultations provided a range of services, such as feeding advice, baby weighing and medical examination, but they rarely provided medical treatment, other than the milk, vitamins and sometimes food which the medical officer might supply for infants or mothers.

It is difficult to assess how widely the clinics were used and who used them. Despite fears that they might become relief agencies for the poor, the limited evidence available suggests they were used by the 'respectable' working class. Although the glowing accounts of the popularity of the centres written by their sponsors may be discounted as prejudiced, the views of more independently-minded working-class women such as Hannah Mitchell indicate that, once they had lost the taint of philanthropy and patronage, they provided a useful service to working-class women.[8]

In the early days of the movement reformers regarded health visitors, who worked closely with infant welfare centres, as the lynchpin of the service. Systematic supervision in the mother's own home was doubtless the most effective method of instruction and regulation but the one for which the mothers themselves showed least enthusiasm. Supervision became even more efficient after the 1907 Notification of Births Act, which facilitated early visiting by requiring notification of birth within forty-eight hours. Typically, it was permissive only.

Health visiting was also administered through a combination of municipal and voluntary effort. It emerged from nineteenth-century sanitary reform and philanthropic visiting which aimed to promote both cleanliness and godliness.[9] In 1890, however, the Manchester Corporation agreed to pay half the salaries of the health visitors of the Manchester and Salford Ladies' Sanitary Association. The corporation took over supervision of health visiting, which was subsequently concerned with domestic hygiene and infant welfare. The Manchester scheme was promoted heavily in the Physical Deterioration Report as a model for other authorities to emulate. It was stressed in the Report that health visiting was for instruction and was not intended as a means by which working people should receive material assistance.[10]

The social class of health visitors seems to have varied regionally, but this period saw a definite shift towards the recruitment of middle-class women, which would have further increased their unpopularity with the mothers they visited. There was a heated debate at the 1906 Infant Mortality Conference about the relative merits of the educated 'Girton girl' and women with practical knowledge and their ability to 'sympathise with the working women in their domestic trials and troubles'. A resolution was carried to the effect that: 'the appointment of qualified women, specially trained in the hygiene of infancy is necessary as an adjunct to public health work'.[11] Two years later, the LCC (General Powers) Act made training compulsory for local authority health visitors. The regulations allowed for a wide range of qualifications, but with an overall graduate and/or medical bias. Health visiting was to undergo substantial transformations during and after the war.

In the absence of a widespread consensus for state intervention in the family, child welfare reforms could only be achieved piecemeal. Legislation was permissive and organized through various local agencies and voluntary bodies. There was no comprehensive reform or centralized administration. The extent of patriarchal resistance to child welfare becomes apparent if we compare it with legislation affecting men. Sickness and unemployment benefit (1911) and old age pensions (1908) were all introduced by Act of Parliament which established national schemes; these distributed cash benefits to male workers. With the exception of maternity benefit, maternal and infant welfare never involved cash, but was always provision in kind. Cash payments to the mother would have contravened the ideology of the male breadwinner and female homemaker.

Child welfare during the war

The First World War led to further state intervention in child welfare. Anxiety about the population level deepened as deaths at the front increased and the birth-rate at home declined. Thus beneath the recurring nationalistic rhetoric about the value of child life and its conservation as 'a matter of war urgency'[12] lay a real fear of population decline and the hope that reducing infant mortality would act as a countervailing influence. One important effect of the population scare was the inclusion of unmarried mothers and their children as acceptable targets for state aid. After the moralistic 'war babies' scandal of 1916, concern was expressed in the 1917–18 Annual Report of the Local Government Board about the high mortality rate among the children of unmarried mothers – which was approximately double that of children born in wedlock. The National Council for the Unmarried Mother and her Child (founded in 1918) skilfully articulated its appeal for a more humane attitude to unmarried mothers in populationist terms: 'In view of the fact that the nation can ill afford this great drain on its infant population . . . their attention was drawn to the urgent need for the skilled care of every woman in childbirth.'[13] In addition, central government involvement became more acceptable as wartime conditions encouraged the expansion of state intervention in other spheres. Just before the declaration of war a circular was sent to local authorities outlining a range of maternity and child welfare measures which henceforth would be eligible for a 50 per cent grant from the Local Government Board. The Notification of Births (Extension) Act, again only permissive, extended eligibility for grants to county councils, which greatly facilitated provision in rural areas. The net result was a staggering increase in provision between 1914 and 1919. By 1918, there were 3038 full- and part-time salaried health visitors, in contrast to only 600 in 1914. The number of maternity and child welfare centres also increased in the same period from 650 to 1365.

The focus on maternal education was not just a cheap alternative to material improvement. Dried milk, malt extract and vitamins were already available at most centres and the Local Government Board was subsidizing local authorities for the provision of cheap milk to mothers and children. By 1916 Newsholme himself appears to have softened his line and explicitly demanded that 'the environment of the infant of the poor should be levelled up towards that of the well-to-do'. He denounced the notion that the working-class mother was more ignorant than the middle-class mother as 'a facile and unbalanced explanation of the excessive infant mortality among the working classes'.[14]

Another important wartime development was the move towards a more clinical approach to childbirth and the training of health visitors and midwives. In part this was due to the relative shortage of doctors, but it was also indicative of the general move towards the creation of state experts, particularly in areas related to the medical profession. If trained at all, health visitors were usually trained as nurses. The official Local Government Board view was that they should possess the sanitary inspector's certificate, as well as a full nurse's and midwife's training. More widely, nurse's training was often criticized as inappropriate for health visitors, as it stressed cure rather than prevention. In addition, because of the institutional environment in which it took place, it left the nurse ill-equipped to understand the problems of a working-class mother trying to make ends meet.[15] The debates in *Maternity and Child Welfare* at this time reveal widespread agreement among professionals in all branches of child welfare work on the need for a broader and more practical training for health visitors and many imaginative training schemes were suggested. However, the gradual and piecemeal standardization of health visiting, and the final abolition of unqualified practice which occurred between 1918 and 1928, confirmed the original medical and/or graduate bias of the 1908 LCC regulations. This would have driven any surviving working-class practitioners from the field and increased the unpopularity of the health visitor with working-class mothers.

The health visitor was ousted from her position at the centre of maternity and child welfare by the midwife. This was the result of growing state concern about health standards and a shortage of doctors. Not only did midwives deliver babies – nearly 75 per cent of all those born in 1917–18[16] – but they were also the first people consulted by the mother about her pregnancy. The midwife was the only person in a position to refer pregnant women to ante-natal clinics, and her co-operation in ante-natal provision was therefore essential. Once this was realized, attempts were made not only to integrate her more closely into the work of ante-natal centres but to improve her training and status.

The Registration of Midwives Act (1902) was beset with administrative difficulties from the start. The clause forbidding unqualified practice 'habitually and for gain' was not to become operational until 1910. Although the act obliged midwives to call a doctor in an emergency, it made no provision for paying the doctor's fee. Local supervision varied enormously. Some authorities like London and Manchester appointed well qualified inspectors who gave some training to bona fide midwives, i.e. those still allowed to practise on the basis of their experience although untrained. In other areas, however, supervision was conducted by health visitors who were of higher social status than the midwives but lacked experience, or alternatively by sanitary inspectors who came 'straight from rubbish tips and drains'.[17] It is scarcely surprising, given this regional variation, that there is evidence of unqualified practice as late as 1932.

The 1902 act outlawed the traditional 'handywoman' or midwife's assistant, who both helped at the delivery and also carried out household duties during the lying-in period. This important function was completely ignored in the act. The handywoman was popular with working-class women although her medical inadequacies were recognized by working women's organizations such as the Women's Co-operative Guild.[18] Nevertheless, general practitioners were willing to cover for handywomen, who posed less of a threat than the trained midwife, so they too continued to practise throughout the 1920s.

In addition, there was a shortage of trained midwives, especially in rural areas. Training required three months absence from home (extended to six months from 1916) and many competent practising midwives failed the examination because it was too academic.[19] Of those midwives who trained, few took up district midwifery, a career which carried both low status and low pay. Many worked as private nurses or with district and county nursing associations. Others took up the 'less arduous and better paid work of health visitor'.[20] It was estimated by the Central Midwives Board that in 1918 only some 20 per cent of those on the trained midwives' roll were practising midwives.

The Local Government Board's attempts to remedy inadequate training culminated in the 1918 Midwives Act which made grants available for training midwives. It also made the local supervising authority responsible for the payment of doctors called by midwives in an emergency, and tightened up regulations for the inspection of midwives. From this date also, the shortage of trained midwives in rural areas was partially solved by grant-aided co-operation between the Local Government Board and County and District Nursing Associations. This policy of government aid to voluntary organizations was continued by the Ministry of Health, so that by 1923 73 per cent of the population had access to a trained midwife.[21]

During and after the war, local authorities were encouraged to set up salaried or subsidized midwifery services. This afforded some financial security to midwives. It also encouraged their integration into the two main wartime developments: better co-ordination of the maternity and child welfare services and the development of ante-natal care. The latter was initiated solely in the interests of the infant. Since deaths after the first month had declined, it was believed that the remaining deaths, which occurred shortly after birth, were caused by the ill health of the mother in pregnancy. Particularly invidious was the link between ante-natal care and campaigns to eliminate venereal diseases, believed to cause a high proportion of miscarriages, still births and childhood diseases. Treatment was dangerous, involving the use of arsenic. Because the secondary and tertiary stages of syphilis were difficult to detect, diagnosis was often based on sociological rather than strictly medical evidence. For example, the 1917–18 Annual Report of the Local Government Board suggests that in view of the high infant mortality among workhouse births ante-natal and especially anti-syphilitic treatment should be concentrated on these patients. It was even suggested by one Medical Officer of Health[22] that venereal disease in pregnancy should be notifiable, treatment compulsory, and patients with two previous still births deemed to be suffering from syphilis.

Ante-natal care was therefore heavily influenced by the link between medicine and morality, discussed by Lucy Bland in her contribution to this volume. For the mother, it brought little immediate benefit. While it enabled some diseases to be detected early in pregnancy and led to the demand for better treatment facilities and more lying-in hospitals, on balance the gains were small when set against the otherwise detrimental effects of ante-natal supervision on working-class women.

More optimistic conclusions can be drawn regarding the related question of the professionalization and registration of midwives. Although these developments undoubtedly reduced the number of working-class practitioners, they also brought better medical skill and knowledge. While maternal mortality remained high until the 1930s, it was lower among midwife deliveries. After 1928 mortality was lower among the poor, who tended to be delivered by midwives at home, than among the rich, who were more often delivered by doctors in hospitals. Most important, however, is the fact that the registration of midwives preserved for women a profession (albeit an inferior, underpaid and undervalued profession) that would otherwise gradually have been taken over by the predominantly male medical profession.

The final wartime development in the field of child welfare was a further attempt to establish a unified central authority in the form of a Ministry of Health. Lord Rhondda saw it as a relatively uncontroversial measure; as he wrote to Lloyd George in 1917: 'Public opinion is now keenly aroused on the deficiency and inefficiency of our public medical service, especially for maternal and infant welfare.'[23] However, Rhondda underestimated the vested interests involved. The new ministry was not established until 1919, after much negotiation between different sections of the medical profession, Poor Law administrators, insurance companies and friendly societies. Honigsbaum argues convincingly that the 1918 Maternity and Child Welfare Act was an attempt, in the face of strong opposition, to head off the demand for a ministry with a weaker measure which would satisfy the child welfare lobby.[24] The 1918 act was again permissive. Its only real innovation was the requirement that local authorities should appoint maternity and child welfare committees, which should include at least two women, in order to be eligible for a Local Government Board grant.

Given the weakness of the ministry as a whole, the record of its Maternity and Child Welfare Department, under Janet Campbell, was impressive. There was a steady expansion in services generally, an increase in the number of local authorities employing women doctors with gynaecological and paediatric experience as assistant Medical Officers of Health, and grants given to both local authorities and voluntary organizations. However, the department was still severely hampered by the fact that the National Health Insurance Commission (including control of maternity benefit) and the Poor Law (which controlled many lying-in wards) remained outside its jurisdiction. Thus while the war had some effect in accelerating welfare reforms and helping to legitimize both provision in kind and state intervention generally, this was a haphazard process and did not lead to the establishment of an effective and unified system of public health administration.

Conclusion

The child welfare reforms achieved in this period were negligible. The pragmatic and piecemeal method of implementation primarily resulted from an inability to counter the ideology of family 'privacy' and parental responsibility. Thus child welfare, unlike some other reforms of the period, could not become a mass popular campaign.

It was, however, in the labour movement that the effects of patriarchal ideology were most significant. In failing to promote child welfare reforms, working-class men were defending their patriarchal privileges within the family. This not only failed to secure maximum material benefits for working-class families, but also came to exploit women, who shouldered the main burden of bearing and rearing children in appalling conditions. Most important of all, for both sexes, was the fact that the lack of working-class support left the field open to the dominant classes. Divisions within the labour movement, between those who advocated state maintenance and those who defended the privacy of the family, prevented the creation of a counter strategy.

Those reforms which were achieved were probably too insignificant to have any immediate effect on the quality of labour power, although they doubtless contributed to a greater awareness of the problem of working-class health. However, their long-term effects in restructuring working-class family life were enormous, in their implications for both class and gender relations. The new ideologies of motherhood and the education of working-class mothers in idealized bourgeois patterns of domesticity laid the foundation for precisely the kind of family which was conducive to a stable and responsible work routine. This is not to say that working-class families simply copied or assimilated middle-class habits. But for those families which achieved a measure of affluence in the 1920s and 1930s, family life was influenced by the powerful ideology of domesticity in which the mother's role was central.

The political consequences for women were that their domestic duties were more clearly defined and rigorously enforced by an army of health visitors, experts and educators. These were no longer concerned, as their Victorian predecessors had been, with religion and morals, but with the minutest detail of domestic and personal hygiene in the name of the welfare of the child.

Nevertheless, if the home was invaded by the expert, it was also opened up for political struggle. The mother did gain status in relation to the father. The national importance of her work as a mother was used by feminists as an additional reason for granting her both the vote and family endowment. If childrearing was a political issue, so were the conditions in which children were raised. The basis had been laid for the struggle for improved living conditions for working-class women as *their* right, not merely in relation to their children. The concern with infant mortality gave way in the 1930s to a concern with maternal mortality and morbidity. The shift in emphasis to the mother's own rights is clearly seen in *Working-Class Wives*, the results of a survey conducted by the Women's Health Enquiry Committee and published in 1939, which was explicitly inspired by the WCG maternity survey of 1915.[25]

It is clear that direct regulation by the state of the working-class family through the construction and supervision of a particular mother–child relationship substantially transformed patriarchal relations within the family itself. What is less clear is whether the position of women was strengthened or weakened. But given that much of the private sphere was made 'public' and that feminists used this public space for political struggle, on balance the increase in supervision of domestic duties was outweighed by the new opportunities this opened up.

Notes and references

1   *Interdepartmental Committee on Physical Deterioration* (3 vols.) Report, Evidence, Appendix and Index (Cmd. 2175, Cmd. 2210, Cmd. 2186, 1904).
2   *The Times*, 7 November 1900, quoted in B. B. Gilbert, *The Evolution of National Insurance in Great Britain: The Origins of the Welfare State* (Michael Joseph 1966), p. 72.
3   G. F. McCleary, 'The state as overparent', *Albany Review*, 2 (1907), p. 47.
4   J. Gorst, *Children of the Nation* (Methuen 1906), p. 9.
5   ibid., p. 61.
6   A. Clay, 'The feeding of school children', in J. St. Loe Strachey (ed.), *The Manufacture of Paupers: a Protest and a Policy* (John Murray 1907), pp. 15–23.

7 *Annual Reports of the Women's Labour League* (Women's Labour League, 1906–18).
8 H. Mitchell, *The Hard Way Up* (Virago 1977), p. 102.
9 For differing views of the relative importance of these two aspects, see R. J. Dingwall, 'Collectivism, regionalism and feminism: health visiting and British social policy 1850–1975', *Journal of Social Policy,* no. 6 (July 1977), pp. 291–315 and W. C. Dowling, 'The Ladies' Sanitary Association and the origins of the health visiting services' (unpublished MA dissertation, London School of Economics 1963).
10 *Interdepartmental Committee on Physical Deterioration*, vol. 1, pp. 58–9.
11 *Report of the Proceedings of the National Conference on Infant Mortality* (National Association for the Prevention of Infant Mortality, 1906).
12 *Annual Report of the Local Government Board 1916–17* (Cmd. 8767).
13 *Maternity and Child Welfare* (October 1918).
14 *Annual Report of the Local Government Board 1917–18, 'Supplement on Child Mortality at ages 0–5'* (Cmd. 8496).
15 See, for example, 'The aims of education for health visitors, an open letter by Via Media', *Maternity and Child Welfare* (April 1917).
16 *Annual Report of the Local Government Board 1917–18* (Cmd. 9169).
17 J. Donnison, *Midwives and Medical Men* (Heinemann 1977), pp. 182–3.
18 Women's Co-operative Guild, *Maternity: letters from working women* (1915, reprinted Virago 1978), p. 211.
19 Women's Co-operative Guild, *Life as we have known it* (Hogarth 1931, reprinted Virago 1977), pp. 42–6 for the example of Mrs Layton.
20 *Maternity and Child Welfare* (February 1917).
21 *Fourth Annual Report of the Ministry of Health* (Cmd. 1944, 1923).
22 *National Conference on Infant Welfare Report* (National League for Health, Maternity and Child Welfare 1919), contribution by Dr J. J. Buchan, Medical Officer of Health for Bradford.
23 Quoted in A. Marwick, *The Deluge: British Society and the First World War* (Macmillan 1965), pp. 241–2.
24 F. Honigsbaum, *The Struggle for the Ministry of Health 1914–1919* (G. Bell 1970).
25 M. S. Spring (ed.), *Working Class Wives: their health and conditions* (1939, reprinted Virago 1981).

12 Managing the delinquent: the Children's Branch of the Home Office, 1913–30*

John Clarke

The 'youth problem' is an English obsession. The disorders of the young have persistently attracted the attentions of the media, moral reformers, commercial entrepreneurs and last, but by no means least, the state.[1] The turn of the century is no exception to this preoccupation with the young. As at other times, 'criminal' youth is at the heart of public anxiety. However, while social concern is continuous, the issues and concepts through which it is publicly articulated are not.

One major change was in the age location of the youth problem. Mid nineteenth-century moral reformers such as Mary Carpenter identified the dangers of disorder with childhood in the course of their discoveries of the 'children of the streets'.[2] By the end of the century the focus of attention was moving towards the disturbances of 'adolescence'. This changing focus was partly a result of the advent of mass education, as schools restricted the formerly unsupervised freedom of the children of the street.

In the eyes of the reformers one of the key explanations for the disorderliness of youth, was the lack of institutional supervision. They increasingly identified the problem with the post-school young. The late nineteenth-century indentification of the 'hooligan' and the classification and analysis of adolescence as a distinct stage of physical and psychological development, were indicative of this changing focus. A variety of voluntary and state initiatives were directed at supervising, civilizing and disciplining the youthful agents of disorder.[3] Voluntary youth movements and clubs were widely established to provide 'rational recreation'. Advice to young school leavers became a feature of the expanding state interest in the labour market and campaigns for 'continuing education' emerged.

This transition was neither abrupt nor absolute, but in general, childhood became a more private concern while adolescence became the public face of the youth problem. Although there was no sudden appearance of a fully

* My thanks to Susan Boyd-Bowman, Alan Clarke and Tony Jefferson for their comments on earlier drafts, and to Bill Schwarz and Mary Langan for their sustained editorial work. This chapter emerged from collaborative work with Mary Langan, to whom I owe a special debt of gratitude.

developed theory and practice of 'adolescence', the period is characterized by the gradual and uncertain 'discovery of adolescence'.[4]

My concern here is relatively narrow. I consider one particular element in the array of theories and practices which surrounded the youth problem – the Children's Branch of the Home Office. Created in 1913, this agency dealt with the legal regulation of the young and with the institutional mechanisms through which that regulation was exercised. The legal apparatuses of regulation specified the generalized 'problem of youth' in the particular form of the delinquent. The Children's Branch was where conflicts were fought over the best means by which the delinquent could be managed.

Charters and scandals

The 1908 Children Act – the 'Children's Charter' – gained its accolade because it drew together and extended existing legislation concerned with the abuse of children. It expanded the intervention of the state into the 'private' world of the family. In addition the act established both the legal apparatus and powers of the juvenile court, where cases concerning either deprived or delinquent juveniles would be considered. Twelve varieties of disposal were available to juvenile magistrates, two of which will be the main focus of attention here: the reformatory and industrial schools, and probation (itself established in 1907 under the Probation of Offenders Act).

The Children's Charter summarized past protective legislation – on employment, education, begging, and parental cruelty or neglect – and constructed a court designed for the regulation of the young. In conventional histories of juvenile justice, the act marks the inauguration of modern juvenile justice. In these histories, a strange silence follows the 1908 act until the 1927 Departmental Committee with its commitment to 'the welfare of the young person' as the main principle of the juvenile court. The acceptance by the Home Office of this principle, expressed in the 1933 Children and Young Persons Act, is often identified as the arrival on the public stage of those concerns which shape contemporary debates about juvenile justice. Particularly important in these debates were the contending models of intervention based on the tension between concepts of 'justice' and 'welfare'.

The silence which marks the space between these two legal landmarks is one which conceals considerable turmoil and activity around state provision of justice to juveniles. This chapter examines some of the internal reorganizations of the state's regime for juvenile offenders which took place betwen these acts.

The 1908 act laid down the legislative framework for the creation of the Children's Branch within the Home Office. Yet the branch did not finally take shape until after the Report of the 1913 Departmental Committee on the Reformatory and Industrial Schools. As with many other innovations in social policy relating to children, the immediate spur to action was a public scandal. In 1910 the journal *John Bull* revealed a story of deaths and excessive cruelty at the Akbar Nautical Training School – a reformatory school for young offenders. An investigation by a Home Office inspector and a subsequent inquiry by C. F. G. Masterman for the Home Office failed to quiet the outraged *John Bull*, and others, including the *Nation*, joined the fray. *John Bull* added accusations of bribery, corruption, and Home Office whitewashing. Masterman's report recommended the establishment of a committee to examine the regimes of the reformatory schools. In 1911 the Home Secretary, Winston Churchill, appointed the committee with Masterman as its chairman.[5]

The Akbar scandal, although the immediate stimulus to the formation of the committee, was not an isolated expression of concern about the reformatory schools. Established in the 1850s, they were primarily the product of voluntary initiatives and subject to relatively little central government supervision. From the 1890s they had become the target of accusations from the penal reformers (notably the Howard Association and the Penal Reform League) of maltreatment, inefficiency and the inadequacy of the reformatories in dealing with juveniles. These criticisms were coupled with demands for new methods (particularly probation) to replace the archaic methods of institutional confinement.

The 1913 Committee

The Committee reported fairly favourably on the overall practice of the schools, but stressed unevenness in standards, an argument which enabled Committee members to propound their general strategy for the future of the schools. Diversity of standards was identified in every facet of the schools' organization and practice. Two major explanations for this variability were adduced by the Committee. One was the funding of the schools, some of which were inadequately funded and could neither maintain standards nor effect improvements. The second was that the powers of the central authority were inadequate to the task of maintaining standards. The Committee's approach was summed up in the following general assessment:

The main reasons why progress has not been faster are, first, that the managers have been hampered by the lack of funds, and, secondly, that the Central Authority, which is the chief instrument of levelling up, has had little power to enforce changes of which managers failed to recognise the value or urgency.[6]

This approach established the dominant themes of the Committee's argument for reorganizing the relation between the schools and the Home Office. They stressed the need for greater powers of inspection, control and direction by an expanded inspectorate in the Children's Branch. Inspection, certification and funding were the means through which the schools were to be 'conformed' to the desirable standards. The Home Office was to provide a standardized and comprehensive set of guidelines for the schools which were to be checked in practice by the school inspectors. Only if the schools attained the established standards would they receive certification by the Home Office. Certification for the schools became vital, since it was to be attached to a more elaborate and generous system of central government funding.

Another crucial question for the Committee was the quality of every grade of staff working in the schools, from the superintendents down to the technical and craft inspectors. In relation to superintendents, they expressed concern that the field of choice in the appointment of suitable men was too limited,[7] and recommended raising salaries and the establishment of provision for superannuation following the appeals of the Association of School Superintendents for a better and more secure career structure. Teachers in the schools were also considered not sufficiently well-qualified. The Committee recommended that the proportion of certified teachers needed to be increased, and that teachers should be allowed better facilities to keep up with developments in their professional field.

The same strictures were also applied to the standard of the technical instructors in the schools. The Committee argued that instructors should hold technical certificates before they were eligible for such posts. Similar standards were needed in the field of domestic training in the girls' schools.

The Committee also proposed the appointment of properly qualified medical officers, with extensive responsibilities, including:

(1) the careful examination of all children on admission in regard to infections and contagious diseases, before they are allowed to mix with the other inmates of the schools; (2) thorough medical inspection . . . of all inmates at regular intervals; (3) periodical re-examination of children found to be defective or of other children needing it before undertaking special training or work; (4) keeping necessary physical records; (5) undertaking or obtaining adequate medical treatment in all cases requiring such attention; (6) subject to the control of the Central Authority, the effective supervision of the sanitation of the buildings, diet, corporal punishment, physical training and the general arrangements of the school routine and curriculum in their relation to the health and growth of the children.[8]

The importance which the Committee attributed to the medical officer's role (and to its recommendation of a specialist medical inspector within the Children's Branch) reflected the growing professional dominance of medicine in the sphere of childhood and adolescence.

Centralization, professionalism and progressivism

The Committee's concern to establish greater central powers over the schools was not solely a matter of the minimum standards. It also reflected a commitment to transform the practice of the schools themselves. The report's emphasis on professionalism expressed a fear of the isolation of the schools from new developments in related fields. The 'progressivism' of the report did not cohere around the question of *delinquency* nor did it identify a 'delinquent subject'.[9] The inmates of the schools were first and foremost identified as *children*.

The central thrust of 'modernizing' the schools in the Committee's recommendations were the two knowledges of medicine and education. Medical knowledge defined the *nature* of children, classifying their characteristics and their potentialities. Educational knowledge constructed the *transformation* of children, identifying the practices by which they could be matured. We have already seen how extensively the medical role was to be incorporated into the daily routine of the schools. The Committee's grave fear about the place of education within the existing schools pointed in a similar direction regarding the place of education in the reformed system.

The committee, while recognizing merits in the present system of education in the certified schools, are of the opinion that improvement could be effected if a knowledge of the more modern methods of education in the elementary and other schools were more widely spread among the teachers.[10]

The Committee acknowledged a third and subordinate knowledge – 'female knowledge'. It gave some attention to the special relation of women to such regimes and recommended the appointment of a further woman inspector because 'A woman will often notice points seriously affecting the comfort and welfare of children especially points connected with matters of domestic arrangement that may escape the notice of a man'.[11]

We have already noted one of the suggestions made by the Committee to overcome the isolation of the schools from the 'more modern' developments in education in their recommendations to provide teachers with greater free time to keep up with professional developments. The Committee also argued for the *educational* practice of the schools to be inspected by the Board of Education rather than by the Children's Branch. In the Committee's view such inspectors would bring with them knowledge of progressive educational practices. This commitment to modernize the schools' educational role was most visible in the discussion of physical education:

It is not too much to say that physical health lies at the root of all true education in the wide and modern sense of the term, and in physical training, rightly conceived and properly applied an instrument is at hand by means of which the whole physique of the child may be readily influenced for good.[12]

The existing schools were castigated for providing no systematic approach to physical training. Consequently, the Committee argued for a training regime to be prescribed by the Children's Branch. It recommended that they adopt the 'Swedish system' of physical training taken up by the Board of Education in 1909. This attention to physical training is not surprising since it condenses the two knowledges – medical/physiological and pedagogic – on which the Committee's 'modernization' was based. As a modernizing and progressive influence on the practice of the schools, the central authority would itself be 'expert' – transmitting knowledge through the inspectorate. It would also be aided in maintaining its expertise by the formation of an advisory committee, representing knowledge about youth, education and social work.

The 1913 Committee made the reform schools financially dependent on the Home Office. It tied this finance to an expanded set of powers of the Children's Branch over the schools, and identified the inspectorate as a directive force.[13] It did not modernize the schools, but rearranged the institutional balance of power to establish the conditions for modernization. The 1913 Committee established the basis for Home Office hegemony over the schools.

Subordinating the superintendents

The inspectorate of the Children's Branch set about strengthening the directive power of the Home Office over the schools. The first two chief inspectors appointed to the Children's Branch after the 1913 Committee embodied the ideal of expertise. The first, Charles Russell, had himself been an influential member of the 1913 Committee. He had previously been active in settlement and youth work in Manchester, and had researched and written extensively on social problems, delinquency and the problem of 'boy-labour'.[14] Russell arrived as an acknowledged expert in the field of youth. He wielded his expertise as chief inspector in the Children's Branch's attempts to persuade the schools to improve their standards. In 1917, he was succeeded by A. H. Norris, a former medical inspector in the Children's Branch. Norris, too, represented the new professional, but in a rather different style from Russell. He had worked with Russell in settlement and youth work in Manchester, but his expertise lay less in the general field of youth than in the medical and organizational aspects of child-care and institutional management.[15]

From taking up his appointment Norris expressed some hostility to the schools. His first address to the Reformatory and Refuge Union was entitled 'The Limitations of Institutional Training'. In 1919 he produced an unpublished but highly critical account of the schools. This was reviewed by the Howard Association which congratulated Norris on presenting 'The most damning indictment of the privately managed, publicly financed certified schools that we have yet seen.'[16] The Howard Association's attack was only one of a long series of criticisms on the schools mounted by the Association, the Penal Reform League and the authors of various books on the reformatories in the immediate post-war period.

Criticism by influential public lobbies coincided with a further major problem for the schools which, by the mid 1920s, seemed to threaten their very existence. During the post-war period magistrates increasingly (though unevenly) began to use probation as an alternative to the schools. By 1925, 6357 offenders were placed on probation, while only 578 were sent to reformatory schools, half that of the 1913 figure.[17] The schools felt that they were being increasingly and unfairly squeezed out by these changes.

Representatives of the schools persistently called on the Home Office to defend their interests. Their persistent complaint was that the Children's Department failed to represent in public the work and successes of the schools – a substantial point since the reconviction rate of the schools, at 10 to 15 per cent, was then at the lowest it has ever been.

The Children's Branch played an ambiguous role in relation to the reform schools. While privately assuring the schools of their support, it made few interventions on their behalf in the public debate. It did, however, make use of the pressures of public debate and declining use of the schools by pressing more firmly for the schools to improve their regimes, and to modernize their educational and training practices. It also took advantage of the beleaguered position of the schools to assert more decisively the leadership of the Home Office over them.[18] As Carlebach argues, by 1926, when the school heads and managers were summoned to a conference by Norris, the autonomy of the schools had been effectively destroyed.

The expansion of probation

The main development which brought the schools under tighter control of the Home Office was the creation of a probation system. This had been established by permissive legislation in 1907, which allowed courts to appoint probation officers into whose supervision offenders could be released. (Previously 'probation' had merely permitted the release of offenders on recognizances for good behaviour, with no necessary supervision.)

The main suppliers of probation workers were the charitable societies. Most important were the police court missionary societies, established by bodies such as the Church of England Temperance Society (CETS). The charitable societies were the focus of the second major struggle fought around the Children's Branch over the direction and staffing of probation. Russell's observations on the role of officers from charitable bodies prefigured the controversy that was later to emerge:

An officer provided by a denominational body would be under a certain obligation to promote its aims, and would often in the mind of the probationer be open to the suspicion of trying to 'get at' him for religious purposes. It is his *temporal* welfare that must be the prime object of the probation-officer's solicitude.[19]

Probation was used as a lever to accomplish school reform. However, criticisms of the work of the charitable bodies, particularly their emphasis on religion, led to questions about the staffing of the probation service. Reformers called for the professionalization of the probation service and its reorganization on a basis of expertise. The drive for reform came from the penal lobbying groups (the Howard Association and the Penal Reform League again), in alliance with the National Association of Probation Officers (founded in 1913) and the Magistrates' Association (founded in 1920). The campaign attacked the charitable societies, calling for an end to 'dual control' – the system by which missionaries who worked as probation officers were paid by the charitable bodies and by the courts. The reformers also demanded the creation of a national service of full-time, salaried probation officers, who would in their practice draw on contemporary developments in the social and medical sciences.

Dual control: denominationalism versus professionalism

Between 1907 and the war the arguments against the unsuitability of the missionaries were repeated in representations to the Home Office by the Penal Reform League, the Howard Association, the State Children's Association and the Committee on Wage Earning Children (an offshoot of the Howard Association). These groups pressed the Home Office to advise magistrates to make greater use of the probation system as a means of dealing with offenders. Evidence collected by the 1909 Departmental Committee on the Probation of Offenders Act showed that there was substantial variation in the use of the provisions of the act by the courts. In 1910, in response to this campaign, the Home Office circulated information to all magistrates on the possibilities of probation provision. Yet, despite the evidence justifying the criticism of the missionaries' work as probation officers, the Home Office took no steps to prevent their appointment.

By 1914, the reforming campaigns were developing a more coherent vision of what a probation service ought to be. They placed greater emphasis on the necessity for systematic investigation and classification of offenders and their circumstances before the court passed sentence and argued that such work, together with counselling, could only be properly achieved by qualified professionals. In 1914 Cecil Leeson published *The Probation System*, in which he argued for a centralized system of direction and inspection, the appointment of chief probation officers to oversee work at a local level, and the necessity of recruiting well-trained personnel. He particularly stressed the need for the development of social studies courses. This was followed in 1915 by the publication of Sir William Clarke-Hall's *The State and the Child*, which argued for the abandonment of the system of dual control.

The Home Office's first open admission that missionaries might not always be ideal appointments came in 1917, following a deputation from the

State Children's Association (which included Lord Henry Bentinck, who was also a leading figure in the Penal Reform League). In the same year the Penal Reform League organized a conference on juvenile delinquency. Shortly afterwards the League published a series of proposals entitled *A National Minimum for Youth*, in which they called for a national probation commission and for the appointment of trained officers.

The shift of the Home Office into open criticism of the missionaries proved to be only the beginning of the CETS's problems. After the war magistrates showed a greater willingness to use probation as a means of disposal, both for young and adult offenders. This was reflected in the founding of the Magistrates' Association in 1920. With Cecil Leeson as its secretary, the association took as one of its immediate aims the expansion of probation. The courts also began to demonstrate a greater willingness to appoint full-time officers and to recruit from outside the ranks of the missionaries. In 1920 Liverpool magistrates decided to end the system of dual control in the appointment of full-time officers, thus excluding missionaries. The CETS expressed concern at this fall from grace and requested that missionaries employed as probation officers should be so identified in the Home Office directory of probation officers.[20] These insecurities were reinforced by the establishment of a departmental committee on the probation service which recommended that changes were needed in the CETS in order to bring about 'A more progressive spirit in probation work and to attract better candidates to the service.'

The Society thus faced a threat from three sides: public criticism from the penal groups, loss of appointments for their members, and the demand to modernize or be further excluded from the development of probation.

The departmental committee gained some success in that the CETS was forced to follow the committee's advice on reorganization in order to survive. In other respects the committee proved a disappointment to the reformers. It failed to establish a full career structure for probation officers, and took very little account of the demands for training made by both the Howard League (formed by an amalgamation of the Penal Reform League and the Howard Association) and the National Association of Probation Officers (NAPO). It did, however, recommend extension of central government funding, an increase in the staffing of the Children's Branch to provide for supervision of the probation system, and the establishment of an advisory group on probation.

Under further pressure from the reform groups, a clause permitting provision of central government funding towards the cost of probation officers was included in the 1925 Criminal Justice Act. The appointment of a probation officer was made mandatory in every petty sessional division, and this became the responsibility of a probation committee composed of magistrates from the division.

The struggle concluded

Between 1927 and 1933 the reform groups finally succeeded in achieving their main objectives. In 1930 the Home Office Advisory Committee on probation persuaded the Home Office to organize a system of training for entrants to the service. In the same year the Howard League sponsored a private members' bill which proposed the abolition of the voluntary societies' role in staffing the probation service. The bill ran aground, but the end of dual control was not long delayed. In 1933 the terms of reference of a committee established to review matrimonial proceedings in the summary courts were extended to cover the whole question of social work in the courts.

This committee was persuaded by the arguments levelled by NAPO, the Magistrates' Association, the Incorporated Society of Justices' Clerks and the Howard League, and recommended the abandonment of dual control. It also pressed for the appointment of chief probation officers to supervise and organize probation work, and for the creation of a separate department of the Home Office specifically concerned with probation and after-care practice. The 1933 Committee identified the probation officer as the appropriate person to prepare reports, not just for the juvenile, but for all courts thus overturning the earlier defeat suffered by NAPO. Finally, the committee favoured the other long-standing demand of the reformers – organized training for probation officers. Thus, the conflicts over the forms through which the state should control the delinquent ended with the reformers triumphant on all fronts. After a thirty-year struggle the 'progressives' had built up a fully professionalized probation service based on a 'scientific' and 'rational' expertise.

The progressive alliance

Three features of the 'progressive' alliance are particularly striking. First, its main organizational forms existed outside the state. It was organized through bodies such as the Penal Reform League, the Howard Association, and the State Children's Association. These bodies pressurized and lobbied institutions of the state, both Parliament and the bureaucracy. Propaganda included the sponsoring of meetings and conferences, and the publication of journals, pamphlets and books. It also included individual publishing activities, for example the works of Leeson, Clarke-Hall, and Russell.

Second, not only were the reforming organizations closely integrated but the voluntary bodies were also closely tied to associations representing state agents – most notably NAPO and the Magistrates' Association. Cecil Leeson, for example, author of *The Probation System*, went on to work as secretary to the Howard Association, and subsequently became secretary to the newly formed Magistrates' Association. Lord Feversham, an enthusiastic supporter of probation, was active in the Penal Reform League, became vice-president and president of NAPO, and subsequently served on the council of the Magistrates' Association. These interconnections were also visible in the careers of Gertrude Tuckwell, who served as president and vice-president of NAPO and on the executive committee of the Magistrates' Association, and William Clarke-Hall, active in the Penal Reform League, chairman of NAPO and of the Magistrates' Association.

Third, the representatives of these organizations operated both inside and outside the state. The trajectories of this move from 'pressure group' to integration in the state are complex and diverse. Some figures were MPs; others, like Feversham, assumed positions in government; still others, like Russell and Norris, were recruited from 'voluntary' practice as acknowledged experts to staff the state institutions. Another pattern of recruitment was through appointment as expert 'advisors': thus Russell was appointed to the 1913 Committee; while others were appointed to those advisory groups established to involve 'external' expertise in the practice of the Children's Branch.

These figures form what Gramsci called the intellectual 'general staff' of an ideology: its directive leadership, co-ordinating and organizing both inside and outside the state. Their task was to produce a new stratum of 'intellectuals' – functionaries within the state who embodied the modernizing and progressive vision of the reformers in state practice. Between 1907 and 1937 this alliance attempted to create a new conception of the relation of the state to delinquent youth. The reformers also sought to win the state to 'progressivism' – in the parliamentary domain, in the bureaucratic apparatus, and in the practices of state agents in the schools and courts. What took place in those thirty years was not the inexorable rise of 'enlightenment', 'liberalism' or any such spirit. It was a systematic campaign, a struggle to transform, destroy and supplant an existing ideology and practice embodied in the voluntary schools and charitable societies.

What sort of modernization?

Up to this point, we have accepted the orthodox characterization of these developments as 'modernizing' and 'progressive'. But the character of this emergent ideology of state practice needs more careful representation. It would be churlish to deny that there were 'improving' influences. For example, the improvement of conditions in the certified schools and the removal of religious zeal from probation must be counted as genuine benefits. But it is important not to mistake such 'improvements' for the embodiment of some abstract ideal of 'civilization' or 'benevolence'. Such improvements are profoundly implicated in the transformation of social arrangements – in the case of the Children's Department the relation between the state and its clientele. State practice was not reconstructed according to an abstract ideal of civilization but to a very particular vision of it.

It was a vision which was predominantly anti-institutionalist. The attack on the schools was not conducted merely to make them 'conform' to new methods of institutional management and education. It also aimed to displace them from a central position in the management of juvenile delinquency by the state. The attack persistently coupled the negative (the failing and backwardness of the schools) with the positive (supervision in the community). The progressive ideology aimed to add a further strand to the presence of the state, not as an external power, but as an integral part of the life of civil society.[21] The probation officer represented one further outpost of the state established to regulate civil society, constituting another element of surveillance alongside teachers, school attendance officers, midwives, health visitors, social workers from the Charity Organization Society (COS) and the police. Regulation *within*, rather than removal *from* the community was constructed as the dominant strategy for the delinquent. This approach rested on a crude psychology of 'personal influence' as the commanding mode of intervention.

A psychology of improvement had been most clearly established in the theory and practice of the COS's conception of case work and in the missionary work of the CETS. But the task of this modernizing alliance was to transform the *theory* of this 'improving' impulse from one of Christian virtue and the moral economy of the COS to one with a secure footing in *science*. Early concerns with the social sciences and the later influence of American psychological casework theories formed the cutting edge of the attempt to transform the theory of supervision and improvement.[22]

The particular concern with science in relation to casework was only part of the progressives' wider commitment and persistent stress that the practice of state agents must be based on a scientific knowledge. The aim was to create a body of state functionaries who were salaried, trained, knowledgeable, professional experts. The mode of state intervention, whether through schools or the probation service, was to be constituted and channelled as rational 'expertise'. This commitment united diverse demands for more free time for teachers in the certified schools, for better pay and conditions of service to attract 'educated' personnel, and for the establishment of advisory groups to carry 'external' expertise into state practice. It also led to the elaboration of demands for new systems of classification and record keeping, and for the 'investigative' task of the probation officer.

The commitment of the progressive alliance to expertise converged with a number of emergent 'sciences' and drew them into the field of state intervention in delinquency. The main knowledges which were written into the delinquency problem were educational pedagogy, medicine and empirical psychology – disciplines which were themselves closely interlinked, most visibly in the work of Cyril Burt. The progressive alliance constructed not only a theory of welfare practice, but also a new conceptualization of the relation of the state to delinquency. The issue of delinquency was transformed from a social problem to one which was technical, universal, scientific and professional. Furthermore, delinquency, as an object of intervention, was constructed through a specific 'universal' and 'neutral' category – the law. The intersection of law and professional knowledge produced a double dislocation from the social relations of youth, which in turn was represented and reconstructed through these two sets of universal categories.

Theory and practice: uneven developments in the state

We have encountered this modernizing ideology in its most developed form – at its most 'theoretical'. There was, however, no simple correspondence between the theory and the practice of state agents. Magistrates, probation officers and the workers in the schools were not immediately transformed into 'expert professionals'. At best, it could be suggested that the modernizing influence of the alliance constructed the conditions under which new forms of state agents could emerge. The gap between theory and practice has remained a major concern within the social work and probation professions.[23] A more accurate conception of the growth of professionalism may be that it constructed *an ideology of practice* – a set of representations of the social relations within which practice took place. State power in these fields was thus organized *through* the ideology of the professional.

Furthermore, I have presented these conflicts as a stark confrontation between the 'modernizers' and their traditionalist opponents. But in practice the relations between these ideologies was more blurred. The 'old ways' were not simply defeated and therefore banished from social life. They were subordinated to the new ideology, and forced into a new mould to achieve a closer fit with the dominance of 'the modern'. Both the COS, and later the CETS, became 'converts' to the value of social science. But traces of the old lingered on. These traces and continuities should also warn us about another aspect of these ideological transformations. The pyrotechnics of ideological conflicts (and the seemingly endless sequence of 'new' theories which followed this professional colonization of delinquency) should not distract us from the powerful continuities in state practice.

The analysis of changing ideologies can be misleading. We can too easily read such changes as if they directly determine transformations in state practice. However, although theoretical and ideological shifts do influence practice, they may also conceal certain continuities.

This period saw the delinquent on the one hand as the subject of the law, and on the other as the object of scientific analysis and professional intervention. But *practically*, he (or, more occasionally, she) remained a troublesome and intransigent member of a particular class and gender. The 'raw material' was persistently working class and male. Delinquency was a 'censure' which was targeted at a specific social position and at particular social practices.

In this period delinquency engaged both what is conventionally under-stood as the criminal law (offences against property and the person), and a whole range of regulations dealing with public space, which accounted for over a quarter of the offences before the courts in 1925.[24] Both Gillis and Cohen have described how criminalization was developed as a strategy to control sections of 'rough' working-class youth at this time. They point to interventions aimed at regulating both the informal economies of the street (street trading by the young was included in the 1908 act) and 'unsupervised' leisure in the street. Criminalization formed one part of a more elaborate set of interventions aimed at making male working-class youth conform. It worked on the distinction between the 'respectable' and the 'rough'. 'Volun-tary' measures were directed to the 'respectable' strata, aiming to provide supervised 'rational' recreation. Those who refused, resisted or remained outside these practices were exposed to the risk of criminalization.[25]

This was the shape of the 'public' regulation of working-class youth by the law. But the state also intervened into the 'private' sphere of family and domestic relations. The 1908 act provided the criminalizing support and legal machinery for interventions by other state agencies into the working-class family – concerning child labour, school non-attendance, and the categories of neglect, cruelty and moral danger. The moral danger category referred particularly to girls' 'delinquency', and provided for legal inter-vention into matters ranging from keeping bad company, to prostitution and incest.[26] Female delinquency, very much a secondary question, revolved almost completely around sexuality. State intervention was directed to the reconstruction of girls' 'domesticity' – either as mothers, or as domestic servants (the main occupation for training in the certified schools for girls).

The law supported the regulation of youth by establishing coercive powers which could be used to enforce the initiatives taken by a vast array of state and voluntary institutions – the schools, clubs, organizations, juvenile employment centres. This relationship between the 'consensual' and the 'coercive' is captured in Gramsci's observation that the state: 'operates according to a plan, urges, incites, solicits and "punishes"; for, once the conditions exist in which a certain way of life is "possible", then "criminal action or omission" must have a punitive sanction with moral implications, and not merely be judged generically as "dangerous". The Law is the repres-sive and negative aspect of the entire positive, civilising activity undertaken by the state'.[27]

Notes and references

1   See G. Pearson, *Hooligan. A history of respectable fears* (Macmillan 1983).
2   See J. Manton, *Mary Carpenter and the Children of the Streets* (Heinemann 1976); and M. May, 'Innocence and experience: the evolution of the concept of juvenile delinquency in the mid-nineteenth century', *Victorian Studies*, **XVII**, no. 1 (1973).

3   See J. Gillis, *Youth and History* (Academic Press 1974), M. Blanch, 'Imperialism, nationalism and organized youth' in J. Clarke, C. Critcher and R. Johnson (eds.), *Working-Class Culture* (Hutchinson 1979); J. Springhall, *Youth, Empire and Society* (Croom Helm 1977); J. Parr, *Labouring Children* (Croom Helm 1980); and S. Humphries, *Hooligans or Rebels?* (Blackwell 1981).

4   The phrase is taken from John Gillis's suggestive discussion of the emergence of adolescence in this period.

5   For a fuller account see J. Carlebach, *Caring for Children in Trouble* (Routledge and Kegan Paul 1970).

6   Home Office, *Report of the Departmental Committee on Reformatory and Industrial Schools* (HMSO 1913), p. 7.

7   ibid., p. 19.

8   ibid., p. 26.

9   This may seem a strange claim since the period sees the publication of a variety of texts and pamphlets on the young criminal. But two points need to be made. First, there is no definite *theory* of delinquency being elaborated within them. Rather they contain an amalgam of moral tales, case histories, and particular representations of family life, bad surroundings, bad company, juvenile unemployment and the 'natural' consequences of growing up in deprived circumstances. Such texts tend to be both moral and empiricist, little concerned with generating aetiological theories. Second, state policy-making in this field remained systematically uninterested in precise theories of causation tending towards agnostic pragmatism, to say the least. The strategies of reform in this period tended to work from an assumption of the normality of the deliquent charges.

10   *Departmental Committee on Reformatory and Industrial Schools*, p. 31.

11   ibid., p. 15.

12   ibid., p. 37.

13   Jill Pellew's recent history of the Home Office details the failure of earlier attempts to expand the control exercised by the Home Office over the schools and points to the importance of financial control as a basis for centralized direction through the inspectorate; *The Home Office, 1848–1914* (Heinemann 1980), pp. 164–82.

14   For example, C. E. B. Russell and L. M. Rigby, *The Making of the Criminal* (Macmillan 1906); C. E. B. Russell, *The Young Gaolbird* (Macmillan 1910); C. E. B. Russell and L. M. Rigby, *Working Lads' Clubs* (Macmillan 1908); and C. E. B. Russell, *Social Problems of the North* (Christian Social Union 1913).

15   Carlebach, p. 131.

16   Quoted ibid., pp. 89–90.

17   *Departmental Committee on the Treatment of Young Offenders*, p. 13.

18   Particularly important were the 'Model Rules' issued by the Children's Branch to the schools in 1922.

19   ibid., p. 146.

20   D. Bochell, *Probation and After-Care* (Scottish Academic Press 1976), p. 72.

21   For an interesting discussion of the development of patterns of supervision, see D. Melossi, 'Institutions of social control and the capitalist organization of work', in NDC/CSE (eds.), *Capitalism and the Rule of Law* (Hutchinson 1979).

22 For fuller discussions of these issues see N. Timms, *The Development of Psychiatric Social Work in Great Britain* (Routledge and Kegan Paul 1964); and C. Jones, 'Social work education, 1900–1977', in N. Parry *et al.* (eds.), *Social Work, Welfare and the State* (Arnold 1979).

23 See H. Walker and B. Beaumont, *Probation Work: Critical Theory and Socialist Practice* (Blackwell 1982).

24 *Departmental Committee on the Treatment of Young Offenders*, p. 12.

25 Gillis, *Youth and History*; and P. Cohen, 'Policing the working-class city' in *Capitalism and the Rule of Law*.

26 See Home Office, *Report of the Departmental Committee on Sexual Offences Against Young People* (HMSO 1925); J. Weeks, *Sex, Politics and Society* (Longman 1981); and the chapter by Lucy Bland in this volume.

27 A. Gramsci, *The Prison Notebooks* (Lawrence and Wishart 1971), p. 247.

13 Popular control or control by experts? Schooling between 1880 and 1902*

Kevin Brehony

Education is always a sensitive point because any settled practice of training the young really rests on certain moral and intellectual assumptions which are exactly the things challenged by those eager for sweeping change (Michael Sadler).[1]

Nineteenth-century liberalism expressed strong ties between a conception of the ethical role of the state and a broad philosophy of education. These ties grew stronger as the prospect of franchise reform loomed closer. The extraordinary campaign for the wholesale reconstruction of the education system and for state regulation of secondary schooling conducted by Matthew Arnold – as a 'Liberal of the future'[2] – is a telling example of the forcefulness and political resources of the liberalism of the 1860s. To Arnold and many of the liberal commentators of the time education was the key to a much larger but much more precise political mission: 'to reform the state in order to save it, to preserve it by changing it'.[3] Reform of the state was conceptualized by Arnold pre-eminently as not only a bureaucratic task, but one which was to be organized in terms of the intellectual and moral leadership of the governing classes – in which education was to be of absolutely central importance.

The Taunton Commission of 1868 recommended that middle-class or secondary education be brought within the sphere of state regulation. Two years later in Forster's Education Act the state's role in the provision of elementary schooling was significantly expanded. By 1902 a national system of state-regulated education was in existence, based on a concept of universal provision. In this period schooling became accepted as a social right, and it was within the field of education that a commitment to universalism first became embodied in state policy. This marked a decisive moment in the re-ordering of the social relations of citizenship. However, the forms in which universalism became institutionalized – both in the practices of the schools themselves and in the reorganization of the apparatuses of the state – are of equal significance. By the end of the century the dominant connotations fixed to the notion of universalism cut back much that was

---

* I would like to thank Roger Dale for discussing this chapter with me.

potentially democratic in the very idea of a universalist programme. The primary determinations on schooling came to be provision for the masses organized and dictated by a central bureaucracy staffed by experts.

This chapter assesses only the most crucial themes in the debates on educational policy at the turn of the century, concentrating on the development of secondary schooling. It surveys arguments about the curriculum. Significant controversies took place between those who favoured a more utilitarian and science-based curriculum and those who emphasized cultural preparation for citizenship. The predominant configurations of the various collectivist pressure groups and alliances, which drew in both state and private agencies and cut across formal party-political boundaries are also examined. This raises questions about the form in which middle-class 'interests' were constituted and came to be represented. Both Liberal organizations and various royal commissions played a crucial role in constructing the terms of the debates on education and in winning consent in and beyond the political parties. The chapter finally traces the shift in regulation from school boards to local education authorities and assesses the contribution to education of the bureaucratic collectivism of the Fabians and Sir Robert Morant.

Secondary education

The extension of education in the last two decades of the nineteenth century was due to a number of factors. The educational literature of the 1880s and 1890s contains ample evidence of perceptions of British economic decline. The example of the centralized German educational system attracted most attention. German industrial success was repeatedly attributed to its unified system of state-regulated elementary and secondary schooling.[4] That many of those who made this connection were scientists was clearly significant, for their aspiration to establish institutions for the teaching of science was easily translated into pleas on behalf of the 'national interest'.

The growing debate about industry and education was fuelled by the Reports of the Royal Commissions chaired by Devonshire (1872–5) and Bernhard Samuelson (1882–4). The latter Commission identified the lack of technical study in middle-class schools as 'the greatest defect of our educational system'.[5]

The threat of increasing German industrial competition was not the only pressure for educational reform. Conditions were also changed by the 'arrival' of the working class in education. Increased demand for extended elementary education forced the Education Department in 1882 to add another standard (class) for older children. The directly-elected local authorities for elementary schooling, the school boards, established higher grade schools which catered for the upper sectors of the working class and the lower middle class.[6] Some of these children managed to ascend the fragile examination ladder to the endowed grammar schools and thence to university but the majority entered skilled and clerical occupations. The curriculum of these higher grade schools was often of a scientific nature. In addition to fees and rate-aid, they received grants from the Science and Art Department at South Kensington for passes in science subjects.[7]

The demand for secondary schooling was stimulated by the expansion of the elementary school system. In addition to clerical work, elementary school teaching provided another route to respectability for working-class children, especially for girls. In 1885, the London school board opened its first pupil-teacher centre, which was soon emulated by other large school boards. Evening classes also expanded rapidly during the 1880s. The combination of higher grade schools, pupil-teacher centres and evening classes made up a school board controlled system of schooling which encroached upon the field regarded as secondary. This expansion of the school boards' legal domain had two principal effects. First, it threatened to disrupt the prevailing notion of liberal secondary education by providing a vocational education to older children. Second, the higher grade schools provided unwelcome competition to the lesser endowed grammar and private schools.[8]

In addition to working-class boys, girls from the middle and upper classes were also entering secondary education. The Endowed Schools Act had made it possible for funds to be made available for the schooling of girls. In 1868 only about fourteen endowed secondary schools for girls existed; by 1897 the number had risen to eighty-six. Proprietary schools were opened by the Girls' Public Day Schools Company founded in 1872 while schools which approximated more closely to the public schools were also founded in the 1870s. With the opening of Girton in 1873 and Newnham Hall in 1875, women's access to higher education was extended. As a consequence women demanded representation on the bodies which controlled schooling.

While some girls' schools tended to imitate the curriculum of boys' secondary schools, in many the stress was on vocational aspects of schooling. Furthermore, women like Dorothea Beale were at the forefront of the movement to improve teacher-training and constitute education as a science.[9] Such tendencies to professionalization were alien to the majority of secondary school headmasters. As Mary Louch, a founder of the child study movement noted: 'Teachers of the higher social class do not care to appear too anxious to gain professional knowledge.'[10]

Science and technical instruction

The forces pressing for greater educational provision envisaged a transformation in the curriculum. This was most frequently expressed in terms of a commitment to scientific instruction. The British Association for the Advancement of Science was an important focus for agitation for more science teaching. In the 1880s it set up a committee to inquire into the teaching of science in elementary schools.[11] In its composition this committee represented the dissenting Liberal tradition. Because of its exclusion from the tradition of literary humanism and its close contact with industry, dissenting liberalism had consistently advocated a science-based curriculum. But the campaign to advance science and technical teaching in the elementary schools was largely unsuccessful. The issue was discussed by the Cross Commission which reported in 1888 on the working of the act of 1870. The Church/Tory majority declared itself convinced stating: 'We believe that technical instruction would exert a decided influence in the direction of preventing too large a proportion of boys becoming clerks and shopmen. . . .'[12] The Liberal Nonconformist minority characteristically disagreed with the majority proposal that technical instruction in voluntary elementary schools should be rate-aided,[13] and reiterated the famous Nonconformist argument that 'local public support implies local public management'. The religious question blocked the development of technical instruction and the course of the 1889 Technical Instruction Bill. This in turn led Liberals active in promoting science and technical education to search for a different form of local control other than the school boards for elementary schooling, even though this step carried the risk of conflict with their Nonconformist and radical supporters.

The NAPTSE and state regulation

After 1887 Liberals continued to campaign for educational reform through the National Association for the Promotion of Technical Education. Two years after its formation the Association added the word Secondary to its title to become the NAPTSE. NAPTSE had its origins in the 'X' Club organized by Thomas Huxley and others in 1864 to promote scientific education. Its more immediate heritage was the Samuelson Commission on Technical Instruction. Unlike previous royal commissions on education, this one was thoroughly bourgeois in its composition. Significantly not one of its members had attended a public school. The entire Samuelson Commission joined NAPTSE, and its programme was similar in most respects to the recommendations of the commission. The two main objectives in the NAPTSE programme were: 'The more extended provision of higher elementary schools. . . . The development, organization, and maintenance of a system of secondary education throughout the country. . .'.[14]

The NAPTSE was a microcosm of Liberalism – an alliance of industrialists, manufacturers, scientists, radical dissenters, 'labour aristocrats', and Oxford educated collectivists. Commercial capital, the established Church and the labouring poor were the only major constituencies not represented in its ranks. But such an alliance was bound to be strained by divisions between those who were prepared to abandon the directly-elected school boards and those who were not. Between 1887 and 1889 seven bills were promoted to provide technical instruction, two of which were sponsored by Roscoe on behalf of the NAPTSE. Speaking on the first of these, Arthur Acland, a commanding figure in educational policy, echoed Arnold by calling for state organization of secondary education. He also argued that a sound general education was an essential condition of technical education.[15] Acland was careful to make his priorities clear. Whatever the importance of science and technical instruction, he believed that education of the working class for citizenship was the most critical objective.

In 1889 Acland attempted to placate the Liberal Nonconformist school board supporters. He argued that 'a thoroughly satisfactory . . . system of technical education for the working classes of this country' could only be brought about by a universal establishment of school boards in England and Wales.[16] However, when the Technical Instruction Bill of 1889 was debated the NAPTSE leaders, with the exception of Broadhurst, withdrew their demand for technical instruction in the elementary schools fearing that otherwise the bill would fail. The Conservative government, which had introduced the bill, excluded the school boards from its provisions and instead gave the recently established county and borough councils the power to levy a penny rate for the purpose of promoting manual and technical instruction in secondary schools. The religious question had thus weakened the claim of the school boards to be the local authority for secondary schooling and strengthened the claim of the councils established by the Local Government Act of 1888.

Experts and representation

The establishment of council control over some, though not all, technical instruction led to an influx of experts to join elected representatives in administering education services. This prefigured the form of local control adopted by what Michael Sadler, an educationalist who was centrally involved in these debates, termed 'the democratic collectivist' state.[17] In London, after a survey of existing technical education by Hubert Llewellyn Smith, the council's technical education committee was replaced by a technical education board which Sidney Webb chaired. This board consisted of thirty-five members. Twenty were members of the London County Council and the remaining fifteen were co-opted from the City livery companies, the London school board and the London trades council. In Birmingham and in Liverpool (where no representative of labour was ever elected to the school board because of the religious question) trade unionists were co-opted to their respective technical instruction committees.[18] These committees therefore combined elected members with 'experts' and representatives of constituencies which were politically too important to be excluded.

There were two arguments to support this state of affairs. The first was the need to insulate schooling from what Sidney Webb described as 'religious quarrels' which attended the school board elections. This 'deplorable strife' was not to 'infect' secondary and technical schooling.[19] For Webb, this meant attempting to depoliticize the question of schooling and to present it as an ideologically neutral practice. The second strand was the emphasis on expertise. This was open to interpretation by the various forces opposed to the school boards, as well as by their supporters. When Balfour introduced the Education Bill of 1902, he referred to 'the best educational elements in the country' and argued that: 'They will not have to go through this elaborate electoral process, or not necessarily; and we shall be able for our educational needs to reach strata of experts not now accessible.' If this could be taken as evidence of Balfour's conversion to the themes of 'national efficiency' his subsequent description of the experts had a more traditional flavour. They were: 'representatives of universities, of higher education in all its forms, who now cannot, from the nature of the case, submit themselves to the laborious tests of a school board election'.[20]

The Bryce Commission and the control of secondary schooling

In arguing this case, Balfour followed the recommendations of the Bryce Commission which had proposed that the local authorities for secondary schooling in rural areas should be the county councils and in the towns, the county borough councils. Direct election was ruled out on the grounds that, 'there were already elections enough in England'.[21] Bryce stressed that women ought to be eligible for appointment to the authorities. In the Commission's view there was a risk that women would not be chosen. This view was more than justified. In 1901 in the *Fortnightly Review*, Honnor Morten, a feminist member of the London school board, claimed that only fourteen technical instruction committees included women. In London there was only one woman out of thirty-four members. After showing that a disproportionate number of technical education board scholarships went to boys, Morten commented: 'just as historians are stating that the world is widening to women, the Technical Education Board tries to thrust them back again to the everlasting saucepan and washtub'.[22]

Bryce also considered the co-option of teachers, which was strongly urged by Michael Sadler and Sophie Bryant, [23] the only woman on the London technical education board. The Commission's lame conclusion was that the presence on the proposed local authorities 'of persons possessing such educational experience as teachers should be required'. In contrast, the Sadler/Bryant memorandum argued forcefully for the representation of 'professional expertise'. They made great play of teachers' 'expert knowledge'. Yet they carefully distinguished their argument for the representation of teachers from any hint that this was an argument for the protection of teachers' 'pecuniary or other interests'. Sadler and Bryant differed with the dominant view of the Commission that direct elections to education authorities turned 'a question which ought to be in its essence non-political, into a distinctly political question'.[24] They felt that this danger might be aggravated by the establishment of the proposed new local authorities, but believed that 'common sense' and 'right feeling' would prevail.[25]

Bryce's recommendation to establish a central authority for secondary and elementary schooling was enacted in the Board of Education Act of 1899. The act rationalized the central administrative apparatus by merging the Education Department, the Science and Art Department and the Charity Commission. But it did not allow the appointment of a minister for education as Bryce recommended. Prior to this act, Sadler and his lieutenant, Robert Morant, had successfully fought off an attempt by the Science and Art Department to gain control of secondary schooling. Such an outcome in Sadler's view would: 'degrade and weaken the position of the great public schools and of Oxford and Cambridge'.[26] The defence of the public schools and their curriculum lay behind much of the Bryce discussion of an educational council to assist the minister. This notion had been put forward by Matthew Arnold in 1886 as part of a proposed educational system designed to combine the need of modern states for free institutions and for 'a rationally planned and effective civil organization'.[27] While the teachers' organizations supported the establishment of an advisory council the view of the Bryce Commission on the utility of such a council was rather different. For the Commission, secondary education could not possibly be made a government monopoly as 'It has been largely dependent on individual enterprise; it has been served by men whose genius has been the passion to instruct, and by their invention and enthusiasm, which no Department could have created.'[28]

The educational council, far from being a forum for technical expertise, was in Bryce's view a means to protect 'liberal education' from the ravages of bureaucracy, science and democracy. It aimed to achieve its goals by installing within a semi-public body those who were guardians of 'culture' in civil society. The proposed composition of the council makes its objectives clear. One-third of its members were to be crown appointees, one-third to be chosen by four universities and the other third selected by those members from among the ranks of 'experienced' teachers. This would have given the universities and the public schools a measure of control over the inspection of state-organized secondary schools and the membership of local authorities. Its other main function was to keep a register of teachers in order, as some witnesses sought, to maintain 'some form of discipline within the profession'.[29]

In his 1899 mission to the head teachers of the 'seventeen great schools' Sadler secured consent to state inspection. Inspectors were to be recommended by the educational council (by then referred to as the consultative committee). In the debate on the Board of Education Bill, which provided for the establishment of a consultative committee, several Conservatives opposed a move which sought to develop a connection between the state and the public schools. The Lord President of the Council, the Duke of Devonshire, who had instigated Sadler's mission, met their objection by pointing out that:

The headmasters indicate a great dread on their part of anything in the nature of bureaucratic interference or any attempt to impose upon them uniformity of instruction or curriculum. They therefore attach great importance to the permanent existence of a Consultative Committee in which they see a guarantee against any such attempts on the part of a Government Department.[30]

In speaking of 'bureaucratic interference' and 'uniformity', Devonshire was referring to working-class elementary schooling. The Education Department imposed uniformity on schools through annual codes and inspectors' annual examinations. This was considered an unfortunate but necessary concomitant of mass schooling, but as Bryce put it: 'We should deprecate the extension to schools of a more advanced type of the methods and principles hitherto generally applied to primary schools.'[31]

Popular control: the school board alternative

Many urban school boards set up working-class higher grade schools, and these were subjected to much scrutiny by the Bryce Commission. The Commission was confronted with the problem of higher grade urban schools which by this time occupied the role designated by Taunton as third grade. Their special function was to train boys and girls for the higher handicrafts, or the commerce of shop and town. The Commission's response was to pursue a tactic of assimilation. The higher grade schools, it suggested, should be treated as secondary schools and placed under the control of the proposed local authorities for secondary education. Organic links should be established between the higher grade schools and other secondary schools, which meant, in practice, selection by examination of the more able. Having incorporated, in theory, the higher grade schools, Bryce then tried to incorporate technical instruction into the Commission's general notion of secondary education. The result was mystifying: 'Secondary education, therefore, as inclusive of technical, may be described as education conducted in view of the special life that has to be lived with the express purpose of forming a person fit to live it.'[32] In this notion of 'fitness for life', the 'cultural' and 'the special' were brought together to form a basis of education for citizenship.

If the curriculum offered by the higher grade schools was capable of being incorporated into a broader form of secondary education, what of popular control? The relation between access to secondary schooling and the way in which the school boards were controlled was perceived by labour and socialist organizations as the principle argument for the retention of school boards. The Exeter Hall Conference of trade unionists held in May 1902 declared that 'the abolition of the School Boards will be detrimental to the interests of the education of the people and will take away the advantages which the workers have in direct representation in the management of School Boards'.[33]

The school boards had been established by Forster's Education Act of 1870, to 'fill the gaps' left in the provision of elementary schools by the voluntary societies. In his speech introducing the bill, Forster ruled out the central funding of elementary schooling through taxation in favour of a system of rate-aid, fees and parliamentary grant 'expended under local management, with central inspection and control'.[34] The Nonconformist leader of the opposition to the 1902 act, Dr John Clifford, elevated the system of local control into a political principle. Citing the rights of free-born Englishmen, and not forgetting John Bunyan and the struggle against Charles I, Clifford proclaimed the rights of citizenship: 'state education is the work of citizens, paid for by citizens, and ought to be controlled and authorised by citizens'.[35] But the system of direct election to the school boards owed more to expediency than to democratic theories. It was granted as a concession to the Nonconformist sects. They feared that if, as was originally proposed, the school boards were appointed from the members of the town councils (in rural areas from the parish vestries), they would be dominated by the Anglican Church and its Tory supporters.

'With very great reluctance', Forster accepted rate-payer control and the system of cumulative voting, which enabled small minorities to return candidates.[36] A uniquely democratic system of election to the school board thus emerged almost by accident. Voting for candidates to the boards was conducted on a wider franchise than any other election at the time. Women, if they were independent rate-payers, were entitled to vote. Married women were excluded from voting, but anyone – man or woman, resident or non-resident, lodger or householder – was eligible for election to the school board. They were only required to be an adult and not subject to penal disqualification.[37]

The advantages enjoyed by the board schools over the voluntary schools derived from their ability to apply for a precept from the rates. As a result school board elections were frequently polarized on sectarian lines. The object of the 'Church Party', which frequently comprised the 'parson's majorities' of which Engels complained, was to keep school board expenditure low so that the position of the voluntary schools would not be too adversely affected. Their principal school board rivals, the Liberals and the Nonconformists, however, pursued a policy of expansion which led to charges of 'extravagance'.

Despite the obstacles to their membership, working-class candidates were successful in being elected to the boards from the outset, though in many instances on a church or Liberal slate. From the 1880s socialist organizations managed to secure representation. Once elected they constituted the 'left wing' of the Progressives. The school boards also attracted women suffragists like Emily Davies and Helen Taylor who were elected to the London board.

If Nonconformist support for the school boards can be explained in terms of opposition to the doctrines of the established church, and that of the urban bourgeoisie in terms of the social discipline imposed upon the 'dangerous classes', how can working-class support be explained? It appears that the elementary schooling provided by the school boards appealed most to the 'respectable' sections of the working class. 'Respectable' workers demanded post-elementary schooling, while the 'rough' resisted attempts to get their children to attend school until at least the end of the century. These distinctions are clearly revealed in the evidence to the Cross Commission given by the three 'representatives of the working class'.[38] The evidence of Thomas Smyth, an Irishman who had been elected as a representative of the London trades council, is the most significant. In answer to the question why he preferred board to voluntary schools, he replied

On the ground that we feel that they are more our own, that they are more the people's schools. They are freer to the people and they are cheaper to the people. We believe also that they are capable of being made a great deal better. We feel that we have some control over them whereby we can affect their efforts and make them better than they are.[39]

It was this prospect, rather than the abstract theories of Clifford or Bryce, which motivated Labour and socialist support for the school boards.

The demise of popular control and the crisis of Liberalism

In his article for the *Nineteenth Century*, 'Lord Rosebery's Escape from Houndsditch', Sidney Webb launched a blistering attack on Gladstonian Liberalism. Michael Sadler endorsed Webb's sentiments. Contemplating the destruction of the school boards in 1902, he wrote that 'collectivism was ousting Benthamite Liberalism'.[40] In the same memorandum, Sadler referred to the disenchantment of leading Liberal theorists with electoral systems, which they began to see not as 'a panacea but a means of ventilating grievances; an intermittent clue to public opinion. . .'.[41]

Sadler was more than a passive observer of the crisis of Liberalism. He described himself not as a Liberal but as a 'Wordsworthian Radical'.[42] At Oxford, his formative political influences were Ruskin, T. H. Green, Arnold Toynbee and Arthur Acland in whose 'Inner Ring' he had participated. Subsequently, Acland appointed Sadler as Director to the Office of Special Inquiries and Reports. This was a new office created by Acland to lay 'the foundations quietly for a great unification of the attitude of the State to National Education'.[43] On the recommendation of Canon Barnett of

Toynbee Hall Robert Morant was appointed as Assistant Director to Sadler.

The Office produced a wide range of national and comparative reports on education. These prepared the ground ideologically for the unification of the central control of schooling, the establishment of local authorities for secondary schooling and the regulation of such schooling by the state. Through his involvement with Gorst's abortive bill of 1896, Sadler – in Acland's view – had compromised the work of the Office. This bill would have established local education authorities in every county and county borough through which all public money would have been channelled to schools.

Sadler continued at the Office until after the 1902 Education Bill was passed, although he played no direct part in its implementation. He was out-flanked by Morant, who became Permanent Secretary at the Board of Education. Although Sadler was personally antagonistic to Morant, he shared some of the latter's commitment to 'national efficiency'. In many ways, Sadler was also the inheritor of the legacy of Matthew Arnold. A key phrase of Sadler's was 'feverish unrest'. This he attributed to 'the victorious advance of applied Science; the quickening of commercial competition between nations or between huge aggregates of capital employing labour on an immense scale. . .'.[44] The effect of these conditions was to tear 'the web of influences, which lies with its invisible restraints over every settled community'. These educative influences were now no longer located in a 'stable social environment', diffused throughout the whole of civil society, but concentrated in the institution of the school. English politics, he argued, were moving towards 'more stringent forms of collective organization in industry, in commerce and in social regulation'. This tendency was mirrored in educational thought, which was modifying educational methods 'with a view to social unification and increased collective efficiency'. He was convinced that the time had come 'for dealing with the residual deposit which consists of the physically and mentally deteriorate, especially in the great centres of the population'.[45] Artisans outside the slums required 'a superior kind of elementary school'. As in the case of secondary schooling, a 'greater differentiation of type' of schools was necessary.[46]

To achieve greater differentiation within secondary education the state had to intervene: 'economic reasons alone and considerations of social order' compelled the state to act.[47] Sadler argued for better secondary education for boys who left school at 16, more organized research and more of the highest kinds of professional and technical training.[48] The emphasis on the 'highest' kinds of specialized training was consistent with his Arnoldian view that a general 'liberal' secondary education must precede specialization. His invective was particularly intense against those who, like some of the NAPTSE supporters, demanded a secondary education which prepared its recipients 'for different kinds of modern industry and commerce'. If education were to be reduced to such utilitarian functions, there was a danger that

we should destroy what is of infinitely more value to the nation in the long run than would be the most successful manufacture of specialists in money making and of experts in the art of pushing cheap . . . wares.[49]

Sadler favoured an education system which combined 'collectivist principles' with 'semi-feudal traditions'. He wanted a half way house between the 'Prussian' and the 'American' systems.[50] For the 'residuum' he planned a very different future; one with a distinctly 'Prussian' flavour.

The Fabians, national efficiency and schooling

According to H. G. Wells, Michael Sadler was a member of the Coefficients, a dining club set up by the Webbs in 1902 dedicated to national efficiency. Whether Wells's recollection was accurate or not, Sadler's famous remark that 'the very existence of the Empire depends ·on sea-power and school-power' was consistent with the Webbs' views.[51] Sadler's concern with the 'perilous tendencies to physical and mental deterioration' exhibited by slum dwellers also fitted the Webbs' outlook.[52]

Sidney Webb's close involvement with education began in 1892 when he became Chairman of the London Technical Education Board. He threw himself into the board's activities working closely with Hubert Llewellyn Smith. Webb joined the executive of NAPTSE ten years later when its leadership had all the appearances of the kind of cross-party coalition so favoured by the Webbs. The Webbs' permeation tactics came into play at an early stage in planning state intervention into secondary schooling. Their efforts culminated in the 1902 act. Acland frequently dined with the Webbs and the Liberal Imperialist group. This circle, which included Richard Haldane, was composed principally of those whom Beatrice Webb called the 'collectivist Ministers' – Asquith, Edward Grey, Arthur Acland and Lord Rosebery.[53]

The principal difference between Webb's proposals on education and those of Roscoe, Philip Magnus and Sadler was one of emphasis. While they called for partial state action in education, Webb demanded universal state action. He deplored 'particularism' in schools, 'sectarian and unsectarian narrowness' and the inefficiency of the Education Department. He concluded, in terms similar to Sadler's, that: 'It is in the class-rooms of these schools that the future battles of the Empire for commercial prosperity are being already lost.'[54] Webb's approach to educational politics was thus very different from that of the socialist groups. At the time of Gorst's ill-fated bill in 1896, Sidney 'enjoyed colloquy with Gorst, Sadler and Llewellyn Smith'. Through these contacts and because of his position as Chairman of the Technical Education Board Beatrice Webb wrote: 'he is able to be constantly suggesting amendments which are favourably considered by those in authority'.[55] Acland, A. J. Mundella and Graham Wallas – Fabians opposed to the Webbs on this – rallied the National Education Association behind the defence of the school boards. Meanwhile Sidney Webb lectured to the Teachers' Guild on the benefits of local control of schooling being placed in the hands of a combination of directly-elected representatives and outsiders 'chosen for their special knowledge'.[56] He saw popular control or 'primitive democracy',[57] as outdated and an obstacle to national efficiency. In Webb's view the social 'organism' was evolving towards the differentiation of political functions into those of administration, representation and citizenship. For Webb 'socialism' was a matter for disinterested experts who would solve the problem of combining 'administrative efficiency with popular control':[58] 'popular control' meant not the active participation of citizens in administration as in the school boards, but consent at elections to policies formulated by trained, professional representatives.

For Sadler, education had a double purpose: individual self-development and the training of pupils to perform social duties. In Webb's view the social function was dominant:

the perfect and fitting development of each individual is not necessarily the utmost and highest cultivation of his own personality but the filling in the best possible way, of his humble function in the great Social machine.[59]

This was his alternative to thinking 'in individuals' of which he accused the Gladstonian Liberals. Thinking 'in communities' was the model appropriate for the future. 'What collectivists demand', wrote Sidney Webb

is the equipment of the whole body of citizens, each in accordance with his particular aptitudes and capacities for the service of the community, as far and as freely in each case as the interests of the community require.[60]

Thus schooling was to be functionally differentiated and hierarchical. His detailed proposals were explained in a letter to Graham Wallas in which he criticized the higher grade schools. Elementary schools, Webb wrote, which took the ordinary working-class boy or girl up to the age of 14 or 15 should not 'lead up to any higher school'. Their function was to prepare for 'the counting house, the factory or the kitchen'. Secondary schooling, on the other hand, was to continue to 17 or 19 and was to be reserved for 'scholarship boys and girls' and fee-payers. Its function was to prepare for the first grade school and the university.[61]

In a retrospective account of the debates on the 1902 act Beatrice Webb distinguished two contrasting ideals. The first, supported by the leaders of the National Union of Teachers and the school boards, consisted of a 'publicly maintained and democratically controlled educational administration, extended to meet the needs of the whole population'. While she pleaded a lack of competence to form an opinion on the contrasting ideals, the second that she outlined corresponded very closely to the Webbs' own position of 1902. This denied the practicality of a 'secondary education for all' and favoured instead selection of those from the manual working class who could be trained as 'the pioneers, the directors, and the organisers of industry, commerce, art, science, and government. . .'. Such training required 'the best educational atmosphere' which could not be provided in the board schools as the teachers themselves were from the working or lower-middle class and therefore 'had never enjoyed the advantages of outdoor sports and games or a cultivated leisure'.[62] For the Webbs and other supporters of the national efficiency position the question of the education of teachers of the working class lay behind the debates on secondary schooling. In attacking the pupil/teacher system of training, Sidney Webb referred to the benefits of removing prospective teachers from working-class homes to colleges so that they could receive a broader education. He wanted to ensure that they would be fit to be the 'intellectual guides and inspirers of the masses'.[63]

It is debatable how far the Webbs broke with prevailing notions of 'culture'. However, it is clear that they pushed the notion of the 'special' much further than anyone had previously. The function of higher education was clearly defined as that of producing 'experts'.[64] In turn these experts were to control schooling both at the local and at the central level. Indeed, the whole range of social life was seen as a field for the practice of experts. As Sidney Webb declared: 'We have come, at the opening of the twentieth century to an era of professional expertness, in which the merely cultivated amateur is hopelessly beaten out of the field.'[65] Nevertheless the Webbs stopped short of the position adopted by their ally, Robert Morant, who argued that democracy could only be saved by the 'many ignorant' submitting voluntarily to 'the guidance and control of the few wise'. This in turn required the 'willing establishment and maintenance' of 'special expert governors or guides or leaders' to subordinate individual notions 'to the wider and deeper knowledge of specialised experts in the science of national life and growth'.[66] Beatrice Webb noted that 'Robert Morant and the Webbs have different ends' and that Morant was an 'aristocrat'.[67] Sadler was less generous. Writing in 1941 he saw Morant as 'an early arrival of the Fascist mentality'.[68]

Conclusion

The achievements of those alliances and coalitions of collectivist intellectuals considered here were many but at the same time limited. With the exception of the public schools and independent private schools, secondary schooling was brought directly under state regulation by the Education Act of 1902. Rate-aid was given to the voluntary elementary schools. The school boards, with the temporary exception of London, were replaced by local education authorities based on the county and county borough councils. These local authorities were given the responsibility to supply, or to aid in the supply of 'education other than elementary'. The quality of teacher training was improved through the establishment of local colleges. Science barely entered the secondary schools; where it did it occupied a place subordinate to the traditional grammar-school curriculum.[69] In this area, in particular, outcomes fell far short of the NAPTSE ambitions.[70] 'Imperial' rather than 'industrial' needs were perceived as the most urgent at the turn of the century.[71] Despite the significant extension of centralized state regulation, a distinctive characteristic of the state system of schooling in England and Wales after 1902 was the enormous intellectual and directive influence of private institutions, most of all Oxford and Cambridge and the public schools.

At one level, a process of conservation and dissolution may be discerned in the transformation of schooling in this period. The prominent position of the public schools was conserved along with the educational notion of the 'gentleman' which proved far more resilient than Webb had imagined. But this was of far less importance than the bureaucratization of the control of state schooling and the dissolution of popular control.

What is so remarkable in this process of conservation and dissolution is the ease with which the reforming, ethical impulse of the liberalism of the Arnoldian stamp became appropriated by the bureaucratic collectivism and statism of Morant's experts. This is not to underestimate the disciplinary core which cohered in the early liberal philosophies of education, nor the extent to which they were activated by a powerful fear of the working class. Both these points are valid. But it also appears to be the case that, ideologically and politically, there was little intrinsic to liberalism which could curb the incursions of a profound bureaucratism once the philosophy became translated into policy and lodged deep inside the institutions of the state. Once Arnold and Taunton had conceded the question of the state regulation of a national system of schooling, the line from Acland to Sadler to Morant came to look increasingly plausible. One of the paradoxes of the formation of state education at the end of the nineteenth century was that Arnoldian liberalism was so speedily and thoroughly Fabianized.

Notes and references

1   Michael Sadler, 'The unrest in secondary education in Germany and elsewhere', in Board of Education, *Special Reports on Educational Subjects*, **IX**, Education in Germany (HMSO 1902), p. 32.

2   W. F. Connell, *The Educational Thought and Influence of Matthew Arnold* (Routledge and Kegan Paul 1950), p. 86.

3   Quoted, ibid., p. 167.

4   This literature is surveyed in G. W. Roderick and M. D. Stephens, *Education*

and Industry in the Nineteenth Century: the English disease? (Longman 1978), pp. 156–60.

5 J. S. Maclure, *Educational Documents: England and Wales 1816 to the present day* (Methuen 1973), p. 125.

6 Anon., 'Higher-grade schools, *Ecoles Primaires Supérieures*, and *Realschulen*: a comparison', *Journal of Education*, **XX**(1898), p. 24.

7 Sir William de W. Abney, Presidential address, Section L – Educational Science, *Report of the British Association for the Advancement of Science* (1903).

8 C. Birchenough, *History of Elementary Education in England and Wales* (University Tutorial Press 1932), p. 158. Also the speech made by Miss Blackmore of the Headmistresses Association, Conference of Secondary Education, *Journal of Education*, **XV** (1893), pp. 627–8.

9 D. Beale, 'Notes on Psychology', *Journal of Education*, **VIII** (1886), pp. 107–9.

10 M. Louch, 'Educational progress in America', *Journal of Education*, **XV** (1893), pp. 591–3.

11 W. H. Brock (ed.), *H. E. Armstrong and the Teaching of Science 1880–1930* (Cambridge University Press 1973), pp. 22–4.

12 *Report of the Royal Commission on the Elementary Acts. Final Report* (Cross Commission), (HMSO 1888), p. 142.

13 ibid., p. 218.

14 The full programme appears in *Report of the British Association for the Advancement of Science* (1887), p. 167.

15 G. M. Holmes, 'The parliamentary and ministerial career of A. H. D. Acland, 1886–97', *Durham Research Review*, **IV**, no. 15 (1964), p. 130.

16 Quoted, ibid., p. 131.

17 M. E. Sadler, 'The state and English education', *Sociological Review*, **IV**, no. 2 (1911), p. 97. Sadler did not define the term but he probably had in mind the state that he described in 'National education and social ideals' in D. A. Reeder (ed.), *Educating our Masters* (Leicester University Press 1980), pp. 232–3.

18 For Birmingham, see W. P. McCann, 'Trade Unionist, Co-operative and Socialist Organizations in relation to Popular Education, 1870–1902' (unpublished PhD thesis, University of Manchester 1960). Liverpool is discussed in G. C. Fidler, 'The Liverpool Trades Council and technical education in the era of the Technical Instruction Committee', *History of Education*, 6 (1977). G. C. Fidler, 'The Liverpool labour movement and the School Board: an aspect of education and the working class', *History of Education*, 9, no. 1 (1980).

19 S. Webb, 'The education muddle and the way out', in W. Van der Eyken (ed.), *Education, the Child and Society* (Penguin 1973), pp. 55–72.

20 ibid., p. 88.

21 *Report of the Royal Commission on Secondary Education* (Bryce Commission) (HMSO 1895), vol. 1, p. 267.

22 H. Morten, 'Technical education for girls', *Fortnightly Review*, **LXIX** (1901).

23 Bryce, vol. V, 'Memorandum by Mrs Bryant and Mr M. E. Sadler on the various methods of securing representation of teachers on the central and local authorities for secondary education', pp. 20–5.

24 ibid., vol. I, p. 121.

25 ibid., vol. V, p. 24.

26   M. J. Wilkinson, 'The Office of Special Inquiries and Reports: educational policy-making under Michael Sadler', *History of Education*, **8** no. 4 (1979), p. 283.

27   Quoted in Connell, p. 88.

28   Bryce, vol. 1, p. 106.

29   ibid., p. 105.

30   *Parliamentary Debates*, Fourth Series vol. 68 (1899), cols. 673–4.

31   Bryce, vol. 1, p. 266.

32   Bryce, vol. 1, pp. 135–6.

33   Report in the *Schoolmaster* (6 September 1902).

34   Quoted in Maclure, p. 102.

35   J. Clifford, 'Mr Balfour's defence of the Education Act of 1902', *New Liberal Review* (January 1903), p. 774.

36   R. Aldrich, '1870: a local government perspective', *Journal of Educational Administration and History*, **XV**, no. 1 (1983), p. 23.

37   M. E. Sadler, 'Syllabus of a course on the history of education in England 1800–1911', in *Outlines of Education Courses in Manchester University* (Manchester University Press 1911), p. 55.

38   Cross, **III**, evidence of Mr H. Williams, pp. 226–9; Mr T. Smyth, pp. 379–97; and Mr T. E. Powell, pp. 397–404. Williams, a jobbing printer, preferred the church schools to the board schools because of the superior 'tone' and 'influence'. Powell, secretary of the Bookbinders and Machine Rulers and Consolidated Union for London, claimed that the board schools catered for the 'street sweepings', 'the rougher and uncontrolled children'; the voluntary schools, on the other hand, had 'a more regular class of children'. Smyth, however, made no such distinction.

39   ibid., p. 387.

40   J. H. Higginson, (ed.), *Selections from Michael Sadler's Studies in World Citizenship* (Dejall and Meyorre 1979), p. 199.

41   ibid., p. 201.

42   ibid., p. 203.

43   Wilkinson, p. 276.

44   M. E. Sadler, 'The unrest in secondary education in Germany and elsewhere', in P. Gordon (ed.), *The Study of Education*, vol. 1 (The Woburn Press 1980), p. 62.

45   M. E. Sadler, 'The school in some of its relations to social organization and to national life', in Higginson, p. 63. On Sadler's politics generally, see S. Cohen, 'Sir Michael E. Sadler and the socio-political analysis of education', *History of Education Quarterly*, **7** (1967).

46   Sadler, 'The school in some of its relations', p. 63.

47   Sadler, 'Unrest in Germany and elsewhere', pp. 16–17.

48   ibid., p. 160.

49   ibid., pp. 11–12.

50   Sadler, 'National education', pp. 238–9. And Sadler, 'A contrast between German and American ideals in education', in Board of Education, *Special Reports on Educational Subjects*, **11**, part 2 (1902), pp. 436 and 462.

51   Sadler, 'Unrest in Germany and elsewhere', p. 163.

52   S. Webb, *The Decline in the Birthrate* (Fabian Tract no. 131, 1907), warns of the

degeneration of 'the stock' by an increase in the number of Jews and Irish; cited by G. K. Lewis, *Slavery, Imperialism and Freedom: studies in English radical thought* (Monthly Review Press 1978), p. 258.

53 *Diaries of Beatrice Webb* (typescript) (Chadwyck Healey 1978) (12 January 1895), p. 1358.

54 Quoted in E. J. T. Brennan, *Education for National Efficiency. The Contribution of Sidney and Beatrice Webb* (Athlone Press 1975), p. 80.

55 *Diaries of Beatrice Webb* (Whitsun 1896), p. 1451.

56 *Journal of Education*, **XIX** (1897), p. 201.

57 See Pierson's discussion of the Webbs' *Industrial Democracy* in S. Pierson, *British Socialists: the journey from fantasy to politics* (Harvard University Press 1979), pp. 93–6.

58 ibid., p. 93.

59 S. Webb, 'The basis of socialism – historic', in G. B. Shaw (ed.), *Fabian Essays* (Allen and Unwin 1889), p. 60.

60 Quoted in A. M. McBriar, *Fabian Socialism and English Politics 1884–1918* (Cambridge University Press 1966), p. 208.

61 Quoted in McCann, pp. 535–9.

62 B. Webb, 'English teachers and their professional organization', *New Statesman*, 25 September 1915, pp. 18–19.

63 S. Webb, *London Education* (Longmans Green 1904), pp. 19–22.

64 E. J. T. Brennan, 'Educational engineering with the Webbs', *History of Education*, **1**, no. 2 (1972), p. 185.

65 Van der Eyken, p. 106.

66 Quoted in B. M. Allen, *Sir Robert Morant* (Macmillan 1934), pp. 125–6.

67 *Diaries of Beatrice Webb* (14 November 1916), p. 3544.

68 M. Sadler, *Michael Ernest Sadler* (Constable 1949), p. 195.

69 M. Smith, 'The evaluation of curricular priorities in secondary schools: regulations, opinions and school practices in England, 1903–4', *British Journal of Sociology of Education*, **1**, no. 2 (1980).

70 M. Sanderson, *The Universities and British Industry 1850–1970*, (Routledge and Kegan Paul 1972), p. 213.

71 B. Simon, 'The 1902 Education Act – a wrong turning', *History of Education Society Bulletin*, no. 19 (1977), pp. 8–9.

Index